KU-523-456

ICAEW

The Institute of Chartered Accountants in England and Wales

BUSINESS PLANNING: TAXATION

For exams in 2019

Question Bank

www.icaew.com

Business Planning: Taxation
The Institute of Chartered Accountants in England and Wales

ISBN: 978-1-50972-065-1
Previous ISBN: 978-1-78363-753-9

First edition May 2013
Seventh edition 2018

The content of this publication is intended to prepare students for the ICAEW examinations, and should not be used as professional advice.

British Library Cataloguing-in-Publication Data
A catalogue record for this book is available from the British Library

Contains public sector information licensed under the Open Government Licence v3.0.

Originally printed in the United Kingdom on paper obtained from traceable, sustainable sources.

Contents

The following questions are exam-standard. Unless told otherwise, these questions are the style, content and format that you can expect in your exam.

Question Bank topic finder

Set out below is a guide showing the Business Planning: Taxation syllabus learning outcomes, topic areas, and related questions in the Question Bank for each topic area. If you need to concentrate on certain topic areas, or if you want to attempt all available questions that refer to a particular topic, you will find this guide useful.

Topic area	Syllabus learning outcome(s)	Question number(s)	Study Manual chapter(s)
Administration/liquidation/ winding up	2b, 2c	9, 12, 14, 32, 46	17
Annual Tax on Enveloped Dwellings (ATED)	1g	13	19
APR and BPR	2a, 2c	4, 10, 24, 30, 35, 39, 44, 49	7
Choice of trading entity – single company, group, consortium	1h	26	21
Choice of trading entity – unincorporated v company	2a	1, 28	21
Close companies	1j	7, 15, 31, 42, 60	13
Controlled foreign companies	1g, 1h, 1m	18, 27, 30, 34, 43, 52	16
Corporate interest restriction	1g, 1k	40	16
Deferred consideration	1w	40	5
Disincorporation	1k	32	23
Diverted profits tax/hybrid mismatch	1g	21, 22, 34, 52, 56	16
Dividend v salary	2a	1, 3, 28	21
Employment income incl. benefits	1v	2, 5, 6, 13, 21	3
Entrepreneurs' relief	2a	1, 3, 4, 31, 44, 50	6
Ethics – fundamental principles, threats, PCRT	1f	6, 11, 12, 19, 21, 24, 25, 29, 35, 43, 46, 52	1
Ethics – tax planning, avoidance and evasion, incl GAAR, BEPS, disclosure, AML	1q, 3d	6, 11, 18, 21, 31, 38, 41, 50, 57, 59	1
Foreign exchange	1g, 1s, 1t	13, 48, 60	11
Gains groups	1k, 2a, 2d	16, 18, 20, 37, 51	14
Gift relief	2a	4, 10, 24, 49	6
Gifts with reservation of benefit (GWROB)	2c	5, 39, 47	7
Hive down	2c	19, 25, 29, 36	24
IHT and CGT interaction	2a	39, 41, 44	7

Topic area	Syllabus learning outcome(s)	Question number(s)	Study Manual chapter(s)
Incorporation	1h	3, 24, 38, 54, 55	23
Incorporation relief	2a, 2d	3, 24, 38, 54, 55	6
Inheritance tax computations	1w	8, 35, 39, 44	7
Intangible fixed assets (including patent box)	1g	17, 23, 28, 34, 37, 40, 48, 59	10
Leases – finance v operating	1g, 2b	14	11
Loan relationships	1g, 1s, 1t	17	11
Losses – change in ownership	1k, 2a, 2d	16, 40	12, 14
Losses – consortia	1k, 2a, 2d	17, 26, 36, 37	14
Losses – corporation tax single company	1n, 2a, 2d	12, 17, 20, 46	12
Losses – groups	1k, 2a, 2d	16, 17, 20	14
Losses – income tax	1b, 1c, 1n, 2d	3, 4, 10, 24, 28, 38, 54	4
Losses – successions	1k, 2a, 2d	32	14
Management buyout	2c	25, 36	24
Overseas corporation tax – double tax relief	1r	18, 20, 30, 57	15
Overseas corporation tax – incorporation of a PE	1o	22, 34, 51	15
Overseas corporation tax – migration	1o, 2a	43	15
Overseas corporation tax – OECD	1q	30	15
Overseas corporation tax – residence	1o	21, 43	15
Overseas corporation tax – subsidiary/permanent establishment	1h, 1i	18, 20, 27, 34, 57	15
Overseas gains – temporary non-residence	1z	18, 53	8
Overseas income tax – double tax relief	1x, 2a, 2d	41	8
Overseas income tax – remittance basis	1z	11, 41, 56	8
Overseas income tax – residence and domicile	1y	10, 11, 18, 21, 34, 53	8
Overseas VAT	1g	22, 36, 53	18

Topic area	Syllabus learning outcome(s)	Question number(s)	Study Manual chapter(s)
Pension schemes	1v	5, 14, 35, 45	3
Personal service companies (IR35)/managed service companies	1h	1, 4, 14, 58	13
Property leases	1g	14, 59	22
Purchase of own shares	1m	7, 8, 23, 31, 47, 59	17
Research and development	1g	17, 23, 24, 28, 37, 48, 57	10
Rollover relief	2a	18, 26, 37, 44, 48	6
Sale and leaseback	1f	7, 29, 42	20
Sale/purchase of shares	1m, 2c	7, 9, 18, 19, 25, 29, 40, 49, 50, 59	24
Sale/purchase of trade and asset	1m, 1n, 2c	4, 9, 18, 19, 25, 27, 29, 40, 50	24
Self-employed v employed	2a	11, 58	21
Share schemes	1v	2, 6, 17, 26, 33, 40, 45	3
Stamp duty land tax (SDLT)	1g, 1k, 1m, 1n, 2b, 2c	14, 19, 24, 25, 26, 27, 29, 37, 42, 50, 55	19
Stamp duty/stamp duty reserve tax	1g, 1k, 1m, 1n, 2b, 2c	16, 25, 40, 47, 50	19
Substantial shareholding exemption	1g	12, 14, 19, 20, 23, 37, 51	10
Takeovers and reconstructions	2a, 2c	5, 16, 23, 30, 34	6
Termination payments	1v	1, 33, 48	3
Trading profits – income tax	1b, 1n, 2d	2, 13, 54	4
Transfer of a going concern (TOGC)	1m, 2c	3, 4, 18, 24, 25, 27, 38, 32, 40, 50, 54, 55	18
Transfer of trade in a group	2c	29	24
Transfer pricing/thin capitalisation	1l	20, 21, 22, 23, 27, 30, 43, 52	16
Trusts – capital tax	1bb, 1cc	35, 39	9
Trusts – income tax	1bb, 1cc	2	9
Trusts – inheritance tax	1bb, 1cc	11, 39, 49	9
Value shifting/depreciatory transactions	1m	19	16
Variation of wills	2c	8, 41	7
VAT groups	1k	17, 20, 60	18

Topic area	Syllabus learning outcome(s)	Question number(s)	Study Manual chapter(s)
VAT on property	1g	4, 14, 18, 20, 26, 37, 42, 55, 60	18
Venture capital schemes (EIS, SEIS and VCT)	1u	1, 2, 5, 24, 28, 33, 56, 58	2

Exam

Your exam will consist of:

3 questions	100 marks
Pass mark	55
Exam length	2.5 hours

The ACA student area of our website includes the latest information, guidance and exclusive resources to help you progress through the ACA. Find everything you need, from exam webinars, past papers, marks plans, errata sheets and the syllabus to advice from the examiners at **icaew.com/exams**.

Question Bank

Individuals – owner managed businesses

1 Thomas Evans

Assume it is September 2019. You are a tax adviser, working for a firm of ICAEW Chartered Accountants.

Your manager, Elspeth Grey, has left a memo on your desk concerning a new client, Thomas Evans (**Exhibit 1**).

Thomas has approached your firm for tax advice, because he is about to be made redundant from his employment with Limpet Ltd. He intends to start his own business, but is unsure of the tax implications.

Thomas has already had a meeting with Elspeth and she has made two notes on Thomas's file:

- a file note concerning the financing needs of the new business (**Exhibit 2**);
- a file note concerning the choice of trading entity for the new business (**Exhibit 3**).

Requirement

Prepare the two items listed in Elspeth's memo (Exhibit 1).

Total: 40 marks

Exhibit 1

Memo from Elspeth Grey

From:	Elspeth Grey, Tax Manager
To:	A Tax Adviser
Subject:	New Client – Thomas Evans

Thomas Evans is a new client. He is 50 years old and will be made redundant from his job at Limpet Ltd on 30 September 2019. Thomas intends to set up his own business, providing marketing services, with effect from 1 November 2019.

He is negotiating a contract under which the new business will provide Limpet Ltd with services from 1 November 2019 onwards. Limpet Ltd will be the sole client of the new business.

I am meeting with Thomas next week and need the following items prepared in advance of that meeting:

(a) a briefing note estimating the amount of the business bank loan required to start the new business. Use the information Thomas has given us concerning his financing needs (Exhibit 2), explain any calculations you make and provide a list of any further information you require to finalise your calculations.

(b) an appendix, capable of being added to a letter to Thomas, explaining the differences, for tax purposes, between operating as a sole trader or as a company, specifically addressing the areas Thomas has identified (Exhibit 3).

Ignore the tax implications of exit strategies from the business.

Exhibit 2

File note – Thomas Evans new business financing needs:

Thomas has calculated that he will need £150,000 initial working capital to finance his new business.

Thomas wants to invest his own capital in the business, using the termination payment he is due to receive from Limpet Ltd and the proceeds from the sale of his investment in the loan stock of Rebus plc. If these finance sources are insufficient to provide all of the £150,000, the remaining working capital will be provided by a business loan from a bank.

Thomas understands that taxes and national insurance contributions payable may reduce the amounts he can invest in the business. He wants us to prepare calculations, which will allow him to estimate the amount of the bank loan the business will need.

Termination payment

Thomas will be made redundant from Limpet Ltd on 30 September 2019.

His gross annual salary was £95,000 and was paid monthly.

He will be receiving a termination payment made up as follows:

	£
Statutory redundancy pay	3,375
Payment in lieu of notice (non-contractual)	23,750
Compensation for loss of office	35,000

Rebus plc loan stock

Thomas owns £100,000 of 10% loan stock in Rebus plc, with a current market value of £50,000. Thomas intends to sell this loan stock for its current market value of £50,000 to help finance the new business.

Thomas originally owned 100% of the share capital of Morse Ltd. In August 2019, Morse Ltd was taken over by Rebus plc (a quoted company). For each 25 Morse Ltd shares, Thomas received £1,000 of Rebus plc loan stock, with a market value of £500.

In March 2016, Thomas's Aunt Miriam had given him 2,500 shares in Morse Ltd (100% stake), when the market value of these shares was £20,000. No claim for gift relief was made on this gift.

Miriam, who is now 90 years old, gave her shares to Thomas because, due to old age and illness, she was finding it difficult to continue to run the company. Thomas became a director of Morse Ltd on 1 April 2016.

Thomas was paid directors' fees of £10,000 (gross) from Morse Ltd between 6 April 2019 and the date of takeover. He no longer holds any position with Morse Ltd or with Rebus plc.

Exhibit 3

File note – Choice of trading entity

Thomas requires further information to help him choose which type of trading entity he should use for the new business. The two options for the trade are:

(1) a sole trader unincorporated business
(2) a limited company

He expects the trade to be loss-making for tax purposes for the first accounting period, but from the beginning of the second accounting period to be making taxable trading profits.

He would like to understand, for each type of trading entity:

- the tax implications of trading losses, in the first period of trade;
- when and on whom the profits would be taxed and at what rates of taxation; and
- if there are likely to be any tax implications arising from the fact that his former employer, Limpet Ltd, will be the sole client of the new business.

His cousin William is interested in investing in the business in the future and Thomas would like to know the differences, for tax purposes, between William investing in an unincorporated business or in a company. He would also like you to provide brief details of any tax incentive schemes available for such investments.

2   Josh Reynolds

You are a tax adviser in the tax department of a firm of ICAEW Chartered Accountants.

You have a new client, Josh Reynolds, a 40-year-old UK resident, married to Martha.

The terms of the engagement letter state that Josh will prepare his own draft, income tax computation, which is then reviewed and corrected by the tax department of your firm, before the agreed version is submitted to HMRC.

Josh has prepared a draft computation of income tax payable for the 2018/19 tax year (**Exhibit 1**), and you have also been provided with notes from the file about the contents of this computation (**Exhibit 2**).

Requirement

Prepare a corrected 2018/19 income tax computation for Josh Reynolds, based on the draft income tax computation in Exhibit 1, and calculate the client's income tax payable/repayable for 2018/19. Make brief notes for the client explaining any amendments made and dealing with the client's query concerning the sale of his shares in Gallery Ltd.

Total: 25 marks

Exhibit 1

Josh Reynolds
Draft 2018/19 income tax computation

	Note	Non savings income £	Savings income £	Total £
Painters Ltd directors' fees (£100 × 12)	1	1,200		1,200
Mileage allowance payment	2	1,500		1,500
Income taxable on exercise of share options in Painters Ltd [(£8 – £4.75) × 10,000]	3	32,500		32,500
Trading profits (period ended 30 June 2018)	4	10,000		10,000
Building society interest	5		15,000	15,000
Income from discretionary trust	6		22,550	22,550
Tax relief on investment in EIS shares (£100,000 × 30%)	7	(30,000)		(30,000)
Net Income		15,200	37,550	52,750
Personal allowance		(11,850)		(11,850)
Taxable Income		3,350	37,550	40,900

Tax:	£
Non-savings	
£3,350 × 20%	670
Savings	
£31,150 × 20%	6,230
£6,400 × 40%	2,560
Income tax liability	9,460
Less tax deducted at source:	
PAYE	(240)
Income tax payable	9,220

Exhibit 2

File notes – Josh Reynolds's draft 2018/19 income tax computation

1   Josh Reynolds became a director of Painters Ltd on 1 April 2018. His director's fees were £100 (gross) paid on the last day of each month from April 2018 onwards. In 2018/19, PAYE of £240 was deducted from these fees. On 1 May 2019 Josh also received a bonus of

£15,000, net of £5,000 tax. This bonus was paid in respect of the results of the company for the year ended 31 March 2019 and was credited to his director's loan account on 31 March 2019.

2   Josh uses his own car to carry out business trips for Painters Ltd. He drove 6,000 business miles in 2018/19 and Painters Ltd reimbursed him 25p a mile.

3   Josh was granted options in an Enterprise Management Incentives (EMI) share scheme in Painters Ltd on 1 August 2017. He was granted options over 10,000 shares, with a market value on that date of £5 each. He exercised all of these options on 10 August 2018 when the shares had a market value of £8 each, for an exercise price of £4.75 per share.

4   Josh started a self-employed business as a financial adviser on 1 January 2018. The profits, as adjusted for tax purposes, have been as follows:

Accounting Period	Profits as adjusted for tax purposes £
Period ended 30 June 2018	10,000
Year ended 30 June 2019	50,000

5   Interest on building society accounts.

	Interest received in 2018/19 £
ISA account in the name of Josh Reynolds	5,000
Joint account: in the names of Martha Reynolds and Josh Reynolds	10,000

Josh provided all the capital invested in the joint account.

6   Josh is a beneficiary of the Reynolds Family Discretionary Trust. In September 2018 the trustees made a payment to Josh of £22,550.

7   Josh invested £100,000 in the shares of Gallery Ltd, an unquoted, UK trading company, in January 2019. This investment qualifies for income tax relief under the Enterprise Investment Scheme.

8   Josh is considering selling his entire shareholding in Gallery Ltd for £125,000 in January 2020. He would like you to provide him with a brief explanation of the tax consequences of this proposed disposal.

3   Owen and Michael

Assume it is February 2019. You work as a tax adviser in the tax department of Gibbons and Co, a firm of ICAEW Chartered Accountants. The tax partner, Matthew Gibbons, has asked for your assistance in preparing for a meeting with Owen and Michael Jones, twin brothers who are aged 25 and have been clients of your firm since 1 October 2016.

Background information

On 1 October 2016 Owen and Michael set up a VAT-registered partnership to run a business (StudentEat), providing easy, online, ordering of hot takeaway food for students in London. The business was an immediate success and expanded into other university cities in the UK.

Although the StudentEat partnership has yet to make a taxable profit, the business shows such promise that Owen and Michael have been approached by a potential purchaser.

Orlando Ltd, an unconnected company, would like to purchase the StudentEat business, but recognises that it needs to keep Owen and Michael's expertise and industry contacts for at least nine months after purchase, to ensure the business continues to be a success. A summary of the offer made by Orlando Ltd for the purchase of the StudentEat partnership is set out in **Exhibit 1**.

Matthew Gibbons has had a telephone conversation with Owen Jones to discuss the brothers' plans after the sale of the partnership and the notes of this conversation are in **Exhibit 2**.

A summary of the tax adjusted losses of the StudentEat partnership from commencement to the cessation of trade, on disposal on 31 March 2019, is shown below.

	Six-month period ended 31 March 2017 £	Year ended 31 March 2018 £	Year ending 31 March 2019 (Estimated) £
Tax adjusted (loss)	(20,000)	(10,000)	(12,500)

The loss of £12,500 for the year ending 31 March 2019 is shown before amending for balancing adjustments on the sale of office equipment. The office equipment will be sold for £50,000 (Exhibit 1) and the tax written down value of the office equipment on 1 April 2018 was £45,000.

Owen and Michael have a partnership agreement sharing all profits and losses equally.

Owen has never had any taxable income from any other sources and he has never used his capital gains tax (CGT) annual exempt amount.

Michael has built up substantial savings as a result of successful share dealings. He receives gross bank deposit interest of £35,000 a year on his savings and he always uses his CGT annual exempt amount. Michael has also used his share of partnership trading losses against his income of the current tax year, under s.64 loss relief against total income. Michael has brought forward capital losses of £25,000.

Michael also owns a small office building which cost him £40,000 and has always been used by the StudentEat partnership. He will sell this to an unconnected third party for £90,000 on 31 March 2019, because the partnership should no longer need to use the premises. Michael has never charged StudentEat any rent for the use of the office.

On the sale of the StudentEat partnership business to Orlando Ltd, Owen and Michael will become shareholders and directors of Orlando Ltd. The existing directors of Orlando Ltd have asked them to decide how their remuneration will be structured (**Exhibit 3**).

Requirements

Prepare a briefing note for Matthew Gibbons, for his use in preparing for the meeting with Owen and Michael Jones, containing explanations, with calculations where appropriate, of the following matters:

3.1 The taxation consequences arising for Owen and Michael Jones from the proposed disposal of the StudentEat partnership's business to Orlando Ltd.

3.2 The taxation consequences for both Owen and Michael Jones, for 2019/20, of receiving the additional remuneration in the form of either a salary or a dividend, together with a recommendation about which option you consider the brothers would prefer for tax purposes (Exhibit 3).

Total: 40 marks

Exhibit 1

Summary of Orlando Ltd's offer to purchase the StudentEat partnership's business

Date of Purchase: 31 March 2019

Estimated total purchase consideration: £1,050,000.

Comprising £50,000 for the office equipment and £1,000,000 for the goodwill of the business, to be paid as follows:

Date	Value of purchase consideration £	Form of consideration
31 March 2019	50,000	Cash for office equipment
31 March 2019	500,000	500,000 £1 'A' ordinary shares in Orlando Ltd
31 December 2019 (Estimated)	500,000	500,000 £1 'A' ordinary shares in Orlando Ltd
	1,050,000	

The consideration payable on 31 December 2019 will be contingent on the results of the StudentEat business. The best estimate of the payment at today's date is that it will be worth £500,000; however, if the results of the business are better or worse than expected, this payment could increase or decrease accordingly.

Orlando Ltd has offered Owen and Michael the opportunity to receive up to £55,000 of the consideration for the goodwill in cash, rather than in shares in Orlando Ltd.

Owen and Michael have been guaranteed that they will each receive a minimum 6% stake in Orlando Ltd, whatever the format or amount of the consideration finally agreed and that they will both become directors of Orlando Ltd with effect from 1 April 2019.

Orlando Ltd is not a close company.

Exhibit 2

Note of telephone conversation between Matthew Gibbons and Owen Jones

Owen rang to discuss plans for his and Michael's futures following the potential sale of the StudentEat partnership to Orlando Ltd.

Owen intends to work for Orlando Ltd until 31 December 2019, when he will benefit from the earn-out on the sale of the partnership. On 31 December 2019 he will terminate his employment with Orlando Ltd and go travelling for a few years. The other shareholders of Orlando Ltd are aware of this and are prepared to buy his shares on 1 January 2020.

Michael intends to work for Orlando Ltd for many years.

Exhibit 3

Details of remuneration payable to Owen and Michael Jones by Orlando Ltd

Owen and Michael will become directors of Orlando Ltd, with effect from 1 April 2019.

The remuneration policy of the existing directors of Orlando Ltd is to take a small salary with the balance of their remuneration being taken as dividend income.

The company is issuing a new class of ordinary shares to Owen and Michael ('A' ordinary shares), which have identical voting rights to the ordinary shares held by the other shareholders, but will give Michael and Owen some choice over how they are remunerated.

Orlando Ltd will pay Owen and Michael a basic salary of £11,850 per annum each.

In addition to this basic salary, they will each be entitled to further remuneration. The total cost of this additional remuneration to Orlando Ltd must be £50,000 pa, per director. Owen and Michael would like us to help them decide if it is more tax efficient to receive this additional remuneration in the form of an extra salary or in the form of a dividend.

4 Phillip Hassan

Assume it is March 2019. You work as a tax adviser for a firm of ICAEW Chartered Accountants. Your firm acts as personal tax advisers to Phillip Hassan who, until recently, was a sole trader, running an online party decoration and fancy dress business.

Lynn Svletka, the engagement manager, has asked for your assistance in preparing for a meeting with Phillip, to advise him on his tax affairs for 2018/19 and to discuss the implications of a consultancy contract he will undertake from 2019/20.

Lynn Svletka has provided you with notes of an initial meeting held with Phillip.

Meeting notes:	Meeting with Phillip Hassan
Prepared by:	Lynn Svletka
Date:	4 March 2019

Cessation of trade

Phillip ceased trading as a sole trader on 30 September 2018 and on that date, transferred the trade and assets of the business to his son, Nicholas. Phillip had started trading in June 2001. His recent tax adjusted trading profits/(losses) are:

	£
Nine months ended 30 September 2018	(54,000)
Year ended 31 December 2017	12,500
Year ended 31 December 2016	26,000
Year ended 31 December 2015	18,000

As at 30 September 2018, Phillip had unrelieved overlap profits of £1,200 brought forward from commencement of trade.

Nicholas believed he could improve the profitability of the business. Nicholas paid £600,000 to Phillip in respect of the building owned by the business, but no other purchase consideration was paid.

The cost of the assets of the sole trader business and their market values at 30 September 2018 were as follows:

	Cost £	Market value 30 September 2018 £
Plant and machinery (Note 1)	10,000	25,000
Building (Note 2)	500,000	600,000
Goodwill	Nil	75,000

Notes

1   The cost and market value of all items of plant and machinery were less than £6,000.

2   Phillip operated his business from a building, which had originally cost £500,000 plus VAT on 1 October 2012. At that date, the building was a new commercial building. Until 31 December 2016, Phillip had used the building 100% for business purposes, but from 1 January 2017 he had rented 20% of the building to an unconnected company.

Phillip did not opt to tax the building. On cessation of trade, the building was transferred to Nicholas for £600,000, with the existing tenant in situ. No option to tax has been exercised. Both Phillip and Nicholas are VAT registered, and have a VAT year end of 31 March.

Other income

Phillip's only other income in all years until 2018/19 is building society interest totalling £2,200 (gross) per annum. He expects to have no income in future years other than that mentioned below.

Consultancy work

Phillip will start work as a computer consultant on 6 April 2019. He will operate through a limited company, PH Ltd, which will have a 5 April year end. Phillip will own 100% of the shares in the company. A two-year consultancy contract has been negotiated with Logan Ltd, a marketing company.

PH Ltd will invoice Logan Ltd £5,000 per month in respect of Phillip's services. Logan Ltd has stated that while Phillip is engaged on the contract, he must work exclusively for Logan Ltd and be on Logan Ltd's premises during normal working hours.

Logan Ltd will supply him with all of the equipment he needs to undertake work on the contract. The terms of the contract are that Phillip provides a personal service to Logan Ltd. Logan Ltd has stated that Phillip is not an employee and does not have any sickness benefits or annual leave entitlement with the company.

In 2019/20, Phillip will draw £30,000 as salary from PH Ltd on which employers' national insurance of £2,977 will be paid.

Phillip has expressed some concern that operating via a limited company is an administrative burden. However, other consultants have informed him that doing so is far more tax-efficient, because if he treats the £30,000 which he draws from PH Ltd as dividends, instead of salary, there is much less tax to pay.

Requirements

4.1 Explain, with supporting calculations, how the trading loss for the nine months ended 30 September 2018 may be relieved.

4.2 Advise Phillip of the capital tax consequences of the transfer of the trade and assets of his sole trader business to Nicholas and explain the availability of any reliefs, which may be used to mitigate his overall tax liability. Ignore the impact of VAT in this part of the question.

4.3 Explain, with supporting calculations, the VAT and Stamp Duty Land Tax implications of the transfer of the building to Nicholas.

4.4 Determine the factors which would be considered to evaluate whether the contract between PH Ltd and Logan Ltd falls within the scope of the personal service company (IR35) legislation. Assuming the personal service company legislation applies, calculate Phillip's deemed employment income payment and advise Phillip if there are any tax advantages for him by taking dividends from PH Ltd in the future.

Total: 35 marks

5 George Assenga

Assume it is March 2019. You work as a tax adviser at Pippin & Potts, a firm of ICAEW Chartered Accountants. George Assenga is a personal tax client of your firm. George is 50 years old and has recently commenced employment with Crowther Ltd. He has been resident in the UK for tax purposes since 2009, but he remains domiciled in the country of Erehwon, where he was born. He intends to return to live in Erehwon within the next five years.

Your manager, Meryl Walker, has had an initial telephone conversation with George and is due to visit him to discuss a number of issues. Meryl has asked for your help in preparing for this meeting. She has provided you with a copy of the following email which she has received from George:

To:	Meryl Walker
From:	George Assenga
Re:	Personal tax affairs

Further to our telephone conversation, please find below the issues I would like to discuss at our meeting:

Crowther Ltd employment

My current salary is £60,000 pa and this is likely to increase to £400,000 pa in three years' time. As part of my remuneration package, in addition to my salary, I can either take a cash bonus each year, equal to 20% of my salary, or be part of the Crowther Ltd occupational money purchase pension scheme.

Under the terms of the scheme, Crowther Ltd contributes an amount of 20% of my salary to the scheme, and I contribute a further 12% of my salary.

I do not understand how this type of pension scheme operates and I am concerned about the risk of only having one pension scheme. Ideally, I would like to make contributions in excess of 6% and so I may also set up a private pension scheme. I do not know if I am allowed to do this and I am also unclear about how tax relief is obtained for pensions.

I do not know which is the best alternative for me; either taking additional salary or joining the occupational pension scheme.

I am keen to plan for retirement and although I do not require Pippin & Potts to produce detailed calculations at this stage, I would like to understand the overall tax implications of each alternative.

Investment in Winstanley plc

I currently hold 1,500 £1 ordinary shares in Winstanley plc, a quoted trading company specialising in the manufacture of ready meals for sale to supermarkets. My shareholding equates to a 0.5% holding. I originally purchased the shares in Winstanley plc on 1 July 2010 for £1.20 each and I have never worked for the company. Last week, Winstanley plc agreed in principle to an offer from Pepper plc, a large supermarket, to purchase the entire share capital of the company.

Pepper plc's offer for each £1 ordinary share in Winstanley plc is:

	Market value £
1 Pepper plc 25p ordinary share	3.20
1 Pepper plc 50p preference share	1.80

In addition to the shares, Pepper plc is also offering Winstanley plc shareholders the choice of either taking £5 in cash for every share currently held in Winstanley plc or to take Pepper plc loan stock, with a market value of £5, for every share currently held. I would like to understand the tax implications of the takeover of Winstanley plc for me and whether opting for cash or loan stock, would be the most tax efficient. I utilise my annual exempt amount for capital gains tax every year.

Plans for the future

I have savings of £75,000 and I am considering investing the full amount in one of two alternative businesses. I would like to invest in the business which generates the best tax advantage for me. I have attached further details on the two alternative businesses to this email (**Exhibit**).

I would also like to transfer ownership of my house in London to my son Arnold to mitigate any future inheritance tax liability.

My home in London has a current market value of £850,000. I believe that the transfer to Arnold, will limit any future liability to inheritance tax. I intend to continue living in the house and, when I eventually move back to Erehwon, I expect to visit the UK for at least three months every year, during which time I will stay at the house.

Requirement

Prepare notes for your manager, to be used at the meeting with George Assenga, which include an explanation of the tax implications for George of each issue raised in the email and in the Exhibit and advice on the most tax efficient courses of actions for George to take. Detailed tax calculations are not required.

Total: 25 marks

Attachment to email

I would like to invest my savings of £75,000 as soon as possible but want the opportunity to be able to withdraw the funds in the next three to five years. I can invest in the shares of either Bemmers Ltd or Markland Ltd. Although my initial investment will give me a minor shareholding, both companies have indicated that there will be an opportunity for me to buy additional shares in the future.

Bemmers Ltd

Bemmers Ltd is an unquoted company which has become very profitable. Lee and Dianne Oliver formed the company five years ago and are the sole shareholders and directors. They each own 50 £1 ordinary shares. As at 31 March 2019, Bemmers Ltd will have 25 full-time employees and gross assets of £1 million.

Bemmers Ltd needs to raise additional funding and as I am a good friend of Lee and Dianne, they have approached me to invest in the company. In return for this investment, I would be issued shares. A new issue of 10 £1 ordinary shares would be made for consideration of £75,000.

Markland Ltd

Markland Ltd is an unquoted company which commenced trading on 1 January 2018 and has issued share capital of 100 £1 ordinary shares. As at 31 March 2019, Markland Ltd will have 10 full-time employees and gross assets of £60,000.

If I invest in this company, £16,500 of my initial £75,000 will be spent immediately in purchasing plant and machinery, with the remaining £58,500 being spent during 2019/20 to fund an expansion of the business. I will receive 10 £1 ordinary shares in the company in exchange for my investment of £75,000.

6 Gamble and Watts plc

You are Alex Robertson, an ICAEW Chartered Accountant specialising in advising on the tax consequences of employee remuneration packages.

Your client Gamble and Watts plc is a UK-registered company, in a capital intensive industry.

Gamble and Watts plc would like your advice on three unrelated employment tax issues.

Issue 1: Graduate recruitment scheme

Gamble and Watts plc recruits large numbers of ambitious graduate trainees every year, with employment contracts starting on 1 September annually.

The economic upturn has increased competition for high quality graduates and the recruitment department of Gamble and Watts plc has struggled to fill all the places on the graduate recruitment scheme in 2019. As a result, the company wishes to improve the graduate employment package for recruitment in September 2020, to give the company a competitive advantage over other graduate employers.

The starting salary for each graduate trainee in 2020 will be £22,000. Gamble and Watts plc also intends to offer an additional incentive as part of the 2020 graduate employment package, but need to ensure that the after-tax cost of this incentive is affordable to the company.

The recruitment department of Gamble and Watts plc have proposed three, mutually exclusive incentives, one of which may be added to the employment package for the 2020 graduate recruitment scheme.

The three incentives proposed are as follows:

(a) One extra week of paid holiday for each graduate, for each of the first three years of the graduate trainee contract. The recruitment department originally planned to recruit 500 graduate trainees; if this incentive is implemented it would need to recruit an additional 10 graduate trainees.

(b) An introductory bonus of £3,000, to be paid with the first month's salary, to each graduate starting with the company on 1 September 2020, together with an interest-free loan of £12,000, to help with travel costs and accommodation expenses. The loan would be made to staff on 1 September 2020 and would be repaid in two, equal, annual instalments, starting on 31 August 2021.

(c) On 1 September 2020, in addition to being provided with a laptop for business use, each graduate would also be provided with a tablet computer, for personal use. The tablet normally retails at £750 each, but Gamble and Watts plc would be able to negotiate a bulk discount and would pay only £500 per tablet.

The recruitment department would like to understand the differences between these incentives for both the employee and the employer, from a tax perspective. These incentives are not salary sacrifice schemes.

Issue 2: Non tax-advantaged share scheme

Gamble and Watts plc currently operate a non tax-advantaged share scheme, under which all new employees receive share options worth £1,750 on joining the company. Following discussions with existing employee groups the company is considering setting up a share incentive plan to replace the non-tax advantage scheme for all new employees. All new employees will receive £1,750 of free shares on joining the company.

Issue 3: Tax-saving scheme

The finance director of Gamble and Watts plc is always looking for legitimate ways to reduce the costs of employing staff. He has been approached by a firm of tax advisers, who have proposed a tax-saving scheme, which the advisers claim can reduce the amount of employers' national insurance contributions payable by the company. The finance director has emailed you asking for your advice about whether Gamble and Watts plc should participate in this scheme (**Exhibit**).

Requirements

6.1 For each of the three, mutually exclusive, graduate trainee incentives listed (a) to (c) above (Issue 1):

- explain, with the aid of calculations the tax implications for a graduate trainee commencing employment on 1 September 2020, for both the 2020/21 and 2021/22 tax years; and

- calculate the net, after tax, cost to the employer, for the period from 1 September 2020 to 31 March 2022.

Do not consider:

- the finance costs associated with the timing of the use of the funds;

- any savings arising from the possible participation by the company in the scheme referred to in the Exhibit.

6.2 Explain the tax implications, and any tax planning opportunities, arising from the proposed changes to the company's share scheme (Issue 2).

6.3 Provide a response to the finance director's email concerning the tax-saving scheme in the Exhibit (Issue 3).

Total: 35 marks

Note: Assume the official rate of interest is 2.5%.

> **To:** Alex Robertson
> **From:** Finance Director Gamble and Watts plc
> **Subject:** Tax-saving scheme
>
> I have been approached by a firm of tax advisers with a proposal for a tax-saving scheme.
>
> They claim that they can reduce our employers' national insurance contributions by up to 50%. The figures they have provided make impressive reading, but it all looks too good to be true. They would charge us 10% of any savings we make as a fee for the advice.
>
> As you are our adviser on employment tax issues, I would welcome your views about how we should approach this scheme. I am not sure I fully understand how the scheme works, but they have told me:
>
> - the scheme is legal;
>
> - it takes advantage of a loophole in the law;
>
> - it does require a few extra steps to be put in place to pay an employee, but the extra work is worth it, to save so much tax.
>
> Can you let me know whether this is a scheme we should pursue?

Individuals – capital taxes

7   Boxit Ltd

You are Fiona Farr and you work as a tax assistant for Kilps ICAEW Chartered Accountants. Boxit Ltd is a UK resident trading company which designs and manufactures card packaging for the food industry. Boxit Ltd is a tax client of your firm. Two of the directors Adam Kard and his daughter Jane Furness are also tax clients of your firm.

Background information on Boxit Ltd

Adam Kard and Jane Furness bought the entire 100,000 £1 ordinary shares of Boxit Ltd in 2001 for £5 per share. In 2010, Adam and Jane accepted an offer from DrinkUp plc, a company operating in the plastic bottling industry, to purchase 10% of the ordinary shares in Boxit Ltd. Using DrinkUp plc's expertise and customer base, Boxit Ltd expanded its operations to include the production of plastic packaging.

The current shareholdings in Boxit Ltd are:

	Number of £1 ordinary shares
Adam Kard	70,000
Jane Furness	20,000
DrinkUp plc	10,000
	100,000

Adam and Jane are directors of Boxit Ltd and work full-time in the business.

Summary statement of financial position for Boxit Ltd at 31 March 2019

	£'000
Property – Ben Lane factory (bought in 2000)	840
Plant and machinery	385
Cash and other net current assets	750
	1,975
Share capital	100
Revaluation surplus	550
Retained earnings	1,325
	1,975

Email from Adam Kard

To:	Kilps ICAEW Chartered Accountants
From:	Adam Kard
Date:	5 June 2019
Subject:	Sale of shares in Boxit Ltd

I had serious concerns when the business moved to producing plastic packaging as I feel strongly about the adverse impact of plastic on the environment. I have also been very unwell and have therefore decided to retire and make way for Jane to take on my role in the business.

Boxit Ltd is a profitable company and although DrinkUp plc has offered to buy my 70,000 shares in Boxit Ltd for £20 per share, I do not want Jane to lose control of the business. I am personally wealthy and my income in the tax year 2019/20 will be over £150,000. Therefore, I am in no hurry to sell my entire holding and will consider selling just 20,000 shares for now. I have decided that I will either sell shares to Boxit Ltd as a purchase of own shares for £20 per share or at a discount to Jane for £16 per share. DrinkUp plc, as the minority shareholder, has agreed to the sale of my shares.

The date of the sale of my shares will be 1 September 2019. I have set out below two alternative scenarios:

Scenario 1: Sale of 20,000 shares to either:

- Boxit Ltd for £20 per share as a purchase of own shares; or
- Jane for £16 per share.

Jane has no spare cash. Therefore if Jane buys the shares, Boxit Ltd will make an interest-free loan to her of £320,000. Jane will ultimately have control of the business as she will inherit my remaining 50,000 shares when I die.

Scenario 2: Sale of all 70,000 shares to Boxit Ltd.

Boxit Ltd has only enough spare cash to buy 20,000 shares at £20 per share. However, it will raise additional finance to purchase the remaining 50,000 shares by a sale and lease back of the company's Ben Lane factory. I have provided you with details of this proposed transaction (**Exhibit**).

Exhibit

Proposed sale and operating lease back transaction

Boxit Ltd will sell its Ben Lane factory to BB Bank on 1 August 2019 for £1 million and immediately lease back the factory under a 15-year sale and operating leaseback agreement. The terms of the lease are a premium payable on 1 August 2019 of £35,000 and annual rentals of £75,000 pa.

There is a chargeable gain arising on the disposal of the Ben Lane factory of £500,000 and there is no option to tax on the factory. However I do not know what the tax implications of this information are for Boxit Ltd or whether there will be any other tax implications of the sale and lease back of the Ben Lane factory.

Requirement

Explain the tax implications for Boxit Ltd, Jane and Adam, of the sale of Adam's shares in Boxit Ltd for each of the Scenarios 1 and 2. Include in your explanation the tax implications of the proposed loan of £320,000 from Boxit Ltd to Jane and the sale and operating lease back of the Ben Lane factory.

Total: 35 marks

8 David Brimelow

You are an ICAEW Chartered Accountant, running your own general accountancy practice. One of your clients is David Brimelow, a 53-year-old businessman. You provide personal tax advice and carry out tax compliance work for David.

David's father, Frank, died on 30 June 2019. Frank's wife, who had made no gifts in her lifetime, had died in 2013 and left her entire estate to Frank. David is an only child and divorced and has one child Henry, aged 20, from his former marriage. David is wealthy in his own right, having built up and sold various business enterprises over a number of years. He usually has taxable income of approximately £60,000 pa. Henry is studying at university and has no taxable income.

David has approached you for advice about the tax consequences resulting from his father's death. He has provided you with a list of the assets making up his father's estate, details of the lifetime gifts his father made leading up to his death and details of the terms of his father's will (**Exhibit 1**). David would like an estimate of the inheritance tax liabilities arising on his father's death, so plans can be made for payment of the tax.

Despite David's personal wealth, he is concerned that he will not have enough cash available to pay the inheritance tax due on his father's estate. Most of David's wealth is tied up in business assets, which he cannot realise and his father left him assets and not cash. To help David pay the inheritance tax due he could sell some of the assets his father left him. Frank's estate includes shares in Dumpling Ltd. The other shareholders of Dumpling Ltd have approached David, suggesting that Dumpling Ltd could buy back the shares. Details of the proposed share repurchase by Dumpling Ltd are set out in **Exhibit 2**.

David would also like to know if there is any tax planning possible to reduce current or future tax payable by the Brimelow family on Frank's assets, even at this stage, after Frank's death.

Requirements

8.1 Calculate and explain the inheritance tax due as a result of Frank's death on 30 June 2019.

8.2 Explain, with calculations, the alternative tax treatments that may apply to the repurchase of David's Dumpling Ltd shares. Advise David which tax treatment you expect HMRC to apply to the proposed transaction.

8.3 Identify and explain any post-death tax planning opportunities for Frank's estate, which will reduce the current or future tax burden on the Brimelow family.

Total: 25 marks

Exhibit 1

Frank Brimelow (date of death 30 June 2019)

Lifetime gifts

Date	Asset	Value at date of gift	Recipient of gift
20 January 2014	Holiday home in Wales (Note 1)	£350,000	Son: David Brimelow
1 April 2015	House in London (Note 2)	£640,000	Son: David Brimelow

Notes

1 Following his wife's death Frank gifted this property to his son, although he continued to visit for a week's holiday each summer, for which no rent was paid. By 30 June 2019 the market value of the holiday home had risen to £500,000.

2 This was Frank's home and he continued to live there, rent-free, until his death. By 30 June 2019 the market value of the house had risen to £1 million.

Since his wife's death in 2013, Frank had also gifted £1,500 pa each to David and Henry.

Probate value of death estate 30 June 2019

	£
10,000 shares in Dumpling Ltd (Note 1)	220,000
Share portfolio (consisting of shareholdings of less than 5% each in a number of quoted companies)	200,000
Cash (Note 2)	25,000
Vintage Rolls Royce car	175,000
25% share in a racehorse	250,000

Notes

1 Frank invested in Dumpling Ltd, on incorporation, four years ago. Frank paid £1 per share (par value) for the 10,000 shares he held at death – a 10% stake in the company. Dumpling Ltd is a UK resident, unquoted trading company.

2 Under the terms of Frank's will, the £25,000 cash is left to a UK registered charity and the remaining assets are left to David.

Exhibit 2

Proposed repurchase of shares by Dumpling Ltd

The other founder shareholders in Dumpling Ltd now feel they would like to take the company forward without any other investors having influence on the company's direction. Frank had a seat on the Dumpling Ltd board of directors and had attempted to block some of the other shareholders' plans for the diversification of the business - because he had thought they were too risky. David, who did not previously hold any shares in Dumpling Ltd, has taken over his father's seat on the board of directors, but he does not agree with his father's view and has indicated he would be supportive of the other directors in any future expansion plans.

The offer by Dumpling Ltd is to repurchase all 10,000 shares for £25 a share, payable in December 2019. The share valuation has increased since Frank's death, as a result of excellent trading results and new contracts won by the company. The shares would be cancelled on repurchase.

9 Riverbrook Farm Ltd

Assume it is December 2018. You are an ICAEW Chartered Accountant in practice. Riverbrook Farm Ltd and its shareholders, David Fletcher and Shona Bridge, are your tax clients.

Background Information

Riverbrook Farm Ltd was incorporated in 2000 by Phil Fletcher (David Fletcher and Shona Bridge's father). Phil Fletcher immediately gave the entire assets and liabilities of Riverbrook Farm (an unincorporated business) to the newly incorporated company. The assets gifted were worth £2.5 million. In exchange for the gift of the Riverbrook Farm business to the company, Phil Fletcher received 100% of the shares in Riverbrook Farm Ltd. Riverbrook Farm was owned by the Fletcher family for many years, prior to the gift to Riverbrook Farm Ltd. Phil did not claim any tax reliefs in relation to this gift.

In 2000, shortly after setting up the company, Phil died. On his death, Phil left 75% of the shares in Riverbrook Farm Ltd to David and the remaining 25% of the shares to Shona.

David has worked for the company, as a farmer, since Phil's death. Shona has never worked for the company, and has her own separate business. Both David and Shona are higher rate taxpayers and each has taxable income of £130,000 per tax year.

In November 2018, a local businessman, Charles Gentry, offered £10.9 million to purchase Riverbrook Farm. After purchase, Charles intends to convert one of the farm buildings into living accommodation and live there with his family. He will not carry on any farming business himself. Charles would like to complete the purchase on 1 May 2019. David and Shona have asked for your advice to determine the most tax efficient method of structuring the sale of the business to Charles. Notes setting out the two alternative methods proposed for the sale to Charles are in **Exhibit 1**.

David intends to buy another farm with his share of the sale proceeds. He has sent you an email asking for advice about how to minimise the tax cost of passing his new farm business onto his three children. An extract from this email is set out in **Exhibit 2**.

Shona intends to place her share of the sale proceeds from the business into a discretionary trust for her children and grandchildren. She would like to understand the tax implications of doing so and has sent you an email asking for your advice (**Exhibit 3**).

Requirements

9.1 Using calculations where appropriate, advise David and Shona of the amount of tax payable on the disposal to Charles, under each of the two alternatives for disposal suggested (Exhibit 1). Explain the impact of any available reliefs and recommend which of the two alternatives is the most tax efficient for the shareholders.

9.2 Advise David on the difference in tax implications between a lifetime transfer and a gift on death of the new farm business to his children (Exhibit 2).

9.3 Reply to Shona's email, advising her on the tax consequences of creating a discretionary trust and explain the tax charges that will apply on the operation of the trust in future years (Exhibit 3).

Total: 40 marks

Exhibit 1

Notes on the disposal of Riverbrook Farm

Two alternative methods of disposing of the business to Charles Gentry have been proposed.

- Alternative 1: Charles will pay £10.9 million to Riverbrook Farm Ltd, to purchase all assets and liabilities of the company.

- Alternative 2: Charles will pay £10.9 million to David and Shona to buy their shares in Riverbrook Farm Ltd.

If Alternative 1 is chosen, the company will then enter a solvent liquidation in the form of a members' voluntary winding up and will distribute the proceeds of sale to its shareholders.

Whichever alternative is chosen David will reinvest his share of the proceeds in a new farm business (Exhibit 2).

Riverbrook Farm Ltd has always been profitable. The main asset of the company is the farmland and buildings which are currently valued at £10.9 million. The farmland and buildings were valued at £2.5 million, immediately prior to the farm business being transferred to the company in 2000. Indexation allowance on the farmland and buildings from the creation of the company to December 2017 is £900,000.

Exhibit 2

Extract from an email from David Fletcher

New Farm purchase

I have found a new farm to buy using my share of the sale proceeds from Riverbrook Farm Ltd. My new farm will be run as an unincorporated business.

This new farm currently has a market value of around £7 million, but an agricultural value of considerably less at just £2 million. Estimates show that in 10 years' time these figures may have appreciated by up to 10%. I am a 50-year-old widower and in the future I intend to gift the farm business to my three children in equal shares.

I would like your advice about whether I should give the farm to my children, in equal shares:

(1) in 10 years' time, when I retire; or
(2) under the terms of my will, on death.

Exhibit 3

Email from Shona Bridge

To:	Tax Adviser
From:	Shona Bridge

As you know I already have my own business and have taxable income of £100,000 each tax year, so I don't need the proceeds from the sale of Riverbrook Farm Ltd for my own use.

I would like to give the cash I receive from the sale of Riverbrook Farm Ltd to my children and grandchildren, but they are young and reckless with money. My solicitor has advised that I set up the Bridge Family Discretionary Trust in June 2019 and put all of the proceeds I receive from the sale into the trust. I have never given any assets away before.

Once you know how much cash I will receive from the sale, please give me an idea of the tax costs that will be attached to creating and running this trust for the next 10 years or so.

Regards Shona

Overseas aspects of personal taxation

10 Bill Mickelson

You are a tax adviser working for Grandal LLP, a firm of ICAEW Chartered Accountants.

Bill Mickelson, his daughter Wilma and her husband-to-be Jorge are tax clients of your firm. Bill is the owner of a bicycle business. He started his business in 1996 when he inherited a workshop from his father which he still uses in his business. You have received an email from Bill (**Exhibit 1**). Your assistant has had a short meeting with Wilma and Jorge and has left you some notes (**Exhibit 2**).

Exhibit 1

Email from Bill

To:	Tax Adviser
From:	Bill Mickelson
Date:	5 June 2019
Subject:	Retirement plans

I have been offered a job touring round the world as a mechanic with an international cycle team and I have decided to sell my business to my daughter, Wilma. I will leave for a three month trip to Australia on 1 August 2019. After I return from Australia I will be in the UK until the cycling season starts again in May 2020.

I need you to explain to me whether I have any tax to pay. The date of the sale has been agreed as 1 August 2019. I have set out below valuations of and information about my business assets and some notes of the terms I have agreed with Wilma:

Business assets of bicycle business

	Notes	Market value at 1 August 2019 £	Information
Retail building	1	130,000	Purchased in 2006 for £55,000
Workshop	2	250,000	Inherited in 1996 with probate value of £128,000
Goodwill	3	175,000	Created since 1996
Inventory	4	45,000	All purchased since January 2019
Plant and machinery	4	1,000	The tax written down value of plant and machinery is £1,000

Notes of terms agreed with Wilma

1   Wilma will eventually inherit the retail building when I die so I have agreed to gift it to her. As I will receive no cash from her for the retail building, I believe that this will save me tax.

2   I would like to retain ownership of the workshop. Wilma has agreed to pay me £9,000 for the first six months' rent in advance on 1 August 2019. She will pay this £9,000 rent direct to a bank account in Australia which I recently opened. Therefore I believe that this amount will not be taxed in the UK.

3   On 1 August 2019 Wilma will pay me £175,000 for the goodwill of my business.

    I cannot believe I would have to pay any tax on this amount received for goodwill as I have worked hard to build up the reputation of the business.

4   Wilma has agreed to pay me £1,000 for the plant and machinery on 1 August 2019. For the inventory, we agreed she will pay me three instalments of £15,000 with the first instalment due on 1 September 2019.

Exhibit 2

Notes from meeting with Wilma and Jorge

Jorge is a professional cyclist and was born in Spain where he is currently tax resident. Jorge and Wilma are getting married on 1 October 2019 in the UK. After the wedding, Jorge will retire as a professional cyclist and live in the UK working for Wilma in the bicycle business. Jorge's only stay in the UK since 6 April 2019 is a nine day visit to make the wedding arrangements. Jorge intends to settle in the UK and needs advice on his residency status. He owns a property in Barcelona, Spain. He is unsure whether to sell this property before or after his wedding on 1 October 2019.

In June 2013, Wilma's grandmother gifted a holiday home to Wilma which was valued at £445,000. Wilma decided to let out the holiday home for the first time in December 2018. The property was actually let out for 31 days during the period from 1 December 2018 to 31 March 2019 and Wilma received net rental income of £16,000 for this period. On 31 March 2019, in order to raise finance to buy her father's business, Wilma sold the holiday home for £485,000. Wilma would like us to confirm that because she did not actually buy the holiday home, she will not have any tax to pay on its sale.

Sadly Wilma's grandmother has just died and she has received a letter from her grandmother's executor asking for details of the gift of the holiday home. Wilma was very concerned that she would have tax to pay as a result of the gift and needs more information on this.

After buying her father's business, Wilma intends to invest in new plant and machinery and shop fittings and therefore projects that the business will, in the first 12 months to 31 July 2020, make a tax adjusted trading loss of £240,000 but that thereafter the business will make taxable profits in the year ending 31 July 2021.

Wilma does not intend to withdraw any money from the business. She will pay Jorge an annual salary of £30,000 starting from 1 October 2019 which she has included as a cost in her projections above.

On 1 May 2019 Wilma resigned from her position as marketing director for an international cycle manufacturer. Her gross salary for the period from 6 April 2019 to 1 May 2019 was £10,000. In 2018/19 her salary was £120,000. Wilma made no other capital disposals in 2018/19 but she does have a capital loss brought forward at 6 April 2018 of £5,000.

Requirements

10.1 Reply to Bill's email explaining the capital gains tax implications for him of the sale and gift of his business assets to Wilma and the income tax liability in respect of the rental income.

10.2 Prepare briefing notes for a meeting with Jorge and Wilma which include:

- advice for Jorge on his residency status in the tax year 2019/20 and the tax implications of the timing of the sale of his property in Barcelona;

- an explanation and calculation of Wilma's income tax and capital gains tax liabilities for 2018/19 after taking into account any reliefs and elections available to her; and

- advice for Wilma of the inheritance tax implications of the gift to her by her grandmother of the holiday home.

Total: 30 marks

11   Gooch Food

Shar Gooch is a sole trader operating as Gooch Food. Shar's business manufactures ready meals for sale to supermarkets. Shar is married to Neeta and they have three children. Shar was born in Ganda, a non-EEA country where his parents still live. He came to the UK in January 2009 to set up the Gooch Food business and has been UK tax resident since then. Shar prepares and submits his own tax returns. Gooch Food has a 5 April year end.

You are a newly-qualified ICAEW Chartered Accountant and have recently started working as the accountant at Gooch Food. Shar gives you the following briefing:

"I have just been to a meeting with a firm of business advisers called Tx3 who I may appoint as my tax advisers. I would like you to help me understand the advice given to me by Tx3. At the meeting, which was free-of-charge, the Tx3 adviser made the following tax planning proposals:

Proposal 1 – Make my wife Neeta a partner in Gooch Food

My business, Gooch Food, has made a taxable profit of £150,000 for the year ended 5 April 2019. This is after the deduction of a salary of £8,424 per annum paid to Neeta, my wife who works in product development at Gooch Food. The Tx3 adviser suggested I could save tax by making my wife a partner in the business. If I do this, it will be from 6 April 2020 and Neeta will receive a partnership profit share of £45,000. I expect Gooch Food profits to remain at £150,000 per annum for the foreseeable future before the deduction of Neeta's profit share.

Proposal 2 – Set up a discretionary trust for my granddaughter

As I have recently become a grandfather, I would like to set some assets aside for my granddaughter who was born last month. I have a portfolio of UK quoted shares with a market value of £300,000. I expect to receive dividends of £36,000 from these shares in the tax year 2019/20.

The Tx3 adviser suggested that I set up a discretionary trust and gift my portfolio of UK quoted shares to the trust making my granddaughter the beneficiary of the trust. Tx3 advised that this would ensure that no inheritance tax would be payable in respect of these shares when I die. My granddaughter doesn't need any money just yet but it would be good to set aside funds for her future education.

Proposal 3 – Paying key employees using an off-shore company

The Tx3 adviser proposed the following tax planning scheme which he claimed would save my business national insurance contributions (NIC) as it effectively 'hides' employees from HMRC. The scheme involves making key members of the Gooch Food management team redundant. These key employees, who each earn £100,000, would continue to work at Gooch Food but would become employees of an off-shore company called LK O/S which is managed by Tx3. LK O/S would invoice Gooch Food for the services of these employees together with a small administration fee.

LK O/S would then pay the salaries direct to the key employees without paying NIC or tax to HMRC on behalf of these employees.

Moving to Ganda

We also discussed my move to Ganda on 1 November 2019, the country where I was born. I will live there for 10 months and will set up a spice production factory in partnership with my brother. Although it will be difficult to be separated from my wife and children who will remain in the UK, I feel that the move is necessary to ensure that Gooch Food is supplied with good quality raw materials. I will be returning to the UK for the holidays; in December 2019 for four weeks and in the summer of 2020 for five weeks.

The Tx3 adviser told me that the move would save tax as I will not be taxed on any of the profit from Gooch Food after the date of my departure from the UK. Gooch Food's taxable profit for the year ending 5 April 2020 will be £150,000. My share of the partnership profits in Ganda for the period to 5 April 2020 will be £75,000. The Tx3 adviser told me that as long as the Ganda partnership profit share was not remitted to the UK, I would not pay any UK tax on these profits."

Requirements

11.1 Explain to Shar and Neeta the tax and NIC implications of Neeta becoming a partner in Gooch Food (Proposal 1). Detailed calculations are not required.

11.2 Explain to Shar the inheritance tax implications of setting up a discretionary trust for his granddaughter (Proposal 2).

11.3 Advise Shar whether he should consider entering into the scheme to pay employees through the off-shore company LK O/S managed by Tx3 advisers (Proposal 3).

11.4 Determine whether Shar will be tax-resident in the UK in the tax years 2019/20 and 2020/21. Calculate the income tax payable by Shar in 2019/20 and identify any relevant claims or elections available, making appropriate recommendations on whether these claims or elections should be made.

11.5 Evaluate the ethical and professional issues for you in advising Shar and Neeta in respect of the tax planning proposals made by the Tx3 advisers.

Total: 25 marks

Single companies

12 Valese plc

Assume it is June 2019. Valese plc is a UK resident parent company which has a number of subsidiaries operating in the software engineering industry. You are a trainee ICAEW Chartered Accountant working at Valese plc as the financial controller. Your manager is the Valese plc finance director who is currently away on annual leave; therefore you report directly to the CEO, Ken Kingsley.

Valese plc has a 70% shareholding in Mendit Ltd, a UK resident company which provides software support for the aerospace industry in the North of England. The remaining 30% of the shares are owned by Gary Jones who is the technical director at Mendit Ltd. Mendit Ltd has a 31 March year end. Following a strategic review, the Valese plc board has decided to divest itself of its investment in Mendit Ltd. The board decided that Mendit Ltd should be wound up.

At a recent board meeting, the directors of Mendit Ltd determined that a resolution would be presented to shareholders to commence the winding up of Mendit Ltd under a members' voluntary liquidation. The liquidation will take place on 1 September 2019 when the company will cease to trade. The Mendit Ltd board made a statutory declaration of solvency.

Ken Kingsley gives you the following briefing:

"Gary has agreed to the winding up of Mendit Ltd and would like to understand the tax implications for his personal tax position. Gary has accepted the position as technical director at another of Valese plc's subsidiaries on a salary of £250,000 pa. Gary also has substantial investments that use his dividend nil rate band.

Mendit Ltd's finance director has prepared some information for the Valese plc board which includes information regarding the liquidation of Mendit Ltd **(Exhibit 1)** and two alternative proposals for the timing of the sale of Mendit Ltd's office building **(Exhibit 2).**

I would like you to do the following:

Explain the possible loss reliefs for Mendit Ltd's trading losses arising in the year ended 31 March 2019 and projected for the five-month period ending 31 August 2019 and recommend the most tax efficient use of the losses. Calculate the amount of tax repayment due to Mendit Ltd as a result of your recommendation. (Ignore for this purpose the disposal of Mendit Ltd's office building.)

For each of the two alternative proposals for the timing of the sale of Mendit Ltd's office building (Exhibit 2):

- explain and calculate the tax implications for Mendit Ltd, Valese plc and for Gary of the liquidation of Mendit Ltd on 1 September 2019;

- calculate the cash receivable post liquidation by both Valese plc and Gary; and

- recommend which proposal should be chosen.

On another matter, I have heard a rumour that the Valese plc's finance director has been buying and selling Valese plc shares without informing the board. I understand that he has given you the password for his personal email account. I want you to access his personal email account and read any emails concerning share transactions. Report your findings to me so that I, together with the Valese plc board, can determine our response."

Requirements

12.1 Prepare a working paper responding to the briefing from Ken Kingsley.

12.2 Evaluate the ethical and professional issues for you arising from Ken Kingsley's request for you to access the finance director's personal email account. Determine the actions you should take.

Total: 40 marks

Exhibit 1

Information for the Valese plc board — Liquidation of Mendit Ltd

Mendit Ltd's share capital comprises of 250,000 £1 ordinary shares. Gary incorporated the company in 2001 when he subscribed for 100% of the shares at par. In 2004, he sold 175,000 shares to Valese plc for £5 per share.

Recent tax results for Mendit Ltd

Years ended 31 March	2016 £'000	2017 £'000	2018 £'000	2019 £'000
Tax adjusted trading profit/(loss)	234	121	148	(350)
Property income	16	13	15	18
Tax rate	20%	20%	19%	19%

A further tax adjusted trading loss of £321,000, including all closure costs is projected for the five months ending 31 August 2019. No non-trading profits are expected to arise in the five months ending 31 August 2019.

Mendit Ltd - projected carrying amounts and amounts realisable on liquidation on 1 September 2019

	Notes	Carrying amounts £'000	Amounts realisable on liquidation £'000
Office building	1	1,500	1,600
Other assets	2	800	400
Bank loan	3	(500)	
Bank overdraft	4	(200)	
Trade and other payables		(300)	

Notes

1   Mendit Ltd purchased the office building in 2007 and a chargeable gain of £300,000, after indexation allowance, will arise on its disposal.

2   These assets are non-chargeable assets.

3   The bank loan is secured by a fixed charge over the office building.

4   The bank overdraft is secured by a floating charge over the other assets.

Exhibit 2

Alternative proposals for the timing of the sale of Mendit Ltd's office building

Hakett Ltd, an unconnected company, has made an offer to buy Mendit Ltd's office building for £1.6 million.

Proposal 1

The office building will be sold for £1.6 million to Hakett Ltd on 1 August 2019, before the appointment of a liquidator. This will enable Mendit Ltd to pay a total dividend of £900,000 to its shareholders. The liquidator will then be appointed on 1 September 2019 and will sell all the other assets for £400,000, settle all liabilities and make a final distribution to the shareholders.

Proposal 2

The liquidator will be appointed on 1 September 2019. The liquidator will sell the office building for £1.6 million to Hakett Ltd and the other assets for £400,000, settle all the liabilities and make a distribution to the shareholders.

13 Fastmole Ltd

You work for a firm of ICAEW Chartered Accountants, which has recently been engaged by Fastmole Ltd on corporation tax matters.

Fastmole Ltd is an unquoted, UK resident trading company, making taxable supplies. Its taxable total profits exceed £2 million each year.

The new finance director of Fastmole Ltd, Ben, is concerned that several transactions during the year ended 31 March 2019 have been treated incorrectly for tax purposes (**Exhibit**). The financial controller submitted the corporation tax return for this period before Ben started work at Fastmole Ltd.

Ben wants you to prepare a briefing paper in which you:

(a) explain, with supporting calculations, the correct tax treatment of the transactions in the Exhibit, assuming the company does not make any elections;

(b) summarise the additional corporation tax, and other tax liabilities, as a result of the correct treatment; and

(c) advise Ben of any further implications of the incorrect treatment and of the actions he should now take to comply with administrative obligations.

Requirement

Prepare the briefing paper as requested by Ben.

Total: 25 marks

Note: The RPI for December 2017 is 278.1. Ignore stamp taxes.

Exhibit

Transactions during the year ended 31 March 2019

Sale of residential property

Fastmole Ltd sold a residential property for £3,718,000 on 30 June 2018. The company bought the property on 1 April 2011 for £2,568,000.

The company values the property each year and has recorded the following valuations:

	£
1 April 2012	2,735,000
1 April 2013	3,112,000
1 April 2014	3,175,000
1 April 2015	3,250,000
1 April 2016	3,375,000
1 April 2017	3,560,000

One of the directors of Fastmole Ltd has lived in the property rent-free since the company bought it. The annual value of the property is £38,000 for both 2017/18 and 2018/19.

The tax charges paid in respect of this property are as follows:

- **Class 1A on benefit to director**

    The total class 1A included in the accounts for the year ended 31 March 2019 is the annual value of £38,000 at 13.8% = £5,244. This amount was allowed as a deduction in the corporation tax return for the year ended 31 March 2019.

- **Annual Tax on Enveloped Dwellings (ATED)**

  The building had a value between £2,000,000 and £5,000,000 on 1 April 2017 and so the ATED of £24,250 was paid on 30 April 2018.

- **Corporation tax on chargeable gains**

	£
Proceeds	3,718,000
Cost	(2,568,000)
	1,150,000
Indexation allowance (278.1 – 234.4)/234.4 = 0.186	(477,648)
Chargeable gain	672,352
Corporation tax at 19%	127,747

Foreign currency loan

On 1 April 2018, Fastmole Ltd took out a loan for €500,000 for use in financing overseas purchases of components. The loan was repaid on 30 April 2019. Relevant exchange rates are given below. The exchange rate movement to 31 March 2019 was reflected in the company's income statement for the year ended 31 March 2019. However, the financial controller reversed the exchange rate movement in the corporation tax computation as she says such exchange rate movements are not 'real profits or losses' and so should not be taxed or deducted.

Exchange rates:
1 April 2018	€1.24 = £1
31 March 2019	€1.12 = £1
30 April 2019	€1.08 = £1

Sale of machinery

On 1 June 2018, the company sold a large piece of specialist machinery to an unconnected company in the UK, receiving cash of £240,000 from the sale. Fastmole Ltd had originally paid £150,000 cash for the machine in January 2014, importing it from another EU country. The financial controller had deducted the proceeds of £240,000 from the main pool of capital allowances. She had subtracted the profit on the sale in the calculation of tax-adjusted trading profits and had made no other changes to the corporation tax computation.

14 Unele Ltd

Samantha owns 80% of the ordinary share capital of Unele Ltd and 100% of the ordinary share capital of Duote Ltd. Both are UK resident, value added tax (VAT)-registered trading companies.

Unele Ltd

Samantha has decided to liquidate Unele Ltd and invest the funds to expand Duote Ltd.

Samantha has provided details of the shareholdings in Unele Ltd, more information about its shareholders and its recent trade in **Exhibit 1**.

She requires advice regarding whether the company should distribute funds to its shareholders before entering into a formal liquidation.

Duote Ltd

Duote Ltd makes standard-rated and exempt supplies.

Samantha wants to expand the existing business, using £150,000 from the liquidation of Unele Ltd which she will contribute as share capital. Details of the existing supplies and the costs of the expansion are given in **Exhibit 2**.

Samantha would like to know how many freelancer hours she could buy in the first year, if she spends the full £150,000 in year one of the expansion.

Pension contribution

Samantha wants to make a personal pension contribution in 2019/20, using £30,000 of the proceeds she will receive from the liquidation. This is the first year for which Samantha would be a member of a pension scheme.

Requirements

14.1 Explain, with supporting calculations, whether it would be beneficial to each shareholder to distribute the remaining funds of Unele Ltd, prior to a formal liquidation.

14.2 Calculate the number of freelancer hours Duote Ltd could purchase in the first year of the expansion.

14.3 Explain the potential tax risk of engaging with the freelancers as self-employed workers, either directly or through the use of companies.

14.4 Explain the tax implications for Samantha of her proposed pension contribution in 2019/20.

Total: 35 marks

Exhibit 1

Unele Ltd and its shareholders

Shareholdings in Unele Ltd

	Number of ordinary £1 shares
Samantha	8,000
Ian, Samantha's brother	1,000
RK Ltd, a UK resident trading company	1,000
	10,000

All the shareholders subscribed for the shares at par value on incorporation on 2 January 2010.

Shareholders

Ian does not work for the company and is a student who has no income.

Samantha is a director of Unele Ltd. Her annual income for 2018/19 was:

	£
Salary from Unele Ltd	20,000
Dividends from quoted company investments	60,000
Rental income from furnished holiday lets	100,000
Savings income	40,000
	220,000

Except for the salary from Unele Ltd which ceased in December 2018, the income listed is likely to continue at this level in future.

Samantha has not previously made any capital disposals.

Proposed liquidation of Unele Ltd

Unele Ltd was profitable, but Samantha decided to concentrate her efforts on growing Duote Ltd, and as a consequence the trade of Unele Ltd has declined in recent months. It will cease to trade on 30 September 2019. Its results for the nine months ended 30 September 2019 are expected to be as follows:

	£
Trading profits before capital allowances and redundancy payments	98,000
Non-trade loan relationship credits	7,500
	105,500

The tax written down value on the main pool at 1 January 2019 was £24,000. There were no acquisitions during the period, and the only disposal will be of a car held at cessation of trade (see below).

The company had one other employee who was paid a total of £25,000 as a redundancy payment. This amount was five times the statutory amount.

Samantha expects that the company will have no debtors or creditors and that the only assets of the company at 30 September 2019 will be cash of £380,000 and a car which will be sold for a cash amount of £8,000. The car has CO_2 emissions of 53g/km and was bought for £16,000 (inclusive of VAT) in 2016. The only amount owed by the company at 30 September 2019 will be corporation tax for the final period.

Exhibit 2

Duote Ltd

Existing annual supplies by Duote Ltd:

	£
Standard-rated supplies	260,000
Exempt supplies	80,000
	340,000

The VAT de minimis tests are not met.

The expansion plans would involve the lease of a small industrial unit for 15 years. Duote Ltd would pay a premium of £20,000 to lease the property, and then an annual rent of £12,000. The landlord of the property has opted to tax the building.

Duote Ltd would purchase computer and office equipment costing £30,000 for the expansion, and this will be sufficient for up to five freelancers to work at the industrial unit.

The costs of purchasing freelancer services as required by Duote Ltd for this expansion is £50 per hour. The freelancers are not VAT-registered. Some freelancers operate through companies but Duote Ltd would engage with other freelancers directly. The output of the freelancers as part of this expansion would produce standard-rated and exempt supplies for the company in the same proportion to the existing supplies.

The amounts given in this Exhibit are exclusive of VAT.

15 Raffles Ltd

Assume it is June 2019. You are working in the tax department of Woosters, a firm of ICAEW Chartered Accountants. Your manager has asked for some help in preparing for a meeting with the directors of Raffles Ltd.

Raffles Ltd and its directors are new tax clients of your firm. The directors have provided your firm with some background information on the company and its shareholders. The directors have asked for a review of the information to be undertaken to ensure that tax compliance issues for both the company and the shareholders are up to date at the start of the engagement.

Background information provided by the directors of Raffles Ltd

Raffles Ltd was set up on 1 October 2017 by two friends, Kate Kendall and Laura Lark.

The share capital of the company consists of 100 £1 shares and is owned as follows:

Name	% of share capital held	
Kate Kendall	40	Director
Laura Lark	40	Director
Marion Miller	4	Employee
Nathan Noon	4	Not an employee
Owen O'Conner	4	Not an employee
Penelope Phillips	4	Not an employee
Richard Robins	4	Not an employee
	100	

Kate paid £150,000 for her shares, funded by an inheritance from her father. Laura paid £150,000 for her shares, having borrowed £150,000 as a loan from her bank at an interest rate of 15% pa. The other shareholders invested £10,000 each.

Raffles Ltd is an unquoted, trading company, and projected profits suggest it will not be paying corporation tax in instalments. The company has no related 51% group companies and has a 30 September year end. Kate and Laura are both full-time directors of the company and pay tax at the basic rate. The five other shareholders are higher-rate taxpayers, but only Marion Miller is an employee of the company.

Raffles Ltd has made interest-free loans to each of the two directors. Details of the movements on the directors' loan accounts are set out below.

Directors' loan account balances at 30 September 2018

	Kate Kendall £	Laura Lark £
Loan made on 1 May 2018	12,000	
Loan made on 1 June 2018		25,000
Balance on 30 September 2018	12,000	25,000

Laura intends to repay her loan of £25,000 on 30 June 2019. However, she will then take another directors' loan from the company of £30,000 on 2 July 2019.

Marion Miller and Penelope Phillips also borrowed £10,000 each from the company in January 2018 at a beneficial interest rate of 1%. The directors do not believe Penelope will be able to repay her loan and therefore the company will write it off in June 2019. Marion is expected to repay her loan on its second anniversary in January 2020.

Laura Lark and Penelope Phillips have each had private use of a car provided by Raffles Ltd since 1 October 2017 and the car benefit figures calculated for each car are as follows:

Laura Lark   £990
Penelope Phillips   £2,700

Requirement

Prepare a report for your manager, to be used at the meeting with the directors of Raffles Ltd, explaining and quantifying the tax issues arising from the above information for:

- Raffles Ltd; and
- the shareholders and directors of Raffles Ltd.

Total: 25 marks

Note: Assume that the official rate of interest is 2.5%.

Groups and consortia

16   Zesst plc

Assume it is March 2019. You work as an assistant in the finance department at Zesst plc. Zesst plc is the parent company of a UK listed trading group operating in the leisure industry. Zesst plc owns 100% of the shares of VHotels Ltd and 90% of the shares in Mall Ltd. Mall Ltd owns 80% of the shares in Vrange Ltd. All of the companies in the Zesst group have 31 March year ends.

Zesst plc's finance director gives you the following information and instructions:

"I have provided you with information concerning Zesst plc and its subsidiaries (**Exhibit 1**).

"At Zesst plc's board meeting, the directors discussed plans to expand into the beauty market and have identified a potential target acquisition, Hairctz Ltd, which operates beauty salons in the UK. I need your help to prepare a paper for the board setting out the tax implications of both the acquisition of Hairctz Ltd and the proposed financing transactions. I have left you the minutes of the board meeting at which these matters were discussed (**Exhibit 2**)."

Requirements

Assuming that the proposed acquisition and financing transactions (Exhibit 2) take place on 1 April 2019, prepare a working paper for the finance director that includes:

16.1 An explanation of the tax implications for the Zesst group of the proposed acquisition of the shares of Hairctz Ltd by Zesst plc. (Ignore the proposed financing transactions for this requirement.)

16.2 Explanations and calculations of the tax implications for the Zesst group of the financing transactions identified by the board (Exhibit 2). Include your recommendation as to which company (Zesst plc or Mall Ltd) would be best placed to take on the £30 million bank loan in order to maximise tax relief for the group.

16.3 A calculation of the taxable total profits for Zesst plc, VHotels Ltd, Mall Ltd and Vrange Ltd for the years ending 31 March 2019, 2020 and 2021 and Hairctz Ltd for the years ending 31 March 2020 and 2021. Use your calculations and recommendations from part 16.2 and assume that all relevant claims for group relief are made.

Total: 40 marks

Note: Ignore indexation allowance.

Exhibit 1

Information concerning Zesst plc and its subsidiaries

Zesst plc

Zesst plc's income is derived entirely from investments.

In the year ended 31 March 2019, Zesst plc received dividends of £10 million from UK investments, including £8 million from its subsidiary Mall Ltd.

Zesst plc incurred deductible management expenses of £2 million in the year ended 31 March 2019 and forecasts similar expenses for each of the next three accounting periods.

Zesst plc purchased 25,000 shares in Wize Ltd in 2005 for £4 million which represented a 5% shareholding. Following a period of rapid success, Wize Ltd was taken over by Digital plc on 21 June 2012 when Zesst plc received 15 ordinary shares in Digital plc and a £100 non-convertible 8% debenture in Digital plc for each share it owned in Wize Ltd. The ordinary shares in Digital plc were quoted at £12 on 21 June 2012 and the £100 debenture stock at £120.

Zesst plc received debenture interest of £200,000 arising on the debentures in Digital plc in the year ended 31 March 2019. This interest is taxable as a non-trading loan relationship profit. (These debentures are treated for financial reporting purposes as available for sale financial assets. Gains and losses arising from changes in the fair value of the debentures have been recognised in reserves.)

There are no tax losses brought forward at 1 April 2018 in Zesst plc.

VHotels Ltd

VHotels Ltd owns and manages a chain of city hotels. VHotels Ltd will make a tax trading loss for the first time in the year ending 31 March 2019.

Mall Ltd and Vrange Ltd

Mall Ltd supplies exclusive toiletries and linen goods to VHotels Ltd and other hotel chains. Mall Ltd also re-brands and sells its products on-line through its 80% owned subsidiary Vrange Ltd. Neither Mall Ltd nor Vrange Ltd have tax losses brought forward at 1 April 2018.

Projected taxable trading profits/(losses) for Zesst plc and its UK subsidiaries for the years ending 31 March

	2019 £m	2020 £m	2021 £m
Zesst plc (management expenses)	(2.0)	(2.0)	(2.0)
VHotels Ltd	(14.0)	(8.0)	1.5
Mall Ltd	1.8	1.0	1.0
Vrange Ltd	20.0	32.0	45.0

The projections do not include any adjustments for the transactions relating to the proposed acquisition of Hairctz Ltd (**Exhibit 2**).

Exhibit 2

Board meeting minutes

Proposed acquisition of Hairctz Ltd

Zesst plc has identified a potential new target acquisition, Hairctz Ltd. Preliminary information provided by the seller, Softsope plc, was presented to the board as follows.

Hairctz Ltd has beauty salons in London and other cities in the UK. Its premises are leasehold except for the freehold of a salon in London which was transferred to Hairctz Ltd by its parent company, Softsope plc, in January 2003 when its market value was £9 million. The original cost of the London salon to the Softsope group was £7 million. The market value of the London salon is now £25 million.

Softsope plc will sell 100% of the shares in Hairctz Ltd for £40 million. Hairctz Ltd's tax trading losses have been used by the Softsope group.

The projected taxable trading results for Hairctz Ltd for the years ending 31 March 2020 and 2021 are as follows:

	2020 £m	2021 £m
Trading (loss)/profit	(2.0)	3.2

Financing the acquisition of Hairctz Ltd

To raise finance for the acquisition of Hairctz Ltd, the board has identified the following transactions:

(a) Zesst plc will sell its 25,000 £100 non-convertible 8% debentures in Digital plc (**Exhibit 1**). The £100 debentures are currently trading at £130.

(b) Zesst plc will sell 300 shares in EG Ltd for £6.75 million. Zesst plc bought 2,000 shares in EG Ltd for £10 million in January 2000, which represented a 20% shareholding in the company. EG Ltd provides catering services to hotels. Zesst plc sold 1,200 shares in EG Ltd in October 2018.

(c) A £30 million loan from the Zesst group's bank. The loan will be a fixed term loan repayable in 2023 at an annual rate of interest of 4%. The loan will be secured on freehold property owned by VHotels Ltd under existing group cross-guarantee arrangements.

The bank has agreed that the loan can be placed in either Zesst plc or Mall Ltd and a finance cost of £1.2 million will be charged in the appropriate company's statement of profit or loss in the years ending 31 March 2020 and 2021. If the loan is placed in Mall Ltd, there are sufficient distributable reserves in Mall Ltd to enable a dividend to be paid to the shareholders such that Zesst plc holds enough cash to purchase the Hairctz Ltd shares.

17 ICee plc

ICee plc is a UK resident company and the parent company of a UK trading group. The group has 300 employees and group revenue in the year ended 31 March 2019 was £40 million. Details of the group companies and their tax adjusted results for the year ended 31 March 2019 are in **Exhibit 1**. ICee plc researches and develops optical technology and has recently undertaken research into eye-activated technology. It makes standard-rated supplies to customers in the UK.

You are the newly-appointed financial controller at ICee plc and you report to the ICee plc finance director, Joe Day.

Joe Day gives you the following briefing: "Your predecessor prepared the adjustment to profit computation and has submitted the company tax return for ICee plc for the year ended 31 March 2019 to HMRC. I have reviewed the adjustment to profit computation and corporation tax calculation, together with notes prepared by your predecessor and believe there are some errors (**Exhibit 2**). Your predecessor was also responsible for identifying tax planning opportunities and has left a handover note of tax planning proposals (**Exhibit 3**).

"I would like you to do the following:

- Identify and explain the errors in the adjustment to profit computation and corporation tax calculation for ICee plc for the year ended 31 March 2019 (Exhibit 2). Include recommendations of the appropriate tax treatments of the issues in Notes 1–3 identifying relevant reliefs, claims and elections.

- Prepare a revised adjustment to profit computation for ICee plc for the year ended 31 March 2019.

- Explain how ICee plc's trading loss for the year ended 31 March 2019 can be used either by ICee plc or by the ICee plc group companies (Exhibit 1). Make a recommendation of the most tax efficient use of the loss.

- Evaluate briefly the tax planning proposals made by your predecessor (Exhibit 3)."

Requirement

Prepare a working paper responding to the briefing from Joe Day.

Total: 40 marks

Exhibit 1

ICee group companies and tax adjusted results for the year ended 31 March 2019

ICee plc has the following investments in group companies:

Optical Ltd

Optical Ltd is a wholly owned subsidiary of ICee plc. It is a UK trading company manufacturing optical equipment for the electronics industry. In addition to its trading income Optical Ltd receives rental income from surplus warehouse space. Its supplies are standard rated for VAT.

MedEquip Ltd

ICee plc owns 70% of the share capital of MedEquip Ltd, a UK trading company. The remaining 30% is owned by four individual investors who are directors of the company, each of whom own more than 5%. MedEquip Ltd manufactures medical equipment and its supplies are zero rated for VAT. MedEquip Ltd buys electrical parts from ICee plc.

Auge GmbH

ICee plc owns 100% of the ordinary share capital of Auge GmbH which is tax resident in Germany. Auge GmbH develops prototypes for the electronics industry. 20% of its sales are to German companies and the remainder of its sales are to companies located elsewhere in the EU.

Eris Ltd

Auge GmbH owns 80% of the shares in Eris Ltd, a UK resident company. This company fits medical devices for customers in the UK. Eris Ltd sold a brand name for £500,000 and in so doing, realised a taxable profit of £160,000. This amount has been included in its taxable trading profit of £3,645,000 (see below). Its sales are exempt from VAT.

Tax adjusted figures for other group companies – year ended 31 March 2019

	Optical Ltd £'000	MedEquip Ltd £'000	Auge GmbH £'000	Eris Ltd £'000
Trading profit/(loss)	225	(63)	(10)	3,645
Rental income	25	–	–	–

Exhibit 2

ICee plc – adjustment to profit computation, corporation tax calculation for the year ended 31 March 2019 and notes prepared by predecessor

	Notes	£'000	£'000
Profit before taxation per the statement of profit or loss			353.0
Add back tax disallowable expenses:			
Research and development expenditure	1	3,400	
Amortisation of patent costs	2	120	
Interest cost of raising loan finance	3	15	
Other disallowable expenses		550	
			4,085.0
			4,438.0
Less:			
Interest receivable on cash deposits			(82.0)
			4,356.0
Less:			
Capital allowances on plant and machinery			(720.0)
Taxable trading profit			3,636.0
Corporation tax calculation			
Corporation tax at 19%			690.8

Notes

1   Research and development expenditure

During the year ended 31 March 2019, ICee plc incurred research expenditure on eye-activated technology. I was unsure what to do with this expenditure for tax purposes and I have therefore added it back to profit. The following amounts were expensed as research costs in the statement of profit or loss:

	£'000
Staff costs	2,500
Consumable materials	700
Depreciation of laboratory equipment	200
	3,400

HMRC has agreed that ICee plc qualifies as an SME for the purpose of research and development relief.

2   Patent cost

On 1 January 2019, ICee plc acquired the trade and assets of Oogle Ltd, a software engineering company. The assets acquired consisted of the following:

	£'000
Patent	1,920
Goodwill	500
Plant and machinery	50

ICee plc now produces Oogle Ltd's products in the UK and is amortising the patent over four years. ICee plc believes that there has been no impairment of the goodwill since acquisition and therefore no costs have been charged to the statement of profit or loss in respect of this goodwill.

3   Interest cost of raising a loan to buy the investment in trade and assets of Oogle Ltd

ICee plc borrowed £600,000 on 1 January 2019 from its bank to assist in the purchase of the trade and assets of Oogle Ltd. I have added back to the profit £15,000 for the interest cost of this loan.

Exhibit 3

Handover note of tax planning proposals prepared by predecessor

Tax planning proposals

(a)   The preparation of the quarterly VAT returns is very time-consuming. I propose that ICee plc and all its subsidiaries apply to be members of the same VAT group.

(b)   ICee plc has applied for a patent for its eye-activated technology and revenues arising from this new technology are expected to be £10 million per annum starting from 1 January 2020. I have looked into the possibility of ICee plc paying a 10% corporation tax rate on the profits arising from this technology but believe that the administration costs of using this tax rate would be too excessive.

(c)   ICee plc pays its senior managers an annual cash bonus of £30,000. The managers have complained that the bonus increases their tax liability. I therefore recommend that ICee plc sets up a share option scheme which will result in the managers paying tax at 10%.

18 Splite Ltd

You work for a firm of ICAEW Chartered Accountants, which acts for the Splite group and its directors.

Splite Ltd is the holding company for a group of UK trading companies, although the directors are considering expanding the group overseas. Your firm's permanent file contains details of the group structure and loss policy (**Exhibit 1**).

The finance director of the Splite group has provided you with details of the performance of the companies during the year ended 31 December 2018 (**Exhibit 2**).

The directors want to exploit an overseas market in the country of Ritopia. They have identified a possible acquisition target, Trubo Inc. They want your firm's advice regarding the structure of a potential purchase, specifically whether to purchase the shares or the trade and assets of Trubo Inc. The directors want to offer one of their managers, Frank Line, a secondment to Ritopia when the new operation is acquired. Extracts of minutes of a Splite group board meeting are included in **Exhibit 3**.

The finance director has been awarded shares in Splite Ltd and he insists that there are no tax implications in a telephone conversation with your manager (**Exhibit 4**).

Requirements

18.1 Prepare notes for a meeting with the group finance director in which you:

(a) Advise on the impact of the capital transactions on the group's tax liabilities for the year ended 31 December 2018, and any appropriate claims or elections that will minimise the group tax liabilities (Exhibits 1 and 2).

(b) Explain the tax implications of purchasing the Trubo Inc shares or its trade and assets (Exhibit 3).

(c) Advise on the tax treatment in 2019/20 and 2020/21 of Frank's income and any gain if he sells his shares, stating any further information required (Exhibit 3).

18.2 Prepare a file note to your manager, summarising the taxation and ethical issues concerning the award of the shares in Splite Ltd to the finance director (Exhibit 4).

Total: 40 marks

Note: The RPI for December 2017 is 278.1. Ignore stamp taxes.

Exhibit 1

Extract of the permanent file on Splite group

Splite Ltd has owned the following shareholdings for several years:

- 90% of the ordinary share capital of Yogi Ltd
- 80% of the ordinary share capital of Poppie Ltd
- 40% of the ordinary share capital of Lilts Ltd

Poppie Ltd acquired 80% of the ordinary share capital of Qusi Ltd on 1 October 2018.

The remaining shareholdings of Yogi Ltd, Poppie Ltd and Qusi Ltd are owned by individuals. The remaining shares in Lilts Ltd are owned 40% by Rile Ltd, a UK trading company and 20% by a UK resident individual.

All companies except Splite Ltd are trading companies, making standard-rated supplies and preparing accounts to 31 December. Each company is registered separately for VAT and has a VAT year-end of 31 December.

If Splite Ltd or any of its group companies claims losses from another company, the claimant company must pay the surrendering company £0.50 per £1 of corporation tax relief received.

It is group policy to claim maximum loss relief possible in the current year.

Exhibit 2

Results of the Splite group for the year ended 31 December 2018

	Splite Ltd £	Yogi Ltd £	Poppie Ltd £	Qusi Ltd £	Lilts Ltd £
Trading profits/(loss)		3,400,000	1,678,000	5,000,000	(2,800,000)
Chargeable gains		See note		See note	
Property income	100,000	200,000			

Note: Capital transactions

Yogi Ltd sold a factory on 30 October 2018, receiving £2,400,000 from the purchaser. Yogi Ltd had purchased the newly constructed factory, paying £1,800,000 in January 2014. Yogi Ltd had used the factory in its trade until January 2018. From 1 February 2018, the company had rented out the property to a third party, who remained as tenant after the sale.

Qusi Ltd sold an office building in April 2018 receiving £500,000. Qusi Ltd had bought the building, built in 1984, for use in its trade in January 2002 for £800,000. However, the building frequently flooded and was in a state of disrepair.

There have been no options to tax made in respect of the properties.

Exhibit 3

Extract of Splite group board meeting minutes regarding Trubo Inc

Trubo Inc is a trading company which was incorporated in Ritopia on 1 January 2017, and has operated there ever since. Trubo Inc generates trading profits, calculated under Ritopian tax rules, equivalent to £250,000 per annum. Trubo Inc has no other income. The rate of tax on trading profits in Ritopia is 12%. There is no double tax treaty between the UK and Ritopia.

Ritopian tax rules are similar to UK corporation tax rules except that investment in any capital expenditure (plant or buildings) for use in a trade qualifies for 100% tax relief in the year of purchase. Trubo Inc incurs expenditure on plant and machinery of approximately £30,000 per annum, and invests £50,000 in new buildings or building improvements each year.

We have agreed a purchase price of £1 million but do not know whether to buy Trubo Inc's shares or its trade and assets.

If Splite Ltd buys the Trubo Inc shares, the directors would expect an annual dividend of £100,000 to be paid to Splite Ltd. Dividends are paid by Ritopian companies net of withholding tax of 2%.

Our directors will not be involved in the trade of Trubo Inc but will retain the existing local management. However, Frank Line, a manager at Yogi Ltd, will be offered a secondment to Ritopia from 1 July 2019 and this is expected to last for two years. Frank, aged 32, wants to travel in Ritopia for the month of June before starting work in the Trubo Inc business, and we will pay him during this time. We will pay for Frank's accommodation in Ritopia and for his parents to visit him three times during his secondment. Frank owns a house in the UK which he will rent out during his secondment. He also owns shares in UK-quoted companies which he might sell while on secondment.

Exhibit 4

Extract of email to your manager from the finance director

The managing director talked about giving me shares in Splite Ltd in 2012 when I joined the company. They were then worth £2 per share, but I did not actually get them then. I paid the company £20,000 for my 10,000 shares in March 2019. I have completed the share register now, but I put the date of the share transfer in the board minutes as 1 January 2012 as that was when I joined the company and I should have got the shares then.

The shares are now worth £40 per share but I paid the full 2012 value for them, so there was no reason for me to record this on my tax return for 2018/19.

19 Principia Ltd

Assume it is early September 2019. You are an ICAEW Chartered Accountant recently appointed as a tax specialist to the finance department of Principia Ltd, with responsibility for all group activities.

Background information

Principia Ltd is a UK resident holding company of a trading group and was set up by two brothers Johannes and Ibrahim Newton in 1984. The brothers are the only shareholders of Principia Ltd. The group companies manufacture and sell various items of furniture and employ approximately 400 people. Until recently the group had been successful. Due to increased competition and a significant legal issue regarding materials used in some soft furnishings, the group has had financial difficulties. As a result the Newton brothers have decided to reduce the size of the group and focus on the core manufacturing business. All group companies prepare accounts to 31 March each year.

You have been sent the following email by Johannes.

To:	Tax Adviser
From:	Johannes Newton

As you know we are looking to restructure the group and sell off some of the companies that are not part of our core business. At a recent board meeting we agreed to:

(1) sell the shares in Opticks Ltd to Einstein Ltd, a third party company, for £2.2 million. I have given you some background to this company in the first attachment to this email (**Exhibit 1**).

(2) sell the business of Scritti Ltd. The potential purchaser, Plato Ltd has mentioned a couple of methods for this. I have given more detail about the company and the methods mentioned by Plato Ltd in the second attachment (**Exhibit 2**).

I would like you to prepare a report for me on the tax implications of these two disposals, which are both expected to take place in October 2019. Your report should include the following:

(a) Explanations showing the amount of the loss available on the sale of Opticks Ltd to offset against the large gains that we expect to make on the sale of Scritti Ltd. Also set out any other tax implications.

(b) Advise me of the amount of tax payable by any Principia Ltd group companies under the two methods suggested by Plato Ltd, and recommend the most tax efficient method for Principia Ltd.

(c) If you can think of any other method of disposal that may be acceptable to both parties, briefly explain how this works and the advantages and disadvantages of this method for either party compared to our preferred method from your previous analysis. I don't expect you to do detailed calculations for this method.

Finally, I know that you previously worked in the finance department of Plato Ltd and are likely to have a good insight into their negotiation methods. It would really help us if you could have a chat with me about this later. I am particularly interested in whether there is the possibility of an increase in the current price if we suggest one. There may be a bonus in it for you if we get an increase in price!

Regards

Johannes

Requirements

19.1 Using calculations where appropriate, prepare the report requested by Johannes Newton in his email.

19.2 Explain your ethical position from Johannes's request relating to your knowledge of Plato Ltd.

Total: 40 marks

Note: The RPI at December 2017 is 278.1.

Exhibit 1

Information on Opticks Ltd

As the business developed we decided that the group should diversify and in March 2013, Principia Ltd purchased the entire share capital of Opticks Ltd for £3.5 million. Opticks Ltd is a property investment company, investing in both residential and commercial properties.

A large residential property investment owned by Opticks Ltd decreased significantly in value recently due a landfill site being opened close to the property. This had an impact on the value of the company.

Opticks Ltd also owned the office building used as the headquarters of the Principia group. The building will still be required by the Principia group after the sale of Opticks Ltd. Therefore, Opticks Ltd sold the office building to Principia Ltd for £500,000 in August 2019. At that time the office building was valued at £850,000 and it had cost Opticks Ltd £300,000 when new in February 2004.

At the time of the share sale Opticks Ltd is expected to be worth £2.2 million.

Exhibit 2

Information on Scritti Ltd

Scritti Ltd manufactures high-quality bespoke oak furniture. The company was purchased by Principia Ltd for £450,000 in June 1987. Scritti Ltd had trading losses brought forward from the year ended 31 March 2019 of £410,000 and is expected to break even in the year ended 31 March 2020. The directors have decided that the group should focus on mid-range mass-market furniture and so should dispose of Scritti Ltd.

Two alternative methods of disposing of the business to Plato Ltd have been proposed by the purchasers:

- Option 1 – sell the trade and assets of Scritti Ltd for £3.21 million. Plato Ltd will take all assets and liabilities.

- Option 2 – sell the shares in Scritti Ltd to Plato Ltd for an amount such that Plato Ltd's total costs are the same as under option 1.

If option 1 is chosen, the company will undergo a solvent liquidation and will distribute all available proceeds of sale to Principia Ltd.

The trade and assets of Scritti Ltd are as set out below, shown at their expected market value in October 2019:

	£'000	£'000
Freehold factory		2,000
Goodwill (all internally generated since 1983)		500
Plant and machinery (all items valued at less than original cost)		400
		2,900
Current assets		
Inventory	450	
Receivables	270	
Cash	10	
	730	
Current liabilities		
Trade payables	210	
Bank overdraft (unsecured)	110	
Hire purchase liability	100	
	(420)	
Net current liabilities		310
		3,210

The freehold factory was transferred to Scritti Ltd by Principia Ltd in June 2014 when it was worth £1 million. It had cost Principia Ltd £550,000 in January 1998.

The plant and machinery had a tax written down value of £80,000 at 1 April 2019.

20 Expandit plc

You are an ICAEW Chartered Accountant, working in practice. Your manager, Richard Ellis, has asked for your assistance in preparation for a meeting with one of your firm's tax clients, Expandit plc.

Background information

Expandit plc is a UK registered company, trading as a furniture manufacturer. Expandit plc has a draft tax adjusted trading profit for the year ending 31 December 2018 of £3.8 million. The company has experienced rapid growth in recent years and now employs over 500 staff in the UK alone. Expandit plc is VAT registered and its annual period for VAT ends on 31 December.

The financial controller of Expandit plc, Martin Morley, has asked for your assistance in calculating the projected corporation tax payable by Expandit plc for the year ending 31 December 2018. Five issues have been identified by Martin Morley, which have not been taken into account in calculating the tax adjusted trading profits of Expandit plc (**Exhibit 1**).

Martin Morley has recently attended a professional update course on VAT and as a result he has emailed you a number of questions concerning the VAT position of Expandit plc (**Exhibit 2**).

Requirements

20.1 Calculate the corporation tax payable by Expandit plc for the year ending 31 December 2018. Provide explanations on how each of the five issues in Exhibit 1 should be treated for corporation tax purposes and whether any beneficial claims, elections or reliefs can be used to reduce the corporation tax payable.

20.2 Prepare a file note to document all of the tax and ethical issues you would need to consider in replying to Martin's email in Exhibit 2.

Total: 35 marks

Exhibit 1

Outstanding issues

The following five issues are to be taken into account in the corporation tax computation of Expandit plc for the year ending 31 December 2018:

(1) On 1 June 2018 Expandit plc bought 90% of the shares of a UK registered trading company, Foldit Ltd. Foldit Ltd also has a 31 December year end and had brought forward trading losses of £150,000 at 1 January 2018. It is estimated that Foldit Ltd will make trading losses of £360,000 during the year ending 31 December 2018. Foldit Ltd prints and sells newspapers and journals. Expandit plc is looking at ways to return the Foldit Ltd business to profitability.

(2) On 31 May 2018, Expandit plc sold its 75% shareholding in Holdit Ltd, a UK registered trading company. The gain realised on sale was £1.45 million. Expandit plc had owned the shares in Holdit Ltd since 1 January 2012.

Expandit plc had transferred its old office building to Holdit Ltd in January 2015, when the building was worth £200,000. The old office building had cost Expandit plc £95,000 in March 2005. The indexation allowance from March 2005 to January 2015 was £32,395 and from March 2005 to December 2017 was £43,700. The old office building had a market value of £220,000 on 31 May 2018. Holdit Ltd makes up accounts to 31 December.

(3) On 1 May 2018 Expandit plc set up a permanent establishment in the non-EEA country of Beregenia. Profits of the Beregenian permanent establishment for the period to 31 December 2018 are estimated to be £140,000 and these profits will be subject to 40% tax in Beregenia. None of the profits will be remitted to the UK.

(4) On 1 April 2018, Expandit plc bought an 80% shareholding in Grabbit Inc, a trading company incorporated in the country of Faraway. Grabbit Inc is managed and controlled in Faraway.

Grabbit Inc has trading profits of £1 million for the year ending 31 December 2018 and corporation tax will be payable on these profits in Faraway at the rate of 30%.

Expandit plc made a loan of £500,000 to Grabbit Inc on 1 April 2018, at a market interest rate of 5% pa. Grabbit Inc paid interest of £18,750 on 31 December 2018 and tax of 15% was withheld in Faraway.

Grabbit Inc paid a dividend of £200,000 to Expandit plc on 31 December 2018. This dividend was subject to 5% withholding tax in Faraway.

(5) During the year ending 31 December 2018, Expandit plc sold furniture to Grabbit Inc for £500,000. The normal retail price for these goods is £300,000.

Expandit plc does not own shares in any other companies.

Exhibit 2

Email from Martin Morley

To:	Tax Adviser
From:	Martin Morley
Date:	June 2019
Subject:	VAT and Expandit plc and group companies

I recently attended a VAT update course provided by the local ICAEW branch. It was really informative and gave me a number of ideas on how VAT can be minimised for Expandit plc and the companies in the Expandit plc group.

Can you help me understand the following?

(a) Why do we not have a VAT group? The course made it clear that VAT groups are often advantageous. I want to understand why Expandit plc does not form a VAT group with one or more of the other companies in the group.

(b) I now realise that we may have made a mistake on Expandit plc's previous year's VAT return.

On 1 December 2016 we brought a new office building into use. The building cost us £500,000 and was purchased directly from the developer. We did not opt to tax the building. The capacity of the building proved too much for us and so we rented out half of the building to an unconnected company on 1 December 2017. This company are still renting half the building today.

I am quite happy that we should declare the impact of this mistake to HMRC for future VAT accounting periods, but, as the amount of tax at stake is minimal, could we ignore the error for prior VAT accounting periods, just to keep things simple?

Let me know your views.

Martin

Overseas aspects of corporation tax

21   Scandipop AB

Assume it is December 2019. You work as a tax adviser for a firm of ICAEW Chartered Accountants. Your firm has been engaged by Scandipop AB, a non-UK resident company, to provide it with tax advice relating to setting up a manufacturing plant in the UK.

Background information

Scandipop AB is resident in the country of Norwen. The company manufactures a traditional, soft drink called 'Scandipop'. Scandipop has become very popular in the UK and so Scandipop AB is setting up a UK manufacturing plant.

The company intends to send a number of production engineers from Norwen to the UK, on secondment, to set up the manufacturing plant. The details of the secondment package are set out in **Exhibit 1.**

Scandipop AB's tax advisers in Norwen have asked the company to seek tax advice in the UK concerning the UK tax status of the seconded production engineers. Scandipop AB's chief operating officer is sceptical about the need for this tax advice and, in a recent telephone call, he stated:

"If the UK tax regulations are too complicated, we will simply send the employees to the UK and ignore all the related reporting requirements for UK tax and national insurance purposes. In the past I have found that you can get away with this approach in some jurisdictions and it saves a lot of paperwork."

Scandipop AB has also asked for advice about the UK corporation tax implications of setting up a UK subsidiary company and the financing of and supply of raw materials to the UK subsidiary company (**Exhibit 2**).

Requirements

21.1 In relation to the UK secondments to be undertaken by employees of Scandipop AB:

   (a)   Prepare notes on the UK income tax implications for Scandipop AB employees of undertaking the proposed UK secondments. Your answer should explain and justify your conclusions. Ignore national insurance contributions in answering this part of the question.

   (b)   Provide a file note on the response your firm should make to the statement made by the chief operating officer of Scandipop AB.

21.2 Prepare a briefing note for the Scandipop AB board of directors, identifying the UK corporation tax implications of:

   •   setting up Scandipop UK Ltd;
   •   the arrangements for the financing of the UK subsidiary; and
   •   the arrangements for the supply of raw materials to the UK subsidiary.

Total: 35 marks

Exhibit 1

Secondment package for Scandipop AB staff seconded to the UK

The Scandipop AB staff being seconded to the UK are all domiciled in Norwen and have been resident in Norwen for many years. They will be offered an 18-month secondment to the UK operation of Scandipop, from 1 January 2020 to 30 June 2021.

Staff will be required to return to Norwen for three days, four times a year, for training and will work 37 hours per week, whilst in the UK.

Most staff will not bring their families with them and so will expect to return to Norwen at least one weekend per month (travelling to Norwen on the Friday evening and back to the UK in time for work on the Monday morning). None of the staff have ever visited the UK for work before, although some of the staff have taken short holidays in the UK in recent years. Most staff expect to spend their 4 weeks per annum annual holiday in Norwen with their families.

Whilst in the UK, they will be provided with rent free accommodation and have all their travelling costs between the UK and Norwen paid for by Scandipop AB. Their salary will be paid into a UK bank account in pounds sterling, however, the employees on secondment will retain employment rights with Scandipop AB in Norwen and their employment in Norwen will not be treated as ceasing. They will return to their old employment in Norwen at the end of the secondment.

Exhibit 2

Details of the business structure, financing of and supply of raw materials to the proposed UK subsidiary company

Scandipop AB will set up a UK manufacturing plant to produce Scandipop for the UK market. The operation will start trading on 1 January 2020, when a UK resident company, Scandipop UK Ltd will be incorporated for this purpose. Scandipop UK Ltd will make up accounts to 31 December annually.

An initial investment of £2,850,000 will be required to fund working capital and acquire the factory premises and plant and machinery for the production process.

The investment required will be financed by a UK bank loan of £1,500,000, at a fixed interest rate of 7% pa, and a loan of £1,350,000 from Scandipop AB at a fixed interest rate of 15% pa. The UK Bank was prepared to lend a maximum of £2,000,000 to Scandipop UK Ltd, based on the company's ability to service the loan.

The main raw ingredient in the Scandipop soft drink is lingonberries, grown in Norwen. Scandipop AB will purchase lingonberries in Norwen and sell them to Scandipop UK Ltd. In the year ending 31 December 2020 Scandipop UK Ltd will require 500 tonnes of lingonberries to maintain planned production. Scandipop AB buys lingonberries for £100 per tonne, but is planning to sell them to Scandipop UK Ltd for £500 per tonne.

The rate of corporation tax in Norwen is 16%.

Scandipop AB has 5,000 employees based in Norwen.

22 Staplit plc

Assume it is early June 2019. You are an ICAEW Chartered Accountant, working in practice. Chloe Hamer, one of the tax partners is due to meet with a client, Staplit plc, and has asked for your help in preparing for the meeting.

Background information

Staplit plc is a UK registered company, with business interests in the UK and overseas. The company's adjusted trading profits totalled £200 million in the year ended 31 March 2019. In addition to a number of wholly-owned subsidiaries, Staplit Ltd also has some overseas permanent establishments. The company now employs over 400 staff in the UK, plus around 100 staff overseas. Staplit plc is VAT registered and has an annual period for VAT ending on 31 March.

Whilst Staplit plc has an internal tax department that can deal with most UK related issues, it has limited expertise on overseas issues. The company would like some advice on a number of overseas issues (**Exhibit 1**).

During her review of the client files for the year ended 31 March 2019, Chloe identified a deduction for loan interest in one of the Staplit plc group companies. She has sent you an email asking you to look at this in more detail (**Exhibit 2**).

Requirements

Prepare briefing notes for Chloe Hamer that explain, with the aid of calculations where appropriate:

22.1 The tax implications for Staplit plc of each of the mutually exclusive issues in Exhibit 1; and

22.2 How to treat the loan outlined in her email (Exhibit 2).

Total: 35 marks

Exhibit 1

Overseas issues

The following three issues relate to recent and future transactions of Staplit plc:

1   On 1 October 2018 Staplit plc injected cash into Templehof Inc, one of its wholly-owned subsidiaries. Templehof Inc used the monies to purchase machinery which it then leases on a three year operating lease to Pancras Ltd, one of Staplit plc's wholly owned UK subsidiaries for a market rent of £6 million each year. Templehof Inc employees' only involvement in this transaction was to purchase it and to invoice for the lease payments. Pancras Ltd uses the machinery and carries out any maintenance on it.

Templehof Inc is resident in Utopia and pays tax on its income at 8%. The client files confirm that Pancras Ltd and Templehof Inc are large companies and that the CFC charge does not apply to the profits of Templehof Inc.

2   On 1 March 2019 Staplit plc purchased some online distance learning training from a German company for the equivalent sterling cost of £80,000. The training related to a manufacturing process used by a number of different group companies. The online training was undertaken by 50 UK employees, 40 employees elsewhere within the EU and 70 employees in Erehwon (outside of the EU). The finance department treated this as a business-to-business supply for VAT purposes.

3   Staplit plc has received clearance to incorporate a permanent establishment in Ruritania (a non-EU country). The trade and assets valued at £2 million are to be transferred to Hermy SA, a new Ruritania resident company, in exchange for the entire share capital worth £1.8 million and the balance in the form of cash. The disposal of the assets is expected to result in chargeable gains of £500,000 on a freehold factory and £100,000 on an office building.

One of the purposes of the incorporation is to enable local directors to be included in the share ownership. It is anticipated that, six months after the incorporation, 25% of the shares will be sold to the local directors for approximately £550,000. In addition the freehold factory is becoming too small for the expanding business and it is expected to be sold in two years for £650,000, to be replaced by a larger factory.

Exhibit 2

Email from Chloe Hamer

To:	Tax Adviser
From:	Chloe Hamer
Date:	June 2019
Subject:	Felisk Ltd – bank loan

On a review of the tax files for the year ended 31 March 2019 I came across a deduction of £1.4 million for loan interest in the calculations for Felisk Ltd, one of Staplit plc's UK subsidiaries. Felisk Ltd has revenue of about £100 million pa and total assets of £45 million.

I haven't had time to look into this properly and would like you to put together your thoughts on this based on the information that the company's finance director sent through to me. See below for an extract of his email:

"On 1 April 2018 Felisk Ltd took out a bank loan for £20 million over 10 years at a rate of 7%. The bank had originally offered only £10 million over 5 years at a rate of 9%. However, it agreed to the revised loan because of a guarantee provided by Staplit plc (for which Felisk Ltd has not made any payment). Staplit plc does not make guarantees to non-group companies."

Please could you add this onto the end of the briefing notes that you are preparing for me. Look at the impact on current and future accounting periods.

Kind regards.

Chloe

Changing business structures

23 Poachers Products plc

You work for XYZ Accountants, who act as tax advisers to Poachers Products plc. Poachers Products plc is the parent company of a long-established group of UK resident companies, which was formerly quoted on the Stock Exchange. On 15 June 2018, its shares were acquired by Outdoors Holdings Inc, a US quoted company. Both the Poachers and Outdoors Holdings groups manufacture and sell outdoor and sports clothing and equipment.

The tax manager of Poachers Products plc left following the takeover, so the Finance Director Hugo Brockhurst has asked for your assistance in the following:

(a) The Outdoors Holdings group has developed a patented process for manufacturing washable, breathable waterproof fabric from old plastic bottles at its US research and development facility. It is now looking to set up a European operation to complement the US one, and will transfer the European patent rights to the new company. The company will carry on a range of research and development activities, including developing a large-scale manufacturing process for the patent and also to develop new ways in which the patented process can be used. One of the first priorities will be to develop a version of the fabric which can be used at very low temperatures.

It is hoped that the facility will be open by the end of 2020. While it is hoped that low-volume manufacturing will begin within 12 months of the facility opening, over a period of five years it is expected to develop a large and profitable manufacturing business, which will run parallel to its research and development activities.

The Overseas Holdings group chief financial officer has therefore asked Hugo to compile a report which sets out whether the UK would be a suitable location for the facility (similar reports are being prepared by finance officers in other countries).

Hugo has asked your firm to provide a draft of the tax section of the report, using the following assumptions:

- The activities would be undertaken by a new UK resident company, the only activities of which would be the research and development activities set out above and to manufacture products incorporating the patent. All manufacturing unrelated to the patent will continue to be undertaken by other group companies.

- The initial investment in the facility would be £100 million. Of this, £50 million would be spent on land and buildings, £20 million on plant and fixtures, £10 million in the form of the acquisition of the patent rights and £20 million on working capital.

- The company would incur research and development expenditure of approximately £5 million per annum from the time that the facility opens. No research and development expenditure will be subcontracted to either third parties or other related parties. The company would be classed as a large company for research and development purposes.

- Five years after incorporation, it would be expected to make a profit of £8 million per annum. This is based on projected turnover of £20 million, with research and development costs of £5 million, other staff costs of £2 million, brand payments of £0.5 million and other operating costs (including the amortisation of the patent) of £4.5 million.

- The new company would not own any marketing intangibles, so the brand payments made to other group companies would reflect the full arm's length cost of using those intangibles.

- Other UK resident group companies would have sufficient profits to absorb any losses.

(b) Some intra-group restructuring has been undertaken since the Poachers Products group was acquired by Outdoors Holdings Inc. Hugo believes this was to optimise the US tax position of Outdoors Holdings Inc. However, he has realised that no UK tax sign off was obtained for some of the transactions. He has therefore asked your firm to review them, and to provide a note summarising the tax consequences of what has been done.

Before the reorganisation, Poachers Finance Ltd (the group finance company) and Poachers Trading Ltd (the main trading company) were both wholly owned subsidiaries of Poachers Products plc. The transactions undertaken on 30 December 2018 were as follows:

(1) Poachers Trading Ltd bought back 30% of its own shares, with the consideration of £150 million being provided by Poachers Products plc by way of a loan.

(2) Poachers Products plc set up a new UK resident company called Poachers Holdings UK Ltd (PHUK), and transferred 100% of the shares in Poachers Finance Ltd to PHUK in exchange for an issue of shares to Poachers Products plc.

(3) The shares in Poachers Trading Ltd were transferred by way of share for share exchange to Outdoors Holdings Luxembourg SA, a Luxembourg resident company which was previously 100% directly held by Outdoors Holdings Inc. The value of the shares issued by Outdoor Holdings Luxembourg SA was equal to the value of the Poachers Trading Ltd shares transferred.

(4) The shares in Outdoors Holdings Luxembourg SA which were received in (3) were then distributed in kind to Outdoors Holdings Inc. Hugo has confirmed that Poachers Products plc had sufficient distributable reserves for this to be a lawful distribution.

Poachers Trading Ltd has been a 100% owned subsidiary of Poachers Products plc since 1928, and has no non-trading activities. Both the Poachers Products plc group before its acquisition, and the Outdoors Holdings Inc groups are trading groups.

Requirements

23.1 Prepare a draft of the tax section of the report which Hugo Brockhurst has been asked to prepare, using the information set out in (a) above. You should set out any tax incentives which would apply to the investment, as well as any other features of the UK tax regime which would be relevant.

23.2 Prepare the note which Hugo Brockhurst has requested outlining the UK corporation tax consequences of the reorganisation set out in (b).

Total: 30 marks

24 CFR

You are a tax assistant working for CFR, a firm of ICAEW Chartered Accountants. You have reviewed the personal tax files of Fred Bead and his niece Fiona Mare and have ascertained the following information:

Fred Bead

On 30 June 2018, Fred who is 70, retired from his sole trader printing business. On the sale of his business he realised chargeable gains of £300,000.

Fred's projected income and income tax liabilities are as follows:

	Actual 2018/19 £	Projected 2019/20 £
Taxable trading profits	70,000	–
Pension	–	80,000
Bank interest	3,750	3,750
Dividends from UK quoted companies	10,000	10,000
Total income	83,750	93,750
Personal allowance (based on 2018/19 rates)	(11,850)	(11,850)
Taxable income	71,900	81,900
Income tax liabilities	20,260	24,260

Fiona Mare

Fiona is an engineer. She received a large inheritance and set up a sole trader business on 1 January 2017. Her business is designing and installing energy saving technologies and it has a 31 December year end. The business has 25 employees and revenue of £2 million for the year ended 31 December 2018.

Fred has offered to invest £600,000 in Fiona's business which will be incorporated on 1 May 2019. These funds will be used for research and development expenditure to develop a new process which will be a major advancement in energy saving technology.

Fiona has sent you an email (**Exhibit**) setting out details concerning the incorporation of her business which will be called Fiona Mare Ltd.

You also receive the following phone call from Fred:

"I would like to invest £600,000 in Fiona's business in a tax efficient manner. I do not want to be involved in Fiona's business on a day-to-day basis. I intend to gift my shares in Fiona Mare Ltd (Exhibit) to Fiona in four years. I do not want you to tell Fiona my intention as I want her to be motivated to succeed but I want to understand the tax implications of this proposed gift."

Requirements

Prepare notes for your manager which include tax planning recommendations and advice on opportunities to save tax where relevant. In these notes you should:

24.1 Determine and explain the tax implications for Fiona of the incorporation of her business as Fiona Mare Ltd (Exhibit). Include an explanation of the tax implications for the company, Fiona Mare Ltd.

24.2 Explain the tax implications for Fred of investing £600,000 in the shares in Fiona Mare Ltd.

24.3 Explain the tax implications for Fred of the proposed gift by him to Fiona of his shares in Fiona Mare Ltd.

24.4 Identify any ethical conflicts in relation to advising Fred and Fiona and determine what action your firm needs to take.

Total: 35 marks

Exhibit

Email from Fiona Mare

To:	Tax assistant
From:	Fiona Mare
Date:	3 March 2019
Subject:	Future plans for business

My Uncle Fred has offered to invest £600,000 in my business on 1 May 2019 to spend on research and development.

I will first incorporate my sole trader business as Fiona Mare Ltd. Fiona Mare Ltd will then issue new shares to Fred equivalent to a 25% shareholding in Fiona Mare Ltd in return for a £600,000 investment by Fred.

Fiona Mare Ltd will have a 5 April year end and expects to pay a dividend to Fred of £45,000 in the period to 5 April 2020.

The incorporation of my sole trader business will happen on 1 May 2019. At that date, I will cease to trade as a sole trader. My business assets will have the following market values and chargeable gains:

	Market values £	Chargeable gains £
Goodwill	100,000	100,000
Freehold factory unit	560,000	160,000
Fiona's car – 90% business use	50,000	–
Plant and machinery	280,000	–
Net current assets excluding cash	260,000	–
Cash	100,000	–
	1,350,000	260,000

I will keep £100,000 in cash but the remainder of the business assets will be transferred to Fiona Mare Ltd in exchange for shares. The assets transferred will include my car which is a Porsche with a list price of £75,000 and CO_2 emissions of 225g/km.

The adjusted trading profit from my sole trader business and potential capital allowance claims up to the date of incorporation are as follows:

	Trading profits £	Capital allowances £
Year ended 31 December 2018	20,000	(50,000)
Projected for period to 30 April 2019	10,000	(2,000)

An election will be made for Fiona Mare Ltd to take over the tax written down value of the main pool and special rate pool for capital allowances purposes. My business had no taxable profits or losses in the year ended 31 December 2017 and there are no overlap profits.

I have no other taxable income or chargeable gains as my inheritance has met my living expenses.

I anticipate that Fiona Mare Ltd will make substantial taxable profits in the period from 1 May 2019 to 5 April 2020.

Fiona

25 Shandy Ltd

Pickle plc owns 100% of the ordinary share capital of Shandy Ltd. Both companies are UK resident for tax purposes.

You are a tax adviser, working for a firm of ICAEW Chartered Accountants, Tristram and Co. Your firm has been engaged by the management team at Shandy Ltd (the 'MBO team'), to act on their behalf providing tax advice concerning a proposed management buy-out.

Shandy Ltd manufactures and sells one product, a chemical sold under the trade name of 'Shandy Soap' and used by professional tradesmen to prepare wood for painting. Shandy Soap is only sold through trade outlets and is not available to the public. Sales of the product have been declining for many years and in recent years Shandy Ltd has been making trading losses. Estimates of tax adjusted trading profits and losses, for both group companies, for the year ending 30 September 2019, and details of brought forward tax-adjusted trading losses are shown below.

Estimated tax adjusted trading profits and losses

Year ending 30 September 2019	Pickle plc £	Shandy Ltd £
Estimated tax adjusted trading profits/(losses)	800,000	(250,000)

Shandy Ltd had brought forward tax-adjusted trading losses of £60,000 from the year ended 30 September 2017 and £129,000 from the year ended 30 September 2018. There are no brought forward capital losses. Neither company had any other sources of taxable profits.

The MBO team believe they could return the company to profitability if they were allowed to run the company themselves. On 1 April 2019, they entered into negotiations with Pickle plc to purchase either the trade and assets of Shandy Ltd or the share capital of Shandy Ltd (this could be referred to as a purchase of the trade and assets of Shandy Ltd, with or without the company). The proposed structure of the management buy-out and the MBO team's plans for the future of the Shandy Ltd trade are set out in **Exhibit 1.**

You have also received an email from your manager (**Exhibit 2**) detailing some concerns that need to be addressed.

Requirements

Your manager has asked you to prepare a briefing note in preparation for a meeting with the MBO team in which you should:

25.1 Explain the tax implications, for the MBO team, of each of the three different options suggested in Exhibit 1 for the purchase of the trade and assets of Shandy Ltd, with or without the company.

25.2 Recommend which purchase option the MBO team should adopt, giving reasons for your recommendation.

25.3 List any further information you would need to finalise your tax advice.

25.4 Provide an initial response to the concerns raised in your manager's email in Exhibit 2.

Total: 35 marks

Exhibit 1

Purchase of the trade and assets of Shandy Ltd, with or without the company

The purchase is expected to take place on 30 September 2019.

The trade and assets of Shandy Ltd have been valued at £2 million.

The MBO team have three, different, mutually exclusive options for carrying out the purchase of the trade and assets of Shandy Ltd, with or without the company, as detailed in the table below.

Option	Structure of the deal	Description of purchase
(1)	The MBO team pays Pickle plc £2 million.	The MBO team acquire 100% of the share capital of Shandy Ltd. Purchase 'with' the company.
(2)	The MBO team's newly incorporated company pays Shandy Ltd £2 million.	The MBO team set up a newly incorporated company and the company acquires the trade and assets of Shandy Ltd. Purchase 'without' the company.
(3)	• Pickle plc sets up a new, 100% owned, subsidiary company, NewShandy Ltd. • Shandy Ltd transfers its trade and assets to NewShandy Ltd. • The MBO team pays Pickle plc £2 million.	The MBO team acquire 100% of the share capital of NewShandy Ltd. A hive down.

Under all three options, the individuals making up the MBO team would need to borrow approximately £2 million, between them, to finance the purchase. The MBO team would like to know if they would be able to receive a tax deduction for the costs of this loan finance.

The MBO team intend to diversify the trade of Shandy Ltd, whatever purchase mechanism they use, and return it to profitability by:

(1) selling Shandy Soap to the retail, amateur, painting and decorating market by selling the product to 'do-it-yourself' superstore chains; and

(2) retailing a wide range of decorating-related products under the 'Shandy Soap' brand name to the retail 'do-it-yourself' market.

Exhibit 2

Email from your manager

From:	Your Tax Manager
To:	A Tax Adviser
Subject:	Management Buy-Out of Shandy Ltd

I spent time this week with Ian Spencer, the financial controller of both Shandy Ltd and Pickle plc, performing an initial review of the paperwork concerning Shandy Ltd, in preparation for the management buy-out. Ian is not a member of the MBO team.

I asked to see Shandy Ltd's VAT returns and Ian was a little reluctant. Eventually, he admitted that the VAT returns for Shandy Ltd contained some inaccuracies. Because HMRC had not picked up the errors, and there had been no recent VAT control visits, he had decided not to report the errors to HMRC.

The errors had arisen because the company had, due to a clerical error, inadvertently mis-entered figures of output VAT on returns. This had resulted in an underpayment of VAT, amounting to £50,000 over the course of the past year. Shandy Ltd is not in a group VAT registration with Pickle plc.

Please consider the ethical implications of this issue and its impact on the management buy-out, in the briefing note you are preparing for my forthcoming meeting with the MBO team.

26 Upten plc

Assume it is June 2019. You are Tina Yarn and you have just started a new job as financial controller at Upten plc which manufactures clothes and household goods in the UK. Upten plc has one wholly-owned subsidiary, Woren Ltd, which imports electrical goods for sale to retailers in the UK. Upten plc and Woren Ltd both have a 30 September year end. The gross assets of the Upten group are £10 million and the group has 100 employees in the UK.

You report to the Upten plc finance director who has asked you to help with his preparation for the next board meeting and has given you the following briefing:

"The Upten plc board is planning to discuss the following two matters at the next board meeting.

"To motivate senior managers at Upten plc, the board is introducing a share option scheme. The board want to ensure that tax reliefs are maximised for key employees and therefore the scheme will be a tax-advantaged share option scheme. An email will be sent to the employees explaining the scheme and will include a worked example demonstrating the tax benefit of accepting the options. I have provided you with the proposed details of the scheme (**Exhibit 1**).

"Upten plc will expand its operations to include retailing its products in the UK. I have set out in the attached note details of a proposed joint venture to implement this expansion (**Exhibit 2**). The joint venture will be achieved by incorporating a company, DLP Ltd.

"Please draft briefing notes for me in which you:

- recommend the most appropriate share option scheme for Upten plc (Exhibit 1). Assuming an employee sells the shares on 30 June 2021, calculate the after tax cash receivable for one employee under the share option scheme; and

- explain the tax implications for Upten plc, Woren Ltd and DLP Ltd of each alternative ownership structure for the joint venture in DLP Ltd (Exhibit 2). Include calculations of the projected taxable profits or losses for each company for the year ending 30 September 2020, assuming that any losses will be used as early as possible."

Requirement

Draft the briefing notes as instructed by the finance director.

Total: 30 marks

Note: Ignore indexation allowance.

Exhibit 1

Proposed share option scheme

On 1 July 2019, 10 managers will be granted an option over 40,000 shares each at the market price of the shares at that date which is expected to be £2.50 per share. The options will be exercised on 30 June 2021 when the market value is expected to have increased to £6 per share.

Exhibit 2

Joint venture in DLP Ltd

On 1 October 2019, Upten plc will start retailing its products in the UK as a joint venture with either Wohnung GmbH, a German homeware retailer, or Home Ltd, a UK homeware retailer. The joint venture will be achieved by incorporating a company, DLP Ltd with one of the following alternative ownership structures:

Structure 1: Upten plc will own 75% and Wohnung GmbH will own 25% of the ordinary shares in DLP Ltd.

Structure 2: Upten plc will own 65% and Home Ltd will own 35% of the ordinary shares in DLP Ltd.

Consideration for the shares in DLP Ltd will be as follows:

	Structure 1 £'000	Structure 2 £'000
Upten plc contribution		
Warehouse (Note)	5,000	5,000
Cash	4,000	2,800
Wohnung GmbH – cash	3,000	–
Home Ltd – cash	–	4,200
	12,000	12,000

Note: Upten plc owns a warehouse in London, which was used as a distribution centre. Upten plc recently centralised its distribution network and the warehouse will not be used in the future by Upten plc. This warehouse will be transferred to DLP Ltd on 1 October 2019 at its market value of £5 million and, after conversion to a retail unit, will be used by DLP Ltd for its retail trade.

The warehouse was originally purchased by Upten plc's subsidiary Woren Ltd in October 2016 for £4 million and was transferred to Upten plc on 1 October 2017. The market value at the date of transfer was £4 million. A claim to rollover a chargeable gain of £300,000 on a business asset sold by Woren Ltd in March 2016 had been made against the cost of the warehouse.

Projected taxable trading profits and losses for the year ending 30 September 2020

	Upten plc £'000	Woren Ltd £'000	DLP Ltd £'000
Trading profit/(loss)	1,500	4,500	(3,600)

At 1 October 2019, Upten plc is expected to have tax trading losses brought forward of £2.5 million (of which £0.6 million is a post-1 April 2017 trading loss) and capital losses brought forward of £550,000. Woren Ltd has no tax losses brought forward at 1 October 2019. DLP Ltd is expected to make trading profits in the year ending 30 September 2021.

ICAEW 2019 — Changing business structures — 55

27 Montgomery Ltd

You are an ICAEW Chartered Accountant, recently appointed to the finance department of Montgomery Ltd, to provide in-house tax advice.

Background Information

Montgomery Ltd is a UK registered company, set up by two individual shareholders in 2015, to retail clothing. The company has been successful, with taxable trading profits in the year ended 31 March 2019 of £800,000 and in excess of 300 employees. Montgomery Ltd is now expanding its business into manufacturing goods for sale in its own retail outlets.

In April 2019, Montgomery Ltd set up a new, wholly owned subsidiary, Fever Ltd. On 1 July 2019, Fever Ltd acquired the trade and assets of Romulus Ltd; an unconnected, UK-based, T-shirt manufacturer. The details of this acquisition are set out in **Exhibit 1**.

Due to high operational costs in the UK, Montgomery Ltd is also planning to manufacture goods overseas, in countries with lower operational costs. As the first stage in this plan, Montgomery Ltd is setting up a jeans manufacturing business in the country of Asiatica, which will start trading on 1 January 2020. The details of the proposed operation in Asiatica are set out in **Exhibit 2**.

Requirements

27.1 Explain and quantify the tax consequences for Montgomery Ltd and Fever Ltd, of the acquisition of the trade and assets of Romulus Ltd on 1 July 2019 (Exhibit 1).

27.2 Explain the tax implications of the alternative business structures proposed for the factory in Asiatica (Exhibit 2).

Total: 40 marks

Note: Ignore diverted profits tax.

Exhibit 1

The acquisition of the trade and assets of Romulus Ltd by Fever Ltd on 1 July 2019

Relevant information about each company is as follows.

Romulus Ltd

- VAT registered, with a VAT return year ending on 31 March
- Capital losses brought forward as at 30 June 2019; £155,000
- Trading losses brought forward as at 30 June 2019; £245,000
- Tax written down value of the main pool at 30 June 2019; £25,000
- Market values of the assets of Romulus Ltd on 30 June 2019:

  - Plant and machinery in the main pool for capital allowance purposes £75,000
  - Property used in the trade £300,000 (Note)
  - Net current assets £25,000

Note: The property comprises the T-shirt factory which was purchased new from the developer, on 28 February 2015 for the VAT exclusive price of £275,000 and has been used 100% for the purposes of T-shirt manufacturing by Romulus Ltd. Romulus Ltd has not exercised the option to tax the property.

Fever Ltd

- Started trading on 1 July 2019

- Paid £600,000 for the trade and assets of Romulus Ltd on 1 July 2019

- Registered for VAT on 1 July 2019, with a VAT return year ending on 31 March

- The assets transferred include the property which comprises the T-shirt factory. The factory has three floors and Fever Ltd uses two of the floors for manufacturing and rents the third floor out to young fashion designers, running small businesses, which are not registered for VAT

- Fever Ltd has not yet decided whether to exercise the option to tax in connection with the property

Exhibit 2

Jeans manufacturing business in the country of Asiatica

Montgomery Ltd is setting up a jeans manufacturing business in Asiatica, which will start trading on 1 January 2020.

Labour and material costs in Asiatica are low and corporation tax on company profits is 5%. Asiatica is not an excluded territory for the purposes of the controlled foreign company legislation. The calculation of taxable profits is similar under both the Asiatica and UK tax systems.

The low rate of corporation tax in Asiatica is very attractive to Montgomery Ltd, although the management skills of the local work force in Asiatica are not yet fully developed. It is therefore anticipated that the Asiatica management team will require significant support from the UK-based Montgomery Ltd management team. All goods manufactured in Asiatica will be sold to Montgomery Ltd.

The factory is expected to make taxable profits, as calculated for both UK and Asiatica tax purposes, as follows:

3-month period ending 31 March 2020   £200,000
12-month period ending 31 March 2021   £1,000,000

Anticipated profit margins are high at around 45% and profits are expected to continue to increase in future accounting periods.

The factory can either be set up as a separate Asiatica-registered subsidiary company or as a permanent establishment in Asiatica. An understanding of the tax consequences of the two alternative business structures is important to assist Montgomery Ltd in making the decision about which business structure to adopt.

March 2016 exam questions

28 Delia, Chris and Ella

You are a trainee ICAEW Chartered Accountant working for Huy and Hennison LLP (HH), which specialises in advising start-up businesses. Your manager provided you with information concerning two new separate start-up business clients: Delia Schlank (**Exhibit 1**) and Chris Yen (**Exhibit 2**).

Your manager gave you the following briefing: "I have separate meetings scheduled with Delia and Chris tomorrow to discuss how they can each structure their businesses' tax efficiently. Both Delia and Chris intend to take an after tax amount of £20,000 from their businesses in the first year of trading.

Ella Markow is a client of HH who has recently moved to the UK. Ella has £250,000 to invest in exchange for a 20% share in a start-up business. Delia is seeking an investor and has given me permission to discuss with Ella a potential investment in her business. Ella does not require an income return from her investment over the next three years but would like to make her investment tax efficient. I have provided you with details of Ella's projected income and gain for the tax years 2018/19 and 2019/20 (**Exhibit 3**).

I would like you to prepare briefing notes for me in which you:

(a) Explain and recommend a tax efficient business structure for each of Delia (Exhibit 1) and Chris (Exhibit 2).

(b) Calculate and explain, based on your recommendations regarding business structure in part a), the tax implications for each of Delia and Chris of extracting an after tax amount of £20,000 from their businesses in the year ending 5 April 2020.

(c) Explain and calculate, assuming Ella invests £250,000 in Delia's business, any tax savings arising from the investment for Ella for the tax years 2018/19 and 2019/20.

In preparing your briefing notes, you should include advice on any relevant claims or elections available."

Requirement

Prepare the briefing notes requested by your manager.

Total: 40 marks

Note: Assume that the rates and allowances as they apply to the tax year 2018/19 continue to apply for future years.

Exhibit 1

Delia Schlank

Delia works in food research for Nisty Foods plc. Her taxable employment income in the tax year 2018/19 will be £140,000. In 2019/20, Delia will continue to work for Nisty Foods plc on a part-time basis and will have employment income of £55,000.

On 1 March 2019, using her savings, Delia paid £45,000 for computer equipment for her new diet business, D4Diet, which will start trading on 6 April 2019. The business will have two separate income streams:

- D4Diet will trade through a website. It will charge users a membership subscription providing access to information, tailored diet advice and will also sell diet products via its website.

- D4Diet will also receive £85,000 in the tax year 2019/20 for providing Delia's services as a dietician to a private clinic. Delia will attend the private clinic on days specified by the clinic and provide diet advice to the clinic's clients for an agreed hourly rate of pay. The clinic will make all the appointments for clients to see Delia.

Delia needs an investment of £250,000 to provide working capital, to build the website and undertake research and development.

Delia will carry out research and development on a new weight loss product called 'Luzit'. Luzit is expected to be a significant improvement compared to existing products in the market. Delia hopes to patent the 'Luzit' product and to receive income from its development.

Projected results for the years ending 5 April

	2020 £	2021 £	2022 £
Revenue			
Online advice and sales	315,000	415,000	650,000
Dietician service at private clinic	85,000	85,000	85,000
	400,000	500,000	735,000
Taxable trading profit before capital allowances	260,000	360,000	425,000

Costs **not** included in the above calculation of projected taxable trading profit are:

	2020 £	2021 £	2022 £
Website costs:			
Computer equipment (purchased 1 March 2019)	45,000	–	–
Advertising and marketing	8,000	5,000	5,000
Research and development costs:			
Power, water and materials	23,000	8,000	–
Salary costs of research staff	45,000	45,000	–
Plant and machinery	19,000	–	–

Exhibit 2

Chris Yen

Chris is 24 years old. He studied garden design for three years and received no taxable income until the tax year 2017/18 when he was employed as a gardener. Chris has taxable employment income of £35,000 in the tax year 2017/18 and £40,000 in the tax year 2018/19.

On 1 March 2019, Chris was made redundant receiving £2,500 statutory redundancy pay and a discretionary termination payment of £8,000. He used this money to prepare a portfolio of garden designs and to advertise himself as a garden designer and landscaper at a national garden show. His garden design business, CYGarden, will start to trade on 6 April 2019.

Projected results for the years ending 5 April

	2020 £	2021 £	2022 £
Revenue	150,000	350,000	655,000
Taxable trading (loss)/profit before capital allowances	(36,000)	15,000	185,000

Costs **not** included in the above calculation of projected taxable trading (loss)/profit are:

	2020 £	2021 £	2022 £
Workshop building	150,000	–	–
Equipment	22,000	5,000	5,000

Exhibit 3

Ella Markow – Projected income and gain

On 1 November 2018 Ella moved from Poland to the UK to work as a surgeon at a hospital in London. Her contract is for three years. Ella has not visited the UK prior to her arrival on 1 November 2018. Her projected income and gain are as follows:

	2018/19 £	2019/20 £
Income		
Employment income		
6 April 2018 to 31 October 2018 – in Poland	35,000	–
1 November 2018 to 5 April 2019 – in London	124,000	–
6 April 2019 to 5 April 2020 – in London	–	210,000
Gain		
Gain on sale of property in Poland – sold on 1 February 2019	55,000	–

29 ZD Holdings plc

You are Sam Fisher, an ICAEW Chartered Accountant, and you work in the corporate development department of YG. YG has been engaged by ZD Holdings plc to provide tax advice in relation to the sale of its subsidiary, Homewize Ltd. The subsidiary is to be sold to Anacim Ltd, a private equity company. ZD Holdings plc is a UK tax resident company. In 2008, ZD Holdings plc had bought 100% of the shares in Homewize Ltd for £5 million. Homewize Ltd operates a chain of stores selling home products and has no subsidiaries.

Bernie Styl, an ICAEW Chartered Accountant, is the manager at YG responsible for the ZD Holdings plc client work. You receive the following email from Bernie:

> **To:** Sam Fisher
> **From:** Bernie Styl
> **Date:** 4 March 2019
> **Subject:** Sale of Homewize Ltd
>
> Homewize Ltd currently has no finance director and its finance department lacks tax expertise. ZD Holdings plc has asked YG to review Homewize Ltd's corporation tax position. A finance assistant at Homewize Ltd has provided information regarding Homewize Ltd's projected tax results for the year ending 31 March 2019, together with three outstanding issues (**Exhibit 1**).
>
> I attended a meeting last week with the CEO from ZD Holdings plc and a member of the deal team representing Anacim Ltd the purchaser of Homewize Ltd. I have provided meeting notes which set out two alternative methods proposed by Anacim Ltd for the sale of Homewize Ltd's business (**Exhibit 2**). I need you to prepare some briefing notes which provide:
>
> - an explanation of the tax implications of the three outstanding issues (Exhibit 1);
>
> - a revised calculation of Homewize Ltd's tax-adjusted trading loss for the year ending 31 March 2019 and a recommendation of how Homewize Ltd could use this loss. (Ignore the proposed sale of Homewize Ltd for this part); and
>
> - an evaluation of the tax implications for ZD Holdings plc, Homewize Ltd and Anacim Ltd of the two alternative methods for the sale of the Homewize Ltd business (Exhibit 2).

Just before you start work, you receive the following telephone call from the CEO of ZD Holdings plc:

"At the meeting last week, your colleague Bernie Styl was verbally aggressive and gave a negative picture of Homewize Ltd in front of the member of the deal team representing Anacim Ltd, the purchaser of the Homewize Ltd business. If this behaviour is repeated at the next meeting, I will ensure that YG is not appointed again by ZD Holdings plc on any future assignments."

Requirements

29.1 Prepare the briefing notes requested by Bernie Styl; and

29.2 Evaluate the ethical issues for you and for YG arising from the telephone call from the CEO of ZD Holdings plc. Determine and describe the actions you should take.

Total: 35 marks

Note: Ignore the indexation allowance.

Exhibit 1

Homewize Ltd's draft projected tax results for the year ending 31 March 2019 and outstanding issues – prepared by a finance assistant

	£m
Loss for the year per the statement of profit or loss	(90)
Add depreciation and other disallowable expenses	31
Less capital allowances	(17)
Tax-adjusted trading loss	(76)

The tax-adjusted trading loss above does not include any adjustments for tax purposes in respect of the following outstanding issues:

Issue 1

On 1 April 2018 Homewize Ltd sold its freehold stores to a property company, for a gross amount of £73 million. The property company leased the stores back to Homewize Ltd under a 10-year leaseback scheme.

The terms of the leaseback are an initial premium, payable immediately, of £5 million followed by annual rentals of £4 million payable in advance. The transaction costs in respect of the sale of the stores were £1.2 million. Therefore a total of £10.2 million in respect of the lease is included as a cost in the projected loss of £90 million for the year ending 31 March 2019 per the statement of profit or loss.

Homewize Ltd and the property company have not opted to tax the freehold stores. The stores were newly constructed for Homewize Ltd at a total cost of £50 million excluding VAT and became available for use in April 2007. An accounting profit on disposal of £35.2 million has been included in the statement of profit or loss for the year ending 31 March 2019 in relation to the stores. No adjustment for this has been made in the above projected calculation of the tax-adjusted trading loss for the year ending 31 March 2019.

Issue 2

Homewize Ltd has an obligation to repay a loan of $1 million on 30 June 2019. The loan, taken out on 1 May 2018, was used to purchase new plant and equipment for many of the company's stores. Relevant exchange rates are given below. The loan was recorded in the financial statements using the exchange rate at 1 May 2018. The financial controller is not sure how to deal with foreign exchange issues, so no adjustment has been made in March 2019.

Exchange rates:	
1 May 2018	$1.30 = £1
31 March 2019 (expected)	$1.37 = £1
30 June 2019 (expected)	$1.25 = £1

Issue 3

Homewize Ltd has £19 million of trading losses brought forward at 1 April 2018 of which £2 million related to the period before 1 April 2017. The company has no capital losses.

Exhibit 2

Notes from a meeting between Bernie Styl (YG manager), the CEO of ZD Holdings plc and a member of the deal team representing Anacim Ltd

The methods for the sale of the Homewize Ltd business are either:

- the sale of Homewize Ltd's shares to Anacim Ltd for £13.75 million; or

- a hive-down involving the transfer of the trade and certain assets of Homewize Ltd to a newly-incorporated company, NewCo Ltd, followed by the sale of NewCo Ltd shares to Anacim Ltd for £11 million. The assets transferred would exclude the office building (see below).

The proposed sale date is 1 April 2019.

Office building

Homewize Ltd now owns only one property; an office building in London. The office building was newly constructed for Homewize Ltd's administration department on 1 April 2011. The building cost £2.85 million, including VAT, at the rate of 20%, of £0.475 million, which Homewize Ltd recovered in full. Homewize Ltd has always used the whole building entirely for business purposes. The building has a current market value of £2.75 million which is not expected to change before 1 April 2019.

If Anacim Ltd acquires the building as part of an acquisition of Homewize Ltd's shares, it estimates that 40% of the floor space would be surplus to its requirements and it would let this space to a financial services company. The financial services company is exempt for VAT purposes and therefore Homewize Ltd does not intend to 'opt to tax' the office building as there is no possibility of the financial services company recovering VAT.

If Anacim Ltd uses a hive-down to acquire Homewize Ltd's business, it would exclude the office building from the agreement. Homewize Ltd would retain ownership and let out the property.

30 Elexi plc

You are an assistant in the technical advisory department of HJJ, a firm of ICAEW Chartered Accountants.

Elexi plc is a quoted UK tax resident company with 760 employees and annual revenue of £41 million. Elexi plc manufactures audio equipment for the music industry. HJJ provides corporate tax advice to Elexi plc and personal tax advice to the directors including Peter May, a director who has recently joined the Elexi plc board.

You receive the following email from Tonya Jones, the financial controller at Elexi plc:

To:	Assistant
From:	Tonya Jones
Date:	4 March 2019
Subject:	Technical tax queries

Please provide tax advice for the following two issues:

Issue 1: Elexi plc – Acquisition of Delby Ltd

On 1 May 2018 Elexi plc acquired the entire ordinary share capital of Delby Ltd, an audio technology business, by means of a 'paper for paper' share exchange. Following the acquisition, HJJ now also acts as tax advisers to Delby Ltd and to Peter May, the former majority shareholder of Delby Ltd. Peter is tax resident in the UK and domiciled in England.

Peter's grandfather gave Peter 11,000 of the 20,000 ordinary shares in Delby Ltd on 31 March 2013. On that date Peter became the managing director having worked for Delby Ltd for 10 years. Peter's 11,000 shares in Delby Ltd had a market value of £900,000 on 31 March 2013. His grandfather continued to hold the remaining 9,000 shares.

On 1 May 2018, Peter and his grandfather accepted an offer from Elexi plc for all of their shares in Delby Ltd. The agreed consideration was 15 shares in Elexi plc in exchange for each Delby Ltd share. The share price of each Elexi plc share on 1 May 2018 was £10. Elexi plc has 15 million ordinary £1 shares in issue after the takeover of Delby Ltd.

I have explained to Peter that there will be a tax liability arising as a result of the share for share transaction but I do not know how to calculate this. The Elexi plc share price is increasing and Peter is considering selling his shares in July 2019 to finance the purchase of a new house.

Peter's grandfather, who was tax resident in the UK and domiciled in England, has recently died. Peter sent me a letter from the executor of his grandfather's estate. The executor needs to know whether Peter still holds the shares in Delby Ltd which were given to him on 31 March 2013. Peter is unsure how to reply to the executor and wants to understand the tax implications for him arising from his grandfather's gift of the Delby Ltd shares and the subsequent 'paper for paper' share exchange. The executor is not asking for calculations on this matter.

Issue 2: Elexi plc – Overseas transactions

Elexi plc's taxable trading profits for the year ended 31 December 2018 were £4.2 million before any adjustments arising from the following transactions:

Acquisition of Crea Inc

In July 2018, Elexi plc bought a 100% shareholding in Crea Inc, a company resident in Erewhon, an overseas tax jurisdiction with a 16% rate of corporation tax. Crea Inc is a customer of Elexi plc. After acquiring the shares in Crea Inc and as a result of a group internal pricing agreement, Elexi plc reduced the selling price of goods to Crea Inc by 25%. This resulted in Elexi plc's taxable profits being reduced by £1.5 million to £4.2 million in the year ended 31 December 2018.

Crea Inc paid a dividend of £1.62 million (after the deduction of 10% withholding tax) to Elexi plc in September 2018 which is not included in Elexi plc's taxable profits.

Manufacturing branch in Germany

In February 2018, Elexi plc set up a manufacturing branch, which is a permanent establishment, in Germany. It has 500 employees and operates from a rented factory near Berlin, Germany. All plant and machinery used in the manufacturing process is held on operating leases. A taxable profit of £1.2 million was made by the branch in the period ended 31 December 2018 and German tax on the branch's profits was paid at 29.6%. If the branch proves successful, Elexi plc intends to set up similar branches in other European Union countries.

Requirements

30.1 Explain and calculate the capital gains tax implications for Peter of the 'paper for paper' acquisition by Elexi plc of his shares in Delby Ltd (Issue 1). Recommend any appropriate claims or elections and set out any additional information you would need in order to make a recommendation.

30.2 Advise Peter of any further tax implications for him arising from his grandfather's gift of the Delby Ltd shares and the subsequent 'paper for paper' share exchange (Issue 1) and his grandfather's death.

30.3 Explain the implications for Elexi plc's taxable trading profits for the year ended 31 December 2018 of the overseas transactions (Issue 2). Identify and explain any relevant tax claims or elections and make appropriate recommendations. Calculate revised taxable trading profits for Elexi plc for the year ended 31 December 2018 including any adjustments you recommend.

Total: 25 marks

June 2016 exam questions

31 Marmalade Ltd

You are an ICAEW Chartered Accountant working in the tax department of Brown and Co, ICAEW Chartered Accountants. Marmalade Ltd and two of its directors and shareholders are tax clients of your firm.

Background Information

Marmalade Ltd was originally incorporated many years ago by two friends, Paddy and Lucy, to manufacture traditional English marmalade (a preserve made from oranges), for sale to supermarkets. Paddy and Lucy are both UK resident for tax purposes.

At incorporation, Paddy and Lucy each subscribed for 50% of the company's original 66,000 £1 ordinary shares, at par. In 2006, Marmalade Ltd issued 33,000 new, £1 ordinary shares to Cooper Ltd, in exchange for an investment in the company of £100,000. Paddy, Lucy and Cooper Ltd each owned one third of the company's total share capital.

Paddy and Lucy continued to work for the company full-time. Marmalade Ltd has been successful and its marmalade is now a well-known product, sold in all major supermarkets in the UK.

Lack of agreement over potential expansion of the product range

Lucy would like to exploit the company's successful branding and expand the company's product range into manufacturing jams and other types of preserves. However, Paddy does not agree with this strategy. Recent board meetings have been unpleasant and inconclusive.

As a result, Paddy has decided to sell his shares in the company and leave Lucy to expand the business. Cooper Ltd has also decided that now would be the right time for the company to realise its investment in Marmalade Ltd. Shares in Marmalade Ltd have a current valuation of £50 each, which has been agreed with HMRC's Shares and Assets Valuation team.

Marmalade Ltd has been successful and has distributable reserves of £2 million. Marmalade Ltd is prepared to repurchase shares from the current shareholders but £2 million is the maximum the company is prepared to use to repurchase shares. Any shares repurchased by Marmalade Ltd will be cancelled.

Marmalade Ltd will repurchase all of the shares owned by Cooper Ltd on 1 August 2019 and it will then use what remains of the £2 million of distributable reserves to repurchase some of Paddy's shareholding on 2 August 2019.

The remainder of Paddy's shareholding will be purchased by Lucy. In order to do so Lucy will need to raise a personal loan from her bank. Her bank is happy to lend her up to £1.5 million to buy the shares from Paddy, at an annual interest rate of 8%.

Paddy is a higher rate taxpayer for income tax purposes, having taxable income of around £130,000 each tax year. Paddy has never realised any capital gains. Cooper Ltd is a UK registered, trading company.

Tax-saving scheme

The current directors of Marmalade Ltd have been approached by an external consultancy firm specialising in tax-saving schemes. You have received an email from Lucy, asking for your professional opinion on the tax-saving scheme on offer.

Requirements

31.1 Prepare notes to be used at a meeting with Paddy and Lucy. These notes should:

(a) Advise on the tax consequences of the repurchase of shares by Marmalade Ltd for both Cooper Ltd and Paddy. Include calculations and explanations to support your advice.

(b) Determine the amount of the personal loan Lucy needs to take out in order to finance the purchase of the remainder of Paddy's shares and explain the tax consequences to Lucy of this loan.

(c) Based on your answer to part 31.1 (a) and (b) above, and taking account of any tax reliefs available, calculate and explain the tax payable by Paddy on the disposal of his shares in Marmalade Ltd to Lucy.

31.2 Prepare a reply to Lucy's email, providing initial advice about the ethical and legal consequences of the tax saving scheme.

Total: 40 marks

32 Kamran Siddiqi

You are an ICAEW Chartered Accountant, working in practice as a taxation adviser within a firm of ICAEW Chartered Accountants.

Kamran Siddiqi is a new client of your firm. He attended a meeting at your office yesterday to discuss the tax implications of a change he intends to make to the structure of his business.

Kamran owns a restaurant, which he originally ran as a sole trader when the restaurant was opened in 2001. On 1 August 2010, Kamran incorporated the business as Siddiqi Restaurant Ltd. Siddiqi Restaurant Ltd has an accounting year end of 31 December.

In order to simplify his business administration, Kamran intends to revert back to running the restaurant as a sole trader on 31 July 2019.

Background information

In order to incorporate the business, Kamran purchased Siddiqi Restaurant Ltd 'off the shelf'. The share capital of the company consists of 200 £1 ordinary shares. Kamran is the sole shareholder and has always been employed as a director of the company.

On incorporation of the business, the only chargeable assets were the goodwill and the freehold restaurant property. Kamran gifted the goodwill of the business to the company, but retained ownership of the freehold restaurant property himself. He claimed gift relief to defer the gain on the goodwill.

Kamran has provided you with details of the most recent trading results of the company and the costs and market values of the company's assets (**Exhibit**).

On 31 July 2019, a liquidator will be appointed and the total assets of Siddiqi Restaurant Ltd will then be transferred back to Kamran.

You have agreed to provide calculations and explanations to Kamran to enable him to understand the taxation implications of these transactions.

Requirements

Prepare notes for your files to document the tax advice you are going to give Kamran on the following matters:

32.1 Calculate the taxable total profit for Siddiqi Restaurant Ltd for the period ending 31 July 2019, explaining how you have treated the outstanding items numbered (1) and (2) in the Exhibit. You should consider any available claims, elections or reliefs and make recommendations on whether these should be claimed.

32.2 Calculate the total amount available for distribution by the company to Kamran as at 31 July 2019.

32.3 Explain the tax treatment of any distribution made to Kamran on 31 July 2019 and calculate the tax cost to Kamran of the distribution, assuming any beneficial reliefs are claimed.

32.4 Explain the VAT consequences for Siddiqi Restaurant Ltd and Kamran of the transfer of the trade and assets of the restaurant business from the company to Kamran.

Total: 30 marks

Exhibit

Recent actual and estimated results of Siddiqi Restaurant Ltd

* Year ended 31 December 2018

  The corporation tax computation for the year ended 31 December 2018 has been prepared and shows taxable trading profits of £165,000.

* Period ending 31 July 2019

  The draft taxable trading loss for this period is projected to be £115,000. This figure is before taking account of the items numbered (1) and (2) below.

Issues yet to be dealt with in calculating the taxable trading profits/(losses) of the period ending 31 July 2019

(1) Capital allowances for the final period of trading have yet to be calculated. No new items of plant and machinery were purchased in the final period. All items of plant and machinery will be sold to Kamran on 31 July 2019 at the estimated total market value of £65,000. The tax written down value of these items at 1 January 2019 was £50,000.

  None of these items cost more than £6,000.

(2) The company's assets have been/are expected to be valued as follows:

	Cost £	Market value on 1 August 2010 £	Market value on 31 July 2019 £
Goodwill	0	45,000	95,000
Other net assets	5,500	52,000	105,000
Total	5,500	97,000	200,000

33 John

Assume it is June 2019. You are an ICAEW Chartered Accountant working in general tax practice for a firm of ICAEW Chartered Accountants.

Your firm's client, John, has been working in the IT department of Thanet University, for the past five years, on a salary of £70,000 pa. After a reorganisation of the university, John was made redundant on 31 March 2019. Details of the termination package he received on redundancy are set out in **Exhibit 1.**

Because his skills are in demand, he has received a job offer and his new employer has given him the opportunity to decide between two alternative employment packages. The details of the employment packages on offer are set out in **Exhibit 2**. His new job will start on 1 July 2019.

John does not need to use the cash from his termination package for daily living costs and if he combines the cash from his termination package with some of his savings he will have £25,000 cash to invest. He has wanted to invest in shares for some time and he is attracted by the tax incentives attached to venture capital share schemes, but wants to be aware of the risks to his capital.

Requirements

33.1 Identify and explain the income tax and employees' national insurance contribution treatment of each part of John's termination package (Exhibit 1).

33.2 Advise John which employment package he should choose (Exhibit 2). Assume he will choose the option that provides him with the highest amount of net (ie, after tax) spendable income on an annual basis.

33.3 Identify the venture capital share schemes John could invest in and evaluate the tax relief he would receive from each possible investment and the relative risks of the investments available.

Total: 25 marks

Exhibit 1

Termination package

Employment ceased on 31 March 2019.

On 31 March 2019 John was paid:

	£
Three months' salary, in lieu of notice	17,500
Statutory redundancy pay	3,256
IT equipment (at market value)	5,000

Note: All senior staff made redundant in the last five years have kept their IT equipment on redundancy.

Contribution to his employers' occupational pension scheme	10,000
Non-contractual goodwill payment	3,000

Exhibit 2

Details of the two alternative employment packages offered with John's new job

Employment package one	Employment package two
• Salary £75,000 pa	• Salary £60,000 pa
• Employers' pension contributions to non-contributory pension scheme 5%	• Private use of company car: Cost £29,000 Car benefit percentage 37%
	• Non tax-advantaged share options:
	– Grant and exercise of 3,000 share options pa
	– Exercise price £Nil
	– Estimated market value on exercise and disposal £2 each

John hopes to sell any shares he receives under the share option scheme in employment package two for their market value, immediately on exercise. The shares are in a private company and are not listed on a stock exchange.

If he takes employment package one he will lease his own car at a cost of £5,700 per annum. Under the terms of employment package two, as he is provided with a company car, these costs would not be incurred.

34 Fragmarb plc

You work as a tax adviser for a firm of ICAEW Chartered Accountants. Fragmarb plc is a client of your firm. The marketing director of Fragmarb plc is also a personal tax client of your firm. Your manager is preparing for a meeting with the Fragmarb plc board of directors and has asked for your assistance. Your manager has provided you with some background information.

Background information

Fragmarb plc is a UK incorporated company which makes high-quality kitchen cupboards and worktops which it sells to businesses and individual customers globally. For the year ended 31 March 2019, Fragmarb plc has draft tax adjusted trading profits of £6.85 million. The following three issues have not yet been taken into account in the calculation of the tax adjusted trading profits and need to be addressed with the board of directors:

(1) In 2006, Fragmarb plc set up a permanent establishment (PE) in Faraway, a non-EU country. The PE has made substantial profits in recent years. On 1 April 2018, the trade of the PE was transferred to a company, Toka SARL, which is resident in Faraway. The transfer was made in exchange for 80,000 £1 ordinary shares (an 80% shareholding) in Toka SARL valued at £2.5 million, which was equal to the market value of the trade and assets transferred. The remaining 20% of the shares in Toka SARL are held by unconnected individuals resident in Faraway. Details of the assets transferred to Toka SARL are outlined in Exhibit 1. On 1 January 2019, Fragmarb plc sold 24,000 of the shares in Toka SARL for £800,000. At that date the market value of Fragmarb plc's remaining holding was £1.96 million. The rate of corporation tax in Faraway is 17%.

(2) In July 2018 Fragmarb plc patented a design for a self-cleaning kitchen worktop from which large profits have already been generated. An analysis of Fragmarb plc's tax adjusted trading profits from all products is provided in **Exhibit 2**.

(3) Fragmarb plc has held 20% of the shares in Mokle Ltd, a UK trading company, since 1 March 2010. The cost of the shares was £325,000. On 1 July 2018, Mokle Ltd was taken over by Wemble plc. In exchange for its shares in Mokle Ltd, Fragmarb plc received shares in Wemble plc with a market value of £600,000, resulting in a 12% shareholding in Wemble plc. The indexation allowance from the date of purchase of the shares in Mokle Ltd, to December 2017 was £84,526.

Transactions with Gobo Inc

Fragmarb plc has one other wholly-owned subsidiary, Gobo Inc which is a large company, resident in the non-EU country of Glubeck. During the year ended 31 March 2019, Gobo Inc bought goods from an unconnected company in Glubeck to sell to UK customers via Fragmarb plc, however, the contracts for sale are between Gobo Inc and each customer. Fragmarb plc provides an after-sales service and marketing services to these customers. Gobo Inc generated income of £14 million and profits of £5 million from sales to these UK customers on which tax of £750,000 was paid in Glubeck for the year ended 31 March 2019.

Your manager has also received an email from the marketing director of Fragmarb plc, asking for advice in relation to a secondment overseas at Toka SARL (**Exhibit 3**).

Requirements

34.1 Calculate the corporation tax payable by Fragmarb plc after making adjustments to the draft tax adjusted trading profits for the three issues identified. You should include an explanation of the tax treatment of each issue and consider any beneficial claims, elections or reliefs.

In answering this part of the question do not consider the transactions with Gobo Inc.

34.2 Explain how the transactions with Gobo Inc are likely to be treated for tax purposes and whether Gobo Inc will be liable to pay any UK tax. You should consider any relevant anti-avoidance legislation.

34.3 Draft a response to the email from Fragmarb plc's marketing director (Exhibit 3).

Total: 40 marks

Exhibit 1

Details of assets transferred to Toka SARL by the PE on 1 April 2018

Asset	Date of purchase	Indexation factor from date of purchase to December 2017	Cost £	Market value on 1 April 2018 £
Factory (Note)	January 2006	0.438	150,000	600,000
Warehouse	January 2008	0.326	450,000	400,000
Fixed plant and machinery	May 2014	0.087	100,000	150,000
Goodwill	January 2006	0.438	–	1,000,000
Trading stock	N/A	N/A	100,000	350,000

All of the assets transferred are located in Faraway

Note: Toka SARL sold the factory to an unconnected third party on 31 December 2018 for £800,000.

Exhibit 2

Analysis of Fragmarb plc's draft tax adjusted trading profits for the year ended 31 March 2019

	Non patented cupboards and worktop £'000	Patented self-cleaning worktop £'000
Turnover	10,155	7,000
Allowable trading costs	(7,555)	(2,750)
Tax adjusted trading profits	2,600	4,250

A transfer pricing study has concluded that a rate of 5% of related turnover should be used to remove a return on marketing assets used to generate the patented self-cleaning worktop income. The nexus fraction for this patent is 90%.

Exhibit 3

Email from marketing director

To:	Manager
From:	Marketing Director
Subject:	Secondment to Toka SARL
Date:	6 September 2019

Hi,

As you are aware, I have worked for Fragmarb plc in the UK for the past 20 years and I have been offered the opportunity of a secondment to work at Toka SARL in Faraway for a period of 18 months. I have never travelled abroad before having been born in the UK and lived here all of my life.

I will either leave the UK on 31 December 2019 and start work at Toka SARL on 1 January 2020 or I could delay leaving the UK to 31 July 2020 and start work at Toka SARL on 1 August 2020 instead. My current annual salary in the UK is £125,000. When I am on secondment working in Faraway, my salary will be paid by Toka SARL into a bank account which I will open with a bank in Faraway. My salary will be £135,000 pa when on secondment.

Please explain briefly if I am liable to pay UK tax when working for Toka SARL and advise me if there will be any difference in my UK tax liability, depending upon when I start the secondment.

Marketing Director

35 Derek Woodhouse

You are an ICAEW Chartered Accountant employed by a firm of ICAEW Chartered Accountants. Your firm acts for Derek Woodhouse and his wife Veronica in personal tax matters. Derek has built up a successful unincorporated floor tiling business, 'DW Floors' over the past 30 years. He is planning to retire from the business in the near future due to ill health. Derek wants to make plans to ensure his son Andrew and his grandchildren are financially secure. Derek has sent you the following email.

Hi,

Please could you advise me on the following matters.

Retiring from my business

I would like to pass my business on to my son, Andrew. He currently works in the business as a sales representative. I will pass the business on using one of two alternative methods:

- transfer of the business to Andrew during my lifetime; or
- leaving my business to Andrew in my will when I die.

I am not sure if there would be any difference for tax purposes, but I would like to retire from the business on 31 December 2019.

If I transfer my business in my lifetime, I will do this on 31 December 2019. On this date, Andrew would pay me £600,000 for the business premises. On the same date, I would then gift the remaining assets to Andrew. The assets of my business are:

	Cost £	Projected market value on 31 December 2019 £
Premises	225,000	625,000
Goodwill	Nil	500,000
Plant and machinery	100,000	60,000
Inventory	10,000	6,500

The cost and projected market value of each item of plant and machinery is less than £6,000.

Providing for my grandchildren

I own a 5% shareholding in Fiestar plc, a UK quoted company. I inherited the shares from my mother when she died in April 2017 and £25,000 inheritance tax was paid in relation to the shares. At the time, the probate value of the shares was £425,000. The current market value is £500,000. I would like to gift the shares to my two grandchildren, Ella and Daniel, who are 8 and 13 years old respectively, so that they have funds to pay for their future education. I want to minimise any tax liabilities which may arise from this gift and have three alternative courses of action:

Alternative 1: Gift the shares to them on 31 December 2019.

Alternative 2: Set up a trust for their benefit on 31 December 2019 by gifting the shares to the trust.

Alternative 3: Leave the shares to them in my will.

I believe that if I gift the shares to a trust under alternative 2, then, as these are quoted shares, there will be no tax liability as inheritance tax was paid when I inherited the shares.

Payment to senior manager

I have recently recruited a senior manager from a competitor. The manager has many trade contacts from his former employment and, as I am keen to leave my son a successful business, I have asked the senior manager to pass me a list of these contacts in exchange for a one-off bonus of £25,000. I will be advising payroll to describe this as a 'restraint of trade payment'. I believe this payment to be capital in nature, so no PAYE or NIC will be deducted from it.

Veronica would also like some advice and has sent you a separate note which I have attached **(Exhibit)**.

Regards

Derek

Requirements

Draft a response to Derek's email in which you:

35.1 (a)   Advise of the capital tax consequences of each alternative method suggested for his retirement from the business, including a calculation of the estimated tax due and a recommendation on which method will minimise the overall tax liability.

   (b)   Explain the inheritance tax implications of the transfer of the quoted shares to Derek's grandchildren, under each of the three alternative methods for transfer considering any beneficial claims, elections or reliefs which may be applicable.

   (c)   Explain the tax treatment of the senior manager's bonus and identify any threats to the fundamental ethical principles and any action you should take.

35.2 Respond to Veronica's note (Exhibit).

Total: 35 marks

Note from Veronica

Hi,

I am employed by Star Ltd as an HR Director earning a basic salary of £120,000 pa. I am a member of Star Ltd's money purchase pension scheme and over the past three years I have utilised my annual allowance for pension contributions (including a small contribution from my employer), paying the maximum amount, to provide for my retirement.

My salary is likely to increase and I am concerned what this might mean for my pension contributions. Without doing detailed calculations could you please let me know how to work out my annual allowance?

Veronica

36 Baluga Ltd

You are an ICAEW Chartered Accountant and have been seconded to the finance department of Baluga Ltd, a client of the firm where you work.

Baluga Ltd is a trading company which sells handmade cosmetics to retail businesses and individual customers in the UK. Historically, Baluga Ltd has been profitable and its taxable total profits for the year ended 31 March 2019 were £1.3 million.

Joint venture

On 1 October 2018, Baluga Ltd entered into a joint venture, acquiring shares in Cosmo plc from an unconnected company Actifirm Ltd. Cosmo plc sells eco-friendly perfumes to retailers in the UK. Following the share acquisition, Baluga Ltd owns 60% of the shares in Cosmo plc and Actifirm Ltd, a company resident in Cyprus, owns 35% of the shares, with the remaining 5% of the shares held by employees of Actifirm Ltd. Actifirm Ltd has taxable total profits for the year ended 30 June 2019 of £755,000.

Cosmo plc has three subsidiaries, Parfum SpA, which is resident in the non-EU country of Utopia, Clarouge Ltd and Perfect Skin Ltd, both UK resident companies. Cosmo plc owns 65% of the share capital of Parfum SpA, 75% of the share capital of Clarouge Ltd and 77% of the share capital of Perfect Skin Ltd. The remaining shares in all companies are held by unconnected individuals.

The finance director of Baluga Ltd has provided you with the following information on the trading results of the Cosmo plc group of companies for the year ended 31 March 2019:

	Cosmo Plc £	Parfum SpA £	Clarouge Ltd £	Perfect Skin Ltd £
Tax adjusted trading profit/(loss)	(775,000)	(65,000)	355,000	(35,000)
Chargeable gain	30,000	–	–	7,500
Property income	–	–	25,000	–

Potential restructuring

Baluga Ltd has experienced a significant downturn in its trading results, as new competitors have entered the market. The forecast trading loss for the six months ending 30 September 2019 is £575,000. During a recent board meeting, the management team of Baluga Ltd presented an outline plan to return Baluga Ltd to profitability by diversifying its product range into mass-produced cosmetics and by restructuring its ownership.

The management team has put forward a proposal for a management buy-out (MBO) of Baluga Ltd. The Finance Director has been asked by the management team to give advice on this. The proposal is for Baluga Ltd to set up a 100% owned, newly incorporated subsidiary, Maxxi Ltd, on 1 October 2019. On that date, Baluga Ltd will transfer its trade and assets to Maxxi Ltd. The shareholding in Cosmo plc will not be transferred as part of the deal. On 31 October 2019, the management team will buy 100% of the shares in Maxxi Ltd from Baluga Ltd for £800,000. This represents the forecast market value of the trade and assets. The management team will borrow £800,000 to buy the shares in Maxxi Ltd.

Once the transfer is complete, the management team wishes to expand the business overseas. A contract is being negotiated with a third party retailer in Germany (an EU country). Maxxi Ltd will sell its products to the retailer which will then sell them to individual customers. If this expansion is successful, Maxxi Ltd will also sell its products via a website direct to individual customers in Germany.

Requirements

Draft a report to the finance director in which you:

36.1 Explain the loss relief options available in respect of the tax adjusted trading loss in Cosmo plc for the year ended 31 March 2019.

36.2 Explain the tax implications for the management team of the MBO of Baluga Ltd.

36.3 Explain how the supply of products by Maxxi Ltd to customers in Germany via the retailer or online will be treated for VAT purposes.

Total: 25 marks

37 Ant plc

You are an ICAEW Chartered Accountant, and you have recently started a new job as an in-house corporate tax specialist, in the finance department of the Ant plc group. You have replaced the group's previous corporate tax specialist who left the group on 1 November 2018.

Background information

Ant plc is a UK resident, investment, company. The companies in the Ant plc group are as follows:

Company	% of ordinary shares owned by Ant plc at 1 October 2017	Country of residence	Trading activity
Bat Ltd	100	UK	Retailer of car parts
Cod Ltd	80	UK	Wholesaler of car parts
Dog Ltd	40 (Note 2)	UK	Manufacturer of specialist engines
Elk GmbH	100	Gerbera	Manufacturer of engine components

Notes

1 All companies are registered for VAT in their own jurisdiction.

2 The remaining 60% of the ordinary share capital of Dog Ltd is owned by Monkey Ltd, a UK resident company. Ant plc and Monkey Ltd set up Dog Ltd as a joint venture and Dog Ltd started trading on 1 October 2017.

Exhibit 1 is a list of transactions carried out by Ant plc and its group companies, in the year ended 30 September 2018. The finance director has asked you to determine the tax implications of these transactions. The shareholdings shown above have not been adjusted to reflect these transactions.

On starting work in the finance department you reviewed the corporation tax returns and computations of all group companies for the year ended 30 September 2017. You have identified substantial errors in Ant plc's corporation tax return submitted to HMRC for the year ended 30 September 2017. These errors mean that Ant plc has underpaid corporation tax of £1.2 million for that year.

The finance director, who is also the Senior Accounting Officer (SAO) of Ant plc, has asked you to advise him about the actions that should be taken now that the errors have been discovered and the implications of these errors for Ant plc and for him as SAO of the company.

Requirements

37.1 Prepare a report for the finance director of the Ant plc group explaining the tax treatment of each transaction listed in Exhibit 1.

In considering each transaction, you should mitigate the tax liabilities of group companies as far as possible and include calculations, where appropriate, to support your explanations.

37.2 Advise the finance director of the implications, for both Ant plc and for himself as SAO of Ant plc, of finding errors in Ant plc's corporation tax return for the year ended 30 September 2017, and the actions that should be taken as a result.

Total: 40 marks

Exhibit 1

Ant plc group – year ended 30 September 2018

The tax implications of the following transactions have yet to be determined.

Ant plc

On 1 March 2018 Ant plc sold 20% of its shares in Elk GmbH for £500,000 (see Elk GmbH below).

In January 2018, Ant plc sold a patent to an unconnected company for £750,000. The patent had originally been acquired in January 2012 for £250,000. Ant plc had elected immediately on purchase to receive a WDA of 4% pa on the patent.

Bat Ltd

On 30 September 2018, Bat Ltd purchased 100% of the shares of Rag Ltd for £800,000. Rag Ltd owns a patent for a new car parts distribution system, with an original cost of £700,000 and a TWDV of £644,000.

Cod Ltd

In May 2018 Cod Ltd sold its warehouse to an unconnected company for £1 million. The warehouse had been purchased new, from the developer, in March 2012 for £700,000, inclusive of VAT. At that time stamp duty land tax on a property of that cost was a flat rate of 4% of the full consideration. The option to tax the building was not exercised and the building was used 100% for trading purposes throughout the period of ownership. The RPI for December 2017 is 278.1.

A new warehouse was purchased in April 2018 for £1.5 million, inclusive of VAT, from the developer. As the warehouse is expected to have spare capacity for the first five years, Cod Ltd has rented one third of the warehouse to an unconnected party for rent of £250,000 pa. The tenant uses the warehouse for its business which makes zero rated supplies.

Cod Ltd is yet to decide whether to opt to tax the new warehouse.

Dog Ltd

Dog Ltd has a tax-adjusted trading loss for the year ended 30 September 2018 of £450,395.

Since February 2018, substantial expenditure has been incurred on qualifying research and development (R&D), developing new engine technology. Dog Ltd is a large company for R&D purposes.

The R&D expenditure incurred in the year ended 30 September 2018 was as follows:

	£
Salaries paid to research staff (incl. PAYE/NIC of £82,600)	250,000
Power and light	162,500
	412,500

In addition to the revenue expenditure above, £750,000 was spent on constructing test laboratory buildings for use by the R&D staff. In arriving at the tax-adjusted loss of £450,395 the only deduction made in respect of R&D expenditure was the expense of £412,500.

Dog Ltd has no other source of income in year ended 30 September 2018.

Elk GmbH

The shares in Elk GmbH were acquired as a result of Ant plc's incorporation of a permanent establishment (PE).

Ant plc originally set up a PE in the non-EU country of Gerbera in 2012. In March 2016, Ant plc incorporated the PE as Elk GmbH. One million shares were issued to Ant plc, in exchange for the assets of the PE, which were then worth £1 million. The indexed cost of the shares from March 2016 to December 2017 is £1,065,000.

On incorporation, chargeable gains of £550,595 were deferred.

38 Jolene and Kenton

You are an ICAEW Chartered Accountant, working in practice, as a tax adviser.

Your clients, Jolene and Kenton, started trading as estate agents on 1 January 2016, when they formed a partnership and registered for VAT. Prior to commencement of trade, neither Jolene nor Kenton had any taxable income or gains, having set up their business straight after finishing university. You act as tax adviser to the partnership and also to the individual partners.

Tax-adjusted trading profits and losses for the partnership from commencement to 31 December 2019 are as follows:

Year to 31 December:	2016 £	2017 £	2018 £	2019 (Estimated) £
Tax-adjusted trading profit/(loss)	(150,000)	(55,000)	20,000	50,000

Jolene and Kenton have equal shares of both income profits and losses and capital profits and losses.

The partners plan to incorporate the business on 31 December 2019, for commercial reasons.

Kenton intends to retire from the business in the next six months.

The partners have identified two alternative ways to structure Kenton's retirement from the partnership and the incorporation of the business:

Alternative 1: Jolene will pay Kenton £475,000 for his 50% share of the partnership on 31 December 2019. Jolene will then incorporate the business, exchanging the business' assets for 100% of the ordinary shares in Jolene Ltd, a newly incorporated company.

Alternative 2: Jolene and Kenton will incorporate the business on 31 December 2019, exchanging the partnership's assets, so they each receive 50% of the ordinary shares in Jolene Ltd, a newly incorporated company. Jolene will then purchase Kenton's 50% shareholding in Jolene Ltd for £475,000 at some time in the following six months.

The estimated market values of the partnership assets at 31 December 2019 and their original costs, where applicable, are as follows:

	Estimated market value as at 31 December 2019 £	Original cost £
Land and buildings (Note 1)	350,000	200,000
Plant and machinery (Note 2)	75,000	100,000
Goodwill	525,000	Nil

Notes

1   The land and buildings were purchased new, from the developer, on 1 January 2016. No option to tax has been exercised in respect of the land and buildings.

2   Plant and machinery consists of cars and office equipment; each item having an individual cost and estimated market value of less than £6,000.

Your tax manager is happy for you to advise Jolene and Kenton on any of these matters, but has asked you to make sure that in giving any advice you make the clients aware of possible challenges to their tax planning from anti-abuse legislation.

Jolene and Kenton have confirmed that there is no conflict of interest in advising both of them on the tax consequences of the dissolution of the partnership.

Requirements

38.1 Advise Jolene and Kenton of the tax consequences of each of the two alternatives for structuring Kenton's retirement from the partnership and the incorporation of the business; make a recommendation as to which of the two structures is the most tax efficient.

You should use calculations to justify your advice and recommendations, where appropriate.

38.2 Discuss whether the structures proposed by Jolene and Kenton might be challenged under anti-abuse legislation.

Total: 35 marks

39 Royston Clark

Assume it is January 2019. You are an ICAEW Chartered Accountant in practice. Royston Clark, aged 55, is a client of your firm. He has a successful company, Clark Ltd, which he incorporated in 1990 by issuing 100,000 shares at their nominal value of £1 each. Clark Ltd buys and sells shares and other tradeable commodities.

The current ownership of ordinary shares in Clark Ltd is as follows:

Shareholder	Percentage of issued ordinary shares owned %
Royston Clark	20
Margaret Clark (Royston's wife)	10
Claire Clark Discretionary Trust	20
Other, unconnected, individual shareholders	50

Royston has been diagnosed with a terminal illness. He expects to live between four and eight years from today's date. He has asked your firm to help him plan his affairs to minimise the tax liabilities which could arise as a result of his death.

His illness means that he will be unable to work in his current role as Chairman of Clark Ltd. He intends to retire in the near future.

His mobility will reduce as the illness progresses, so he needs to live in a property specially adapted for his needs. Royston and Margaret intend to adapt the current family home to enable Royston to remain at home throughout his illness.

Royston and Margaret have two children:

- Claire, aged 30; and
- Brian, aged 35.

Brian has three children, aged 10, 12 and 14 from his first marriage. Brian married his second wife in November 2016.

Royston has provided you with:

- a list of all the lifetime gifts he has made to date **(Exhibit 1)**; and

- a list of all his assets and liabilities and their current market values and original costs **(Exhibit 2).**

Royston wants to ensure that he gives his assets to his immediate family (wife, children and grandchildren). He is willing to make either lifetime or death gifts, so that he can minimise the overall tax liability arising on the gifts.

Requirements

Prepare a report for the client which:

39.1 Quantifies the taxes that may already be payable or become payable on death based upon the lifetime gifts already made by Royston; and

39.2 Recommends the assets which Royston should consider gifting during his lifetime to minimise any tax liabilities arising.

You should provide explanations and calculations to support your answer.

Total: 25 marks

Exhibit 1

Lifetime Gifts made by Royston Clark

Date	Asset	Donee	Market value at date of gift
8 May 2014	Gift of 10% of the shares in Clark Ltd	Margaret, Royston's wife	£200,000
12 August 2016	Gift of 20% of the shares in Clark Ltd	Claire Clark Discretionary Trust	£400,000
21 November 2016	Cash	Brian Clark on the occasion of his second marriage	£400,000

Exhibit 2

Royston Clark

Asset/liability	Estimated market value at 31 December 2018 £
Family car – Range Rover	35,000
Vintage car – Rolls Royce Silver Shadow	100,000
Family home – owned jointly with his wife Margaret as joint tenants	1,500,000
Joint mortgage secured on the family home	(200,000)
Holiday home in Wales	700,000
Vintage watch	150,000
Antique furniture	300,000
Shares in Morrell Ltd (Note 1)	550,000
20,000 shares in Clark Ltd (Note 2)	600,000
Cash	1,500,000
	5,235,000

Notes

1   Morrell Ltd was incorporated by a friend of Royston's. Royston subscribed £400,000 for a 20% stake in the company on 1 June 2017. This investment qualified as an Enterprise Investment Scheme investment and income tax relief was given in the tax year of investment.

2   Shares in Clark Ltd have the following values agreed with HMRC:

Holding	Estimated value per share December 2018 £	Value per share August 2016 £
75% or more	60	50
More than 50% but less than 75%	50	40
Exactly 50%	45	35
More than 25% but less than 50%	35	25
Less than 25%	30	20

March 2017 exam questions

40 Taul plc

You are a trainee ICAEW Chartered Accountant and you work in the finance department of Taul plc, a UK tax resident company, which employs 350 people in the UK. Taul plc is an unlisted company owned by a US parent company. Taul plc operates shops selling beauty products and makes standard-rated supplies. Taul plc has a number of wholly-owned subsidiaries, which trade in different industries in the UK. Taul plc plans to list on the Alternative Investment Market (AIM) of the London Stock Exchange in the near future.

Your manager is Taul plc's finance director, Pat Swift, who gives you the following briefing:

"Taul plc is negotiating to buy the business of HG Ltd. HG Ltd trades as an optician business in the UK. The entire share capital of HG Ltd is owned by Val Howey who works full-time for the company.

"I have provided you with some background information together with a summary projected statement of financial position for HG Ltd at 31 March 2019 (**Exhibit 1**), and two alternative methods for Taul plc to buy HG Ltd's business (**Exhibit 2**). Assume that the proposed acquisition date is 31 March 2019.

"Taul plc wants to avoid a restriction of interest deduction under the corporate interest restriction rules. Taul plc and its subsidiaries do not have any unused interest allowance from earlier accounting periods. For the year ended 31 March 2019 the group has the following results:

	£m
Aggregate net tax-interest expense	47
Aggregate tax-EBITDA	158
Fixed ratio debt cap (ANGIE)	103

"Taul plc has enough cash to buy HG Ltd's shares but would need to borrow £2 million from a bank at a rate of 10% pa if it buys HG Ltd's trade and assets.

"Because of Val's reputation as an optician, Taul plc would like to employ her after buying HG Ltd's business. Taul plc has proposed a remuneration package for Val (**Exhibit 3**). I will be meeting Val next week to discuss the purchase of the business further and need to understand the tax implications for Val, HG Ltd and for Taul plc. Please prepare notes for me which provide:

(a) an explanation of the tax implications for Val and HG Ltd of the two alternative methods of buying HG Ltd's business.

(b) calculations and an explanation of the impact of the two alternative methods of buying HG Ltd's business on Taul plc's ability to receive tax deductions for interest in the UK.

(c) a brief evaluation of other tax-related factors which Taul plc should consider when evaluating the alternative methods of buying HG Ltd's business. Calculations are not required.

(d) an explanation of the tax implications for Val and for Taul plc of the share option (Exhibit 3). Assume that the option is exercised on 4 April 2020 when Taul plc's share price will be £4.50."

Requirement

Prepare the notes requested by Pat Swift, finance director.

Total: 40 marks

Exhibit 1

Background and summary projected statement of financial position for HG Ltd at 31 March 2019

Val Howey started the HG business in 2003 when she incorporated HG Ltd with £100,000 of share capital. HG Ltd operates a chain of optician shops in the UK. HG Ltd has expanded its business by buying the trade and assets of other optician businesses in the UK. It makes a mixture of standard-rated, zero-rated and exempt supplies. HG Ltd has forecast a tax trading loss of £1.2 million for the year ending 31 March 2019 before any adjustments for the sale of the business. HG Ltd has made taxable profits in each of the last three years.

Projected summary statement of financial position for HG Ltd at 31 March 2019:

	£'000
Intangible asset: trademarks	6,300
Equipment (Note)	2,200
Inventory	2,500
Cash and receivables	1,000
	12,000
Share capital and reserves	3,000
Non-current liabilities: bank loans	8,000
Current liabilities	1,000
	12,000

Note: The tax written down value of the equipment is £2 million and comprises computer and optical examination equipment. The average cost of a single piece of equipment is £60,000.

Exhibit 2

Two alternative methods of buying the business of HG Ltd

Method 1

Taul plc will buy the entire share capital of HG Ltd for a consideration of £5 million in the form of:

	£'000
Ordinary shares in Taul plc representing a 3% shareholding	4,000
Cash	1,000
	5,000

The shares will be newly issued by Taul plc to Val Howey on 31 March 2019. The payment of £1 million cash will be deferred until 1 April 2020 and is contingent on the HG business meeting performance targets set by Taul plc.

Method 2

Taul plc will buy the trade and assets of HG Ltd for £13 million in cash. The purchase will include the following assets of HG Ltd:

	£'000
Trademarks	9,700
Equipment	1,500
Inventory	1,800
	13,000

Under both methods, trade would continue without interruption.

Exhibit 3

Proposed remuneration package for Val for the year ending 5 April 2020

Val will be employed by Taul plc from 6 April 2019 on a salary of £200,000 pa. Val will be granted an option in April 2019 to acquire 80,000 shares in Taul plc at £2.50 each. The scheme is not a tax-advantaged scheme. The current market value of Taul plc's shares is £3.75. This has been agreed with HMRC Shares and Assets Valuations team. The option can be exercised before 5 April 2020 provided that Val continues to work for Taul plc.

41 Marie Gao

Assume that the date today is 1 December 2019. You are an ICAEW Chartered Accountant and you work as a tax assistant for a firm of ICAEW Chartered Accountants. Marie Gao is a new tax client of your firm. Marie has previously always prepared her own self-assessment tax return but has asked your firm for help with her 2018/19 self-assessment tax return. She has sent you an email (**Exhibit**) with information concerning her tax affairs for 2018/19 and the property and shares in Lemion plc which she inherited from her mother who died in February 2018. Marie is a sole trader operating a business in the UK called Go-Gym which operates fitness gyms. Marie is married to Jon Gao. Marie and Jon were both born in Ozland, a non-EU country.

Marie came to live in the UK in January 2010 and set up the Go-Gym business. Marie has been a UK tax resident since 2010. She has told you that Jon lives in Ozland where he has an import business. Marie spends three months each year visiting Jon in Ozland.

Earlier today, you researched Ozland tax rates on the internet and found that in Ozland trading income is taxed at 20%, capital gains are not taxable and that there is a withholding tax of 25% on interest income.

As you were searching the internet, you came across a news story published on an Ozland news website. The news story reported that Jon Gao, Marie's husband, had allegedly evaded Ozland taxes. Details of his tax affairs had been leaked by an employee of a firm of tax advisers operating in a tax haven where Jon had allegedly hidden income by investing in offshore businesses. The news website reported that Jon was now living permanently in the UK with his wife Marie and that the Ozland tax authorities were investigating his business and tax affairs.

Requirements

41.1 Calculate the income tax and capital gains tax payable by Marie in 2018/19 and explain any relevant claims, elections or reliefs available. Make appropriate recommendations on whether these should be made.

41.2 Advise Marie on how the transfer of her shares in Lemion plc to a trust for her children's education can be done tax efficiently to minimise any capital gains and inheritance tax liabilities.

41.3 Evaluate any professional and ethical issues for you and your firm arising from the news story published on the Ozland news website. Set out the actions that you and your firm should take.

Total: 30 marks

Exhibit

Email from Marie Gao to tax assistant

Income and gains

During 2018/19, I continued to operate my UK business as a sole trader and also sold some shares in UK quoted companies, which I bought five years ago.

My UK income and gains were as follows:

	2018/19 £
Trading profits for Go-Gym – year ended 28 February 2019	140,000
Rental income from house inherited from my mother – see below	20,000
Gains on disposal of UK quoted shares	15,000

I have a trading loss of £60,000 from my Go-Gym business brought forward from the tax year 2017/18.

Apart from the gains on disposal of UK quoted shares, I made no other UK capital disposals in 2018/19.

Last tax year (2017/18), I sold a property in Devon in England which I had bought in 2010 and used as my holiday home. This property had never been rented to tenants and was not a furnished holiday let. The value of the property had fallen because it was damaged by floods. I made a tax loss on its sale of £5,760.

Inheritance from my mother

My mother, who came to live in the UK in 2010, died on 27 February 2018. In her will, she left me her house in England. I have never lived in the house. The house has been rented to tenants since 6 April 2018 for an annual net rental income of £20,000 pa. I also inherited some shares in Lemion plc, a UK quoted company. These shares represented a 1% shareholding in Lemion plc.

My mother's estate has now been settled and all UK taxes paid in full. I would like to transfer the shares I inherited in Lemion plc to a trust for my children's education. The shares had a probate value of £200,000 at the time of my mother's death but they have now increased in value to £225,000. I am not sure whether to transfer the shares to the trust in the current tax year 2019/20 or wait until the next tax year 2020/21.

Income and assets in Ozland

In July 2018, I became a partner in my husband Jon's import business in Ozland. My share of the profits from this business for the tax year 2018/19 is £200,000. In 2018/19, I remitted only £25,000 of this to my UK bank account as Jon told me he needed the money to be kept in Ozland to make investments. I have £175,000 in a savings account in Ozland on which I received net interest of £9,000 in the tax year 2018/19.

In December 2018, Jon sold our house in Ozland. I had a 50% ownership share in the property although I stayed there for only three months of the year. Jon lived there for most of the year. The total chargeable gain on the sale of the house was £75,000, and the proceeds were retained in Ozland.

42 Lyre Ltd

Assume that the date today is 1 May 2019. You work for HED, a firm of ICAEW Chartered Accountants. Lyre Ltd is a tax client of your firm. HED also acts for the directors and shareholders of Lyre Ltd in respect of their personal tax affairs. You are provided with the following information on Lyre Ltd and its shareholders.

Background information for Lyre Ltd

Lyre Ltd is a UK tax resident company operating in the publishing business. The company was set up by Diane Bens and her brother Sam on 1 April 2012. The share capital consists of 100,000 £1 shares and is owned as follows:

Name	Number of shares held	Description
Diane Bens	35,000	Director
Sam Bens	30,000	Director
Mark Carn	5,000	Director
Ann Bens	10,000	-
John Smith	2,500	Employee
Printoff Ltd	17,500	-
	100,000	

Mel Granger, the newly appointed financial controller at Lyre Ltd, has sent you the following note.

Note to HED: Request for advice

I have recently joined Lyre Ltd. My predecessor has prepared a draft corporation tax computation for the year ended 31 March 2019. I need your help in explaining the tax implications of the following three issues in relation to Lyre Ltd's tax situation:

(1) **Sale and lease back transaction**

Lyre Ltd sold its warehouse to BB Bank on 1 August 2018 for £750,000 and immediately leased back the warehouse under a 7-year sale and operating leaseback agreement.

Under the terms of the lease Lyre Ltd paid a premium on 1 August 2018 of £50,000 and will pay annual rentals of £66,250 pa. A rental charge of £44,167 has been included in the income statement. There is a note on the file to say that there is 'no option to tax' on the warehouse.

My predecessor calculated correctly that there is a chargeable gain of £375,000 and included this in the draft corporation tax computation for the year ended 31 March 2019. It appears no other adjustments have been made or taxes paid.

(2) **Company flat**

Lyre Ltd owns a flat in London which until 1 May 2018 was available to all employees who were required to attend meetings in London and to stay overnight. On 1 May 2018, Ann Bens who is the mother of Diane and Sam Bens, moved into the flat because her house in Oxford had been damaged in a fire. The flat has an annual value of £62,000 and Lyre Ltd pays all the heat and light and maintenance costs which were £7,500 for the period from 1 May 2018 to 31 March 2019. Lyre Ltd also agreed to pay the council tax and to pay a cleaning company to clean the flat each week. The council tax and cleaning costs for the year to 31 March 2019 were £12,000. Ann believes that she should have no tax liability arising from her living in the flat. She told me that she already pays tax at 40% on her income and does not want to pay any more.

(3) **Loans**

The following director and employee loans are included in the statement of financial position at 31 March 2019:

£	
108,000	Lyre Ltd made an interest-free loan of £150,000 to Diane Bens on 1 May 2015 to help her to move house. The notional tax arising on the loan was paid on the normal corporation tax payment date. Diane repaid £42,000 of the loan on 1 May 2016. I have been told by Diane, who is the Lyre Ltd managing director, that the board voted to write off this loan in mid-April 2019.
5,450	Lyre Ltd made a loan to Sam Bens on 1 January 2018. This balance was outstanding at 31 March 2018 and at 31 March 2019. No notional tax has ever been paid for this loan and the loan is interest-free.
11,000	On 1 April 2018 Lyre Ltd made a loan to John Smith to buy a car. Interest of 3% pa is charged on the loan.

Requirement

Prepare notes for a meeting with Mel Granger, explaining and quantifying the tax implications arising from the above three issues, where relevant, for:

- Lyre Ltd;
- Ann Bens;
- Diane Bens;
- Sam Bens; and
- John Smith.

Total: 30 marks

Note: The official rate of interest is 2.5%.

43 Tea Group

You are an ICAEW Chartered Accountant, working as a corporate tax specialist, within the finance department of the Tea Group of companies. The recently appointed Chief Executive Officer (CEO) of the Tea Group is planning changes to the group to take place in September 2019. You have been asked to provide advice about the tax implications of the CEO's plans.

Background information

The Tea Group of companies consists of Tea plc and three, wholly owned, subsidiary companies:

Tea plc	UK registered holding company
Tree Ltd	UK registered manufacturing company
Trunk OOD	Bulgarian registered wholesale company
Leaf Ltd	UK registered retail company

All of the group companies have a 31 March year end. Tree Ltd produces Forest Tea, a traditional English tea, in a factory in the north of England, using tea leaves imported from international suppliers.

Trunk OOD buys the finished tea from Tree Ltd and acts as wholesale distributor of Forest Tea to both Leaf Ltd (the retail arm of the Tea group) and other unrelated third party retailers. Trunk OOD is registered in the EU country of Bulgaria, but its central management and control and its trade are both currently in the UK.

Leaf Ltd sells Forest Tea in its chain of UK-based Tea Shops.

Each company pays 100% of its profits to Tea plc each year, in the form of both management charges for group services and dividends. Tea plc provides human resource, finance and administration functions to the group.

Proposed changes to the group

The recently appointed CEO of the Tea Group plans to make changes to increase group profitability. He believes that profits could be increased by relocating the management of some of the subsidiary companies to overseas jurisdictions. As a result, he is proposing:

- relocation of the effective management of Tree Ltd to the non-EEA country of Estaban; the trade of Tree Ltd would continue to operate within the UK; and

- relocation of the central management and control and the trade of Trunk OOD to Bulgaria.

Further information about the proposed changes is set out in **Exhibit 1**.

In addition, the CEO has provided you with details of his proposals for future pricing structures for the transfer of goods and services between group companies, from September 2019 onwards (**Exhibit 2**).

Requirements

43.1 Prepare a report for the CEO using the information in Exhibit 1, which:

(a) Sets out the tax implications and the tax costs of the relocation of:

- the management of Tree Ltd overseas; and
- the management and the trade of Trunk OOD overseas.

(b) Briefly identifies and outlines the impact of anti-avoidance legislation, which may be applicable to the relocation of the management of Trunk OOD to Bulgaria, given that the rate of corporation tax in Bulgaria is currently 10%.

43.2 Identify the issues arising from the information in Exhibit 2 and explain your response to these ethical and tax issues.

Total: 40 marks

Exhibit 1

Further information about the proposed changes to the group

Tree Ltd

Tree Ltd, is incorporated in the UK. The effective management of the company will relocate to the non-EEA country of Estaban from 1 September 2019, although the trade will continue to operate in the UK. The relocation of the management will be deemed to have happened because:

- all future board meetings will take place in Estaban;
- two of the four directors will be resident in Estaban; and
- the company will have its head office in Estaban.

Estaban and the UK have a double tax treaty, which allows Estaban resident companies to be treated as non-resident in the UK.

Tree Ltd will have the following assets at 31 August 2019:

Asset	Cost plus indexation allowance up to December 2017 £	Estimated market value at 31 August 2019
UK factory used in the trade	750,000	£2,000,000
UK office building	100,000	£750,000
UK investment property	20,000	£950,000
Headquarters of the company in Estaban (Note 1)	100,000	E$1,250,000
Fixed plant and machinery used in the trade	500,000	£400,000
Pre-2002 goodwill of the trade	0	£1,500,000

Notes

1   All figures are quoted in pounds sterling (£), apart from the market value of the headquarters in Estaban, which is quoted in Estaban dollars (E$). The spot rate for Estaban dollars on 31 August 2019 is estimated to be E$2.5 to £1.

2   All buildings are more than three years old and no elections have been made to opt to tax any of the buildings.

All of these assets will be retained by Tree Ltd, apart from the UK office building, which will be sold for its market value on 31 August 2019 to a third party.

The CEO is also considering moving the tax residence of the parent company, Tea plc from the UK to Estaban in the future.

Trunk OOD

Trunk OOD, is incorporated in Bulgaria. The company will relocate the central management and control and the trade of the company to Bulgaria, from the UK, on 1 September 2019. Bulgaria is not an excluded territory for the purposes of the controlled foreign company anti-avoidance legislation. There is no commercial reason for situating the wholesale business in Bulgaria. Trunk OOD normally has taxable profits in excess of £2 million pa.

Trunk OOD will have the following assets at 31 August 2019:

Asset	Cost plus indexation allowance up to December 2017 £	Estimated market value at 31 August 2019 £
Warehouse in the UK	500,000	1,500,000
Post-2002 goodwill of the trade	0	250,000

Exhibit 2

MEMO

To: Tea Group finance staff
From: The CEO
Subject: Tea Group transfer prices

I have decided for commercial reasons that we should make the following changes to the transfer prices charged between companies in the Tea group from 1 September 2019:

	Change in transfer price	Financial effect pa
Sales of product from Tree Ltd to Trunk OOD	Decrease the transfer price charged by 50%.	Decrease profits in Tree Ltd by £1 million; Increase profits in Trunk OOD by £1 million.
Sales of product from Trunk OOD to Leaf Ltd	Increase the transfer price by 50%.	Increase profits in Trunk OOD by £1 million; Decrease profits in Leaf Ltd by £1 million.
Management charges from Tea plc to group companies	The management charge from Tea plc to Trunk OOD will be reduced by £500,000 pa	Increase profits in Trunk OOD by £500,000; Decrease management income in Tea plc by £500,000.

After sending this memo, the CEO called you into his office for a private conversation. During this conversation, he said:

"I know that the transfer pricing changes I am suggesting could be contested by the transfer pricing anti-avoidance legislation, which would make these changes ineffective for tax purposes.

"However, I am also aware that we self-assess our UK corporation tax liabilities.

"I will be asking you to submit the UK corporation tax computations for our group companies, taxed in the UK, using the new transfer prices to calculate group taxable profits, with effect from 1 September 2019.

"This should reduce our UK corporation tax bill by £500,000.

"If I increase the group after tax profits by at least £300,000 in my first year, I will receive a substantial bonus.

"I will ensure that if we hit the £300,000 target, you will also receive a substantial bonus."

44 Ben and Martha

You are an ICAEW Chartered Accountant working in practice as a tax adviser.

Your clients, Ben and Martha are partners in a farming business, Redmires Farm. They have received an offer from a property developer to buy the land farmed by their business, and have asked for advice concerning the tax consequences of the transaction.

Background information

Ben is 68 years old and is Martha's son. Martha is 96 years old and in poor health.

Martha and her husband Phil bought Redmires Farm in 1983 for a total cost of £27,500.

Phil and Martha traded in partnership, sharing profits and losses 50:50, until Phil's death in 2000. The farmhouse at Redmires Farm has always been let out to tenants.

Under the terms of Phil's will, his half share in Redmires farmhouse was left to his wife Martha and his half share of the farmland to Ben. Phil also left other assets to Ben totalling £400,000.

The cost of the farmhouse and the farmland in 1983 and the market value in 2000 were as follows:

Asset	Cost 1983 £	Market value 2000 £
Redmires Farmhouse	2,500	400,000
Farmland	25,000	900,000

The farming partnership business currently makes taxable total profits of £120,000 pa, and has a 30 June year end. In addition to her share of the farm profits, Martha receives rental income of £12,000 pa for the rent of the farmhouse.

Sale of the farmhouse and the farmland

Martha will sell the farmhouse to a property developer in July 2019 for £750,000. The property is a residential property.

The property developer has also offered Ben and Martha a total of £2,000,000 for the farmland, which reflects the development value of the farmland. The agricultural value of the farmland is £1,200,000.

If Ben and Martha agree to sell the farmland, the sale is expected to conclude in August 2019. The farmland will be developed into a housing estate and a small retail park.

Future plans

Ben will use some of his sale proceeds from the farmland to buy new farmland with solely agricultural value and no development value and he will commence farming as a sole trader. Any cash he does not reinvest in farmland will be used to buy new farm plant and machinery.

Ben has one child, Sharon, who works as a hairdresser and has no interest in farming. He would like to know if there is any tax advantage to be gained from giving the newly purchased farmland to his daughter, during his lifetime, or, if he should wait and leave all the farmland to his daughter on his death.

Martha has no reinvestment plans and will leave all of her estate to her daughter Helen. Her other assets are her own home currently worth £1.5 million and other assets totalling £500,000.

Requirements

44.1 Calculate and explain the capital gains tax consequences of the sale of the farmhouse and the farmland. Your answer should consider any available reliefs.

44.2 Advise Ben on the differing tax consequences of gifting the farmland to his daughter during his lifetime or on death and provide a recommendation as to the best course of action.

44.3 Explain, with supporting calculations, the consequences of the sale of the farmland and the farmhouse on the amount of inheritance tax that will be suffered on Martha's death.

Total: 30 marks

45 Stollen Ltd

You are an ICAEW Chartered Accountant working for a firm of ICAEW Chartered Accountants as a tax adviser. Both Stollen Ltd and its managing director, Amy Crisp, are clients of your firm.

Background information

Stollen Ltd is a UK registered company, incorporated in 2010, and trades as a bakery, with 25 full-time employees and gross assets of £500,000.

Amy owns 22% of the ordinary share capital of the company. The company has a 31 March year end.

Stollen Ltd has been successful and Amy plans to take additional remuneration from the company during the year ending 31 March 2020.

The bakery is outgrowing its current business premises and new, larger premises will be needed in the near future. Amy has located a suitable industrial unit for the company to purchase at a cost of £200,000 and she hopes the purchase will be completed in the next few months.

Amy's remuneration

Amy normally receives a gross salary of £68,600 pa and a dividend of £2,000 pa from Stollen Ltd. She would now like to receive an additional, gross remuneration of £100,000 from Stollen Ltd.

Amy wants to take the additional £100,000 as follows:

- Stollen Ltd is to make the maximum tax deductible pension contribution to the Stollen Ltd small self-administered pension scheme (SSAS), on Amy's behalf; and

- The balance of the £100,000, remaining after the pension contribution, is to be paid into a tax-advantaged share scheme, which will be set up for Amy's sole benefit.

The only change in Amy's remuneration package from Stollen Ltd between 2018/19 and 2019/20 will be the payment of the additional gross remuneration of £100,000. Amy is the only member of the Stollen Ltd SSAS scheme.

Amy's history of pension contributions

Pension contributions in respect of Amy, to the Stollen Ltd SSAS from the start of the fund in 2015 onwards have been:

Tax Year	Amount of contribution £
2015/16	30,000
2016/17	45,000
2017/18	40,000
2018/19	30,000
2019/20	to be determined

Pension input periods for this scheme have always aligned with the tax year.

Requirements

45.1 In relation to Amy's pension scheme:

- determine the maximum pension contribution that Stollen Ltd can make into its SSAS in 2019/20 without Amy incurring an annual allowance charge; and

- advise Amy on how the funds in the SSAS could be used to help purchase the industrial unit.

  Ignore any potential payment into the share scheme for this part.

45.2 Advise Stollen Ltd on which tax-advantaged share scheme should be used to reward Amy and the tax implications for both Stollen Ltd and Amy.

45.3 Based on your advice in parts 45.1 and 45.2 above, calculate Amy's income tax due for 2019/20.

Total: 30 marks

46 LM Ltd

You are an ICAEW Chartered Accountant and you work in the finance department of LM Ltd. LM Ltd operates as a hotel business in the UK and made a taxable total profit for the year ended 31 March 2019 of £1.4 million. LM Ltd owns many subsidiaries and has a 45% investment in the shares in Fall Ltd. Fall Ltd operates a theme park in the north of England.

Your manager David Fury, the finance director at LM Ltd, has left you the following briefing note on LM Ltd and its investment in Fall Ltd:

Briefing note from David Fury

As finance director of LM Ltd, I represent LM Ltd as a director on the Fall Ltd board. I do not own any shares in Fall Ltd.

The shareholders and other directors of Fall Ltd are as follows:

Name	Director	% shareholding
LM Ltd	n/a	45
Ken Haw	CEO/finance	24
Jan Brown	Operations	n/a
RXX Inc - tax resident in Utopia	n/a	31

Fall Ltd has issued share capital of 500,000 £1 ordinary shares. The shareholders subscribed for the shares at par in 2005.

Because I was on holiday, I did not go to the Fall Ltd board meeting last week. Ken Haw sent me the minutes of that meeting. These minutes show that the directors proposed to close Fall Ltd and that a resolution will be presented to the shareholders to commence winding up of Fall Ltd under a members' voluntary liquidation. The reason for the closure is poor trading results caused by bad weather. The directors intend to appoint a liquidator as soon as trade ceases.

Two alternative dates for cessation of trade were discussed: 30 September 2019 or 31 October 2019. Jack Cee, the Fall Ltd accountant, sent me Fall Ltd's tax results for the year ended 31 March 2019 and the previous three years and also its forecast tax results to 31 October 2019 (**Exhibit 1**).

Ken sent me some information about the forecast amounts of Fall Ltd's assets and estimated disposal proceeds (**Exhibit 2**). The LM Ltd board has asked for a report about Fall Ltd's tax position and proposed closure.

Last night you were in a restaurant and overheard a conversation between Jack Cee, Fall Ltd's accountant, and his wife. You made a note of this conversation.

Jack was complaining to his wife about the stress he was suffering in his job at Fall Ltd. In his conversation, he said that in August 2019, Fall Ltd paid £75,000 to a visitor to the theme park. The visitor had taken a video of a theme park worker who was asleep when he should have been operating Fall Ltd's major attraction called 'WhiteRide'. The visitor threatened to put the video on social media and the amount of £75,000 was paid to the visitor in exchange for a promise not to publish the video. The worker was clearly in breach of health and safety rules and Ken dismissed him. Ken told Jack Cee to 'hide' the payment of £75,000 in sundry expenses because if the payment was discovered by the media, the bad publicity could lead to claims against Fall Ltd.

Requirements

46.1 Prepare a draft report for the LM Ltd board of directors, which:

(a) explains, without calculations, the key tax implications to consider in determining the date that Fall Ltd should cease to trade (Exhibit 2). Recommend the most tax efficient date of cessation of trade for Fall Ltd.

(b) explains the tax implications with calculations for Fall Ltd and LM Ltd if the liquidation of Fall Ltd takes place on 31 October 2019. Assuming a distribution is made to shareholders after the liquidation of Fall Ltd, estimate the cash receivable by LM Ltd and by Ken Haw.

46.2 Identify and explain the ethical implications for you and for LM Ltd arising from the overheard conversation. Set out the actions that you should take.

Total: 40 marks

Exhibit 1

Fall Ltd – Tax results prepared by Jack Cee, Fall Ltd accountant

Fall Ltd: Tax results

Years ended 31 March	2016 £'000	2017 £'000	2018 £'000	2019 £'000
Tax adjusted trading profit/(loss)	608	315	385	(810)
Property income	42	34	39	47
Tax rate	20%	20%	19%	19%

Fall Ltd: Forecast results	Notes	7 months to 31 October 2019 £'000
Tax adjusted trading loss before any adjustments for plant and machinery and brand name	1	(626)
Property income	2	36
Tax rate		19%

Notes

1   At 1 April 2019 the tax written down value for the main pool for capital allowances was £920,000. At 1 April 2019 the tax written down value of the brand name 'WhiteRide' was £352,800.

2   Property income relates to the profit from rents received from holiday homes on land owned by Fall Ltd.

3   If Fall Ltd ceases to trade on 30 September 2019, the tax adjusted trading loss will be £600,000 before any adjustments for plant and machinery and the brand name.

Exhibit 2

Fall Ltd – Forecast amounts and estimated disposal proceeds – prepared by Ken Haw, CEO

The board has proposed two alternative dates for the cessation of Fall Ltd's trade: 30 September 2019 or 31 October 2019.

I believe that the preferred date is 30 September 2019 as we can save the cost of employing staff for an extra month.

I have set out below the amounts that will be shown in the statement of financial position for Fall Ltd at cessation. Please assume that the amounts are the same regardless of whether Fall Ltd ceases to trade on 30 September 2019 or 31 October 2019.

Financial position before cessation	Notes	Forecast amounts £'000
Holiday homes and land	1	3,900
Other assets – plant and machinery	2	2,080
Brand name 'WhiteRide'	3	273
Bank loan	4	(516)
Cash at bank		280
Net current liabilities		(300)

Notes

1   On 10 October 2019 Fall Ltd will sell the holiday homes and land and estimates that it will receive cash of £4,160,000. A chargeable gain will arise on the sale of the holiday homes and land after indexation of £543,000.

2   Other assets are non-chargeable for chargeable gains purposes. Capital allowances have been claimed on these assets as part of the main pool. When the trade ceases Fall Ltd will sell these assets and receive £1,040,000.

3   Fall Ltd operates a ride using the brand name 'WhiteRide'. It bought the brand name on 1 April 2015 for £420,000. Fall Ltd elected to claim a 4% pa straight line writing down allowance. Fall Ltd will sell this brand for £280,000 on 20 September 2019.

4   The bank loan is secured by a fixed charge over land owned by Fall Ltd.

47   Aldo, Zeta and Greg

Aldo and Zeta were married in 1990. They each own 50% of the 100,000 £1 issued share capital of Luca Ltd which they subscribed for at par on incorporation in 2005. Luca Ltd operates takeaway shops selling pizzas. Aldo and Zeta have one son, Greg, who is employed in the business. Aldo, Zeta and Greg are the directors of Luca Ltd.

Aldo and Zeta were divorced last year but continued to work together in the business. However, they have now found that working together is too difficult and Zeta would like to resign as a director and dispose of her shares in Luca Ltd.

You are an ICAEW Chartered Accountant working in practice as a tax adviser. Your firm acts for Luca Ltd and its three directors, Aldo, Zeta and Greg. The directors have sent you details of three proposed methods for the disposal of Zeta's shares. They have agreed that you are initially to act for them and for Luca Ltd in this matter. However, Zeta will take independent advice at a later stage.

Disposal of Zeta's shares

The directors have agreed with HMRC Shares and Assets Valuations that the shares in Luca Ltd will have a market value of £8 per share on 1 October 2019 which is the proposed date of the disposal of Zeta's shares. They have set out three alternative methods for the disposal:

Method 1:   Bella plc, an unconnected company, will purchase Zeta's shares for £8 per share.

Method 2:   Greg will purchase Zeta's shares for £6 per share.

Method 3:   Luca Ltd will repurchase some of Zeta's shares on 1 October 2019 and the remainder of her shares on 1 October 2020. Luca Ltd will pay £8 per share on both dates.

At the next board meeting on 20 September 2019 a dividend of £450,000 will be proposed to be paid on 30 September 2019. This will leave Luca Ltd with distributable reserves at 30 September 2019 of £120,000.

Luca Ltd's legal adviser has stated that Luca Ltd must be able to make a payment out of capital to buy Zeta's shares. The legal adviser has informed the directors that Luca Ltd will not have enough distributable reserves or other reserves to buy all of Zeta's shares on 1 October 2019.

Zeta leaves you the following telephone message.

"I have been diagnosed with a serious illness. I think it may be simpler if, instead of selling my shares in Luca Ltd, I make an outright gift of them to Greg. He will inherit them anyway when I die. I will, however, need to receive the dividends from the shares. I have spoken briefly to Greg and he agreed that he would be happy to own the shares but to pass the right to receive the dividends to me if I need the income."

Requirements

47.1 Draft an email to the directors which includes:

    (a) an explanation of the tax implications for Aldo, Zeta, Greg and Luca Ltd for each of the three methods of selling Zeta's shares, considering any beneficial claims, elections or reliefs.

    (b) a summary comparing Zeta's tax liability, effective tax rate and after-tax cash receivable for each method. Include the key points Aldo, Zeta and Greg should consider in deciding which method to choose.

47.2 In a separate note, explain the tax implications for Zeta of an outright gift of her shares in Luca Ltd to Greg.

Total: 30 marks

48 Gig plc

You work for ERD, a firm of ICAEW Chartered Accountants. Gig plc, a tax client of your firm, is a UK tax-resident company which owns subsidiaries in the UK and other countries. Gig plc researches and develops electronic technology. The CEO of Gig plc has sent you the following note.

Note to ERD

Issue 1 – Tax adjusted profit for the year ended 30 June 2019

The finance director is on maternity leave and her team has prepared a draft corporation tax computation for the year ended 30 June 2019. The tax adjusted trading profit for the year ended 30 June 2019 is as follows:

	£m
Profit before tax	48
Add depreciation and other disallowable expenses	61
Less capital allowances	(64)
Tax-adjusted trading profit	45

The tax-adjusted trading profit above does not include any adjustments for tax purposes in respect of the following three outstanding matters:

(1) **Research and development (R&D)**

    In July 2018, Gig plc commenced a qualifying R&D project to develop a new product which is a major technological advance. Gig plc purchased research laboratory equipment for £2.2 million. The following amounts were deducted as research costs in the statement of profit or loss:

	£m
Staff costs	3.4
Consumable materials	1.1
Externally provided workers (Note)	0.8

Note: The externally-provided workers are from an unconnected company. HMRC has agreed that Gig plc qualifies as a large company for R&D relief.

(2) **Ruritanian customer**

The currency in Ruritania is the Ruritanian dollar (R$). Gig plc is owed money by a customer in Ruritania for a sale made in March 2019 for consideration of R$3 million, at a time when the exchange rate was R$1.39:£1. The receivables are recorded in the financial statements using the exchange rate at the date of sale. The balance remains unpaid at 30 June 2019 when the exchange rate is R$1.33:£1.

(3) **Sale of patent**

On 1 July 2018 Gig plc sold a patent for £21 million which it had purchased on 1 July 2015 for £14 million. Gig plc was amortising the patent over seven years. A profit of £13 million is included in the profit before tax for the sale of the patent.

On 1 September 2018, Gig plc bought 100% of the shares of Techo Ltd, a software company, for £20 million. Techo Ltd owns intellectual property rights with an original cost of £20 million and a tax written down value of £17 million.

Issue 2 - Cost saving proposal

The IT department has 15 employees and a manager, Frances Hobb. Sometimes the department is busy, but at other times, the employees have little to do. At the next board meeting, Gig plc's board of directors will discuss the commercial implications of closing the department and issuing new contracts on a self-employed basis to some of the staff.

Details of the proposal

All the IT employees including Frances will be made redundant and will be offered the following redundancy packages:

- Frances Hobb will receive statutory redundancy of £12,000 and an ex-gratia payment of £100,000. Frances has been employed by Gig plc for 17 years.

- The other employees will each receive statutory redundancy of £12,000. The employees will also each receive an ex gratia payment of £15,000.

- Frances and six of the other former employees will each be offered a contract for services on a self-employed basis. Extra IT consultants will be recruited also on a self-employed basis as required.

Requirements

Prepare a report for the CEO which includes the following:

48.1 An explanation of the tax implications for Gig plc of each of the three outstanding matters in Issue 1. Your answer should identify any beneficial reliefs, claims and elections.

48.2 A calculation of the revised taxable profit and the corporation tax payable for Gig plc for the year ended 30 June 2019.

48.3 A calculation of the tax implications of the redundancy payments for Gig plc, the IT employees and Frances Hobb.

48.4 An evaluation of the tax implications and risks for Gig plc of the proposal to issue Frances and six of her team with contracts on a self-employed basis.

Total: 30 marks

49 Philip and Estelle

Assume it is January 2019. You are an ICAEW Chartered Accountant employed in the tax department of a firm of ICAEW Chartered Accountants. Your firm's clients Philip and Estelle Thompson have requested some tax advice in relation to their plans for retirement.

Background information

Philip and Estelle have been married for many years and are both UK resident and UK-domiciled. Thompson Ltd was incorporated by Philip and Estelle in March 1990 when they subscribed, at par, for 50,000 £1 ordinary shares each (100,000 shares in total) in the company.

Thompson Ltd is a successful company in the retail sector. The company has generated surplus cash, some of which was used to purchase a portfolio of residential properties, which the company rents out. In the most recent accounting period ended 30 September 2018, 37% of net profit was from residential property letting income.

Although Philip and Estelle still own 100% of the shares in Thompson Ltd and work as full-time company directors, their roles are now mainly administrative. Alan and Sandra, (Philip and Estelle's children) have taken over the management of the company together with Francis (the company's managing director, who is not related to the Thompson family).

Philip and Estelle would like to retire from the company in the near future. They have e-mailed you, outlining their plans for retirement (**Exhibit 1**). In preparation for this, valuations of shares in Thompson Ltd as at 31 December 2018 were calculated (**Exhibit 2**). You were also sent information by Thompson Ltd about the values of the company's tangible net assets on 31 December 2018 (**Exhibit 3**).

Philip and Estelle are higher rate taxpayers and each has capital losses brought forward of £10,000, from an unsuccessful property investment they made many years ago.

Alan works full-time at Thompson Ltd for a salary of £55,000 pa. Sandra works part-time at the company for 21 hours a week and she earns £25,000 pa.

Philip and Estelle have requested a meeting with you to discuss the tax consequences of their retirement plans.

Requirements

In preparation for the meeting with Philip and Estelle Thompson:

49.1 Set out the current and future taxation implications of Philip and Estelle's retirement plans, as explained in Exhibit 1;

49.2 Recommend and justify the most tax efficient course of action from the alternatives suggested by Philip and Estelle; and

49.3 Identify any further information you would need in order to make a full recommendation to Philip and Estelle.

Total: 40 marks

Exhibit 1

Email received from Philip and Estelle Thompson

To: Tax Adviser
From: Philip and Estelle Thompson
Subject: Retirement plans
Date: 2 January 2019

As you know, we intend to retire from Thompson Ltd in February 2019. Although we still work full-time for the company, our children, Alan (aged 35) and Sandra (aged 32) together with Francis, the managing director, are already running the company on a day-to-day basis and can manage without us. We are not getting any younger and would like to enjoy some well-earned time off. We plan to:

(1) Sell 40% of the total shares in Thompson Ltd (20% from each of us) to Francis. Francis has just inherited a large sum of money following the death of his father and has offered us £800,000 for the 40% stake in the company.

(2) Gift the remaining 60% of the company's shares (30% from each of us) either:

- to Alan and Sandra directly, in equal shares (so 30% of the company each); or

- to a trust, under the terms of which Alan and Sandra would be among the beneficiaries.

We know very little about the types of trusts available, the differences between them in terms of tax consequences, and the advantages or disadvantages of using a trust for this purpose. Any advice you could give would be helpful.

(3) We would also like to consider if there are any tax advantages in distributing the current cash balance in the company of £300,000 prior to the share sale and gift. The cash balance was being held for the purchase of more residential property and is surplus to the working capital requirements of the company.

Can we arrange a meeting next week, to discuss the tax consequences of the three issues above? We would also like your advice about the most tax efficient course of action to take.

It would also be useful if you could let us know at that meeting if there is any further information you need in order to finalise your advice.

Best wishes

Philip and Estelle

Exhibit 2

Valuation of Thompson Ltd shares

A valuation of Thompson Ltd shares was carried out in December 2018, which values the shares as follows:

	£m
100% shareholding	3.25
60% shareholding	1.75
50% shareholding	1.2
40% shareholding	0.8
30% shareholding	0.6

Exhibit 3

Information provided by Thompson Ltd

Thompson Ltd's tangible net assets are made up as follows:

	Carrying Amount 31 December 2018 £	Market Value £
Property plant and equipment:		
Plant and equipment	24,500	24,500
Retail premises	50,000	250,000
Residential investment properties	225,000	750,000
Cash	300,000	300,000
Total of other assets less liabilities	21,400	21,400
Net assets	620,900	1,345,900

Note: All individual items of plant and equipment were bought for and have market values of less than £6,000.

50 TabletTech Ltd

You are an ICAEW Chartered Accountant, employed as a tax specialist at TabletTech Ltd (TT Ltd). The company manufactures and sells accessories for tablet computers.

The directors of TT Ltd identified a potential company to purchase; PhoneCharger Ltd (PC Ltd), which manufactures and sells phone chargers compatible with popular mobile phones.

PC Ltd was incorporated by Alice Crane in 2010, when she subscribed £2 million for 2 million ordinary shares of £1 each. She still owns 100% of the share capital of PC Ltd and continues to work full-time for the company.

The latest balance sheet of PC Ltd is attached (**Exhibit**). All assets on the balance sheet are shown at a carrying amount of historic cost less accumulated depreciation, apart from the property, which is shown at market value. The property was purchased on incorporation in 2010 for £2.4 million. The indexed cost of the property to December 2017 is £3.12 million. In addition, the business has significant non-purchased goodwill, which has been created since incorporation. The company has always been profitable.

Alice stated that she expects to receive net cash, after tax, for the sale of PC Ltd of £20 million. As part of the deal to sell her company Alice has also asked that at least £5 million of any purchase consideration is paid into a bank account held by a nominee in the Cayman Islands (a tax haven).

The directors of TT Ltd have asked for your advice about how to structure the purchase of the business of PC Ltd. The purchase can be either:

- 100% of the shares in PC Ltd; or
- 100% of the company's trade and assets.

If TT Ltd buys the assets of PC Ltd, PC Ltd will cease to trade and will then be liquidated.

Alice is a higher rate taxpayer and uses her capital gains tax annual exempt amount each tax year against gains she makes on her investments.

Requirements

Prepare extracts for inclusion in a report to the board of directors of TT Ltd. The extracts should:

50.1 Identify the amount of consideration that would need to be paid to Alice Crane, so that she received cash of £20 million, net of tax, under each of the alternative methods of purchasing PC Ltd.

50.2 Determine which method of purchase would be the most tax efficient for TT Ltd.

50.3 Identify and explain the implications for you, as an ICAEW Chartered Accountant, of Alice Crane's request that £5 million of purchase consideration should be paid to a nominee account in the Cayman Islands

Total: 35 marks

Exhibit

PhoneCharger Ltd – balance sheet as at 30 September 2018

	£'000	£'000
Tangible fixed assets		
Property		3,600
Plant and equipment		1,000
		4,600
Current assets		
Stock	6,800	
Trade debtors	6,600	
	13,400	
Less creditors: amounts falling due within one year		
Trade creditors	(1,800)	
Net current assets		11,600
Net assets		16,200
Capital and reserves		
Called up share capital		2,000
Revaluation reserve		1,200
Profit and loss account		13,000
		16,200

51 Elm plc

Assume it is June 2019. You work for a firm of ICAEW Chartered Accountants and are asked to assist your manager in preparation for a meeting with Lewis Gordon, the finance director of Elm plc, a UK quoted company.

You have been provided with some background information on the structure of the Elm plc group and details of outstanding issues to be considered in order to prepare corporation tax computations for the group companies for the year ended 31 March 2019.

Background information

The Elm plc group companies all have a 31 March year end.

On 31 March 2019, the group structure was as follows. Elm plc owned:

- 75% of the ordinary share capital of Terrapin Ltd;
- 51% of the ordinary share capital of Labrador Ltd;
- 76% of the shares in Walker SARL, which is registered in Ruritania, a non-EU country.

Terrapin Ltd also owns 75% of the share capital of Cat Ltd. Terrapin Ltd's 75% shareholding in Cat Ltd was acquired on 31 January 2019 for £4 million. Cat Ltd had brought forward capital losses of £550,000 at the date of acquisition.

Outstanding issues

Lewis Gordon asked for your firm's advice on the tax treatment of the following issues which need to be resolved in order to complete the corporation tax computations of the Elm plc group companies for the year ended 31 March 2019:

(1) In 2007, Elm plc set up a permanent establishment (PE) in Ruritania, a non-EU country. The PE made substantial profits in recent years. On 1 April 2018, the trade of the PE was transferred to a company, Walker SARL, which is resident in Ruritania. The transfer was made in exchange for 300,000 £1 ordinary shares (an 100% shareholding) in Walker SARL valued at £3.2 million, which was equal to the market value of the trade and assets transferred. Details of the assets transferred to Walker SARL are in the **Exhibit**. On 1 January 2019, Elm plc sold 72,000 of the shares in Walker SARL for £1.35 million. At that date the market value of Elm plc's remaining holding was £2.1 million. The rate of corporation tax in Ruritania is 18%.

(2) On 7 May 2018, Labrador Ltd issued 75,000 shares to a third party, reducing Elm plc's holding from 75% to 51%. In January 2014 Elm plc transferred part of its trade to Labrador Ltd, including an office block which was transferred at its historical cost of £1,400,000 when its market value was £2,400,000. The office block had originally been acquired in May 2003. The indexation factor from May 2003 to January 2014 is 0.392.

(3) On 26 September 2018, Elm plc sold its 100% shareholding in Parrot Ltd to an unconnected third party in exchange for cash of £12 million. The shares were acquired in April 2007 for £14 million. Parrot Ltd owns an investment property that makes up more than 50% of its net assets and accounts for at least 30% of its income.

(4) In October 2018 Elm plc and Terrapin Ltd both sold their shareholdings in Basset Ltd, a trading company, which was originally set up as an industry-wide joint venture. 8% of the shares were held by Elm plc, and 8% by Terrapin Ltd. Each company paid £40,000 for its shareholding in 2008, and received sale proceeds of £125,000. The indexation allowance for each company is £12,540.

(5) In addition to any gains or losses arising from the above transactions, Terrapin Ltd realised a chargeable gain of £140,000 on 4 October 2018 from the sale of land.

Your files show that, before any adjustment for the items noted above, the taxable total profits of companies taxable in the UK for the year ended 31 March 2019 were:

	£
Elm plc	2,500,000
Labrador Ltd	325,000
Terrapin Ltd	10,000
Cat Ltd	1,200,000
Parrot Ltd	60,000

In addition, Terrapin Ltd had brought forward capital losses of £36,000.

The group has no other losses, of any kind, other than those mentioned or resulting from the transactions above.

Requirement

Prepare detailed notes for your manager, to be used at a meeting with Lewis Gordon, outlining the tax implications of each of the outstanding issues.

Notes

1 Where appropriate, include calculations in your notes.
2 You are not required to calculate the corporation tax liability for any group company.

Total: 25 marks

Exhibit

Details of assets transferred to Walker SARL by the Ruritanian PE on 1 April 2018

Asset	Date of purchase	Indexation factor from date of purchase to December 2017	Cost £	Market value on 1 April 2018 £
Factory (Note)	January 2007	0.379	250,000	700,000
Warehouse	January 2009	0.324	550,000	500,000
Fixed plant and machinery	May 2015	0.076	200,000	250,000
Goodwill	January 2007	0.379	–	1,250,000
Trading stock	N/A	N/A	200,000	500,000

All of the assets transferred are located in Ruritania.

Note: Walker SARL sold the factory to an unconnected third party on 31 December 2018 for £900,000.

March 2018 exam questions

52 2B plc

Assume it is March 2019. You are an ICAEW Chartered Accountant. You are working on a short-term contract in the finance department at 2B plc, a UK tax-resident company. 2B plc sells beer and other drinks to shops, hotels and restaurants. Your role is to cover the temporary absence of the financial controller, Gerry Maya, who has gone on a four-week holiday. 2B plc's projected adjusted taxable profits for the year ending 31 March 2019 are £150 million and it employs over 400 staff in the UK.

On your first morning at 2B plc, Trina Hall, the CEO, gives you this briefing on 2B plc's structure:

Briefing from Trina Hall

As you are new to the company I have set out below some background information on 2B plc's four investments; H-Brew Ltd, Toll Ltd, UB Inc and CS Inc.

H-Brew Ltd

2B plc owns 75% of the ordinary shares of H-Brew Ltd, a UK tax-resident company. 2B plc bought its shares in H-Brew Ltd in March 2014. The remaining 25% of the shares are owned by H-Brew Ltd's three individual directors. H-Brew Ltd brews beer which it sells to Toll Ltd, UB Inc and to other UK bottling companies.

Toll Ltd

2B plc owns 100% of the ordinary shares of Toll Ltd, a UK tax-resident company. Toll Ltd operates a factory in the UK, which bottles beer and other drinks. 2B plc bought its shares in Toll Ltd in July 2013.

UB Inc

On 1 July 2018, 2B plc bought 60% of the shares of UB Inc. The remaining 40% of the shares are owned by Gerry Maya's brother, Jin Maya. UB Inc is tax-resident in Utopia where the tax rate on all corporate profits is 9%. UB Inc operates a factory in Utopia which bottles beer and other drinks exclusively for 2B plc. Jin Maya is also tax-resident in Utopia.

CS Inc

2B plc owns 100% of the shares of CS Inc, a company which is also tax resident in Utopia. CS Inc operates an efficient and profitable customer call centre for many different clients including 2B plc. 2B plc bought its shares in CS Inc in July 2015.

The 2B plc board asked Gerry to report on the international tax implications of 2B plc's four investments but he did not have time to prepare the report before he went on holiday. Gerry has summarised projected tax computations for the four companies for the year ending 31 March 2019 and has left you some handover notes concerning details of international tax transactions between the companies (**Exhibit**).

Later the same day you receive the following email from Denise Young, the sales manager at H-Brew Ltd.

> **Email from Denise Young**
>
> **Subject:** H-Brew Ltd selling prices
> **Date:** 13 March 2019
>
> I understand that you are covering Gerry Maya's work while he is on holiday and I need your advice about an email he sent to me last week, just before he left. In the email, he told me to implement changes to H-Brew Ltd's selling prices of beer to Toll Ltd, UB Inc and other bottling customers from 1 April 2019. Gerry told me that the proposed pricing structure would result in a reduction of tax for the 2B plc group overall.
>
> However, staff at H-Brew Ltd have a performance-related bonus which is calculated based on achieving gross profit targets. The new pricing structure will result in a lower bonus for them. Gerry told me not to worry about this and that if we did not tell the sales staff this would save H-Brew Ltd money too.

Requirements

52.1 Prepare a draft report for the 2B plc board of directors, which:

(a)   Evaluates the tax implications of 2B plc's shareholding in CS Inc and UB Inc.

(b)   Explains the key tax implications of Note 1 and Note 2 set out in the Exhibit; and

(c)   Recommends, where relevant, adjustments to be made to the tax results of 2B plc and Toll Ltd for the year ending 31 March 2019.

52.2 Identify and explain the ethical implications for you and for 2B plc arising from the email from Denise Young. Set out the actions that you should take.

Total: 40 marks

Exhibit

Handover notes prepared by Gerry Maya

I have set out below the tax results and information concerning international tax transactions between the group companies.

Tax results for group companies

Year ending 31 March 2019	2B plc £m	H-Brew Ltd £m	Toll Ltd £m	UB Inc £m	CS Inc £m
Tax adjusted trading profit/(loss)	150	(5)	15	25	16
Property income	–	–	–	–	4

Note 1

On 1 October 2018, I arranged a £25 million interest-free loan from 2B plc to CS Inc. CS Inc used the money from 2B plc to buy a warehouse including land in the UK which it then leased to Toll Ltd at an annual rent of £7.2 million. If CS Inc had taken out an equivalent bank loan in Utopia the interest rate would have been 2.5%. Toll Ltd uses the warehouse for its trade to store equipment, empty barrels and Toll Ltd's delivery vehicles. I organised the purchase of the warehouse for CS Inc and used 2B plc's UK legal team to complete the transaction. CS Inc's accounts staff send an invoice to Toll Ltd each month for £600,000 for the rent. Toll Ltd has included a deduction for the rent in its results for the year ending 31 March 2019. This loan and leasing transaction will reduce Toll Ltd's trading profit in the UK and divert profit to CS Inc in Utopia where the tax rate is lower.

Note 2

Instead of charging the same sales price to all customers, I have instructed Denise Young, the sales manager at H-Brew Ltd to implement changes in H-Brew Ltd's sales price of beer to Toll Ltd, UB Inc and other bottling customers as from 1 April 2019. I believe that these new prices will result in a reduction in tax for the 2B plc group overall.

The sales price changes will result in the following projected revenue and gross profit margins for H-Brew Ltd for the year ending 31 March 2020:

Customer	Revenue £'000	Gross profit margin %
Toll Ltd	19,045	35
UB Inc	29,120	15
Other UK bottling customers	5,135	35
	53,300	

I trust that you will ensure that these prices are implemented in my absence.

53 Recruit plc

You work for Merit and Nore (MN), a firm of ICAEW Chartered Accountants. Your firm provides tax advice to Recruit plc and its senior employees. Recruit plc is a UK tax-resident company engaged in recruitment and training in the UK.

Recruit plc owns 100% of the shares in R-India Ltd, a company tax-resident in India which operates a recruitment agency in India.

In October 2018, Recruit plc set up a permanent establishment called Faktur in Poland, a country in the EU. Faktur carries out routine invoice and credit collection functions for both Recruit plc and R-India Ltd. Faktur pays tax in Poland and Recruit plc has made an election to exempt the profits from permanent establishments from UK taxation.

Your manager has forwarded you an email from Peter Murray, an accountant and senior employee in the finance department at Recruit plc:

Email

Date: 9 March 2019
Subject: Faktur – Secondment

Recruit plc's finance director has offered me a two-year secondment at Faktur to replace the Faktur accountant who has recently resigned. I am writing to you for advice on the UK tax implications for me of the following:

I expect my secondment to start on 6 October 2019 and I will work on average 40 hours a week. However, I will visit Faktur's offices in Poland on 6 August 2019 for 8 days to attend an induction course and to organise rental of a house. I will be paid an annual salary during my secondment of an equivalent amount of £80,000 starting on 6 October 2019. This is an increase of £10,000 on my current salary. Recruit plc has agreed to pay my living costs and to pay for my trips home to visit my family.

I will return to the UK for one weekend each month. I will arrive on Thursday evening and attend meetings at Recruit plc on Friday and spend the weekend with my family before returning to Poland on Monday morning.

I will return to the UK for an additional 10 days in December 2019 and December 2020 and spend all my other holidays in Poland. My wife intends to live with me in Poland from January 2020.

Each tax year I invest the maximum amount I am allowed in ISA accounts but I am unsure when and if I should make a £20,000 investment in the tax year 2019/20.

I intend to buy a holiday home in Poland and to raise the money I will sell either a UK rental property which has a market value of £225,000 or my 20,000 shares in EEW plc which are currently quoted at £11.25 each. I have attached details of the cost of these assets and the rental income I will receive from my rental property for the tax year 2019/20 (**Exhibit**). If I do not sell either the rental property or the EEW shares, I expect the rental income will be the same for the tax years 2020/21 and 2021/22. I am not sure whether it would save me tax if I wait until I leave the UK before selling either the rental property or the EEW plc shares.

I own a house in the UK which is my principal private residence. I bought the house in 2016 for £350,000. I will rent my house to a tenant for £1,900 per month after expenses from 1 November 2019.

VAT

I need to resolve a VAT issue before I leave my current position at Recruit plc. I have overseen a project to update the group's accounting software. On 1 October 2018, Recruit plc bought an online accounting software license which is to be used by Recruit plc, Faktur and by R–India Ltd. This license was downloaded through an e-commerce service supplied by a German company at a total cost of £900,000. I did not make any adjustment for this transaction when I completed the 31 December 2018 VAT return. However, I am not sure now that this was correct.

Requirements

Prepare a draft reply to Peter's email in which you:

53.1 Explain and calculate the tax implications for Peter of his two-year secondment to Faktur. (Ignore for this requirement the proposal to sell either the rental property or 20,000 shares in EEW plc.)

53.2 Explain the tax implications for Peter of selling either his 20,000 EEW plc shares or his UK rental property. Include advice on the timing of the potential sale and the impact on his income and capital gains tax liabilities.

53.3 Explain the VAT implications of the e-commerce service supplied by the German company to Recruit plc.

Total: 25 marks

Exhibit

Attachment to email – cost of assets and estimated rental income and dividends

Assets	Cost £	Taxable income in tax year 2019/20 £
UK rental property	150,000	
Annual rental income net of expenses		15,000
20,000 shares in EEW plc	150,000	

54 Frank and Hari

You work as a tax adviser for CCE, a firm of ICAEW Chartered Accountants. The tax partner has asked you to prepare notes for a meeting with Frank and Hari, the partners of DroneTx, who are clients of your firm. Frank and Hari are tax-resident in the UK.

Background information

On 6 October 2016, Frank and his uncle Hari set up an unincorporated partnership business, DroneTx, to develop a drone-mapping application. The partners provided cash to buy computer equipment, software and to fund the initial running costs of the business.

Frank and Hari have a partnership agreement to share all profits and losses equally. Hari owns an office building called Rue House which is used by the DroneTx partnership. Hari has never charged the partnership any rent for the use of Rue House. Hari bought the building in 2006 for £90,000.

Extracts from Frank and Hari's client tax files with information about DroneTx's trading losses, the partners' unused tax losses brought forward and estimated income for 2018/19 are in **Exhibit 1**.

DroneTx is ready to launch its product and the business needs more finance. The partners agree that the business should be incorporated and they have provided information about two alternative methods of incorporating the DroneTx partnership.

Method 1 - Incorporation by selling the DroneTx partnership business to DX Ltd, a newly formed company

Method 2 - Incorporation by selling the DroneTx partnership business to MK Ltd, an unconnected technology company (**Exhibit 2**).

You receive the following telephone message from Hari:

"I want to avoid my estate paying inheritance tax if I were to die soon. If Method 1 is chosen, instead of selling the office building Rue House to DX Ltd, I propose to gift it to Frank on 6 April 2019."

Requirements

54.1 For method 1 and method 2, explain the tax implications for Frank and Hari of the incorporation of the DroneTx partnership. Support your answer with relevant calculations and explanations of any relevant claims, elections or reliefs. Recommend the most beneficial method of incorporation for Frank and Hari. You should include advice and calculations for each of Frank and Hari on the most appropriate use of the partnership trading losses.

Ignore for this requirement, Hari's proposal to gift Rue House to Frank.

54.2 Explain the taxation implications for Frank and for Hari of Hari's proposal to gift Rue House to Frank.

Total: 30 marks

Exhibit 1

Extract from Frank and Hari's client tax files

DroneTx partnership trading losses

DroneTx has made tax trading losses since it was established on 6 October 2016 as follows:

	Six-month period ended 5 April 2017 £	Year ended 5 April 2018 £	Year ending 5 April 2019 (estimated) £
Trading loss	(90,000)	(45,000)	(56,250)

DroneTx has made claims for the Annual Investment Allowance for the full cost of computer equipment and therefore the tax written down value of assets will be nil at 6 April 2019.

The estimated trading loss of £56,250 for the year ending 5 April 2019 is calculated before any balancing adjustments for the sale of the computer equipment on incorporation of DroneTx (Exhibit 2).

Unused tax losses brought forward

	Frank £	Hari £
Share of partnership trading loss b/f at 6 April 2018	(67,500)	See Note

Note: Because Hari has always made a claim to set his share of the partnership trading loss against his income of the current tax year under s64 loss relief, he has no partnership trading losses brought forward at 6 April 2018.

Summary of partners' estimated income for the tax year 2018/19

	Frank £	Hari £
Employment income	–	124,000
Gross income from discretionary trust	25,000	–

Hari's employment income relates to a part-time job as an engineer with an unconnected company. He has paid PAYE of £42,100 on this income.

Exhibit 2

Two alternative methods for incorporation of DroneTx

Proposed date of incorporation: 6 April 2019.

Estimated total consideration: £2,000,000 comprising £1,950,000 for goodwill and £50,000 for computer equipment. The computer equipment cost the partnership £125,000. There was no cost for the goodwill.

Method 1 – Incorporation by selling the DroneTx partnership business to DX Ltd

- The partners will incorporate the DroneTx business by transferring the goodwill and computer equipment to a newly-formed company, DX Ltd. In exchange for the goodwill and computer equipment DX Ltd will issue 10,000 £100 ordinary shares to each of the partners.

- DX Ltd will, in the future, be able to attract investors under the Enterprise Investment Scheme to raise finance to launch the DroneTx product.

- DX Ltd will buy Rue House owned by Hari for £250,000 and will continue to trade from the building.

- Hari will no longer work for the business, but will retain his shares in DX Ltd indefinitely. Frank will work for the business.

Method 2 – Incorporation by selling the partnership DroneTx business to MK Ltd

- MK Ltd, an unconnected technology company, has offered to buy the DroneTx partnership business. MK Ltd will issue 100,000 £10 'B' ordinary shares to each of the partners in exchange for the goodwill and assets of DroneTx which, will guarantee each partner a 7% shareholding in MK Ltd. The 'A' ordinary shares in MK Ltd are owned equally by 25 individual unconnected shareholders.

- MK Ltd will provide all future finance to launch the DroneTx product.

- Hari will sell Rue House to an unconnected party for £250,000 as the DroneTx business will trade from MK Ltd's premises.

- Hari will work for nine months for MK Ltd. On 31 December 2019, he will resign and sell his shares to one of the other MK Ltd shareholders. Frank will work for the business.

June 2018 exam questions

55 Swell Gallery

Assume it is June 2019. You are an ICAEW Chartered Accountant, working in practice as a tax adviser. Hugh Roberts, one of your firm's clients, owns Swell Gallery (SG) an unincorporated sole trader business.

Background information

SG started to trade on 1 July 2012 and has always made up accounts to 30 June annually. The business made losses for the first three accounting periods, but has traded profitably ever since. SG is VAT registered and currently makes wholly taxable supplies, preparing VAT returns quarterly with a VAT year end of 31 March.

SG trades from Tide House, a commercial property, bought new from the developer, in July 2012. Tide House is now too small and is due to be sold and replaced by larger commercial premises, at Beach Lane, which will also be bought new from the developer.

The continued success of SG makes it commercially sensible for Hugh to incorporate the business as Swell Ltd (S Ltd) on 1 July 2019. After incorporation Hugh expects to receive a gross salary of £10,000 per month from S Ltd.

Hugh has asked you to advise him about the tax effects of the incorporation; in particular, the difference between the two alternatives available for the sale of Tide House (**Exhibit 1**) and to advise him which of these alternatives will be the most tax efficient. The attachment to the email (**Exhibit 2**) explains the issues he needs help with and gives you further information about SG in order to enable you to provide him with advice. Hugh is 32 years old and has brought forward capital losses of £50,000 as at 6 April 2019.

Requirements

Prepare notes for use at a meeting with Hugh Roberts, to advise him of the tax consequences of his plans for incorporation. These notes should:

55.1 Identify the tax consequences of incorporation for Hugh and Swell Ltd, taking into account the differing tax effects of adopting either Alternative 1 or Alternative 2 in respect of the sale of Tide House.

55.2 Compare the differing tax costs of Alternatives 1 and 2 and recommend which alternative provides the most tax efficient route for incorporating Swell Gallery as Swell Ltd.

55.3 Identify and explain the tax consequences of buying and letting the Beach Lane premises.

55.4 Briefly suggest how Hugh could structure his affairs differently in order to mitigate his tax liabilities.

Support your notes with calculations, where relevant.

Total: 40 marks

Exhibit 1

Email from Hugh Roberts

To: ICAEW Chartered Accountant
From: Hugh Roberts
Subject: Incorporation of Swell Gallery (SG) as Swell Ltd (S Ltd) on 1 July 2019

I have been advised by my solicitors that I need to incorporate my business, SG, for commercial reasons.

On 1 July 2019, S Ltd will issue two £1 ordinary shares to me, in exchange for the trade and all, or part, of the assets of SG. I need your help in deciding whether I should transfer Tide House to the new company or not (see below).

Tide House, my current commercial premises, has become too small for my business. I plan to sell Tide House and replace it with newly built commercial premises at Beach Lane. The new premises will be ready to occupy around the same time as I incorporate and will cost £650,000, excluding SDLT and VAT.

I have identified two alternatives for the incorporation of my business and the sale of Tide House, as follows:

Alternative 1: I transfer Tide House to S Ltd on 1 July 2019, along with all the other trade and assets of SG. The company then sells Tide House for its market value (see Exhibit 2 below) on 1 July 2019.

Alternative 2: I keep Tide House and do not transfer it to S Ltd with the trade and the remaining assets on incorporation. I then sell Tide House, personally, for market value on 1 July 2019.

The new premises at Beach Lane will be too large for the company and the company will rent out two thirds of the building to tenants for at least three years. Please advise me of the tax consequences resulting from buying the Beach Lane premises and the tax impact of renting out two-thirds of the building to commercial tenants.

The information you may need to give me this advice is included in the attachment below (Exhibit 2).

Exhibit 2

Email attachment
Tax information concerning SG

SG: Trading profits, adjusted for taxation, in recent accounting periods:

Year ended 30 June	£
2017	100,000
2018	105,000
2019	125,000 (Note)

Note: the adjusted profits for the year ended 30 June 2019 have been estimated and are calculated before any balancing adjustments on sale.

Market value of the trade and assets of SG on 1 July 2019

Asset	Notes	Market value
		£
Goodwill	1	500,000
Plant and machinery	2	100,000
Net current assets		50,000
Tide House	3	450,000
Total market value of SG		£1,100,000

Notes

1 **Goodwill**

The goodwill is internally-generated goodwill and has no cost.

2 **Plant and machinery**

The plant and machinery figure is made up of many small items, each with a cost and a current value of less than £6,000. Tax written down value of the plant and machinery at 30 June 2019 is £25,000.

3 **Tide House**

Cost of purchase on 1 July 2012 (excluding VAT and SDLT) was £350,000.

No option to tax has been exercised on this property.

56 Albion Ltd

You are an ICAEW Chartered Accountant, working in practice as a tax adviser. Jim Bell, also an ICAEW Chartered Accountant, is the recently appointed finance director of Albion Ltd, a UK-resident company. Both Jim and Albion Ltd are clients of your firm.

Background information

Jim has been resident in the UK for tax purposes since the tax year 2005/06, but continues to have a domicile of origin in the non-EEA country of Oceania.

Jim has a mixture of UK and overseas income and gains and each tax year he decides whether he should claim the remittance basis. He has yet to make that decision for the 2018/19 tax year (**Exhibit 1**).

As Albion Ltd's finance director, Jim has contacted your manager about some concerns he has over the tax treatment of transactions being carried out between Albion Ltd and its parent company Cliff Ltd (**Exhibit 2**).

Requirements

56.1 Explain the basis on which Jim's income tax and capital gains tax liabilities will be calculated for 2018/19, including an evaluation of whether Jim should take advantage of any claims or elections available to minimise his tax liabilities for the year.

Your answer should include a computation of Jim's income tax and capital gains tax liabilities for 2018/19.

56.2 Provide a briefing note for your manager, in reply to Jim's concerns in Exhibit 2, which explains the role of the Senior Accounting Officer (SAO), analyses the issues raised and identifies the appropriate action to take.

Total: 35 marks

Exhibit 1

Jim Bell's personal tax information

For the 2018/19 tax year Jim has the following income and gains:

Income	£
Directors' fees – Albion Ltd	100,000
Dividends received from Albion Ltd	10,000
Dividends received from Bloomswell GmbH and paid into a bank account in Oceania (Note)	45,000
Gains	
Gain on sale of a painting in the UK	75,450

Note: Bloomswell GmbH is resident in Oceania.

Jim transferred £150,000 into the UK from one of his bank accounts in Oceania on 1 February 2019. The money was sourced from the sale of capital items in Oceania in tax years before 2018/19. These gains have not been taxed in the UK.

On 25 March 2019, Jim invested the £150,000 in 20% of the ordinary share capital of Fisherhead Ltd, a UK, newly incorporated, unquoted, trading company, Fisherhead Ltd has two employees and will use the £150,000 invested by Jim for the purposes of its trade. Jim does not work for or have any other connection with Fisherhead Ltd.

Exhibit 2

Extract from note of telephone conversation with Jim Bell

Jim rang us and as the new FD of Albion Ltd, he is concerned about his accountability for the tax affairs of the company; especially as he is the nominated SAO of the company.

Albion Ltd is 100% owned by Cliff Ltd, a company incorporated and resident in the British Virgin Islands (BVI). The BVI are a tax haven and the rates of corporation tax and income tax are 0%. There is also no tax on dividend income, although there is tax on interest income.

Cliff Ltd lent Albion Ltd £5 million in January 2018, at an interest rate of 8%pa, on arm's length terms. In the UK, this loan is treated as a debt instrument and interest is paid by Albion Ltd to Cliff Ltd. Under the laws of the BVI, this loan is treated as an equity instrument and the payments of interest under the loan are treated as dividend income.

Jim tells us that his fellow directors want Albion Ltd to take a deduction for the interest in the corporation tax computation for the year ended 31 December 2018.

Jim is concerned that this tax treatment of the interest expense on the loan may be incorrect, but when he raised this with his fellow directors, they told him to keep quiet his concerns because no-one will ever find out about them.

His would like our advice as to:

- how the company should deal with the loan interest in the corporation tax computation of Albion Ltd for the year ending 31 December 2018; and

- the implications for him, as SAO, and for the company, of the attitude of his fellow directors to the tax treatment of the loan interest.

57 Dolphin Ltd

You are an ICAEW Chartered Accountant working in the finance department of Dolphin Ltd, a UK registered trading company. You are responsible for preparing the corporation tax computations and returns of Dolphin Ltd, reporting to Laurel Storm, the finance director.

Background information

Dolphin Ltd has been trading for many years, manufacturing and selling equipment to the UK fishing industry and preparing accounts to 31 December. The company recently won a large contract to provide innovative fishing equipment to the nationalised fishing industry in the non-EEA country of Atlantica from 1 January 2020.

Given the size of this contract, Dolphin Ltd will need to set up a business in Atlantica either via a permanent establishment (PE) in Atlantica or a 100% owned subsidiary company resident in Atlantica. Atlantica has a tax rate of 25% on company profits and a tax rate of 5% on the profits of foreign PE's. The tax system is very similar to that of the UK. It is likely that this will be the first of many overseas contracts as Dolphin Ltd's trading strategy is to expand by targeting overseas markets. There is no double tax treaty between the UK and Atlantica and any double tax relief given in the UK is via unilateral double tax relief.

In addition, because of the changes this contract will make to the trading pattern of Dolphin Ltd, it has been suggested that Dolphin Ltd should change its year end from 31 December to 31 March. Laurel has asked you to identify the difference between preparing the next set of accounts for the 15-month period ending 31 March 2020. Alternatively, preparing two sets of accounts; firstly for the year ending 31 December 2019 and then secondly for the three months ending 31 March 2020.

Laurel also provided you with projected figures of income and expenditure, for both the existing UK-based trade of Dolphin Ltd and also the new contract in Atlantica, for the year ending 31 December 2019 and the three months ending 31 March 2020 (**Exhibit**).

Laurel mentioned that a firm of UK-based tax advisers, run by a friend of the CEO, approached Dolphin Ltd a few weeks ago, offering to help set up the business in Atlantica. This firm claim that they have a 'tax-saving scheme', which can reduce the rate of tax on profits made in Atlantica to 0%, whether the profits are taxed in the UK or in Atlantica. They also mentioned that the terms of this scheme are confidential and would only be disclosed to the company on the payment of a one-off fee of £100,000, and the signing of a confidentiality agreement. The board of directors has discussed this offer and is keen to save any tax it can. However, Laurel would like your opinion about the 'tax-saving scheme', because it appears too good to be true.

Requirements

Prepare notes, which Laurel can use to advise the board of directors of Dolphin Ltd which include:

57.1 An explanation of the difference for tax purposes between Dolphin Ltd setting up a permanent establishment in Atlantica or an Atlantica-resident subsidiary company, together with a recommendation as to which structure would be the most tax efficient.

57.2 Provide a recommendation as to whether Dolphin Ltd should adopt a 15-month period of account ending 31 March 2020 or two separate periods of account (year ending 31 December 2019, followed by three months ending 31 March 2020). Assume that you adopt the structure you recommended in Part 57.1 above.

You should prepare calculations, where appropriate, to support this part of your answer.

57.3 Advice about the approach to be taken to the 'tax-saving scheme' offered to Dolphin Ltd.

Total: 25 marks

Exhibit

Prepared by Laurel Storm

Dolphin Ltd
Projected figures

	Year ending 31 December 2019 £	3-month period ending 31 March 2020 £	Totals for 15 months ending 31 March 2020 £
Trading profits from UK trade before capital allowances	2,100,000	550,000	2,650,000
Trading profits from Atlantican contract before capital allowances	100,000	1,450,000	1,550,000
Capital allowances of UK trade	345,000	45,000	390,000
Capital allowances of Atlantican trade	–	500,000	500,000

In addition, Dolphin Ltd, which is an SME for R&D purposes, has incurred qualifying research and development expenditure. The projected trading profits above only take account of a 100% deduction for any revenue costs against trading profits and no capital allowances have been calculated on any R&D capital expenditure:

Expenditure on R&D	**Year ending 31 December 2019** £	**3-month period ending 31 March 2020** £	**Total for 15 months ending 31 March 2020** £
Computer hardware	400,000	95,000	495,000
Computer software	50,000	10,000	60,000
Staff costs	259,000	55,450	314,450
Consumable costs	150,000	35,250	185,250

September 2018 exam questions

58   Joe Gregory

Assume it is September 2019. You are an ICAEW Chartered Accountant employed by a firm of ICAEW Chartered Accountants. Your firm acts for Joe Gregory and JG Ltd. Your manager has provided you with the following information:

Background information

Joe is 45 years old, and is UK resident and domiciled. He is a financial adviser and was employed by a bank until April 2018. On 6 April 2018 Joe started his own business operating through a limited company, JG Ltd. Joe lectures in finance and is the sole director and shareholder of JG Ltd. Details of the lecturing engagements of JG Ltd for 2018/19 and Joe's future plans for the business are in **Exhibit 1**.

Joe recently inherited £20,000 on the death of his father. He would like some advice on how to invest this money and has sent your manager an email (**Exhibit 2**).

Requirement

Prepare a briefing note for your manager which includes:

58.1 (a)   An explanation of whether the personal service company (IR35) legislation is relevant to each of the contracts undertaken by JG Ltd in 2018/19 (Exhibit 1), and the implications for JG Ltd. Include calculations of the deemed employment income, together with the income tax and NIC liabilities for any relevant engagements.

(b)   A comparison of Joe's net disposable income for 2020/21 if he operates as a sole trader or via a limited company. For the purposes of this part of the question, assume that the personal service company (IR35) or managed service company legislation is not applicable.

(c)   A brief explanation of the managed service company legislation and a conclusion on whether or not it is likely to apply in respect of Joe's business plans for 2020/21. Include a recommendation on how Joe should operate his business in the future. Detailed calculations are not required for this part of the question.

58.2 Explain the tax reliefs available for the two potential investments (Exhibit 2) and recommend which one is the most tax efficient.

Total: 40 marks

Exhibit 1

File note – details of lecturing engagements in 2018/19 and future plans

2018/19 client engagements for JG Ltd are as follows:

AM Ltd

AM Ltd provides private tuition for exam training for graduates. AM Ltd entered into a contract with JG Ltd for a fee £80,000. AM Ltd determined the dates and times of the lectures and that Joe had to personally deliver them. AM Ltd provided the textbooks and equipment they felt necessary for delivery of the lectures. JG Ltd purchased some additional textbooks at a cost of £125 and a tablet laptop at a cost of £1,250 to help Joe with additional preparation for the lectures.

During 2018/19, in relation to this work, Joe drew a salary of £46,350 from JG Ltd which was taxed via PAYE and on which employers' NIC of £5,234 is due.

Pennington Local Authority

Pennington Local Authority is a local government body. It engaged JG Ltd to deliver public finance training to its employees. The contract was for 20 days' work for a fee of £20,000. Pennington Local Authority provided the equipment and the course materials to JG Ltd and specified that Joe had to be on the premises from 9am until 5pm, on each of the 20 days. Pennington Local Authority deducted income tax of £8,000 under PAYE and employers' NIC of £1,597 from the fee.

Jupiter Ltd

Jupiter Ltd is a private company which agreed a fee of £10,000 for five lectures on dates to suit JG Ltd throughout 2018/19. JG Ltd contracted to write and supply all training material and stipulated in the contract that any suitably-qualified lecturer could be supplied. The contract did not specifically name Joe.

Future plans for JG Ltd

JG Ltd has no lecturing engagements during 2019/20.

For 2020/21 Joe is considering changing the way his business operates due to the administrative burden involved. He could either operate as a sole trader or outsource the general day-to-day running of JG Ltd to an independent management company. In addition to sourcing work for JG Ltd from third party clients, the management company would operate the payroll and prepare all accounts and tax returns for JG Ltd.

Joe is also negotiating with his former employer to provide in-house lecturing services. He estimates that 80% of his time will be spent working for his former employer whilst the remainder of the work will be for a number of clients sourced by the management company.

Joe estimates that his business will have business income of around £175,000 pa with tax-adjusted profits of £145,000 before deducting salary, if he operates as either a sole trader or as a company through JG Ltd. If Joe operates his business as a limited company, through JG Ltd, he will draw a gross salary of £24,000 per annum and the balance of his income as dividends.

Exhibit 2

Email

To:	Tax Manager
From:	Joe Gregory
Subject:	Investment opportunities

I have inherited £20,000 and would like to invest this in shares during 2019/20. However, I am likely to sell some of these shares during 2021/22, as my daughter will start university in 2022.

I have the opportunity to invest in two alternative companies:

(1) **Belle Ltd**

Belle Ltd is an unquoted trading company which started trading on 1 March 2019. The company currently has issued share capital of 30,000 £1 ordinary shares, gross assets of £55,000 and five full time employees. In return for my investment, I will receive 10,000 new £1 ordinary shares.

(2) **Boo Ltd – issuing new shares**

Boo Ltd is an unquoted trading company, formed seven years ago. It currently has issued share capital of 500,000 £1 ordinary shares and gross assets of £10 million. The company employs 150 staff across the UK. In return for my investment, I will receive 3,125 new £1 ordinary shares.

During 2019/20, I intend to sell shares in Weiner plc, purchased seven years ago. The current market value of my holding is £12,500 and the shares originally cost £3,000. My shareholding is less than 0.5% of the total issued share capital.

I am unsure which investment will be better for me in terms of tax savings. I would also like to understand if there are any reliefs available.

59   Foodpack Ltd

You are an ICAEW Chartered Accountant working in practice as a tax adviser. Your firm acts for Foodpack Ltd, a UK resident trading company that designs and manufactures packaging for the food industry.

Two of the directors of Foodpack Ltd, Ella King and her son Daniel Moseley, are also tax clients of your firm. They work full time for the company.

The engagement partner needs your help to prepare for a meeting with Foodpack Ltd to finalise the corporation tax return for the year ended 31 March 2019 and to advise the directors on a potential restructuring of the company.

Ella King and Daniel Moseley, purchased the entire share capital of Foodpack Ltd, of 100,000 £1 ordinary shares, in February 2007, for £2 per share from the previous shareholders.

In 2013, Ella and Daniel sold some of their shares to Hitchens Ltd, a small trading company. The current shareholdings in Foodpack Ltd are:

	Number of £1 ordinary shares
Ella King	70,000
Daniel Moseley	20,000
Hitchens Ltd	10,000
	100,000

You have been provided with details of Foodpack Ltd's tax-adjusted trading profit for the year ended 31 March 2019 and summary of its statement of financial position as at that date (**Exhibit 1**). Ella has also sent you an email regarding the restructuring of the business (**Exhibit 2**).

Two days ago, a newspaper released details of several high-profile individuals who have invested offshore in order to avoid tax. In the newspaper, Ella King was named as a scheme investor. Ella owns a holiday home in Barbados. Barbados tax law levies stamp duty and capital taxes where a home is sold by an individual or a local company. It has been revealed that Ella has set up a company resident in Luxembourg which owns the home. No liability for stamp duty and capital taxes arises in Barbados because the company is resident in Luxembourg.

Your firm was not aware of Ella's arrangements in this respect and had no knowledge of the holiday home.

Requirements

59.1 Calculate the corporation tax payable by Foodpack Ltd for the year ended 31 March 2019, explaining the treatment of the two outstanding issues, considering any beneficial claims, elections or reliefs (Exhibit 1).

59.2 Respond to Ella King's email (Exhibit 2).

59.3 Identify the ethical issues for your firm arising from the information about Ella King published in the newspaper. Identify and explain any actions that you and your firm should take.

Total: 35 marks

Exhibit 1

Foodpack Ltd, tax-adjusted profit for the year ended 31 March 2019 and summary of its statement of financial position as at 31 March 2019

The tax adjusted trading profit for the year ended 31 March 2019 is as follows:

	£'000
Profit before tax	8,100
Depreciation and other disallowable expenses	60
Less capital allowances	(90)
Tax-adjusted trading profit	8,070

The following two issues may require further adjustment to be made to the tax-adjusted trading profit above.

(1) **Lease of factory**

On 1 April 2018, Foodpack Ltd sold the lease for a factory for £40,000 when there were 20 years left to run. The lease had been granted to Foodpack Ltd as a 25-year lease for £31,000 in April 2013. Foodpack Ltd had immediately started to use the factory as an additional manufacturing site in the north of England. However, as part of the planned restructure, the manufacturing has been centralised and the company stopped trading from the site just before sale.

(2) **Patents**

In June 2018, Foodpack Ltd purchased two patents. The first patent relates to new packaging which extends the shelf life of food.

The second patent is for internal packaging that slows down the defrosting process. Foodpack Ltd has not previously elected into the patent box regime. Profit before tax comprises:

Profit on patent 1	£3 million
Profit on patent 2	£4 million
Other profits	£1.1 million

Profit on patent 1 is made up of patent income of £5 million with expenditure of £2 million. Profit on patent 2 is made up of patent income of £6 million with expenditure of £2 million.

A transfer pricing study has concluded that the notional marketing royalty to be deducted in computing the patent profits is 3% with nexus fractions of 60% for the first patent and 80% for the second.

A summary of the Foodpack Ltd statement of financial position as at 31 March 2018 shows the following:

	£'000
Intangibles	5,000
Property, plant & equipment	5,670
Cash and other net current	(5,010)
Liabilities	5,660
Share capital	100
Share premium	100
Revaluation surplus	4,670
Retained earnings	790
	5,660

Exhibit 2

Email from Ella King

To: Tax Adviser
From: Ella King
Re: Potential restructuring and investment

I have thoroughly enjoyed my time as a director at Foodpack Ltd, but since Hitchens Ltd has become a shareholder, the company is not going in the direction I would like, so I want to retire.

Income from my portfolio of investments and my salary from Foodpack Ltd mean that I am an additional rate taxpayer.

Foodpack Ltd is a profitable company and I want to ensure that it continues to be successful. I am not yet sure if I want to sell all of my Foodpack Ltd shares, so I have been discussing various alternatives with the board. Any sale of my shares will take place on 1 October 2019 when the market value will be £12 per share. There are three alternative ways to structure the sale.

Alternative 1

Daniel would purchase 20,000 of my shares at a discounted price of £9 per share, funded by a bank loan from a third-party bank.

Alternative 2

Foodpack Ltd would purchase my entire shareholding of 70,000 shares, for £12 per share, if it has the reserves available to do so.

Alternative 3

Foodpack Ltd would purchase 20,000 of my shares for £12 per share.

Can you please advise on the tax implications of the three alternatives for Foodpack Ltd, myself and Daniel?

60 Gold Ltd

Your firm acts as tax advisers for the Gold Ltd group of companies and its directors.

Corporation tax year ended 31 March 2019

Gold Ltd is a UK resident trading company, designing and manufacturing jewellery. It supplies items to retail businesses in the UK and overseas. Gold Ltd started trading in 2005.

Gold Ltd has one wholly-owned subsidiary, Silver Ltd. Gold Ltd acquired its shares in Silver Ltd in 2008 for £65,000.

Gold Ltd's share capital is held as follows:

Shareholder	Number of £1 ordinary shares	Percentage holding
Amber Ltd	10,000	50%
Topaz Ltd	5,000	25%
Estelle Thomas	5,000	25%

For the year ended 31 March 2019, Gold Ltd has taxable total profits of £760,000, before any adjustments for the following:

(1) On 1 June 2018, Gold Ltd purchased an investment property in the non-EU country of Anchara (where the currency is the A$), costing A$300,000, when the rate of exchange was £1 = A$3.20. On 31 January 2019, Gold Ltd sold the property for A$380,000 when the rate of exchange was £1 = A$4.00. The proceeds from disposal were left in an overseas bank account and remitted to the UK on 25 March 2019 when the rate of exchange was £1 = A$4.50.

(2) On 30 June 2018 Gold Ltd issued £100,000 of 6% loan stock for the purposes of raising finance for its trade. The cost of issuing the loan stock was £8,000.

(3) Estelle Thomas has been employed as a director of Gold Ltd since incorporation, on an annual salary of £150,000. In August 2011 she borrowed £80,000, at an interest rate of 1%, from the company. This loan was written off on 30 September 2018. Estelle had paid all interest due up to that date and the interest has been correctly recorded in the accounting records. The loan write-off has been treated as a non-trading loan relationship debit for corporation tax purposes. Estelle is an additional rate taxpayer and receives dividends from other investments.

VAT

Gold Ltd purchased Antalya House, a new commercial building, in April 2012 and it exercised the option to tax. In January 2014 the building was transferred to Silver Ltd.

Silver Ltd has decided to sell Antalya House to an unconnected third party. The sale is likely to take place in December 2019 for £2.5 million.

Since Gold Ltd acquired it, Antalya House has always been let to tenants under a short lease. The tenants have the right to terminate the lease should the ownership change but no information has been obtained on whether they will exercise this right.

Requirements

Prepare notes for a meeting with the financial accountant of Gold Ltd that include:

60.1 A revised computation of the taxable profits and tax liabilities of Gold Ltd for the year ended 31 March 2019 including an explanation of any adjustments you have made.

60.2 An explanation, including calculations of the impact for Estelle of the loan write off.

60.3 An explanation of the potential VAT implications on the sale of Antalya House, identifying areas where further information is needed to give accurate VAT advice. Calculations are not required.

Total: 25 marks

Answer Bank

Individuals – owner managed businesses

1 Thomas Evans (September 2014)

Scenario

The candidate is a tax adviser in a firm of ICAEW Chartered Accountants, reporting to a manager in the tax department. The candidate is asked to complete a number of tasks relating to a new client, who has been made redundant from a previous employment and intends to set up a new business venture.

Firstly, the candidate is asked to calculate the after tax contribution to business start-up costs from termination payments and the sale of loan stock. This tested understanding of:

- the tax and NICs due on different types of termination payments;

- the tax consequences of the sale of QCBs, interacting with the tax due on QCBs received as part of a takeover and the availability of entrepreneurs' relief;

- where there is incomplete or ambiguous information, evaluating the additional information required.

In the second part of the question the candidate is asked to demonstrate understanding of the tax differences between trading as a sole trader or a limited company, with particular reference to the use of losses in opening years and the withdrawal of profits. In addition, consideration needs to be given to the tax implications of a potential investment in the company by a close relative.

Marking guide

	Technical	Skills	Marks
Briefing notes with treatment of termination payments and loan stock			
Summary re: bank loan	–	1	
PILON	1	–	
Compensation	–	2	
IT and NIC on PILON	2	1	
IT and NIC on compensation	1	½	
Additional information	–	1½	
	4	6	10
Inheritance from Aunt Miriam			
QCB exemption	½	½	
Takeover – deferral	1	2	
Takeover – election	1	3	
IHT – PET	–	2	
IHT – BPR	½	1	
IHT – Tax	½	1	
Calculation summary	–	1½	
Additional information	–	1½	
	3½	12½	16

	Technical	Skills	Marks
Letter to Thomas explaining sole trader v company			
Losses – unincorporated	1	2	
Losses – company	1	2½	
Taxing profits – unincorporated	1	1	
Taxing profits – company	1	3	
Payment dates	1½	½	
Employed v self-employed	–	1	
IR 35	2	2	
William's investment – unincorporated	–	2	
William's investment – company	1	2	
	8½	16	24½
Total marks	16	34½	50½
Maximum			40

Briefing note: Amount of bank loan finance required

	£
Finance required	150,000
Less termination payment contribution (after tax and NIC)	(48,800) (W1)
Less proceeds from sale of loan stock (after tax)	(41,770) (W2)
Bank loan required	59,430

WORKINGS

(1) Termination payment

As all payments in lieu of notice (PILON) are taxable, contractual and non-contractual, the amount of £23,750 is fully taxable as general earnings.

Discretionary payments for loss of office are exempt up to £30,000 and taxable above this amount. The statutory redundancy pay of £3,375 is not subject to income tax and NIC, but reduces this exemption.

Compensation for loss of office (£35,000), if it is a discretionary payment, will be exempt up to £26,625 (£30,000 – £3,375). The excess of £8,375 (£35,000 – £26,625) is specific employment income. This is taxable as the top slice of Thomas's income and taxed at his highest marginal rate.

Thomas has taxable employment income of £57,500 in 2019/20 [(£95,000/12 × 6) + £10,000]. Assuming his adjusted net income does not exceed £100,000, after deduction of the personal allowance his basic rate band will have been used in full meaning that any incremental income from the termination payments will therefore be taxed at 40%.

The income tax and NIC due on the PILON will be 42% × £23,750 = £9,975.

The compensation for loss of office taxable, after deduction for the exemption of £26,625, is £8,375. Tax due on this at 40% is £3,350.

As the £35,000 payment attracts the £30,000 income tax exemption, there is no NIC on any of the payment.

	£
Total termination payments (£3,375 + £35,000 + £23,750)	62,125
Less tax and NIC on PILON	(9,975)
Less tax on compensation for loss of office	(3,350)
Termination payment contribution to business start-up costs	48,800

Additional information required:

The following are examples of the issues to be mentioned. Credit was given for other valid points made by candidates:

- Does Thomas have any other income, which would affect the rate of income tax payable, or require abatement/loss of the personal allowance?

- Did Thomas have any taxable benefits by virtue of his employment?

- Can the £35,000 compensation for loss of office be regarded as a discretionary payment? If there was any contractual entitlement or a reasonable expectation of payment, the payment would be regarded as a taxable termination payment taxed in full at 40% and liable to national insurance.

(2) **Inheritance from Aunt Miriam**

The sale of the Rebus loan stock, if it is a QCB, is exempt from capital gains tax.

However, on the takeover in August 2019, a gain of £30,000 would have arisen ie, proceeds £50,000 (£100,000/1,000 × £500) less base cost on gift of £20,000.

If Thomas does nothing the gain of £30,000 on takeover will be deferred, until the loan stock is sold.

However, if, in this case, he were to defer the gain he would forfeit his entitlement to claim entrepreneurs' relief on the gain, resulting in CGT due of £3,660 [(£30,000 – annual exempt amount of £11,700) × 20%].

If an election is made not to defer the gain on the QCBs, the whole gain will be taxable at the time of the takeover, however, entrepreneurs' relief could be claimed to reduce the CGT due on the gain to £1,830 [(£30,000 – £11,700) × 10%]. As both events occur in the current tax year Thomas still has the opportunity to make this election and reduce the tax arising with no cash flow disadvantage.

In addition, Thomas has received the Morse Ltd shares as a lifetime gift from his Aunt. At the time of the gift, the gift would have been considered a potentially exempt transfer for IHT purposes. No IHT would have been due in lifetime.

If his aunt were to die within seven years of making the lifetime gift, Thomas, as recipient of the gift would be liable to pay any IHT due.

BPR would probably not be available on Miriam's gift, because, although the original gift was of unquoted shares, presumably eligible for 100% BPR, the shares were converted into securities in a quoted company.

The worst case scenario would be IHT due of £6,400 (£20,000 transfer of value × 40% (death rates) × 80% (1 year of taper relief). If Miriam had some remaining nil rate band, then less or no IHT would be due.

	£
Proceeds for sale of loan stock	50,000
Less CGT due on sale (assuming claims made)	(1,830)
Less maximum IHT due on sale	(6,400)
Contribution from sale of loan stock to business start-up costs	41,770

Additional information required

The following are examples of the issues to be mentioned. Credit was given for other valid points made by candidates:

- Is the loan stock in Rebus plc a QCB? (sterling denominated, non-convertible, normal commercial loan, interest not excessive etc)

- Confirm no other gains in the same tax year, annual exempt amount has not already been used, no capital losses brought forward.

- Confirm the entrepreneurs' relief lifetime limit of £10 million of gains has not been exceeded.
- Has Miriam used her IHT nil rate band?

Appendix

Unincorporated or corporate business?

The tax implications of the choice between an unincorporated and a corporate business will affect how losses of the trade can be utilised and how and when profits will be taxed.

Trading losses

Initial trading losses can be used more flexibly in an unincorporated business. Tax losses incurred in the first four tax years of trade can be carried back against total income of the previous three tax years, setting the loss against the earliest tax year's taxable income first. In your case, depending upon the level of your tax loss, you could potentially carry the loss back to the tax year 2016/17 and claim a repayment of income tax from that earlier year.

Given your high level of remuneration from your job with Limpet Ltd, I presume you would have been a higher rate taxpayer in 2016/17 and would therefore be able to gain a repayment of income tax paid at the rate of 40%.

Until we can quantify the loss it is not possible to quantify the amount of tax repayment available.

Losses in a corporate business would not give rise to an immediate tax repayment. If the loss arose in a company, the company would need to use the loss against its own profits. If the company were loss making initially, the loss would be carried forward in the company until a profit were made in a later accounting period. This would create a time lag between making the loss and receiving the tax relief on the loss. Indeed, if the company were never to make a profit, the loss would never be used. The tax relief given for the loss would then be at corporation tax rates, which are lower than income tax rates you have been liable to in recent years.

Taxation of profits

A sole trader pays tax on all the profits of the business at his marginal rate of income tax, regardless of whether or not they are drawn out of the business. In addition, a sole trader pays class 4 national insurance contributions. Because all profits have been taxed, there is no additional tax due on drawing profits out of the business.

The company will pay 19% corporation tax on its profits, and funds withdrawn from the company could be subject to further taxation. An owner-managed company can choose how profits are paid out to its owners and seek to minimise the tax cost of withdrawing profits by choosing the most tax-efficient method of profit extraction.

Profits could be withdrawn as salary, dividend or pension contributions.

Profits withdrawn as salary will be subject to both income tax (20%/40%/45%) and class 1 national insurance contributions (both employees' and employers'). The amount of the gross salary and employer's NICs will reduce the company's taxable total profits.

Profits withdrawn as dividends will not be deductible from taxable total profits, but will be subject to income tax at lower rates (0%/7.5%/32.5%/38.1%) and will not attract NICs (for employer or employee).

Profits withdrawn as pension contributions will not attract income tax or NICs (for employee or employer) and will be deductible from taxable total profits for the employer. However, pension contributions do not provide any immediate income, because they need to be invested in your pension scheme and only provide an income on retirement. Income tax may be payable on receipt of a pension.

Payment dates

Sole Trader: Income tax and class 4 NICs are payable by self-assessment. Payments on account of half of last year's liability are due on each of 31 January and 31 July in/after the tax year and a final balancing payment is due on 31 January following the end of the tax year. No payments on account will be due in the first year of trade.

Company: The company will probably pay corporation tax nine months and one day after the end of its accounting period.

Income tax and employees' class 1 NICs due on salary will be deducted from gross salary payments and paid over to HMRC under the PAYE scheme each pay period. Employers' NIC will be calculated on top of gross salary and paid over to HMRC by the employer, each pay period (after deduction of the £3,000 employment allowance provided there are other employees).

Tutorial note

The employment allowance is not available to companies whose only employee is the director.

Income tax on dividends is due on 31 January following the tax year.

Employed or self-employed: Trading as a sole trader

If your only client is your former employer we would need to apply the tests of employment v self-employment to confirm that you are self-employed and subject to income tax and class 4 NICs on your taxable profits rather than being deemed an employee, taxed under PAYE and subject to income tax and class 1 NICs on your salary.

Personal Service Company (IR35) Anti-Avoidance Legislation

If you trade as a company you may still have a problem if your only client is your former employer. If you could be classified as an employee of Limpet Ltd, but for the presence of your own intermediary company, then the rules set out in IR35 could apply.

IR35 explains that the profits of contracts from quasi employment situations are subject to income tax and national insurance contributions in the same way as these profits would have been taxed if you had been an employee.

There is little advantage to be gained in setting up your own intermediary company and remunerating yourself via dividends, because income tax and employees' and employers' class 1 NICs would be payable on income from relevant engagements. This would reduce the tax advantages gained by incorporating your business.

For the IR35 rules to apply, you would have to set up as a company. You would also need to be capable of being classed as employed by Limpet Ltd. Given your former employment with them this looks likely, but we would need to ascertain the facts and employ tests to verify that this would be the case.

Future investment by your cousin William

If you set up in business as a sole trader business and your cousin William wished to invest in your business he would have two options. Firstly he could lend the money to your business, and be paid interest on his investment, which would be taxed on him as savings income and deductible for your business as an expense. Alternatively, you and William could enter into a partnership and profits would then be split between you and a proportion of profits (as agreed between you in your partnership agreement) would be taxed on each of you.

If you incorporate your business, your cousin could lend money to the company, the company would then pay him interest on his loan. The company would deduct the interest payable in calculating taxable total profits, either as a trading expense or as a non-trading loan relationship expense, depending on the purpose of the loan.

Alternatively you could issue shares to your cousin in exchange for his investment in the company. The tax advantage of issuing shares to your cousin would be that, provided he satisfied the criteria for the EIS or the SEIS scheme (as you will set up an unquoted company this is likely, provided his level of investment is anticipated to be less than 30% of the share capital of the company), he could claim an income tax deduction for 30% or 50% of his investment in the company, within certain limits. Provided the shares continue to qualify for EIS/SEIS, they would also be exempt from CGT on any future sale by your cousin. There is also a form of reinvestment relief for gains reinvested in EIS/SEIS shares.

The most tax efficient form of investment will depend upon several factors including whether there is any intention for William to play an active part in the business, his proposed level of investment and his personal circumstances.

Examiner's comments

The majority of candidates found the first part of the question relatively straightforward and explained the treatment and differences between fully exempt, partially exempt and taxable termination payments well. The ability to apply their knowledge to the scenario was very impressive and it is apparent that candidates' performance overall in this area is improving. There was some confusion over the gain on the takeover, with a lot of candidates calculating this to be £50,000 (£100,000 – £50,000) which displayed a lack of understanding of the rules. Furthermore, the discussion on the implications of deferring the gain and the loss of entitlement to ER was quite weak and often only very brief answers were produced. However, this was the area where the strongest candidates were able to display their knowledge and understanding.

It was disappointing to note that only a small number of candidates recognised the IHT implications of the transfer of shares in Morse Ltd. The stronger candidates did recognise that IHT was relevant and where this was the case, some very good answers were produced. Candidates need to consider all taxes when dealing with what are in essence, multi tax questions.

Also, a significant number of candidates did not even address the need for additional information to determine tax liability on the termination and on the sale of the loan stock. The ability to think about what would be needed in practice to calculate tax and make a recommendation is a key skill of BP:T and candidates need to refine this skill for future sittings.

The second part of this question was generally well answered.

Candidates had adequate knowledge of the different loss reliefs available for different business vehicles.

However, it was disappointing that candidates were often unable to adequately explain the difference in tax treatment between profit extraction for a sole trader and for a company; BP:T requires answers which address and evaluate alternative taxation and business strategies and unfortunately, candidates seemed more capable of writing answers about a corporate structure, than an unincorporated one. This was quite disappointing as it is a fundamentally basic area of the syllabus.

A significant number of candidates recognised the relevance of IR35 and some excellent answers were produced to this part of the question. Again, candidates should be careful to ensure that they distinguish between the consequences for companies and for sole trader businesses. Only the better performing candidates recognised this distinction.

In terms of the investment in the business by William, candidates were comfortable with discussing EIS and SEIS on the basis that the business was run as a company, but failed to discuss how the treatment would differ if William merely became a partner or simply 'invested' in the unincorporated business.

2 Josh Reynolds (September 2014)

Scenario

The candidate in this question is required to review an income tax computation prepared by a client and revise the computation to correct any errors made and explain the corrections made to the client.

The candidate is required to assess whether the tax treatment given by the client is correct and to explain the corrections needed, where errors have been made, and make and explain the correct calculations.

Marking guide

	Technical	Skills	Marks
Correction of income tax computation for Josh Reynolds			
Director's fees and mileage	2	–	
EMI share options	1	½	
Trade profit	½	½	
Building society interest	1	–	
Personal allowance	1	1	
EIS relief	½	½	
Tax rates	–	1	
	6	3½	
Including notes of amendments required			
Director's fees	1	–	
Car mileage	½	½	
EMI exercise	1	2	
Self employment	½	2	
Building society	½	1½	
Discretionary trust	–	2	
Personal allowance	–	2	
Savings allowance	–	1	
EIS		1½	
	3½	12½	
Notes of client query re: sale of EIS shares			
Income tax	1	½	
Capital gains tax	1	1½	
	2	2	
Total marks	11½	18	29½
Maximum			25

Josh Reynolds – revised income tax computation 2018/19

	Non-savings income £	Savings income £	Total £
Employment income:			
Director's fees (W1)	21,200		21,200
Mileage deduction (W2)	(1,200)		(1,200)
EMI share options (W3)	2,500		2,500
Taxable trading profits (W4)	35,000		35,000
Income from discretionary trust (W5)	41,000		41,000
Building society interest (W6)		5,000	5,000
Net Income	98,500	5,000	103,500
Less personal allowance (W7)	(10,100)		(10,100)
Taxable Income	88,400	5,000	93,400

Tax	£
Non-savings income	
£34,500 × 20%	6,900
£53,900 × 40%	21,560
Savings income	
£500 × 0% (W8)	–
£4,500 × 40%	1,800
Less tax reducer	
EIS (W9)	(30,000)
IT liability	260
Less tax deducted at source	
PAYE (£240 + £5,000)	(5,240)
Income tax on discretionary trust income	
(£41,000 × 45%)	(18,450)
IT Repayable	(23,430)

Explanations of amendments to the Income Tax Computation

WORKINGS

(1) **Director's fees**

Director's fees are assessed as employment income on the receipts basis. The director's fees of £100 per month would amount to £1,200 (12 × £100) for the tax year. In addition, you would also be assessed on the £20,000 bonus, which, although received in the tax year 2019/20, would be treated as received in 2018/19, because the receipts basis for directors requires that director's remuneration is regarded as being received on the earliest of five dates. The earliest date here would be the date earnings are credited in the company's accounts (31 March 2019).

(2) **Mileage allowance payments**

The mileage allowance paid by Painters Ltd for business miles driven in your own car is not subject to income tax. As the payment made, of 25p per mile, is below the statutory rate for mileage allowance payments of 45p per mile, you can claim a deduction from your employment income for the shortfall in allowance of £1,200 (6,000 miles × 20p).

(3) **EMI share options**

You were granted options under an enterprise management incentive (EMI) share scheme in Painters Ltd on 1 August 2017. An EMI share scheme is a tax-advantaged share scheme. No income tax is payable on the difference between the market value of the shares acquired at exercise and the exercise price paid for the shares. If, however, the exercise price payable is less than the market value of the shares, at the date the options are granted, then there will be a charge to income tax, at exercise, on the difference between the exercise price per share and the market value of the share at the date of grant.

	£
Market value at date of grant (1 Aug 2017)	5.00
Exercise price per share (10 Aug 2018)	4.75
Difference per share	0.25
Employment income taxed (10,000 × 25p)	2,500

(4) Taxable trading profits

In opening years of a trade, a sole trader is not taxed on the current year basis of assessment.

The profits taxable in 2018/19 are calculated based on the following rules:

2018/19 is the second tax year of assessment.

The accounting period that ends in 2018/19 is the period ended 30 June 2018. This accounting period is less than 12 months long and so you are taxed on the profits of the first 12 months of trade.

Period 1 January 2018 to 31 December 2018	£
1 January 2018 to 30 June 2018	10,000
1 July 2018 to 31 December 2018 – (£50,000 × 6/12)	25,000
Total	35,000

(5) Discretionary trust

Income paid to a beneficiary of a discretionary trust is paid net of a 45% tax credit. Discretionary trust income is treated as non-savings income regardless of the sources of income of the trust.

The income should be grossed up to include the tax deducted at source then included in the tax computation. The tax deducted at source is deductible from your income tax liability.

(6) Interest

Interest on the ISA account is exempt from taxation and not included in the taxable income in the computation.

Interest on the joint account with Martha should have been split 50:50 between Martha and your income tax computations, regardless of whom had initially invested the capital in the account.

(7) Personal allowance

The personal allowance is reduced by £1 for every £2 of income over £100,000, so is £11,850 less £1,750 ie, £10,100.

(8) Savings allowance

As you are a higher rate taxpayer, you have a savings income nil rate band of £500 ie, the first £500 of savings income is taxed at 0%.

(9) EIS relief

Income tax relief for investment in EIS shares is given by reducing the tax due, and not the taxable income, by 30% of the investment made in shares in unquoted, UK companies carrying on a qualifying trade.

Prospective sale of Gallery Ltd Shares in January 2020

If you sell your shares in Gallery Ltd in January 2020, there will be two tax consequences:

(1) The income tax relief given as a tax reducer in the 2018/19 computation will be withdrawn, because you have disposed of the shares within three years of purchase. This will be achieved by bringing the relief back into charge as miscellaneous income in the tax year of disposal (2019/20).

(2) The disposal of EIS shares is exempt from capital gains tax, provided the shares are held for three years and provided the EIS relief is not withdrawn. Because the shares are sold within three years of purchase and the EIS income tax relief is withdrawn, the gain of £25,000 will be subject to CGT in the tax year of disposal (2019/20). This gain can be reduced by your annual exempt amount, if it has not been used against any other gains in the same tax year. The tax on the gain, net of annual exempt amount will be at the rate of 20%.

Examiner's comments

General comments on candidate performance

In previous examinations we have tested the correction of an incorrect corporation tax computation. This is the first occasion on which we have tested the correction of an incorrect income tax computation. Although the calculation of income tax is very definitely tested at the earlier exam, Tax Compliance, this question tested the ability of candidates to evaluate an incorrect computation and determine when and how that calculation should be corrected. This uses skills that are untested at the earlier exam. The mix of income tax issues tested were also higher skill areas of the income tax syllabus. Although, interestingly, the two most fundamental areas of income tax tested were the worst answered.

Specific comments on sections of the question

Several mistakes were made by candidates in adjusting the income tax computation. The most common errors were as follows:

- Omission of the bonus as candidates assumed it was not taxable. Candidates were also unable to explain the basis of assessment for employment income;

- Inclusion of £1,200 mileage as a taxable benefit or a miscalculation of the amount altogether – £1,500 being a common figure cited (being 25p × 6,000);

- Treating the £2,500 on the exercise of the EMI options as a loss instead of taxable income;

- Failing to gross up the income from the discretionary trust correctly and including it as savings income;

- Including the EIS tax reducer as a deduction from income instead of a reduction against tax liability; and

- Failing to abate the personal allowance as net income was in excess of £100,000.

Candidates were generally quite good at providing detailed explanations of the treatment of each item and calculation of the overall tax liability was very accurate.

Some candidates failed to include an assessment of the tax implications on the sale of the Gallery shares, which displayed an inability to read the question fully and deal with all requirements. Where candidates did address this point, answers were generally very good and correctly identified that there would be potential clawback of the relief and a chargeable gain made on the sale of the shares. Others merely wrote that EIS relief would be withdrawn, which whilst correct, was not enough to be fully awarded the marks on offer.

3 Owen and Michael (December 2014)

Scenario

The candidate is a tax adviser in a firm of ICAEW Chartered Accountants, reporting to a tax partner and is asked to complete a number of tasks relating to two existing clients, who are selling their partnership (unincorporated) business in exchange for shares in a company. The question also addresses the issues of contingent consideration, income tax losses on cessation of trade and the tax consequences of choosing between remuneration in salary or dividend form.

Marking guide

	Technical	Skills	Marks
3.1 Tax consequences of disposal of StudentEat partnership			
VAT	1	1	
Income Tax			
• Final period loss	1	1	
• Allocation of losses	2	–	
• Use of losses	–	4	
CGT			
• Contingent consideration	1	1	
• Gain allocation	1	1	
• Incorporation relief	1	1	
• Entrepreneurs' relief	1	1	
Michael			
• IR and future ER	–	4	
• Premises	–	1	
• Use of loss	–	2	
• Gain	1½	–	
• Future share sale	–	2	
Owen			
• Disapplying IR	1	2	
• Cash consideration	–	1	
• Use of trading loss	–	2	
3.2 Tax consequences of additional remuneration			
Dividend			
• No NIC/not deductible	1	1	
• Net cash for Michael	½	1	
• Net cash for Owen	½	2	
Salary			
• Cost to company (salary calculation)	1	1	
• Net cash for Michael	½	1	
• Net cash for Owen	½	2	
Recommendation	–	2	
Total marks	14½	34	48½
Maximum			40

3.1 Owen and Michael Jones – StudentEat

Briefing note for Matthew Gibbons, Tax Partner

Owen and Michael Jones have received an offer to purchase 100% of the StudentEat partnership. The purchase of the partnership will have the following tax consequences:

1 **VAT**

   The partnership is registered for VAT, on disposal of the partnership business to Orlando Ltd; StudentEat will need to be de-registered for VAT.

   The partnership does not own any property; however it does own some capital assets. VAT will be charged at the standard rate on the value of these assets, when they are transferred to Orlando Ltd. However, if the transfer can be classified as the transfer of a going concern (TOGC), the transaction will be classified as outside the scope of VAT.

   This transfer is likely to be classified as a TOGC, as we appear to satisfy the conditions for a TOGC (transferring all assets to the new owner, the assets being used in the same kind of business, the purchaser being registered for VAT and the trade continuing as a going concern).

2 **Income tax for the partners**

   When the partnership's trade is sold to Orlando Ltd on 31 March 2019, the trade will cease for income tax purposes. The final period of trade is the 12-month period to 31 March 2019. The losses of this period, as adjusted for the balancing adjustment on the sale of plant and machinery are as follows:

	£
Loss for 12 months to 31 March 2019 (per question)	(12,500)
Balancing charge on disposal of plant and machinery (45,000 – 50,000)	5,000
Tax adjusted trading loss	(7,500)

   It will not be possible to make a succession election to transfer the assets at TWDV to Orlando Ltd, because the StudentEat partnership and Orlando Ltd will not be connected persons.

   The trading losses of the partnership will be split equally between the partners, according to their profit sharing agreement, and each partner will be able to decide their own use of their own entitlement to trading losses.

   The losses made to date are allocated as follows between the two partners:

Accounting period	Tax year	Total adjusted loss	50% allocated to Owen Jones	50% allocated to Michael Jones
		£	£	£
6 months ended 31 March 2017	2016/17	20,000	10,000	10,000
Year ended 31 March 2018	2017/18	10,000	5,000	5,000
Year ending 31 March 2019	2018/19	7,500	3,750	3,750

   Owen Jones has had no income to enable him to use the trading losses of £18,750 accumulated up to the point of cessation of trade. These losses cannot be carried forward against future profits of the same trade, as the trade has ceased.

Owen Jones will be able to carry forward his share of the accumulated losses of the partnership, at cessation of trade, against income from the company, under s.86. The carry forward of the losses relies on the consideration for the business being solely or mainly shares (this is taken to mean that the consideration is at least 80% shares) and that the shares are held by Owen throughout any tax year in which loss relief is given under s.86. As he is intending to leave employment and sell his shares during 2019/20 this may not be viable.

Michael Jones has used his share of losses against his current income under s.64 loss relief and will continue to do so for the loss for the final 12 months of trading.

Tutorial note

Credit would also have been given for the extension of loss relief against capital gains on disposal of the business, but only in the correct context and for Owen, not Michael.

3   **Capital gains tax**

The disposal of the partnership to Orlando Ltd, will give rise to a capital gain for each partner.

Because the consideration for the disposal is not all received at the point of disposal, and some of the consideration is contingent on uncertain future events, the disposal proceeds are valued as the amount of the proceeds actually received and the estimated present value of the future consideration.

As the goodwill of the business has no cost, the gain for the business disposal is equal to the proceeds and this gain is split 50:50 between the partners.

Michael will also make a gain on the disposal of the office premises, which he owns personally.

	Owen £	Michael £
Gain on partnership goodwill (split 50:50)	500,000	500,000
Gain on sale of premises	–	50,000
Less annual exempt amount	(11,700)	Already used
Taxable gains	488,300	550,000

The rate of tax payable on the disposal depends on the reliefs claimed on the disposal and on the rate of tax payable by the taxpayer in the 2018/19 tax year.

The reliefs available are incorporation relief and entrepreneurs' relief.

Each partner can make their own decision about whether to claim incorporation relief or entrepreneurs' relief.

As all of the assets of the business are transferred to Orlando Ltd, incorporation relief would be available to defer the proportion of the gain relating to share consideration. The gain is deducted from the cost of the Orlando Ltd shares received. Incorporation relief does not require a claim and is automatically applied, if the conditions are satisfied. Incorporation relief could also be disapplied by either of the brothers if they considered that a claim for entrepreneurs' relief would be more beneficial.

Orlando Ltd has stated that it is willing to provide an amount of cash consideration, if this would help the brothers to manage their tax affairs. Generally cash consideration is taken, if incorporation relief is applied, to provide a gain equal to any annual exempt amount or capital losses, because this will then be a tax free amount of proceeds.

In the case of each of the brothers, the amount of cash consideration they would take from the disposal could be calculated as:

$$\frac{\text{Value of cash received}}{\text{Value of total consideration received}} \times \text{Net gains} = \text{tax free gains}$$

Entrepreneurs' relief for gains on disposal of internally generated goodwill can be denied in certain circumstances. However, as Orlando Ltd is not a close company and the brothers are shareholders of Orlando Ltd, entrepreneurs' relief can apply and the gain will be taxed at 10%.

Michael

As Michael intends to keep his shares for at least one year before disposing of them, will own at least 5% of Orlando Ltd at the time of disposal and also work for the company, he should be able to claim entrepreneurs' relief on any future disposal of the shares. As a result, he could accept that incorporation relief would apply to the sale of the partnership to Orlando Ltd and defer the gain against the base cost of the Orlando shares. This would have the cash flow advantage of not crystallising a taxable gain in 2018/19 and only crystallising a gain in the future, when entrepreneurs' relief would be available to reduce the tax on the gain to 10%.

However, Michael should be aware that this would be the case on the basis of current tax legislation, and this legislation could change in the future.

Michael also has a small gain on the disposal of the premises used for the business of StudentEat, which he owns personally. This gain is not eligible for incorporation relief but, provided the disposal of the partnership share qualifies for entrepreneurs' relief, as an associated disposal, it is eligible for entrepreneurs' relief.

Michael would use the £25,000 of capital losses brought forward against these gains, in preference to using these losses to generate an amount of proceeds he could receive in cash from Orlando Ltd, on the share sale. This is because, from a cash flow perspective, it would reduce his tax bill on the sale of the premises by £2,500 (£25,000 × 10%).

Michael's capital gains tax liability for 2018/19 would be:

	£
Gain on disposal of partnership share	500,000
Less incorporation relief (100% share consideration)	(500,000)
Gain on sale of premises	50,000
Less capital losses brought forward	(25,000)
Taxable gains	25,000
Capital gains tax liability at 10%	2,500

Tutorial note

The examiners have stated that the £50,000 of cash consideration for the plant and machinery resulted in no gain. However, if received as part of the consideration for the incorporation of the partnership, this could have restricted the incorporation relief given on the disposal. Most candidates ignored this, but credit was given to candidates who considered this issue.

On disposal of the Orlando Ltd shares in the future, the base cost of the shares of £500,000 would be reduced by the gain on the disposal of his 50% of the StudentEat partnership of £500,000 and so would be £nil. However, under current legislation he would qualify to claim entrepreneurs' relief on any gain on the sale of the shares and would pay tax at 10%, after deduction of any capital losses and the annual exempt amount, on any gain made on disposal of the shares.

Owen

As Owen intends to leave the employment of Orlando Ltd in nine months' time, sell his shares and go travelling the world, he needs to consider the CGT reliefs he receives on the disposal of the partnership in conjunction with the effect of the taxation of the gains on the sale of the shares in Orlando in nine months' time.

If he were to apply incorporation relief to the disposal of his share of the StudentEat partnership, the gain on the disposal of the partnership of £500,000 would be deferred against the base cost of the Orlando Ltd shares. This would bring the base cost of these shares down to nil and ensure that any gain would be deferred until the disposal of the shares. In nine months' time, when Owen intends to sell the shares, he will not qualify for entrepreneurs' relief on the disposal, because he will not have owned the shares for at least a year, and so the full gain will be in charge to tax at 10% or 20%.

It would therefore be preferable for Owen to disapply incorporation relief on the sale of the partnership and claim entrepreneurs' relief instead, as Orlando Ltd is not a close company. He has until 31 January 2022 to make the claim to disapply incorporation relief, so, if his circumstances change in this time, he could reconsider the claim.

The tax payable on the disposal would be £48,830 (£488,300 × 10%), which is a considerable saving on charging the gain at 10/20% in nine months' time.

Owen will therefore be happy to receive any mix of cash or share consideration from Orlando Ltd on the sale of his share of the StudentEat partnership, given he is not intending to apply incorporation relief to the disposal, but would probably like to receive sufficient cash to cover the amount of CGT payable on the disposal.

As Owen intends to sell his Orlando Ltd shares before the end of the 2019/20 tax year he will be unable to use his brought forward trading losses against the income (salary or dividends) he receives from the company. However, he should be able to use s.261B TCGA 1992 to convert the 2018/19 losses to capital losses and relieve them against the gain on disposal of the business.

3.2 Remuneration strategy: Orlando Ltd

The remuneration from Orlando Ltd can be taken as either a dividend or as a salary.

Michael and Owen will have to decide which option they prefer together. As they both have 'A' ordinary shares, they will need to have the same amount of dividend declared on their shares. Therefore, the decision may advantage one brother and disadvantage the other from a tax perspective.

Dividend receipts are subject to income tax, in the hands of the shareholders, but not to national insurance contributions.

Dividend payments are not tax deductible for the company.

Orlando Ltd wants the cost of dividends to be £50,000 to the company. The £50,000 will therefore represent the dividend payable to each of the brothers.

Given the brothers have different tax situations, the implications of a £50,000 dividend receipt to each of them would be:

	Michael £	Owen £
Dividend	50,000	50,000
Tax cost 32.5% × £(50,000 – 2,000)	15,600	
£2,000 × 0%		–
£32,500 × 7.5%		2,438
£15,500 × 32.5%		5,038
		7,476
Net cash received	34,400	42,524

If the company were to pay additional salary, with a cost to the company of £50,000 per brother, the amount of gross salary paid to each brother would be:

	£
Gross salary (100%)	54,243
Employers' NIC (13.8%)	7,485
Total salary cost to company (113.8%) (£50,000 + CT saving)	61,728
CT saving at 19% (ie, £50,000 × 19%/81%)	(11,728)
Net cost to company	50,000

The gross salary would generate differing amounts of income tax and NIC for each brother, as follows:

	Michael £	Owen £
Gross salary	54,243	54,243
Less income tax at 40%	(21,697)	
Less income tax ((£34,500 × 20%) + (£19,743 × 40%))		(14,797)
Less employees' NICs		
(£46,350 – £11,850) = £34,500 × 12%	(4,140)	(4,140)
(£54,243 – £34,500) × 2%	(395)	(395)
Net salary	28,011	34,911

Both brothers, despite differing tax rates, would receive more cash after taxation if in receipt of a dividend. We should therefore recommend that the additional remuneration for 2019/20 is paid in the form of a dividend, rather than in the form of a salary.

Tutorial note

The answer assumes that both Michael and Owen had a full annual basic salary of £11,850. However, Owen's employment is likely to end on 31 December 2019. The examiners have confirmed that in the real exam there was flexibility in the marking and they accepted answers that used either the full basic salary (with an appropriate comment) or a time apportioned amount.

Examiner's comments

The first part of the scenario related to the taxation consequences of the sale of an unincorporated business and required the interaction of a number of taxes. Most candidates realised the need to consider VAT, income tax and capital gains tax.

This examination differentiates itself from the earlier Tax Compliance examination in a number of ways, but one area of difference is the requirement for students to consider how a range of taxation issues might interact to affect a business decision or transaction. In this scenario, students considered how their knowledge of taxation could apply to and help them make decision about the consequences of a business transaction for two similar individuals. The level of complexity of this question was comparable to questions set at previous BP:T exam sessions, and the issues tested were popular with candidates. Apart from a few, common, technical misconceptions, the majority of answers demonstrated a broad understanding of the issues to be addressed, with some candidates scoring the full 40 marks available for the question.

In part, this was because the question, whilst appearing complex, was well bounded by the particular circumstances set out in the question and by very clear question requirements. Most candidates found that as they worked through the information in the question, that a number of areas that might at first have seemed relevant and distracting, were in fact irrelevant, due to the facts in the scenario. Only the very poor candidates, whose technical knowledge was more tentative, were distracted by irrelevant issues, simply because their knowledge of the tax rules was so poor that they were unable to identify when issues were irrelevant.

The consequences of cessation of trade for the partnership were dealt with very well, along with the capital gains tax consequences of the disposal of the partnership. Poorer candidates became confused about the status of a partnership, with some, in error, treating a partnership as a company (including treating the sale of the goodwill incorrectly as the sale of 'new' goodwill, with no capital consequences!). It was pleasing to see that the majority of candidates noted that the proceeds for the sale of the partnership were contingent and understood the tax consequences and that many, excellent answers considered the carry forward of trading income tax losses against income of the company in the partners' hands.

The confusion between partnership and company led a significant number of candidates to consider the sale of a partnership to a company to be a 'share-for-share' exchange for CGT purposes, in error and to ignore incorporation relief. However, many candidates recognised the associated disposal for entrepreneurs' relief and also the merit of dis-applying incorporation relief, in favour of entrepreneurs' relief, where the subsequent sale of shares was within 12 months – both of which were complex areas of understanding.

The second part of the question asked candidates to evaluate the differences for tax purposes between receiving remuneration as a salary or as a dividend, from the recipient's perspective.

Most candidates made a good attempt at evaluating the differences for tax purposes between the two forms of remuneration and at differentiating between the circumstances of the two individuals.

It was disappointing that a sizeable number of candidates seemed to be unaware that National Insurance Contributions were payable on a salary, but not on a dividend. This is a fairly fundamental issue to be considered when differentiating between the tax consequences of salary and dividend remuneration.

Despite these issues the majority of candidates scored well on this part of the question, with a lot of answers scoring full marks.

4 Phillip Hassan (March 2015)

Scenario

In this question the candidate is a tax adviser in a firm of ICAEW Chartered Accountants providing advice to a client. The client has traded as a sole trader for many years and is transferring the trade and assets of the business to his son. The client is then going to undertake a consultancy contract via a limited company.

Marking guide

		Marks	
		Technical	**Skills**
4.1	**Trading loss**		
	• s.64 relief	1½	½
	• s.83 relief	½	½
	• s.89 calculation of loss	1	1
	• s.89 use of loss	1	1
	• s.89 narrative	–	1
	• s.261B relief	½	1
	• ER	½	1
		5	6

Transfer of trade and assets

• CGT calculation – no reliefs	1	2
• Gift relief	1	2½
• Entrepreneurs' relief	1	3
• IHT	1	2½
• Capital allowances	1	1
	5	11

4.3 **VAT and stamp duty**

• Initial recovery	1	–
• Position for 100% business use periods	½	½
• Position for 80% business use periods	½	1½
• TOGC	1	1
• SDLT	½	1
	3½	4

4.4 **Factors re scope of personal service company legislation**

• HMRC considerations	1½	1½
• IR 35 implications	1	2
• Employment income treatment	1	1
	3½	4½

Calculation of deemed employment income

• 5% deduction and salary costs	½	1
• Employer's NIC	1	1
• Income tax	½	½
• Employee's NIC	½	½
• Dividend alternative	½	1
	3	4

Total marks	20	29½	
Maximum			49½
			35

4.1 **Trading loss**

Phillip can make a claim under s.64 ITA 2007 to set off the loss against his general trading income of the same year and/or the previous tax year in any order. If a claim under s.64 is not made then the losses are automatically carried forward under s.83 and can be set against future profits of the same trade.

A s.64 claim must be made within 12 months from 31 January following the end of the tax year in which the loss arose. Therefore, a claim must be made by 31 January 2021.

However, the use of the loss in this manner is not advisable as Phillip's other income in 2018/19 will be covered by his personal allowance.

Carry forward under s.83 is not possible as Phillip is ceasing to trade.

On cessation of trade, a claim can be made under s.64 to set off the loss against general income of the same tax year or, a claim under s.89 can be made for the loss made on the cessation of trade to be carried back and relieved in earlier years.

The loss available for relief is the loss of the last 12 months of trading. Therefore in Phillip's case this is:

	£
Loss in final tax year 2018/19	
6 April 2018 – 30 September 2018	
6/9 × £54,000 loss	(36,000)
Plus overlap	(1,200)
	(37,200)
Loss relief in penultimate tax year – 12 months of cessation	
1 October 2017 – 5 April 2018	
3/12 × £12,500 profit	3,125
3/9 × £54,000 loss	(18,000)
	(14,875)
Loss available (£37,200 + £14,875)	(52,075)

This loss can be used as follows:

	2015/16 £	2016/17 £	2017/18 £	2018/19 £
Trading income	18,000	26,000	12,500	Nil
s.89 relief	(13,575)	(26,000)	(12,500)	
Interest (gross)	2,200	2,200	2,200	2,200
Net income	6,625	2,200	2,200	2,200
PA – restricted	(6,625)	(2,200)	(2,200)	(2,200)
Taxable income	Nil	Nil	Nil	Nil

If a s.89 claim was made, Phillip would receive a repayment from HMRC. A claim must be made within four years of the end of the tax year that the business operates, so by 5 April 2023.

The loss of the final period of trade which does not form part of the terminal loss (£3,125) is available for Phillip to use in the current year via s.64 relief to set off against other income and gains.

Phillip could also consider converting the trading loss into a capital loss to set off against his 2018/19 capital gains under s.261B TCGA 1992. In order to do this Phillip would first need to make a s.64 claim in 2018/19 against his other income of £2,200 which would leave losses of £53,000 (54,000 + £1,200 – £2,200) which could be allocated against his 2018/19 capital gains. As entrepreneurs' relief is likely to be available on any taxable gains (see below) this would save tax at 10% which is lower than the rate of income tax saved above.

Tutorial note

The examiner did not require a calculation of the comparative tax savings.

4.2 Capital gains

Phillip and Nicholas are connected parties for CGT purposes, therefore, the transfer of assets is deemed to be at market value. Therefore, there will be a capital gain for Phillip of £175,000 as the plant and machinery is exempt under the small chattels exemption having been bought and sold for less than £6,000.

As Phillip has no taxable income in 2018/19 then tax would be due at 10%/20% after using his annual exempt amount of £11,700 as follows:

	£
Gains	175,000
Less annual exempt amount	(11,700)
Taxable	163,300
£34,500 × 10%	3,450
£128,800 × 20%	25,760
	29,210

To mitigate this CGT liability Phillip and Nicholas could consider two alternative CGT reliefs.

Holdover relief for gifts

Phillip and Nicholas could jointly elect for gift relief. If this is done, any gain eligible for hold-over will not be taxed, but instead would be deducted from the cost of the asset for Nicholas.

As Nicholas has paid full market value for the property, the gain of £100,000 will not be eligible for gift relief. However, the gain of £75,000 on the goodwill will be eligible for gift relief.

The base cost of Nicholas's assets would be reduced by the gains held over ie, £75,000. He would therefore have more tax to pay when the assets were sold in the future, but Phillip would have less CGT to pay now. So only a tax saving of £15,000 (£75,000 at 20%) ie, capital gains tax on £88,300 (£100,000 − £11,700) of which £34,500 is taxed at 10%.

Entrepreneurs' relief

Alternatively, Phillip could claim entrepreneurs' relief instead. The conditions for entrepreneurs' relief relate to gains made on the disposal of assets of an individual's business following cessation of the business and have been owned for a period of at least one year ending with the date of the disposal. These conditions appear to have been met.

Under these circumstances, presuming that Phillip has not used his £10 million lifetime allowance already, the gains on the sale of the business would be taxable, but at only 10%.

The optimum position is for gift relief to be claimed on the disposal of goodwill and entrepreneurs' relief to be claimed on the disposal of the business as a whole (after taking account of gift relief). This would give CGT payable of £8,830 after the annual exempt amount.

Entrepreneurs' relief must be claimed. The time limit is 12 months from 31 January following the tax year in which the qualifying disposal is made, so by 31 January 2021.

Inheritance tax (IHT)

IHT may also be due. At the time of the transfer of value, part of the gift would be a PET. Nicholas has paid £600,000 in respect of the transfer so the value of the PET is £100,000 representing the diminution in value.

If Phillip was to die within seven years of the transfer, the value transferred would potentially be in charge to IHT. However, as the assets transferred are the assets of an unincorporated business, which have been owned for more than two years, then 100% business property relief (BPR) should be available.

BPR will exempt 100% of the gift from IHT. However, although 100% BPR is available on a lifetime gift, it is only allocated to a lifetime gift, when calculating tax due on that gift at death, if the asset is still owned by the recipient of the gift on the donor's death.

There will be no balancing allowances or charges if Phillip and Nicholas make a joint election for the transfer of plant and machinery to be transferred at their tax written down value as they are connected persons. A succession election must be made within two years of the date from which the succession takes effect. If a succession election is not made then this could potentially alter the amount of the loss as balancing charges could arise therefore reducing the amount of the loss available for relief.

4.3 VAT

At the time that Phillip acquired the premises it was a new commercial property and Phillip would have suffered input VAT of £100,000 (20% standard rate). As the premises were used wholly for taxable purposes it was fully recoverable. It is, however, subject to the capital good scheme. No adjustment was required for the intervals to March 2013, March 2014, March 2015 and March 2016 but there was a change in use in the interval to March 2017 with no option to tax being made. Therefore, a capital goods scheme adjustment of:

£100,000/10 × (80% - 100%) = (£2,000). This will have to be repaid to HMRC and this will be the same in the interval to 31 March 2018. As the building is sold with a tenant in situ and the other part of the building will continue to be used in the trade, then it is likely to constitute TOGC. As TOGC is outside the scope of VAT then no adjustment on sale is required. However, Nicholas will assume responsibility for the remainder of the adjustment period.

The SDLT would be on the chargeable consideration received. As there is no option to tax, SDLT will be charged on the VAT inclusive amount of sale proceeds of £600,000, ie, £19,500 (£150,000 × 0% + £100,000 × 2% + £350,000 × 5%).

4.4 Consultancy agreement

It appears that but for the presence of PH Ltd, Phillip would be treated as an employee of Logan Ltd. In deciding whether Phillip is actually an employee of Logan Ltd, HMRC would consider:

- control – Phillip is obviously highly skilled but is required to attend Logan Ltd's premises to undertake his duties.

- mutuality of obligations – the contract is for two years and there are specific contract hours suggesting that an employment relationship exists.

- in business on your own account – it does not appear that Phillip has any other clients and there are terms within the contract which preclude Phillip from working for anyone else.

- intention of the parties – the intention in the contract appears to be not to establish an employment relationship.

- status – Phillip is not entitled to sick pay or holiday pay which an employee would normally receive.

- risk – he will be paid a fixed fee and submit monthly invoices. It seems that there is no real financial risk involved pointing to an employee/employer relationship.

The relationship may to fall under IR35 – personal service company anti-avoidance provisions. As PH Ltd are invoicing Logan Ltd, they are avoiding national insurance as Phillip is not an employee. But it is likely this would be deemed to be a 'relevant engagement' under the IR35 legislation.

Any employment income paid to Phillip via PH Ltd should be paid in the normal way via PAYE. Where the amount paid as employment income is less than the amount received from the relevant engagement (as is the case here) then the excess will be treated as deemed employment income.

This will be subject to income tax and NIC. The payment will be deductible for corporation tax purposes in the accounting year in which it is deemed paid. Therefore in Phillip's case the deemed employment income and income tax and NIC will be as follows:

	£	£
Employment income		
Total earned (£5,000 × 12)		60,000
Less 5% deduction		(3,000)
		57,000
Less salary	30,000	
Employer's NIC	2,977	
		(32,977)
		24,023
Employer's NIC (£24,023 × 13.8/113.8)		(2,913)
Deemed employment income		21,110
Income tax		
£16,350 × 20% (34,500 – (30,000 – 11,850))		3,270
£4,760 × 40%		1,904
£21,110		
Income tax on deemed employment		5,174
NIC		
£16,350 × 12% (46,350 – 30,000)		1,962
£4,760 × 2%		95
		2,057

Therefore, the extraction of profits via dividends is not a viable plan as it will not be 'tax free'. The amount drawn will be ignored and the whole of the contract amount – £60,000 will be taken into consideration and treated as earnings from the relevant engagement.

Examiner's comments

The question required candidates to compute terminal losses which was very straightforward and then to give advice on the tax implications of the transfer of business, considering any reliefs or elections to minimise tax liability. This posed quite a few problems and candidate's answers were quite brief and often failed to discuss both CGT and IHT. Candidates also did not do particularly well in relation to part 4 and failed to acknowledge that there was no advantage in taking dividends as the IR35 legislation would mean the whole amount received from the relevant engagement would be taxed in any event.

Part 1 Candidates performed very well in this part of the question with a high number of candidates correctly computing the terminal loss available and producing very detailed answers on how the loss of the final period of trade could be used.

Part 2 was less well answered. Whilst candidates did allude to the fact that entrepreneurs' relief could be claimed to reduce the amount of tax on the gain and that gift relief may be applicable, they failed to appreciate the interaction of both. The scenario outlined that full market value had been paid by the son for the building and so gift relief was not available on this, only on the goodwill of the business. Therefore, the optimum position was for entrepreneurs' relief to be claimed on the building with gift relief being claimed on the goodwill. Candidates needed also to consider what the effect of that would be in relation to reducing the base cost of the goodwill for the son and hence generating a larger gain in the future, which they didn't always do. In addition, it was disappointing that even though the requirements asked for the capital tax consequences to be considered, candidates often failed to deal with IHT aspects and merely concentrated on CGT.

Part 3 was very well answered with a significant number of candidates scoring full marks. This was extremely encouraging as the majority of the knowledge required was brought forward from Tax Compliance. This indicates that the tutorial providers and the candidates are now becoming more aware of the fact that although BP:T is different from TC in the nature of skills that it tests, knowledge gained at TC is very important in setting the foundations and is often required at BP:T to make efficient recommendations. This part of the question also tested the transfer of going concern rules for VAT and again, candidates coped with the question well.

Part 4 produced a mixed standard of answers from candidates. Some coped very well and were able to discuss the relevant employment tests and then apply them to the scenario, which is what the question required. Others merely listed the tests without really appreciating why they were relevant and how they would apply to the scenario. The computation of the deemed employment payment didn't pose any problems and the fact that candidates were clearly directed in the requirements to compute the payment helped them a lot. It was disappointing however to see that where application is required, in this instance in relation to the discussion of whether dividends would be more advantageous, candidates did not cope well. Answers simply regurgitated the learning materials in terms of how a dividend would be taxed and the savings available for the client, without thinking about the scenario presented. In this instance, there was no advantage in taking dividends at all as under the personal service companies legislation, the entire amount earned from a relevant engagement is taxed as salary anyway. Only a small number of candidates picked this up and this section was actually a good discriminator between good candidates and those who were excellent.

5 George Assenga (March 2015)

Scenario

The candidate has been asked by their manager to prepare notes in preparation for a meeting with a personal tax client. The tax client has requested advice on the following matters:

- Remuneration from his employer by way of a cash bonus or contributions into a pension scheme which would eventually be in excess of the annual allowance;

- The treatment of mixed consideration which has been issued after a takeover where the client previously held only shares and whether to opt for cash or a QCB;

- Potential investment in two alternative businesses, where EIS and SEIS need to be considered;

- The transfer of the clients home to his son, which constitutes a GWROB and whether the proposed course of action will mitigate the overall IHT liability.

	Technical	Skills
		Marks
Remuneration		
• Bonus	1	1½
• Pension – current pay	1	1
• Maximum contributions	1	1
• Increased pay	1	2
• Lifetime allowance	–	1
• OPS v PPC	1	½
• Retirement	–	1
	5	8
Investment in Winstanley plc		
• Share for share	½	½
• Allocation of consideration	1	2
• Cash impact	1	2
• Loan stock	1	2½
	3½	7

	Technical	Skills	Marks
Investment opportunities			
Bemmers			
• EIS company conditions	–	1	
• George relief/conditions	1	1	
• Disposal of shares	–	2	
Markland			
• EIS company conditions	–	1½	
• George relief/conditions	1	1½	
• Disposal of shares	–	1	
	2	8	
Gift with reservation	1	2	
Total marks	11½	25	36½
Maximum			25

Remuneration

If George takes a bonus then this will be subject to tax and NIC. The bonus of £12,000 will be taxed at the rate of 40% (assuming he remains a higher rate taxpayer) and NIC will be payable at the rate of 2%.

If George chooses to join the pension scheme then the company will make contributions of £12,000 but George will also make contributions of £7,200.

In terms of the choice of remuneration package for George, pension contributions made by the company are not a taxable benefit for George and any contributions made by George will attract tax relief at source. A bonus will be immediately taxable but George will receive cash, rather than having to wait for the benefits from the pension scheme, which he would only be entitled to in the future.

However, there are several tax advantages to being part of the pension scheme and if George is planning for retirement then this may be the preferred option.

George can contribute up to 100% of his earnings into a pension scheme and obtain tax relief on those contributions. However, the total amount which can be contributed to the pension scheme and qualify for tax relief is subject to an annual allowance of £40,000 for 2018/19. Any contributions over this amount could be subject to a tax charge. This amount of £40,000 can be increased if there is unused annual allowance from the previous three tax years but in order to use this, George must have been a member of a registered scheme previously. There is no information available to confirm this so it is likely that the gross amount which can be contributed during this tax year would be limited to £40,000. In the first few years before the pay rise, the total amount of contributions will be £19,200 so George can pay up to £20,800 gross (£40,000 – £19,200) into a private pension scheme each year with no tax charge.

When his salary increases to £400,000 then the total contributions into the pension scheme from George and his employer will increase to £128,000 (£48,000 + £80,000). As George's income will be so high, his annual allowance will be restricted to £10,000 (as adjusted income exceeds £150,000 and threshold income exceeds £110,000). This will then trigger an annual allowance charge whereby the amount of pension savings which exceed the revised annual allowance is added to other taxable income for the year and taxed under the income tax rules. Therefore the excess of £54,000, at current rates, will be taxed at 45%. However, in the year of increase in pay there will be some unused annual allowance for each of the three years until that date, as only £19,200 out of the £40,000 annual allowance has been used, if George makes no additional contributions to a personal pension scheme.

As George is planning for retirement and his salary is increasing significantly over the next few years, he must also be made aware of the lifetime allowance. This is the maximum value of the pension fund which is allowed to build up over the lifetime of the scheme. This is currently £1.03 million. If the fund exceeds this, there is a tax charge of 55% on funds vested to provide a lump sum and 25% on funds vested to provide pension income.

Normally tax relief for occupational pensions is given under net pay arrangements where the contributions made are deducted from salary before income tax is applied, and so George will receive tax relief of 40% at source on his contributions of £7,200 in 2018/19. If a private pension scheme is taken in addition to the occupational pension then relief for any contributions will be given by extension of the basic rate band. Contributions will be treated as having been paid net of 20% tax. George will save tax at the rate of 40% (20% at source and the balance via his income tax computation).

At retirement, George may take up to 25% of the fund value as a lump sum. Only 25% of the lifetime allowance will be tax free. Any excess will be taxed at the rate of 55%. The balance of the fund could be used to buy an annuity or to make annual draw downs from the pension scheme.

Investment in Winstanley plc

Normally, where there is reorganisation of a company's share capital, the new shares are treated as having been acquired for the same cost and at the same date as the original shares. There is no chargeable disposal on a paper for paper takeover.

However, the takeover of Winstanley plc by Pepper plc is in exchange for mixed consideration – shares and cash/loan stock. Therefore, there will be a part disposal for capital gains tax purposes.

The cost of the original shares is apportioned so the cost of George's original shareholding will be allocated as follows:

	Consideration £	Cost allocated £
1,500 25p ordinary shares	4,800	576
1,500 50p preference shares	2,700	324
Cash/Loan stock	7,500	900
	15,000	1,800

The receipt of cash would give rise to a gain of £6,600 (£7,500 – £900). As George is a higher rate taxpayer then this would be taxed at 20%, giving rise to a liability of £1,320 as his annual exempt amount has already been used. On eventual sale of the shares, the original cost of £576 for the ordinary shares and £324 on the preference shares will be used to compute the gain.

If George opted to receive loan stock, which will probably be a qualifying corporate bond (QCB), this would still give rise to a gain of £6,600 but this would not be immediately chargeable on takeover, but would be held over until the loan stock were sold. Clarification should be sought to ensure the loan stock is a QCB.

The disposal of a QCB itself in the future would be exempt, but the gain held over against the loan stock on the takeover would crystallise on the sale of the loan stock and become chargeable, so George should opt for the QCB.

As George's shareholding in Winstanley plc does not qualify for entrepreneurs' relief, he should not opt to disapply the paper for paper takeover rules.

Investment opportunities

For George to obtain tax relief relating to either of the investments there must be a 'risk to capital' ie, Bemmers Ltd and/or Markland Ltd must have a long term objective to grow and develop the trade, but there must be a risk that there could be a loss of capital.

Bemmers Ltd

George's investment in the shares should qualify under the Enterprise Investment Scheme (EIS) as Bemmers Ltd is a UK unquoted company, with gross assets which do not exceed £15 million before the investment is made or £16 million immediately afterwards. Confirmation should be sought that Bemmers Ltd meets the conditions ie, it has a qualifying trade, has not raised £5 million under EIS in the last 12 months, has a permanent establishment in the UK and does not control other companies (except for qualifying subsidiaries).

Under the EIS rules as George has less than a 30% interest in the company he can reduce his income tax liability by an amount equal to 30% of the amount invested. The maximum amount of investment on which George can obtain relief is £1 million pa (£2 million if Bemmers Ltd is a knowledge-intensive company (KIC)). Therefore, George could obtain relief of £22,500 (£75,000 × 30%) in 2018/19 if he invests in the shares in this tax year. An individual does not need to be UK resident to claim the relief so even if George intends to move back to Erehwon earlier than originally anticipated, the relief still applies.

As George is subscribing for qualifying shares he may claim to carry back the amount subscribed to the previous tax year, therefore accelerating the timing of the relief.

However, the income tax relief may be withdrawn if George disposes of the shares within three years, so he should be advised to retain the shares beyond three years. The relief would be brought back into charge in the year disposal of the shares was made. The dividends from these shares will then be taxable in the normal way.

When George eventually sells the shares, any gains arising on disposal will be exempt, providing the relief has not been withdrawn.

Markland Ltd

This investment appears to qualify under the seed enterprise investment scheme (SEIS) as:

- the company's trade is new (it has been carried on for less than 2 years) – assuming that it is a qualifying trade;

- the gross asset value before the share issue does not exceed £200,000;

- it has fewer than 25 full-time employees.

Confirmation should be sought that the company has previously raised money under EIS or VCT, or more than £150,000 under SEIS. The maximum investment under SEIS is £100,000 and George would be entitled to a tax reducer/reduction of 50% of the amount invested which would be £37,500 or the amount which reduces his income tax liability to nil.

However, no relief can be claimed until the company has spent at least 70% of the funds invested in that year. In this case, relief could not be claimed by George in 2018/19 as the company are only proposing to spend £16,500 of the £75,000 invested.

George could claim SEIS in 2019/20 and could then claim to carry back the relief in the normal way to 2018/19.

The capital gains treatment is the same for EIS. Any gains would be exempt providing the relief has not been withdrawn. This does not apply if the shares are disposed of within three years of acquisition.

Under both options, if George acquires more than a 30% shareholding in either company then he will become connected with the company and the reliefs would be withdrawn. In terms of the amount of relief, the SEIS appears to be the better option.

Gift of house

The gift of the house constitutes a gift with reservation of benefit (GWROB) as the house is being transferred and the possession and enjoyment of the asset is not bona fide assumed by George's son and it is not enjoyed to the entire exclusion of George. Even if George moves back to Erehwon, his proposed use does not meet the definition of 'virtually to the entire exclusion of the transferor' as he will be staying in the property for three months every year.

However, if George pays full market rent for the occupation of the property then a GWROB will be avoided. Payment of rent is therefore advisable at least for the three-month period when George is back from Erehwon. At that point the reservation would be treated as removed.

When a gift with reservation is made, it is treated in the same way as any other transfer. It will be a PET and will still be included in George's death estate at the date of his death. Only the treatment which generates the higher tax liability will actually be payable. Careful consideration needs to be given to this issue, as the house is likely to be an appreciating asset so increasing in value by the time of death. However, the residence nil rate band (RNRB) may be available if the house is in George's death estate – but not available for a lifetime gift. This also depends on the value of George's estate, so if greater than £2 million the RNRB will be restricted. So it is not possible to easily determine which treatment will be adopted.

Therefore, George may be unable to 'mitigate' his IHT liability as the house may be included in the death estate in any event.

Examiner's comments

The stronger candidates who had managed their time well in the previous two questions performed very well on this question. In a number of instances, this question was attempted first by some candidates and high marks were scored. The less able candidates who had got bogged down in the first two questions on the exam produced very weak answers and often wasted time discussing the remittance basis which was not relevant at all in this scenario as no details on overseas income were given. The fact that George was non-domiciled was relevant to the IHT consequences, in particular to the gift with reservation of benefit rules.

Specific comments on sections of the question:

- Pension v salary: For the most part, this was done very well with candidates showing a good understanding of the pension rules in relation to the annual allowance and the maximum amount of contributions which could be made. Candidates also recommended the pension as the most efficient way of saving for retirement. The stronger candidates did point out however that in investing in a pension, there would be a delay in receiving cash until some point in the future, in contrast to receiving salary which was immediate. Some very good answers were produced.

- Share for share takeover: This is a frequently tested area of the syllabus, yet mixed answers were produced. The very weak candidates discussed SSE which conveyed lots of confusion with the basic rules. Others thought that entrepreneurs' relief would be available on disposal of the shares, again showing a lack of skills when it comes to application of the rules in the scenario. The better candidates did recommend that it would not be worthwhile to disapply the paper for paper takeover rules and that taking a QCB as opposed to cash would result in the gain being deferred and this was therefore the preferred option.

- Investments: This part produced some very good answers with candidates showing a sound knowledge of both EIS and SEIS. Again, this part of the question was a good discriminator as the stronger candidates did notice that the income tax reducer under the SEIS scheme would not be applicable until 70% of the invested funds had been spent. This part again set aside the good candidates from the excellent ones.

- Gift of house to son: This part of the question gave candidates a lot of information in an attempt to signpost them to discuss the gift with reservation of benefit rules. Some of them did not discuss this and merely wrote about principal private residence relief in great detail, which the facts of the scenario did not allow. However, the majority of candidates did produce some good answers.

6 Gamble and Watts plc (September 2015)

Scenario

This question asked candidates to consider the tax implications of differing remuneration packages for both employees and employers. The aim of the question was not for students to provide just calculations of liabilities but, in addition, to evaluate the differences in tax treatments of alternative remuneration packages and consider how the tax cost to employee and employer might differ.

The question then moved on to consider share schemes and the ethical considerations of a 'too good to be true' tax avoidance scheme.

Marking guide

	Technical	Skills	Marks
6.1 Additional leave	1	–	
Golden hello/loan	1	1	
Beneficial loans	2	2	
Provision of tablet	2	2	
Net after tax cost to employer			
• Additional leave	1	1	
• Golden hello/loan	1	3	
• Tablet (cost and NIC)	1	2	
• Tablet (CAs)	–	2	
6.2 Non tax advantages share scheme	1	2	
Share incentive plan	1	2	
6.3 Ethics			
• Tax evasion v avoidance	1	1	
• Dislosure: rules	–	2	
• Disclosure: penalties and association	1	2	
• Accelerated payment notice	1	1	
• GAAR	3	2	
• Legality of scheme/risks	1	2	
• PCRT – standards for tax planning	–	2	
Total marks	18	29	47
Maximum			35

Tutorial notes

- At the time of the exam candidates had access to both current and future NIC rates in their open-book materials. As such candidates would not be penalised for using any of the rates available to them. The 2018/19 rates of NIC and FY2018 corporation tax rate are used below are for illustrative purposes only.

- This question was marked based upon the level of skills demonstrated by candidates, as BP:T is a skills-based exam. In marking this question the examiners were interested in how candidates had interpreted the data in the question, to understand the tax implications for both employer and employees of differing remuneration strategies. The calculations produced were reviewed in the light of the impact on the employer and employees in terms of tax costs and cash flows, rather than as numerically correct calculations.

The tax arising on the various incentives will be dependent upon the individual circumstances of the trainees. For illustrative purposes figures are calculated below on the assumption that they are basic rate taxpayers based on a salary of £22,000 and aged at least 21 years. The position may differ if they are in receipt of income from other sources or are less than 21 years old.

Additional paid leave

This is not taxable on the individuals.

Golden Hello

This income will be equivalent to salary and liable to income tax and national insurance for the individuals. For basic rate employees the tax payable will be £3,000 at 20% ie, £600 and national insurance of £263 ((£3,863 – (£22,000/12)) being £2,030 at 12% ie, £244; and (£3,000 – £2,030) being £970 at 2% ie, £19).

Beneficial loans

2020/21 - Assuming the official rate of interest is 2.5% throughout, the benefit of the loan would be:

£12,000 × 2.5% × 7/12 = £175 – tax cost £35

No employee's NIC is payable on the benefit.

2021/22

Lower of:

Average method: ½ (£12,000 + £6,000) × 2.5% = £225

Precise method: (£12,000 × 2.5% × 5/12) + (£6,000 × 2.5% × 7/12) = £125 + £88 = £213

Loan benefit = £213 – tax cost £43

No employee's NIC is payable on the benefit.

Tutorial note

There would be no loan benefit charge in 2022/23 as the total value of the loan outstanding does not exceed £10,000 for the whole year.

Tablets – as these are provided for personal use a taxable benefit will arise.

No employee NIC is payable on the benefit.

The core benefit is £750 × 20% pa = £150 based on the market value of the asset. The cost to the employer would only be relevant if the assets were immediately gifted.

2020/21 £150 × 7/12 = £87.50 Tax cost £17.50

2021/22 £150 Tax cost £30

The net, after tax cost of each alternative to the employer will include the employers' national insurance cost, where applicable and will be net of any corporation tax saving which can be made for the costs of employment.

Incentive cost

		£
1	Salary for an extra 10 trainees (£22,000 × 10 employees × 1 year 7 months)	348,333
	Employers' NIC on additional employees (Note 1) (£1,873 + 1,093) × 10 employees)	29,660
	CT saving on costs (348,333 + 29,660) × 19%	(71,819)
	Net cost	306,174
2	Golden Hello £3,000 × 500	1,500,000
	Employers' NIC on golden hello at 13.8%	207,000
	Employers' class 1A NIC on interest benefit 2020/21 (Note 2)	12,075
	Employers' class 1A NIC on interest benefit 2021/22 (Note 2)	14,697
		1,733,772
	CT saving on costs £1,733,772 × 19%	(329,417)
	Net cost	1,404,355
3	Cost of providing tablets to employees (£500 × 500)	250,000
	Employers' class 1A NIC on tablet benefits (Note 3)	16,388
	CT saving on	
	- Employers' NIC (19% × £16,388)	(3,113)
	- Capital allowances (Note 4)	(15,561)
	Net cost	247,714

Notes

1 Assuming the rates of employers' NIC remain the same in future tax years, the Employers' NIC due on a salary of £22,000 would be:

To March 2021 (£22,000 × 7/12) - (£8,424 × 7/12) = £12,833 - £4,914 = £7,919 × 13.8% = £1,093

Year to March 2022 £22,000 - 8,424 = £13,576 × 13.8% = £1,873

2 2020/21

Employers' NIC on the benefit:

£175 × 500 × 13.8% = £12,075 due July 2021

2021/22

Employers' NIC on the benefit:

£213 × 500 × 13.8% = £14,697 due July 2022

3 2020/21

Class 1A NIC £87.50 × 500 = £43,750 × 13.8% = £6,038 July 2021

2021/22

Class 1 NIC £150 × 500 = £75,000 × 13.8% = £10,350 July 2022

Total = £16,388

4   CT saving at 19% on capital allowances on tablet computers

Capital intensive industry so AIA likely to have been used in full.

Year 1 WDA of £250,000 × 18% = £45,000

CT saving £45,000 × 19% = £8,550

Year 2 WDA £250,000 – £45,000 = £205,000 × 18% = £36,900

CT saving £36,900 × 19% = £7,011

Note: Allowances of £168,100 still to be claimed so future tax saving of £31,939 – total saving therefore £47,500.

6.2   As the current share scheme is non tax-advantaged, employees will be liable to tax at the time of exercise of the options. They will have deemed employment income equal to the market value of the shares at the date of exercise less any amount paid – apparently nil in this situation. NIC will arise only if the shares are readily convertible assets so this will depend whether the shares in Gamble and Watts plc are traded on a stock exchange.

The employee will also be liable to tax on a capital gain on the disposal – being the value of the proceeds less the original cost and the amount charged to income tax on exercise.

A share incentive plan is a tax-advantaged scheme, and as such there will be no income tax implications at the time of the share issue. Income tax and NIC will only apply if the employee leaves employment within five years (the shares leave the plan if the employee leaves employment). In addition there will be no capital gains tax on disposal of shares held for at least five years provided they are still in the plan at the time of disposal (ie, the employee is still employed). If not in the plan at that time, the base cost on disposal of shares is the market value at the date the shares left the plan.

6.3   **To:**   Finance Director
From: Alex Robertson
Subject: Tax saving scheme

Without full details of the scheme it is difficult to reach a definite conclusion about this scheme. However, based on the information you have given me I would have concerns about it.

The tax advisers have informed you that the scheme is legal. Assuming they are correct, this should mean that this scheme falls within the category of tax avoidance rather than tax evasion. However, when reducing the tax burden through legal means (tax avoidance) it is sometimes difficult to identify the difference between what HMRC would deem as acceptable tax planning and unacceptable tax avoidance.

The concerns I would have are as follows:

(1)   If this is a tax avoidance scheme, which takes advantage of a loophole in the tax legislation to reduce a tax liability, it is possible that the scheme should have been notified, by the scheme promoter, to HMRC under the disclosure of tax avoidance schemes regime.

Such disclosure would be required where there was a tax advantage to be gained by a scheme, which is one of the main benefits of the arrangement, and where the scheme bears one of the 'hallmarks' of a tax avoidance scheme. A premium fee contingent on the tax advantages to be gained from the scheme (as here) is a hallmark.

Although any penalties for non-disclosure of the scheme to HMRC would fall on the tax advisers and not on the company, if the scheme is not registered with HMRC, the company should not consider an unregistered tax avoidance scheme.

If the scheme is registered with HMRC the promoter should be able to provide us with details of the scheme registration number.

The company may wish to consider whether ethically the company wishes to be associated with a tax avoidance scheme and the company may consider the impact such an association might have on public opinion of the company's business if they became aware of the company's behaviour.

Disclosure of a tax avoidance scheme is likely to mean that the tax loophole it takes advantage of is likely to be closed by HMRC once details of the scheme are made known to them, so the tax advantage to be gained from the scheme may be short lived.

(2) If the scheme is challenged HMRC powers may also eliminate any cash flow advantage as HMRC have the power to issue an Accelerated Payment Notice requiring payment of an amount in dispute whilst an enquiry is in progress.

(3) A general anti-abuse rule (GAAR) has been introduced to counteract the tax advantages to be gained from 'abusive tax arrangements'.

A tax arrangement is one that involves a tax advantage as one of its main purposes.

Such arrangements are abusive if they use contrived or abnormal steps, or exploit shortcomings in tax provisions to gain a tax advantage.

In the case of the proposed scheme, the fact that extra steps are put into the process of paying employees, in order to produce a tax saving sounds like the scheme could be abusive.

As the GAAR is new, there is still some uncertainty about how the law could be applied. As a result it is possible that HMRC could seek to counteract any tax advantage gained under this scheme by adjusting the company's tax burden upwards on a 'just and reasonable' basis.

Similarly the inclusion of artificial steps could lead to the effect of these being disregarded under principles arising from case law in this area. The Ramsay doctrine may therefore apply to eliminate benefits arising under a strict interpretation of the relevant steps.

(4) As a professionally qualified accountant I would be unable to advocate the use of a scheme which should have been reported to HMRC under the DOTAS regime, but had not been so reported. I would also wish the company to be aware of the risk posed by the GAAR regime to any perceived tax advantages to be gained under the scheme. I would wish to be very certain that the proposed scheme was indeed legal and was not illegal and actually a form of tax evasion. Without full details of the scheme I would not be able to ascertain this. Professional conduct in relation to taxation (PCRT) sets out the five standards for tax planning which include a requirement that professional accountants should not be involved in tax planning arrangements that either aim to achieve results not intended by Parliament, exploit loopholes in legislation, or using artificial or contrived steps. It appears that this scheme may not be in line with the standards for tax planning.

Examiner's comments

Although the subject matter of part 1 was relatively simple, candidates found the layout of their answers a challenge. This part of the question discriminated well between those with sound tax knowledge, who could think through the implications of what was asked for and those with poorer knowledge, who often struggled to be able to think through how to lay out their answers to best effect.

Part 2 has changed since the real exam due to changes in legislation.

Part 3 of the question contained a detailed ethical scenario, requiring knowledge of the general anti-abuse rule, the Ramsay doctrine and the disclosure of tax avoidance scheme legislation, as well as more general ethical principles. This requirement is particularly important to BP:T, in a world of increasing legal challenges to the roles of professional advisers, in the area of tax avoidance. Unfortunately many candidates produced simplistic answers to the problem, citing the aged chestnuts of ethics advice, as follows:

- Call the ICAEW helpline;
- Report the money laundering to the Money Laundering Regulatory Officer;
- Resign.

Sadly, these generic and somewhat thoughtless answers scored little or no marks. The better answers were those that addressed the issue in the light of the specific legislation and case law on tax avoidance schemes, which is fully documented in the open-book learning materials.

Individuals – capital taxes

7 Boxit Ltd (June 2014)

Scenario

In this scenario the shareholder of a close company has decided to retire and sell his shares. The company cannot afford to buy all the shares and therefore needs to carry out a refinancing by means of a sale and lease back of their factory.

A proposal is made by the board to finance the acquisition by the other shareholder by means of a director's loan account. The candidate has to determine the tax implications of this for both the company and the shareholder.

To answer this question well the candidate needed to demonstrate both a technical understanding of the tax implications of the purchase of the shares for different parties and the skills to identify, mediate and recommend a course of action.

Marking guide

	Technical	Skills	Marks
Company purchase of own shares			
Conditions	3	1	
Income distribution calculation	1	1	
Capital loss	1	1	
Stamp duty	½	1	
	5½	4	
Sale of shares to Jane			
Connected party valuation	½	1	
Gift relief	1	2	
CGT valuation	1	1	
IHT	1	2	
Impact on Jane	–	3	
Director's loan account	½	3	
	4	12	
Sale of shares to Boxit Ltd (including sale and leaseback)			
Adam – ER conditions	2	–	
Adam – Gain	–	2	
Stamp duty	½	1	
Sale and leaseback			
• Gain and ROR	1	2	
• Lease premium and rental deduction	1	2	
• SDLT	–	3	
	4½	10	
Total marks	14	26	40
Maximum			35

PURCHASE OF OWN SHARES

It is possible for a shareholder to sell shares back to the company rather than to a third party. Importantly the company must have both the cash available and the ability to make a permissible capital payment (PCP). Essentially this means having distributable reserves in the company. On repurchase the nominal share capital is reduced. The shares can be held as treasury shares, but they are still treated as having been cancelled.

An examination of the statement of financial position at 31 March 2019 shows that the company has distributable reserves of £1.325 million. The cost of the buy back to the company of 70,000 shares is likely to be £1.4 million which would therefore require a permissible capital payment of £1.4m – £1.325m = £75,000.

At 31 March 2019 there are insufficient reserves to enable the full buyback of 70,000 shares. However the proposed date of the buyback is 1 September 2019 and therefore as the company appears to be profitable, a further statement of financial position should be prepared immediately before the buyback to ensure that reserves are available to make the PCP. It is also advised that the company obtains confirmation of the transaction from the company's solicitor.

Tutorial note

The examiner has stated that full marks could be obtained in the question without reference to the PCP, as the question asked only for tax consequences.

SCENARIO 1 SALE OF 20,000 SHARES TO BOXIT LTD AS A PURCHASE OF OWN SHARES

Tax implications for Adam

From Adam's point of view the sale of his shares to Boxit Ltd will automatically be treated as a capital transaction unless the conditions for it to be treated as such are breached.

Applying to the scenario would suggest that most of the conditions are met:

- Boxit Ltd is an unquoted trading company;

- The buyback would appear to benefit the trade as Adam is retiring through ill health and to make way for his daughter to take over the business;

- Adam has owned the shares for at least five years; and

- Adam also needs to be UK resident and there is no information in the scenario to indicate that this is not the case but would need to be confirmed.

However, there is a requirement that Adam's shareholding must be substantially reduced and therefore selling only 20,000 shares to Boxit Ltd would not pass the substantial reduction test. This test involves comparing the relative shareholdings (including associates) before and after the buyback. For this purpose Jane, assuming she is over 18, is not an associate.

	Adam No of shares	Jane No of shares	DrinkUp plc No of shares	Total No of shares
Before the buy back	70,000	20,000	10,000	100,000
Buy back of 20,000	(20,000)			(20,000)
	50,000	20,000	10,000	80,000
Percentage before	70.0%			
Percentage after	62.5%			
75% of the percentage before	52.5%			

As the post-sale percentage is more than 75% of the pre-sale percentage, the test is not met and the income distribution treatment will apply.

As Adam is not the original subscriber of the shares, the situation is as follows:

Income = 20,000 × (£20 – £1) = £380,000

Tax charge (Additional rate payer) 38.1% × £380,000 = £144,780

(If Adam has not used the dividend nil rate band then the tax charge is 38.1% × (£380,000 – £2,000) = £144,018.)

As Adam subscribed for the shares above the nominal value, the income distribution also results in a capital loss.

	£
Proceeds 20,000 × £20	400,000
Less net distribution 20,000 × (£20 – £1)	(380,000)
Deemed proceeds	20,000
Less cost 20,000 × £5	(100,000)
Allowable capital loss	(80,000)

Tax implications for Boxit Ltd

Stamp duty of 0.5% × £400,000 = £2,000 is payable by Boxit Ltd.

SALE OF 20,000 SHARES TO JANE

Tax implications for Adam

For Adam, the sale will be treated as a capital transaction. However as Jane and Adam are connected persons, the market value must be used regardless of the actual amount paid.

There is a market price for the shares as DrinkUp plc has offered £20 per share. Therefore the consideration is potentially £400,000.

However, Jane would be buying a much reduced shareholding and not an outright controlling shareholding. Therefore it may be possible to provide evidence to support the valuation of £16 as a value for 20,000 shares – further information will be required.

Jane and Adam could elect to make a joint election for gift relief under s.165 TCGA 1992 in relation to the undervalue payment for the shares. Gift relief would reduce Adam's gain by £80,000 ((£20 – £16) × 20,000).

If £16 is determined to be a sale at below market value, Adam's capital gains tax liability would be as follows assuming he qualifies for ER relief see below:

	£
Gain chargeable (Market value £400,000 less cost £100,000)	300,000
Gift relief	(80,000)
	220,000
Less annual exempt amount	(11,700)
Chargeable gain	208,300
Tax at 10%	£20,830

Adam will be able to use a 10% tax rate as he is likely to qualify for entrepreneurs' relief (ER) see below.

Adam has suggested that Jane will inherit the remaining 50,000 shares on his death. These shares should qualify for Business Property Relief (BPR) and would therefore be exempt from Inheritance tax when Adam dies.

The 'undervalue' on the sale of shares to Jane is also a potentially exemption transfer (PET) for IHT purposes. This should be covered by BPR if Jane still holds the shares at Adam's death, otherwise by exemptions and the nil rate band, providing there have been no other transfers of value.

Tax implications for Jane/Boxit Ltd

Jane's base cost would be £320,000 (£400,000 – £80,000) if gift relief is claimed.

Stamp Duty for Jane, based on the actual amount paid by her, would be £1,600 (0.5% × £320,000).

There are no VAT implications.

Directors' loan account

Boxit Ltd is a close company and when a close company makes a loan to a participator it must make a notional payment of 32.5% of the loan which is still outstanding nine months after the year end. Therefore £320,000 × 32.5% = £104,000 would be payable.

It is not clear whether Boxit Ltd is subject to the instalments regime. If it is then the notional tax would be payable as part of the company's instalments payments.

Jane will also be taxed on a benefit which would be the difference between the rate of interest charged (0%) and the official rate of interest (2.5%). In the tax year 2019/20 this will be £4,667 (£320,000 × 2.5% × 7/12). Boxit Ltd will pay class 1A national insurance contributions of £644 (£4,667 × 13.8%) on this benefit.

SCENARIO 2 SALE OF ALL 70,000 SHARES TO BOXIT LTD

Tax implications for Adam

The disposal would automatically meet the conditions for a purchase of shares - capital route - and subject to Adam meeting all the requirements for ER, the rate of tax will be 10%.

Conditions for ER relief

Adam will qualify for 10% tax rate for the following reasons.

Adam holds more than 5% of the ordinary shares, therefore Boxit Ltd is a personal trading company; he has held the shares for more than a year; he is a director and an employee.

	£
Proceeds 70,000 × £20	1,400,000
Less cost 70,000 × £5	350,000
Chargeable gain	1,050,000
Less annual exempt amount	(11,700)
Taxable gains	1,038,300
Tax at 10%	103,830

Tax implications for Boxit Ltd

Stamp Duty

Stamp Duty of £7,000 (0.5% × £1,400,000) is payable by Boxit Ltd.

SALE AND LEASEBACK TRANSACTION

The chargeable gain of £500,000 will be taxed as part of the total income for the year at Boxit Ltd's at 19%.

If Boxit Ltd invests in a qualifying asset there is a possibility of rollover relief to defer the gain.

An annual revenue deduction will be available to Boxit Ltd in respect of the lease premium as follows:

(£35,000 × (50 – 14)/50)/15 = £1,680 pa

Boxit Ltd will claim tax relief for the lease rentals as they are charged to profit or loss.

Although the purchaser of the Ben Lane factory, BB Bank, will pay stamp duty land tax (SDLT) on the purchase, Boxit Ltd will also pay SDLT on the lease premium and the lease rentals.

SDLT on lease premium

As the property is non-residential property and the value is below £150,000 the whole of the premium will be chargeable at 0%.

In addition SDLT is also payable on the rental. The rental charge is based on the net present value of the rent payable to the landlord over the term of the lease. However, ignoring discounting only the excess is chargeable over £150,000 at 1% (and 2% over £5 million).

15 years × £75,000 = £1,125,000 – £150,000 = 975,000 × 1% = £9,750

As there is no option to tax there is no VAT charged on the sale as the building is a commercial building over three years old.

Examiner's comments

Candidates did approach the question in a structured way and considered the income v capital route. Often a lot of calculations without explanation were produced and whilst they were correct, one of the skills which the BP:T exam tests is the ability of the candidates to assimilate information, deal with a real life situation and give advice based on an assessment of the circumstances. Producing lots of calculations without explanation should be discouraged, as a lot of what is tested centres on the candidate's ability to give advice as well as being able to calculate the overall tax liability.

The higher scoring answers firstly considered whether the company had enough cash to make a permissible capital payment and discussed how a purchase of own shares would be treated in terms of treasury shares and subsequent cancellation. This was extremely encouraging and conveyed that candidates understood the scenario and the non-tax issues in relation to the scenario.

Sale to Boxit – 20,000 shares

Candidates did not have too many problems in discussing the conditions needed in order for the capital route to apply and correctly concluded that if just 20,000 shares were sold, the conditions would not be met; although some candidates did think the conditions were met and concluded incorrectly that the capital route would apply.

Sale to Jane and director's loan

In terms of the sale of shares to Jane, the majority identified that Jane was a connected person and the sale would be deemed to take place at market value. Some excellent answers were produced which included a discussion on the availability of ER, the IHT consequences and the s.455 implications of the loan made to Jane. It was also very pleasing to see that within their answers, candidates also considered the VAT and stamp duty consequences of each transaction.

Sale to Boxit – 70,000 shares

Some candidates applied 20% without even considering ER.

Sale and leaseback

Some very good answers were produced on this part, with candidates correctly calculating the tax on the gain on the sale, identifying the possibility of rollover relief and the tax relief available on rentals. SDLT and VAT were also considered. Overall, candidates coped very well with this question.

8 David Brimelow (September 2015)

Scenario

This question required the candidate to provide advice to a personal tax client on both personal and business tax issues.

The question concerned a death and simple evaluation of the inheritance tax consequences of that death. The inheritance tax due was then to be financed from the proceeds of a purchase of own shares. Specialist rules can apply to the tax treatment of the proceeds of the purchase of own shares if the proceeds are to be used to finance an inheritance tax liability.

Candidates were asked to evaluate the tax consequences of the purchase of own shares in the light of the need to pay the inheritance tax.

Finally, some simple thought was to be given to the tax planning measures that can happen after death in respect of the estate of the deceased.

Marking guide

	Technical	Skills	Marks
8.1 IHT computation			
• London house	1	2½	
• Holiday home	1	1½	
• Dumpling Ltd	1	1	
• Nil rate bands/RNRB	1	2	
• Other aspects of the calculation	2	2	
8.2 Company purchase of own shares			
• Income route	2	2½	
• Capital route	1	2½	
Conditions			
• Benefit of trade	1	1	
• IHT	1	3	
8.3 Deed of variation			
• For IHT	1	1	
• For CGT	2	2	
Total marks	14	21	35
Maximum			25

8.1 IHT due as a result of the death of Frank Brimelow

Date of death 30 June 2019

	£
House in London (Note 1)	1,000,000
Holiday home in Wales (Note 2)	0
Shares in Dumpling Ltd	220,000
100% BPR on shares in Dumpling Ltd (Note 3)	(220,000)
Share portfolio	200,000
Cash	25,000
Vintage Rolls Royce car	175,000
25% share in racehorse	250,000
Total Estate	1,650,000
Less: Exempt gift to charity	(25,000)
RNRB (£150,000 × 2) (Note 4)	(300,000)
Nil rate band (£325,000 × 2 less £350,000) (Note 5)	(300,000)
Chargeable estate	1,025,000

Tax on death estate

£1,025,000 × 40%   £410,000

Notes

1. The lifetime gift of the house in London is a gift with reservation of benefit, because the donor (Frank) continues to live in the property, rent free, after the date of the gift.

   HMRC could treat this gift as both a PET, at a value of £740,000 and also an asset in the death estate, at a value of £1 million.

   In practice HMRC usually choose one of the two potential charges, the one that will net the largest amount of tax to HMRC.

   In this case the greatest tax will be payable if the asset is included in the death estate at a value of £1 million. Even after the benefit of the RNRB on death the value on death is greater, plus taper relief will apply to further reduce the tax on the lifetime gift.

2. The gift of the holiday home in Wales would have constituted a PET at the time of the gift. It would not have been a gift with reservation of benefit as Frank was virtually excluded from enjoyment of the property. As Frank died within seven years of making the gift, this becomes a chargeable transfer. However, Frank has made no other gifts beyond his annual exemption and so the nil rate band will be available for this transfer.

3. The shares in Dumpling Ltd are shares in an unquoted trading company, which had been owned by the deceased for two years and so attract 100% business property relief.

4. As Frank's wife died before 6 April 2017, leaving the residence to him, he is entitled to 100% of her residence nil rate band (RNRB). It is assumed that her estate was less than £2 million and the RNRB is therefore not restricted. As Frank died in 2019/20 the RNRB is £150,000.

5. Frank's wife left all of her estate to her spouse, Frank. As a result she did not use her nil rate band. Frank is therefore entitled to two nil rate bands to use against his death estate. Of this £350,000 has been used against the lifetime transfer now chargeable.

8.2 The proceeds from a company purchase of own shares for an individual shareholder can either be treated as an income distribution or as a capital disposal.

The capital treatment is mandatory, if certain conditions are satisfied. If those conditions are not satisfied, the income distribution treatment will be applied.

The difference between the tax implications of the two treatments would be:

Treatment 1: Income distribution

	£	£
Proceeds (£25 × 10,000)		250,000
Less subscription price, original owner (£1 × £10,000)		(10,000)
Distribution		240,000

	£	£
Income tax due by David (higher rate taxpayer)		
Additional tax on abatement of personal allowance		
£11,850 × 40% (assuming other income is not dividend income)		4,740
Tax on distribution		
£2,000 × 0% (unused dividend nil rate band)	–	
£88,000 (£150,000 – £60,000 – £2,000) × 32.5%	28,600	
£150,000 × 38.1%	57,150	
		85,750
Total IT due on distribution		90,490

Capital loss on income distribution:

	£
Proceeds (£25 × 10,000)	250,000
Less net distribution	(240,000)
	10,000
Less cost to David (£22 × 10,000)	(220,000)
Capital loss	(210,000)

Treatment 2: Capital distribution

	£
Proceeds (£25 × 10,000)	250,000
Less probate value (£22 × £10,000)	(220,000)
Capital gain	30,000
Less annual exempt amount (assuming unused and 2018/19 rates continue)	(11,700)
Taxable gain	18,300
Capital gains tax at 20% (David is a higher/additional rate taxpayer)	3,660

Entrepreneurs' relief could be available to reduce the tax due on the gain to 10%, however, David has not owned the shares for one year at the date of disposal.

If certain conditions are met the capital treatment is mandatory.

The capital route requires either:

- the repurchase of the shares to be for the benefit of the trade. Although David's father had expressed dissenting views as a shareholder, David has made it clear that he would not do so. However, this condition is also met if a shareholder dies and his beneficiary does not wish to retain the shares; or

- the proceeds are used to settle an IHT liability. The conditions for this route require:

  - the person receiving the payment to use all or virtually all of the proceeds to pay an IHT liability falling on him as a result of death. As the IHT liability on Frank's death is £410,000, it is possible the proceeds of £250,000 could be used towards this liability.

  - the IHT paid could not otherwise have been paid without causing undue hardship. That is, the sale of the shares back to the company is the last resort. We cannot judge whether this condition is met here, and would require further information to form a judgement.

  - the payment of tax must be within two years of death. Given the date of the repurchase of shares, this is likely to be the case.

It seems likely that the repurchase will fall within the capital distribution route which certainly result in a smaller amount of tax being due on repurchase, although the income distribution route gives rise to a large capital loss.

8.3 Post death tax planning is usually in the form of a deed of variation to the original will.

Frank's will left all of his assets to his son David. As David is wealthy in his own right, he has no immediate need for these assets. His son has no taxable income or gains and so has not used his personal allowance or annual exempt amount and is a basic rate taxpayer.

It would be possible to vary Frank's will to leave the shares in Dumpling Ltd, the Rolls Royce car and the share in the racehorse to Henry Brimelow.

For IHT purposes, this would not reduce the burden of the inheritance tax due on Frank's death; however, it would reduce the inheritance tax due on David's death in the future. Effectively we have skipped a generation of inheritance tax by varying the terms of Frank's will for IHT purposes.

It is also possible to include a statement in a deed of variation that the variation has effect for capital gains tax purposes too. In this circumstance this statement would be beneficial, because although the racehorse and the car are exempt from CGT on disposal, and the statement has no effect on the CGT due on these assets, however, the Dumpling Ltd shares are a chargeable asset. If the deed of variation did not apply for CGT purposes, David would be deemed to sell the shares to Henry and would realise a gain on any increase in value of the shares since Frank's death, over and above probate value. Probate value was £22 per share and the value of the shares in December 2019, is likely to be £25, there could therefore be a gain on any transfer between David and Henry. As David is a higher rate taxpayer, we might prefer that gain to crystallise in Henry's hands, rather than David's as the gain would fall within Henry's basic rate band and so would be taxed at 10% in Henry's hands (after deduction of the annual exempt amount), rather than 20% in David's hands.

Examiner's comments

The better candidates realised that part 1 of this question required explanations as well as calculations and there were some inheritance tax planning points to explain in terms of gifts with reservation of benefit, business property relief, transfer of spouse's nil rate bands and the applicability or otherwise of the charitable rate of inheritance tax.

Part 2 was well answered, although not all candidates realised that one of the reasons the capital treatment can be used for the proceeds of a company purchase of own shares, is if the proceeds need to be used to pay an inheritance tax bill.

Part 3 was either very well or very poorly answered. A deed of variation is one of the inheritance tax administration issues at Business Planning: Taxation that is not in Tax Compliance, and many candidates appeared to be unaware of its existence and, instead, considered any inheritance tax planning advice they had ever heard of as an answer to this part of the question.

9 Riverbrook Farm Ltd (December 2015)

Scenario

In this question candidates were working as an ICAEW Chartered Accountant in a tax practice providing advice to the vendors on the sale of a farming company. The sale could either be by way of:

(1) a sale of trade and assets; or

(2) a sale of shares.

Candidates then had to consider the tax planning considerations around the use of the sale proceeds by the vendors, in the purchase of a new business venture or the creation of a discretionary trust.

Marking guide

	Technical	Skills	Marks
9.1 Alternative 1			
Company gain	1	1	
No CGT reliefs for company	1	–	
Net cash company could pay to each shareholder	1	3	
Pre or post winding up	–	1	
Pre-liquidation dividend			
• Discussion	1	1	
• Calculations	1	3	
Post-liquidation dividend			
• Discussion	2	1	
• Calculation	1	3	
Summary	1	2	
Alternative 2			
• Computation	3	–	
Conclusion	–	3	
	12	18	
Max			20
9.2 Gift in lifetime			
CGT consequences			
• Gains	–	1	
• Gift relief	1	2	
• Entrepreneurs' relief	1	1	
IHT consequences			
• PET	–	1	
• APR/BPR	2	2	
• David's death	1	1	
Gift on death			
CGT consequences	–	1	
IHT consequences	1	1	
	6	10	
Max			10

	Technical	Skills	Marks
9.3 No CGT for gift of cash	1	–	
IHT on lifetime CLT	2	–	
Further IHT on Shona's death	1	2	
IT on trust income	–	3	
Exit charges	–	3	
CGT on capital transfers	–	2	
	4	10	10
Total marks	22	38	60
Maximum			40

Tutorial note

In answering the second and third parts of this question, markers took account of candidates' answers to part 1 in terms of the amounts David and Shona had available to invest.

9.1   The disposal of Riverbrook Farm Ltd can be structured in two, different ways:

Alternative 1: The company sells the farmland and buildings for £10,900,000 and the company pays the disposal proceeds to the shareholders.

Under this alternative the gain on disposal of assets will be made by the company and not the shareholders. The company will make a gain of £7,500,000 (£10.9m – £2.5m – £900,000).

No CGT reliefs are available to the company on this disposal.

Corporation tax on the gain of £7.5 million × 19% (CT rate assumed on 1 May 2019) would be £1,425,000.

The company will therefore have net cash of £9,475,000 to pay out to the shareholders.

This will be split between David and Shona: 75% to David £7,106,250 and 25% to Shona £2,368,750.

Tutorial note

The question was deliberately silent on any disposal proceeds for the goodwill of the farm business – given the purchaser was buying the farmland and buildings for non-business use and the sale proceeds for goodwill were therefore nil. Sensible assumptions and comments on the disposal of goodwill would be given additional credit.

The question stated that on incorporation of Riverbrook Farm Ltd, Phil had not claimed any reliefs. Students were given credit for any reasonable assumptions made about incorporation relief on the transfer of the farm business to the farm company.

Riverbrook Farm Ltd is to be liquidated and the cash paid out to the shareholders. There is no information given about any other cash balances in the company or any other assets of value, which may be sold on liquidation, so I have only considered the net proceeds of sale of the farmland and buildings.

The net proceeds of sale can be paid out to David and Shona either before winding up commences or after:

1   A pre-liquidation dividend: a dividend paid out before winding up proceedings have started. This would be taxed as an income distribution. As both David and Shona are higher rate taxpayers (other income of £130,000), the rate of tax on the first £2,000 of the dividend would be 0% (assuming they have not used any of their dividend nil rate

band), on the next £18,000 it would be 32.5%. Thereafter the rate of tax on the dividend will be 38.1%.

The net cash receivable would be:

	David £	Shona £
Dividend	7,106,250	2,368,750
Tax at 0% on £2,000	–	–
Tax at 32.5% on £18,000	(15,600)	(15,600)
Tax at 38.1% on £7,086,250	(2,699,861)	
Tax at 38.1% on £2,348,750		(894,874)
Net dividend after tax	4,390,789	1,458,276

There would be no further reliefs available from tax on income.

2 A post-liquidation dividend: a dividend paid out after winding up proceedings have started, which is treated as a capital distribution to the shareholders.

As both David and Shona are higher rate taxpayers, ignoring any available CGT reliefs, the gain after the annual exempt amount has been deducted would be taxed at 20%.

On receipt of a post liquidation dividend, David would be entitled to entrepreneurs' relief (held 5% or more of the shares for at least one year and works full-time for the company).

Shona would not be entitled to entrepreneurs' relief because she has never worked for the company.

	David £	Shona £
Capital distribution	7,106,250	2,368,750
Less cost of shares (probate value of £2,500,000 75:25)	(1,875,000)	(625,000)
Gain	5,231,250	1,743,750
Less annual exempt amount	(11,700)	(11,700)
Taxable gain	5,219,550	1,732,050
CGT at 10%/20%	521,955	346,410
Net proceeds after tax	6,584,295	2,022,340

A post liquidation dividend is more tax efficient than a pre liquidation dividend for both David and Shona, but, due to the operation of entrepreneurs' relief, is particularly beneficial for David.

So, under alternative 1 David would receive cash of £6,584,295 and Shona would receive cash of £2,022,340.

Alternative 2: David and Shona receive £10.9 million for the sale of the shares in Riverbrook Farm Ltd

David and Shona will each make a gain on the sale of their shares in Riverbrook Farm Ltd, calculated as follows:

	David £	Shona £
Proceeds (£10.9 million 75:25)	8,175,000	2,725,000
Less cost of shares probate value (£2.5 million 75:25)	(1,875,000)	(625,000)
Gain	6,300,000	2,100,000
Less annual exempt amount	(11,700)	(11,700)
Taxable gain	6,288,300	2,088,300
CGT at 10%/20% (assuming no reliefs)	(628,830)	(417,660)
Net proceeds received after tax	7,546,170	2,307,340

It is assumed that, at the time of the sale, no element of the farm represents residential property (as Charles had to convert a building to live in). The net, after tax, cash received under alternative 2 is higher than alternative 1, so David and Shona should dispose of the shares in Riverbrook Farm Ltd, under alternative 2, rather than the company selling the assets to Charles Gentry and the company distributing the proceeds to the shareholders.

Tutorial note

Depending on the assumptions made by candidates, there were a number of outcomes to the calculations of gains and dividends. Credit was given for the underlying understanding and principles demonstrated by candidates. This is a planning paper, and where there is imperfect information, there can be more than one set of numerical responses to the data given. The calculations above are for demonstration only. Any reasonable calculations based on reasonable assumptions by candidates were given credit.

9.2 The choice that David has is between gifting his unincorporated farm business to his children during his lifetime, or waiting to gift the business on his death.

Gift in lifetime

If David gifts the unincorporated farm business to his children in 10 years' time, this will be a lifetime gift.

A lifetime gift will have both capital gains tax and inheritance tax consequences.

Capital gains tax consequences

If David gifts the farm in 10 years' time there would be a capital gain of £700,000 (£7.7m – £7m) on the gift, assuming market value of the farm is deemed to be sale proceeds for the gift. I am assuming that the farm is a single asset of farmland and buildings, we would need to know more about the make-up of the business assets to provide full calculations of any liabilities.

However, because the farm is an asset used for the purposes of trade/business, a gift relief claim would be possible. This would be a joint claim with David and his three children and would have the impact of deferring the gain by reducing the total base cost of the farm. David would therefore pay no CGT on the gift, but his children would have a reduced base cost for any future disposal of the business and also pay more tax if they dispose of the farm in the future.

Alternatively, a claim for entrepreneurs' relief could be made as David would be disposing of a trading business which has been owned for more than one year. This would result in the gain being taxed at the rate of 10%, giving him a tax liability of £68,830 [(£700,000 – £11,700) × 10%].

Inheritance tax consequences

The gift of the business during his lifetime will be a PET.

The gift of an unincorporated business, whether in life or on death, should attract both 100% business property relief (BPR) and 100% agricultural property relief (APR), provided certain conditions are met.

APR is available after two years of ownership, if the land is farmed by the owner themself, but only on the agricultural value of the assets. The agricultural value is usually less than the market value of farming assets.

BPR is available at the rate of 100% on a gift of an unincorporated business, after 2 years of ownership. Therefore the remainder of the value of the partnership, over and above the agricultural value will be covered by 100% BPR.

Thus, on a transfer in 10 years' time, assuming an appreciation in value of 10%, the transfer of value for IHT purposes would be:

	£
Transfer of value (£7m × 1.1)	7,700,000
Less APR on agricultural value (£2m × 1.1)	(2,200,000)
Less BPR on development value	(5,500,000)
Taxable value of transfer	Nil

If this transfer takes place in lifetime in 10 years' time, when David retires, the APR and BPR will be applied at the time of the lifetime transfer.

However, if the transfer comes within the charge to tax, because David dies within seven years of the lifetime transfer, the APR and BPR will no longer be available if the children have sold or gifted the property before David's death (without buying replacement property), or have stopped using the property for business/agricultural purposes. Taper relief would however be available if the gift becomes chargeable.

The lifetime transfer will then be chargeable on death without any APR or BPR being deducted and the unreduced value of the gift will enter the cumulation for IHT purposes, for the purpose of the use of the nil rate band.

If David survives seven years, or the property continues to be agricultural or business property this will not be an issue.

As David cannot guarantee the actions of his children once the farm has been transferred, if he is concerned about the impact of these rules, he should either consider giving away the farm sooner rather than later (to reduce the risk of death within the next seven years) or retain the assets until death, to preserve definite entitlement to APR and BPR.

Gift on death

Capital gains tax consequences

There will be no CGT consequences of a gift on death. The children will inherit the unincorporated business assets at probate value and this will be their base cost for any future CGT disposal.

Inheritance tax consequences

Inheritance tax would be payable on a gift of the unincorporated farm business on death, however, as noted above, the full value of the business would be reduced to nil for IHT purposes by the operation of 100% APR on the agricultural value of the business and 100% BPR on the remainder of the value of the business assets. This is provided the farm business still satisfies the conditions for operation of the relief.

Tutorial note

This question's requirement did not ask candidates to recommend an option for David to take; however, credit was given for commentary on the difference between a lifetime and a death gift.

9.3 Shona would receive net proceeds on sale of £2,307,340.

If she were to gift this to a discretionary trust, the gift of cash would not give rise to any CGT charge.

For IHT, the creation of a discretionary trust is a chargeable lifetime transfer. If Shona has not gifted any assets previously, two annual exemptions of £3,000 each will reduce the value of the gift and the full nil rate band will ensure that the first £325,000 is taxed at 0%.

IHT due on the lifetime transfer would be 20% × the remaining transfer (assuming Shona intends the trust to pay any lifetime IHT due). £(2,307,340 – 6,000 – 325,000) = 1,976,340 × 20% = £395,268 of tax due on the creation of the trust.

Should Shona die within 7 years of creating the trust, there will be further IHT due on her death at 40%. The lifetime tax paid will be deductible from the death tax due.

If Shona dies more than 7 years after making the gift then no further tax will be due.

However, the CLT may still use some of the NRB as part of the 7-year cumulation if later gifts are made.

Once the cash is within the trust, the trustees will invest the cash according to the rules of the trust. Income of the trust will be taxed on the trust itself, with a £1,000 basic rate band and the balance of trust income being taxed at 45% for savings and non-savings income and 38.1% for dividend income.

Trust income is paid out to beneficiaries at the discretion of the trustees and the beneficiary is treated as receiving any payments net of a 45% tax credit.

The beneficiary treats all income from a discretionary trust as non-savings income. The net receipt will be grossed up by 100/55 and then a 45% tax credit will be deducted from the income tax due.

Distributions of property from the trust to beneficiaries are subject to an exit charge for inheritance tax purposes. The exit charge is 6% (reduced by n/40 for the number of complete quarters since the trust was set up/the last 10-year principal charge) × trust property, subject to the availability of the nil rate band to reduce the amount in charge to tax.

Every 10-year anniversary of the creation of the trust, the trust property is also charged to tax at 6%, subject to availability of the nil rate band.

On an exit charge there could also be a charge to CGT, as an asset is being disposed of, by way of gift, by the trust, however, as there is an immediate IHT charge on the same transaction, the CGT can be held over under gift relief against the cost of the asset to the beneficiary.

Tutorial note

Candidates should have used the net proceeds they have identified for the most tax efficient route for Shona in the first part of the question.

Examiner's comments

Part 1 was clear, with unambiguous requirements, and success or failure in answering the question hinged on thinking through the problem before answering. We had a large number of candidates who understood that the difference between the two options for the sale was on whom and when tax would be charged.

There were some areas of the question where candidates had imperfect information and they had to think through the options for how events of the past would affect tax computations in the present (such as the tax implications of the previous incorporation on the base cost of the shares assets). These issues were useful in discriminating between good and excellent scripts. Even good candidates were often unaware of these subtleties in the question.

Candidates performing badly in this part often had insufficient knowledge to be able to analyse the scenario and could not discriminate between the tax differences of selling trade and assets and shares. Some of the poorer scripts simply copied out the checklists from the open book material, writing copious amounts about VAT, Stamp Duty and losses, none of which were relevant to the tax situation of the vendors. An alarming number of candidates thought that you could roll over a gain on shares sold into the purchase of an unincorporated business or that the company could roll over the gain on the sale of its assets into the purchase of an unincorporated business by a former shareholder. This particular issue shows a lack of understanding of the purpose of these reliefs and the rules that apply to their application. Another common error was to imply that individuals who are shareholders could receive the corporate substantial shareholding exemption.

Part 2 was relatively well answered. Poorer candidates failed to address both IHT and CGT. In identifying the effects of IHT on planning for future inheritances, candidates failed to spot the exemptions of agricultural property relief and business property relief (or they spotted APR, but missed BPR; available as the asset was shares in a company as well as a farm).

Part 3 was poorly answered. Candidates are still ignoring the topic of trusts and this is a fundamental part of the syllabus, in terms of tax planning for individuals and their business interests.

Overseas aspects of personal taxation

10 Bill Mickelson (June 2015)

Scenario

The candidate is advising the owner, Bill, of a sole trader business on his retirement and sale to his daughter, Wilma. The question requires a good understanding of owner managed businesses and business start-ups. The candidate is replying initially to Bill and should use appropriate language and style. The candidate then is asked to prepare briefing notes for a forthcoming client meeting with Wilma and Jorge, Wilma's husband-to-be. The clients have some misconceptions about the tax implications of the sale and gift of some of his assets and the candidate must be able to identify these misconceptions and offer appropriate advice in a manner the client can understand.

Marking guide

	Technical	Skills	Marks
10.1 Capital gains/income tax implications			
• Gain on building	–	1	
• Gift relief	1	2	
• Gain on goodwill (incl. ER)	1	2	
• Other assets	–	1	
• Rental income	1	1	
• Residence status	1	1	
	4	8	
10.2 Advice on residency status			
• Automatic overseas test	1	1	
• Automatic UK tests	1	1	
• Split year	1	2	
• Remittance basis	1	1	
	4	5	
Wilma's income and capital gains tax			
• Opening year losses	1	2	
• s.83 relief	1	1	
• s.72 relief	2	2	
• s.64 relief	1	1	
• Restriction	1	1	
• Calculation	1	2	
• Gain	–	1	
• s.261B relief	1	1	
	8	11	
Inheritance tax			
• PET	1	1	
• BPR	1	2	
	2	3	
Total marks	18	27	45
Maximum			30

10.1 Reply to Bill's email

To: Bill Mickelson
From: Tax Adviser
Date: 9 June 2019
Subject: Future plans

Gift of retail building to your daughter

The building is a chargeable asset and a gain needs to be calculated using the market value at the date of the gift as follows:

	£
Market value	130,000
Cost	(55,000)
Gain	75,000

If your daughter agrees it is possible to claim gift relief which would mean that no gain arises for you and hence no tax is payable.

For your daughter however the deemed cost of the building, which would otherwise be the market value above of £130,000, is reduced by the gain which would have been taxable (£75,000). Hence the deemed cost to her would become £55,000. Therefore your daughter may, depending on the law relevant when she sells the building, pay tax on a larger gain when she sells the building. Both you and your daughter must sign a joint election for you to get the gift relief. The time limit for making the election is four years after the end of the tax year in which the gift was made.

You should also consider the possibility that future tax rates may be higher for your daughter than the current 10% rate you would pay on this gain if you were not to claim gift relief.

Goodwill

Goodwill is also a chargeable business asset even though as you point out it is an intangible asset and as your daughter is paying you the market value for the goodwill, a capital gain must be calculated as follows:

	£
Consideration	175,000
Cost	–
Gain	175,000
Annual exempt amount	(11,700)
	163,300
CGT @ 10%	16,330

Entrepreneurs' relief will be available to be claimed as you are disposing of business assets used for your trade. Therefore the gain will be taxed at 10%.

The inventory will not give rise to capital gains tax liabilities as any gains or losses will be taken into account in determining the income tax liability on cessation of your business. Any items of plant and machinery sold at a gain are likely to be subject to small chattels relief.

Rental income

The rental income will be liable to income tax as property income. In the tax year 2019/20 this will be £12,000 (£9,000 plus 2/6 × £9,000). Although you will be receiving the income in Australia, this will form part of your UK taxable income.

You will still be tax resident in the UK as you will have spent more than 183 days in the UK in 2019/20.

Both working in Australia for three months and the receipt of the rental income in Australia may give rise to tax implications in Australia and you should seek the advice of an Australian tax adviser.

10.2 Briefing notes for a meeting with Jorge and Wilma

Advice for Jorge on his residency status

In 2019/20 Jorge will not meet any of the automatic overseas tests because although he appears to have been non-resident in the previous three tax years, he will be spending more than 46 days in the UK.

For 2019/20 it is very probable that he will meet both:

(a) the 183 days in the UK automatic test; and

(b) the automatic UK test for full-time work in the UK (because he intends to be here working for full-time for more than 365 days, working a 35-hour week). If either of these tests is passed he would be automatically UK resident for 2019/20.

Split year treatment should apply ie, he will only be tax resident in the UK from 1 October provided that he has not established sufficient 'ties' in the period before getting married and coming to the UK.

There are 5 whole months prior to the start of his job and therefore the days relevant to the sufficient ties test need to be scaled by 5/12.

In total Jorge will have spent 9 days in the UK in this period which is an annual equivalent of 22 days. As he appears not to have been resident in the previous three years and has less than 46 days in the UK in this period he meets the automatic overseas test for this period.

Should split year be appropriate, Jorge would be liable to capital gains tax on his worldwide assets once he is UK resident. Should he sell his Spanish house before moving to the UK the gain will not be taxable in the UK as the split year also applies to capital gains tax. He may have tax liabilities in Spain and should seek advice.

The remittance basis for foreign income and gains eg, on the Barcelona property, could apply on a claim. However, the effect of a claim would normally be to forfeit both the income tax personal allowance and the CGT annual exempt amount. In view of Jorge's lack of previous UK residence, the remittance basis charge would not apply.

Wilma's income and capital gains tax

Trading losses – opening year

	£
2019/20 – basis period (actual)	
1 August 2019 to 5 April 2020	
8 months to 5 April 2020 = 8/12 × £240,000 (loss)	(160,000)
2020/21	
12 months ending 31 July 2020	(240,000)
Add loss already assessed	160,000
	(80,000)

Loss in 2019/20 – Loss relief choices available to Wilma

s.83 – the loss could be carried forward against future profits of the same trade – however the cash flow effect of this would be sometime in the future.

s.72 – the loss occurs in the first year of trading – Tax losses incurred in the first four tax years of trade can be carried back against total income of the previous three tax years, setting the loss against the earliest tax year's total income first. In Wilma's case, she could potentially carry the loss back to the tax year 2016/17 and claim a repayment of income tax from that earlier year.

I do not have information about Wilma's income for earlier years back to 2016/17 and 2017/18 to determine whether relief for early years' trading losses should be claimed, though I do know that she was a higher rate tax payer in 2018/19 and the level of her income in 2019/20. If such a claim is made for the 2019/20 loss, the claim starts with 2016/17 even if income for that year is wholly or mainly covered by personal allowances.

S.64 permits Wilma to relieve the loss against net income in 2019/20 and/or 2018/19. Given that her income in 2019/20 is likely to be covered by her personal allowance, a claim against 2018/19 would be a better use of the loss.

The loss relief is restricted to the highest of 25% of adjusted total income and £50,000. For 2018/19, 25% of adjusted income is £34,000 (£136,000 × 25%).

	2018/19 £	2019/20 £
Employment income	120,000	10,000
Property income	16,000	
Net income	136,000	10,000
s.64 loss relief	(50,000)	
Personal allowance	(11,850)	(11,850)
Taxable income	74,150	Nil
Tax liability		
34,500 × 20%	6,900	
39,650 × 40%	15,860	
	22,760	

The property income arising on the holiday home gifted to her by her grandmother will be subject to income tax.

Wilma is incorrect to say that the gain on her holiday home is not chargeable.

The asset was gifted to her and she is permitted to deduct the market value at the time of the gift as the allowable cost on its disposal.

Potentially therefore there is a 2018/19 chargeable gain as follows:

	£
Disposal proceeds	485,000
Cost	(445,000)
Gain	40,000

However, Wilma may extend the claim under s.64 for any unrelieved trading loss to be set against chargeable gains for the year of the loss and/or the previous year. The relevant legislation s.261B TCGA 1992.

s.261B loss is the lower of:

	£
The unrelieved trading loss	
£160,000 – £50,000	110,000
And:	
The current year gains less current year losses less brought forward losses	
£40,000 – £5,000	35,000

Therefore the gain becomes:

	£
Gain	40,000
Less current year loss (s.261B)	(35,000)
	5,000
Annual exempt amount	(5,000)
Taxable gain	Nil

Wilma's inheritance tax

The gift of the holiday home to Wilma was a PET. Any IHT due will be payable on her grandmother's estate as she did not survive seven years after the gift. The transfer will be subject to taper relief. The nil rate band may be available dependent on other gifts.

Business property relief is not available if the property was not a furnished holiday let. It seems unlikely that these provisions were satisfied for the brief period that the property was let and would in any case depend upon whether it were used as a furnished holiday let by the donor. In any event it appears the property had been sold before the donor died, so, as there seems to be no question of replacement property, business property relief would not be due.

Examiner's comments

Most candidates scored well with regard to Bill's situation, although many failed to note that the question specifically asked for capital gains tax implications and the income tax liability in respect of the rental income and thus spent unnecessary time discussing issues such as IHT.

However, there were very few answers that were couched in such a way that a non-technical client could really understand the content. A statement like 'Wilma's base cost is £55,000', is really not going to mean much to a bike mechanic.

Some candidates incorrectly thought that gift relief would be available on the goodwill gain even though full market price had been paid by Wilma.

The answers to part 2 were much more variable in quality, although most candidates managed to pick up at least some of the more straightforward marks.

Most candidates considered the application of the statutory residence test to Jorge's situation and identified the relevance of the split year basis with the best candidates going on to consider the relevance to the disposal of his house and the need to consider the Spanish position when deciding on the most tax efficient approach.

The section on Wilma's income tax and capital gains tax liability was often done badly, or not at all. Most candidates managed to say something relevant about her capital gains liability but very often completely missed out her income tax liability. It was disappointing to note errors such as the offset of the capital loss against the tax payable rather than the gain itself. Only the best candidates identified the point about carry back of business losses against other income.

11 Gooch Food (June 2014)

Scenario

In this question the candidate is asked to advise on tax treatments which are intended to minimise or defer tax liabilities. The three proposals were: a partnership arrangement between the client and his spouse; a discretionary trust; and a scheme to pay employees through an offshore company. In this question the candidate needs to understand the interaction of taxes and to be able to discriminate between legitimate tax planning and tax evasion. The candidate is also required to consider the ethical implications of their own position as an ICAEW Chartered Accountant working for a company rather than in professional practice.

	Marks	
	Technical	**Skills**

11.1 Partnership with Neeta
	Technical	Skills
• Income tax savings	1	2
• NIC costs	1	1
• Legal aspects/registration	1	1
• VAT	-	1
• CGT	½	1
• IHT	½	1
	4	7

11.2 Implications of a discretionary trust
	Technical	Skills
• CLT and lifetime tax	1½	2½
• Tax on death	½	½
	2	3

11.3 Paying employees through an overseas company
	Technical	Skills
	2	2

11.4 Shar's residency status in 2019/20 and 2020/21
	Technical	Skills
• Residence status incl. split year	1	2
• Taxation of UK business	-	1
• Remittance basis	2	1
• Calculation – no RBC	2	1
• Calculation – RBC	1	1
• Conclusion	-	2
	6	8

11.5 Ethics
	Technical	Skills
• Objectivity	1	1
• Professional care and competency	1	3
• Tax evasion, avoidance and PCRT	1	3
	3	7

	Technical	Skills	
Total marks	17	27	44
Maximum			25

11.1 Partnership with Neeta

In principle the advice to set up a partnership with Neeta could save tax for the couple as Neeta is not fully using her basic rate band.

Shar's business has a 5 April year end and therefore in the year ended 5 April 2019 Shar saved tax at his marginal rate of tax on Neeta's salary as it was deducted in arriving at his business profits.

If Neeta becomes a partner on 6 April 2020 and receives a profit share in the year ending 5 April 2021, she will use her full personal allowance and basic rate band. She will pay tax at 20% on the income above the personal allowance, saving Shar marginal rate tax at a higher percentage.

However, Neeta's salary will no longer be tax deductible, so the taxable profits will increase by £8,424.

There will be additional class 4 NIC to pay. Neeta will be liable for class 4 NIC on the excess over £8,424 ie, (£45,000 – 8,424) × 9% = £3,292. However, if Neeta had not been a partner, Shar would have only paid NIC at 2% ie, on the £45,000 since this falls above the upper annual profits limit. Overall additional class 4 NIC is payable.

Overall therefore the couple will save tax but pay more NIC.

Tutorial note

Detailed calculations were not required as stated in the question.

A partnership structure is very easy to create although it is advisable that Shar and Neeta obtain legal advice in drawing up a partnership agreement to determine profit sharing ratios and other matters.

A partnership is itself not a taxable person and for Neeta to become a partner in Gooch Food she would need to register as self-employed. She would be taxed on a share of the profits and pay class 4 NIC.

The partnership would need to become VAT registered.

There would be a CGT disposal as Shar is disposing of a share in his business. However, the transfer would be at a no gain/no loss basis as it would be between husband and wife.

There would also be a PET for IHT, but the spouse exemption would apply (because Shar is not UK domiciled, there would be no limit on the spouse exemption even if Neeta is also not UK domiciled).

11.2 Implications of a discretionary trust

All discretionary trusts are relevant property trusts which mean that when an individual sets up a trust it is a chargeable life time transfer. If Shar has not made any other lifetime transfers the transfer would fall within the nil rate band of £325,000 and IHT would be charged at 0%.

The Tx3 adviser however has made this assessment on the basis of a single interview with Shar – in reality he would have to look back seven years from the date of the creation of the trust to determine whether other chargeable transfers had been made.

If other transfers of value have been made then lifetime tax may become payable on the creation of the trust. This would be at the rate of 20% if the trustees agree to pay the lifetime tax and 25% if Shar pays the tax.

If Shar survives for more than seven years then no further IHT tax will be due. In that respect the advice is correct.

11.3 Paying employees through an overseas company

The scheme has the hall marks of tax evasion since there is a deliberate intention to hide information from HMRC. Potentially the scheme would fall within the definition of money laundering.

My clear advice to Shar is not to pursue this scheme further.

11.4 Shar's residency status in 2019/20 and claim for remittance basis

The Tx3 adviser's advice is incorrect in respect of Shar's residency status in 2019/20.

Assuming Shar moves to Ganda on 1 November 2019 and spends four weeks in the UK in December 2019 – he will have more than 183 days in the UK. He therefore satisfies the automatic UK residency test.

The split year rules will not apply since he will almost certainly be UK resident in 2020/21 as he will spend five weeks in the summer in the UK and will return in September 2020 to live in the UK (10 months after his departure on 1 November 2019) – which again is more than 183 days in the UK in 2020/21.

Therefore Shar will be taxed on all the profits of his UK business in the tax year 2019/20 and on his overseas income.

Shar, however, is non-domiciled in the UK. Therefore he could potentially be able to apply to be a remittance basis user in respect of his foreign income.

The remittance basis will not apply automatically as Shar's overseas income is greater than £2,000. Therefore he must make a claim to be a remittance basis user (RBU).

As Shar has already lost his entitlement to a personal allowance due to the level of his income, this is not a factor in the decision of whether to claim to be a RBU or not.

Income tax – arising basis – without remittance basis

	NSI £	Dividend £
Income tax		
UK trading	150,000	
Overseas partnership income	75,000	
Dividends (assuming shares not transferred to discretionary trust)		36,000
Net income	225,000	36,000
Less personal allowance (>£123,700)	Nil	
Taxable income	225,000	36,000
Non-savings income		
34,500 × 20%	6,900	
115,500 × 40%	46,200	
75,000 × 45%	33,750	
Dividend income		
2,000 × 0%	–	
34,000 × 38.1%	12,954	
Income tax liability	99,804	

With remittance basis

	NSI £	Dividend £
Income tax		
UK Trading	150,000	
Overseas partnership income	Nil	
Dividends (assuming shares not transferred to discretionary trust)		36,000
Net income	150,000	36,000
Less personal allowance (RB claim)	Nil	
Taxable income	150,000	36,000
Non-savings income		
34,500 × 20%		6,900
115,500 × 40%		46,200
Dividend income		
2,000 × 0%		–
34,000 × 38.1%		12,954
Remittance basis charge present for at least 7 years out of the last 9 years but less than 12 years		30,000
Income tax liability		96,054

Therefore on the basis of the above calculation, Shar should be advised to become a remittance basis user in 2019/20.

This answer assumes that there are no DTR implications in Ganda, which would need to be investigated.

11.5 Ethical and professional considerations

Objectivity

My relationship with Shar and Neeta is that I am their employee, therefore there are significant threats to my objectivity and independence created by this relationship.

In respect of the advice concerning the partnership for Neeta, I must consider both parties and not present a biased view in favour of Shar or Neeta.

Professional care and competency

I have been requested to provide information about their personal tax positions. I need to take due care that I have all the information available to make recommendations to them. I need to make it clear to them that I am not acting in anyway as their adviser in their tax affairs but offering advice as an employee of the business.

I must also ensure that I have up-to-date technical knowledge before I give my advice to Shar and Neeta.

As a professional I need to be aware of my limitations in terms of technical knowledge. My advice must be caveated with this in mind, and I must advise very firmly that Shar and Neeta consult an independent tax adviser with the appropriate qualifications and knowledge.

Proposal 3 – Tax evasion

If Shar were to accept the advice from Tx3 in respect of proposal 3, I could not allow myself to be involved in tax evasion and would therefore resign my employment. I would also seek legal advice as the transaction may fall within the Money Laundering regulations and seek advice from the ICAEW ethical helpline.

Even if this is not considered to be tax evasion, HMRC may consider this to be aggressive tax avoidance and may challenge the treatment of the arrangement. Shar should be made to consider whether the GAAR applies ie, whether the 'double reasonableness test' applies:

- Is it reasonable to conclude that obtaining a tax advantage was one of the main purposes of the arrangements?

- Are the arrangements abusive (ie, not a reasonable course of action)?

Although I am not providing the tax planning advice, PCRT Standards for tax planning state that I should not become involved in tax planning arrangements that either aim to achieve results not intended by Parliament, or are highly artificial seeking to exploit loopholes in the legislation. Proposal 3 appears to fit these criteria.

Tutorial note

Credit would not be awarded for discussing the managed service company structure, but credit would be awarded for advising Shar whether such a scheme would be appropriate given the circumstances outlined.

Examiner's comments

Partnership

This question required the candidates to consider the overall tax saving, NIC and CGT consequences of making Neeta a partner.

It was surprising how many candidates were clearly unaware that a partnership is an unincorporated business and considered corporate remuneration strategies, such as the payment of dividends.

Whilst some candidates adopted the correct approach and discussed that making Neeta a partner would enable utilisation of her basic rate band and a decrease in profit share for Shar, other candidates produced very confused answers which referred to extraction of profit via dividend with no NIC consequences and quite detailed calculations on the income tax liability as a consequence for both Neeta and Shar. Only a small minority of exceptional candidates considered the fact that making Neeta a partner would be a disposal for CGT but would be at no gain/no loss.

Discretionary Trust

Answers to this part displayed that candidates are very comfortable with questions containing IHT. Most candidates made relevant comments in connection with the establishment of the trust and scored well on this section but failed to appreciate that the question only asked for the IHT implications of setting up the trust, thus providing irrelevant information on CGT and income tax implications.

Unfortunately therefore, candidates wasted time by discussing the income tax consequences of the creation of the trust, 10-year charges and exit charges when the question quite clearly stated that all that was required was the IHT consequences of setting up the trust. This could be interpreted to include the implications of the trust once the funds are in there, but these would be less important than the implications of the initial transfer of funds into the trust. It was worrying how many candidates asserted there would be BPR on the transfer into trust, given the assets transferred into trust were a portfolio of quoted shares, BPR would only ever be available at the 50% rate and only then if a majority stake was held in the quoted company. Clearly this was very unlikely to be the case in this instance.

Where candidates referred to the fact that this was a CLT, that there would be lifetime tax at 20% or 25% and the amount payable would depend upon any other chargeable transfers in the last seven years, full marks were awarded.

Overseas company

Answers to this part were very mixed. The question included lots of signposts for candidates which should have indicated that attempting to 'hide' employees from HMRC was clearly tantamount to tax evasion. Whilst some candidates did recognise this, a significant number went down the route of managed service companies and IR35. Credit was given for appropriate discussion of the operation of DOTAS.

Residence

Whilst the majority of candidates displayed that they understood and could apply the new SRT, others produced very mixed up answers which incorrectly concluded that Shar would be treated as an overseas resident for both tax years. Whilst other answers identified that he would be UK resident in 2019/20, they then went on to consider the split year treatment for 2020/21 which was incorrect. Though the question did ask for calculations, these were not always produced. However, those candidates performing calculations were usually rewarded with high marks on this part of their answers.

A common error made was inclusion of the remittance basis of £60,000 and not £30,000 which indicated a failure by candidates to get to grips properly with the dates and the information in the question.

Ethics

This section was attempted poorly by a significant majority of candidates who mainly just repeated their considerations from part 3 of the question and considered DOTAS, GAAR and evasion. Only a small number of candidates went on to consider objectivity and professional care in terms of the advice. Few mentioned the relevant areas of concern such as the conflict of interest arising in the first part of the question and the independence and intimidation threats.

The main problem with most answers was the failure of candidates to understand their role and recognise that, in this question, they were an employee and not a professional adviser. Those candidates who failed to appreciate the scenario in this question and overlooked the fact that they were actually an employee of Gooch Food discussed engagement letters and separate teams which were clearly not relevant to the scenario. Candidates need to ensure for future sittings that they read the scenarios very carefully.

Some very weak candidates discussed the ethical implications for the Tx3 Advisers.

(The PCRT standards for tax planning became part of the syllabus after this exam but are relevant to the answer.)

Single companies

12 Valese plc (June 15)

Scenario

The candidate is in the role of a trainee ICAEW Chartered Accountant working as the financial controller at Valese plc a UK trading company and a parent company of a UK group. The candidate is reporting to the CEO as his line manager, the finance director is on holiday and therefore is required to communicate in an appropriate manner. The scenario involves the liquidation of a 70% owned subsidiary, Mendit Ltd. The candidate is initially required to:

"Explain the possible loss reliefs for Mendit Ltd's trading losses arising in the year ended 31 March 2019 and projected for the five month period ending 31 August 2019 and recommend the most tax efficient use of the losses. Calculate the amount of tax repayment due to Mendit Ltd as a result of your recommendation. (Ignore for this purpose the disposal of Mendit Ltd's office building.)"

The second half of the question requires the candidate to consider two alternative proposals for the timing of the disposal of the company's main asset and the payment of distributions to the shareholders. If the building is sold prior to the appointment of the liquidator, the company's trading loss can be used to reduce the chargeable gain and hence the amount of tax payable by the company. A distribution before the appointment of a liquidator would be treated as an income distribution and create a relative high personal tax liability for the minority shareholder. The second requirement was therefore:

"For each of the two alternative proposals for the timing of the sale of Mendit Ltd's office building (Exhibit 2):

- explain and calculate the tax implications for Mendit Ltd, Valese plc and for Gary of the liquidation of Mendit Ltd on 1 September 2019.

- calculate the cash receivable post liquidation by both Valese plc and Gary.

- recommend which proposal should be chosen."

The ethics requirement involved the candidate considering the implications of a request by the CEO to access the personal email account of his line manager the FD, who is suspected of dealing in secret in the company's shares. Specifically the candidate is required to do the following:

"Evaluate the ethical and professional issues for you arising from Ken Kingsley's request for you to access the finance director's personal email account. Determine the actions you should take."

Marking guide

	Technical	Skills
12.1 Working paper		
Loss reliefs available		
• Carry forward and group relief	1	1
• Terminal loss	2	2
• Remaining loss	1	1
• Order of relief	1	1
• Calculation of tax relief	1	2
• Calculation of refunds	1	2
	7	9

	Technical	Skills	Marks
Proposal 1			
• Mendit – sale of office	1	2	
• Dividend	1	3	
• Distribution on liquidation	1	2	
• Cash available	1	2	
• Final distribution	1	3	
	5	12	
Proposal 2			
• Mendit	1	1	
• Gary	1	1	
• Valese	–	1	
• Cash available	1	2	
• Final distribution	1	2	
	4	7	
Recommendation			
• Valese	–	1½	
• Gary	–	1½	
• Compromise	–	1	
	–	4	
12.2 Ethical issues			
• Fundamental principles	1	1	
• Intimidation threat	1	1	
• Safeguards	1	1	
	3	3	
Total marks	19	35	54
Maximum			40

12.1 Working paper responding to the briefing from Ken Kingsley

As Mendit Ltd will cease to trade its loss cannot be carried forward. Therefore the best use of the losses is by means of current year and carry back claims.

Mendit Ltd is not a member of the Valese plc group for group relief purposes as the shareholding in Mendit Ltd is less than 75%. A consortium claim cannot be made by a member of the Valese group, as it is not the case that companies owning at least 5% of the shares of Mendit Ltd own at least 75% of its shares.

There is a strict order in which losses are dealt with and the losses of earlier years are dealt with first.

The loss of the last 12 months is available under s.39 CTA 2010 for an extended carry back period of up to three years from the beginning of the 31 March 2019 accounting period under a LIFO basis. There are two elements to the terminal loss calculation as follows:

Calculation of terminal loss relief

		£'000
Loss in the last 12 months		
Year ended 31 March 2019	£350,000 × 7/12	204
Period ending 31 August 2019		321
Terminal loss		525

As some of the terminal loss arises in the accounting period 1 April 2018 – 31 March 2019, part of the loss is eligible to be carried back for three years against profits arising from 1 April 2015.

Part of the loss arising in the year ended 31 March 2019 is not eligible for terminal loss relief and this should therefore be dealt with first and set off against current year profits under s.37(3)(a) CTA 2010 and then carried back under s.37(3)(b).

£350,000 × 5/12 = £145,833

The remainder of the loss of the year ended 31 March 2019 (£204,167) is relieved under s.39 against the three years from the beginning of the accounting period (terminal loss relief), as noted above ie, from 1 April 2015.

Loss relating to 5 month period to 31 August 2019 is dealt with next. The loss arising in the period to 31 August 2019 is eligible for carry back against profits arising from 1 April 2016 ie, 3 years before the beginning of the accounting period. There is no other income in the accounting period and therefore this loss is eligible under s.39 (the question excludes consideration of the disposal of the building for this requirement but see below). However, there are no remaining profits available in the three years prior to the commencement of the accounting period and therefore the loss of £321,000 remains unrelieved.

Years ended 31 March	2016 £'000	2017 £'000	2018 £'000	2019 £'000
Tax adjusted trading (loss)/profit	234	121	148	
Property income	16	13	15	18
	250	134	163	18
CY s.37(a) – Y/E 31 March 2019				(18)
CB s.37(b) – Y/E 31 March 2019			(128)	
TLR s.39 – Y/E 31 March 2019	(35)	(134)	(35)	
	215	Nil	Nil	Nil

Calculation of tax refund arising on use of loss relief

	Loss relief claimed £'000	Tax rate %	Refund £'000
2018	163	19	31
2017	134	20	27
2016	35	20	7
			65

In addition the corporation tax payable for the year ended 31 March 2019 is reduced by £3,420 (£18,000 × 19%), to give a total tax saving of approximately £68,000.

PROPOSAL 1

Sale of office building followed by the appointment of the liquidator on 1 September 2019

Implications for Mendit Ltd

Mendit Ltd will realise a chargeable gain on the disposal of the building. Mendit Ltd has an unrelieved trading loss of £321,000 for the five-month period ending 31 August 2019. Therefore the chargeable gain on the sale of the building will be relieved by this loss and no tax will be payable on this gain.

The building is an old commercial building and no VAT will be payable on its disposal.

Implications for Valese plc and Gary

Distributions of cash or assets, such as the £900,000 dividend, prior to liquidation are treated as normal income distributions.

Gary has already used his dividend nil rate band and will therefore be taxed at 38.1% on the full amount, as he is an additional rate payer.

The distribution received by Valese plc will not be taxable.

Therefore the tax implications of the pre liquidation dividend are as follows:

	Valese plc £'000	Gary £'000
Dividend	630.00	270.00
Tax due at effective rate of nil/38.1%	–	102.87
Net cash received by shareholders	630.00	167.13

A further distribution to the shareholders will be made during the liquidation, the amount depending upon the realisation proceeds of the other assets etc; this distribution will be treated as a capital distribution as under Proposal 2.

Both Gary and Valese will be able to deduct the cost of acquiring the shares of £75,000 and £875,000 respectively.

The capital loss for Valese plc is covered by the SSE and is therefore not available to be used by the Valese plc group.

The capital loss for Gary is available for use against capital gains in the year and if there are none, for carry forward against future chargeable gains.

Calculation of cash receivable by the shareholders

Proposal 1

	£'000
Office building	1,600
Other assets	400
Bank loan	(500)
Bank overdraft	(200)
Trade and other payables	(300)
Add tax repayment (see above)	65
Cash available	1,065

	Valese plc £'000	Gary £'000
Pre liquidation dividend after tax as per above	630.0	167.13
Final distribution 70:30 (£1,065,000 – £900,000)	115.5	49.50
Less cost	(875.0)	(75.00)
(Loss)	(759.5)	(25.50)
Net cash received on final distribution	115.5	49.50
Total cash received	745.5	216.63

Tutorial note

A tax repayment of either £65,000 or £68,000 would be acceptable in the exam ie, including or excluding the tax reduction for the year ended 31 March 2019.

PROPOSAL 2

Appointment of the liquidator on 1 September 2019 followed by the sale of the building

Implications for Mendit Ltd

On the appointment of the liquidator the trading loss arising in the period to 31 August 2019 cannot be carried forward.

If the building is sold after the appointment of the liquidator as under Proposal 2, there are no profits available to set against the gain and therefore corporation tax of £57,000 (£300,000 × 19%) will be payable in respect of this gain.

Implications for Gary

If a distribution is made after the appointment of the liquidator it will be treated as a capital distribution for both Gary and Valese plc who will be able to deduct the cost of acquiring the shares of £75,000 and £875,000 respectively.

Gary should be eligible for entrepreneurs' relief and therefore, as he owns at least 5% of the shares and is a director of the company, will pay tax at 10% subject to the gain not exceeding his lifetime limit of £10 million.

Implications for Valese plc

The conditions for the substantial shareholdings exemption appear to have been met as Valese plc owns at least 10% of the ordinary share capital and has done so for at least 12 months.

Therefore any gain or loss arising for Valese plc on the final distribution will be exempt.

Proposal 2

	£'000
Factory building	1,600
Other assets	400
Bank loan	(500)
Bank overdraft	(200)
Trade and other payables	(300)
Add tax repayment (see above)	65
Less tax on disposal of building	(57)
Cash available	1,008

	Valese plc £'000	Gary £'000
Final distribution (70:30)	705.6	302.4
Less cost	(875.0)	(75.0)
(Loss)/Gain	(169.4)	227.4
Less annual exempt amount		(11.7)
		215.7
Tax at 10%		21.6
Net cash on final distribution	705.6	280.8

Recommendation

Selling the building before the appointment of the liquidator results in a higher post liquidation receipt for Valese plc because the gain on the disposal of the building can be offset against the trading loss arising in the period to 31 August 2019. Neither the dividend nor the distribution results in any additional tax for Valese plc, although the loss arising on the disposal of the shares in Mendit Ltd is not available as it is within the SSE.

However Proposal 2 results in a higher post liquidation receipt for Gary as, under Proposal 1, he is liable to the additional dividend tax rate. The effect may be mitigated if the capital loss of £25,500 can be used against capital gains.

A possible solution would be to sell the building and pay either a lower or no pre-liquidation dividend before the appointment of the liquidator.

12.2 Ethics

I am being asked by the CEO, a person to whom I currently report, to access the personal email account of the Finance Director, who is normally my line manager, and pass information from it to the CEO.

I am not in a position to determine if the finance director has committed an offence as I do not have the information to make that judgement.

I have been asked however to breach the fundamental principles of confidentiality as the finance director has trusted me with his email password only for emergency situations, which would not include the request from the CEO; and also professional behaviour and integrity since I would be becoming party to information to which I was not intended to have access.

The CEO's request leads to an intimidation threat since the CEO is in a position of authority and if I do not comply then he could potentially have a detrimental impact on my career development within the firm.

No safeguards seem to be relevant so, to address these threats, I should inform the CEO that I am not prepared to access the email account for this purpose.

Examiner's comments

The best candidates were those where the answer was properly laid out in a logical form. The question briefing very clearly suggested the appropriate format for the answer: discuss the losses, then each of the alternative proposals, then provide a recommendation. Poorer-quality answers tended to start somewhere in the middle; for example, discussing Gary's options, then moving on to loss reliefs, then going back to the proposals again. Given that the question layout was so clear, it seemed perverse not to use the obvious layout for the answer.

Generally, candidates produced very detailed answers to this question, and covered most of the relevant issues. The best answers were excellent.

Specific comments on sections of the question:

Loss reliefs

Almost all candidates got the point about terminal loss relief and attempted appropriate calculations. Some incorrectly thought that the ownership structure of Mendit allowed for consortium relief, or even group relief. It was however disappointing to see a number of references to overlap profits in the corporate scenario.

Two proposals

Not all candidates made it clear whether they were talking about proposal one or two. A surprising number failed to identify Gary's base cost of his shareholding, and indeed many simply applied the (appropriate or otherwise) tax rate to the gross distribution even in the capital situation. Many candidates also determined the net cash available after deduction of the annual exempt amount rather than deducting the tax payable from the net proceeds. Some candidates were concerned about minimising tax liabilities rather than the cash receivable post liquidation.

Not all candidates managed to make a recommendation at the end of the answer. Those that did provide one, often demonstrated good skills at appreciating the scenario from different perspectives.

Ethics

Answers to the ethics element of the question varied in quality. Some candidates were side-tracked by the suggestion of money-laundering by the finance director, but that was not the focus of the question. The ethical dilemma was clearly posed for the financial controller in relation to accessing the FD's email account. The better candidates were concise in their answers and in a time-constrained examination this was a wise approach to adopt.

13 Fastmole Ltd

		Technical	Skills	Marks
(a)	Class 1A NIC in respect of residential property	1	2	
	ATED	1	1	
	Taxation of gain on property	1	4	
	Foreign currency gain	1	3	
	Sale of machinery	1	3	
(b)	Calculation of change in tax liabilities	2	3	
(c)	Amendments of returns, plus new return	1	2	
	Penalties and interest	1	1	
		9	19	
Total marks				28
Maximum				25

(a) Briefing notes

Residential property

Class 1A NIC

The annual benefit of the property is the annual value plus an additional benefit because the cost of the property exceeded £75,000. The market value when the property was first provided to the employee is used in the calculation ie, the original cost to the company. The corporation tax computation for the year ended 31 March 2019 should include the NIC costs of the 2018/19 tax year.

	£
Annual value	38,000
Additional benefit (£(2,568,000 – 75,000) × 2.5%)	62,325
	100,325
Class 1A NIC @ 13.8%	13,845

The additional class 1A of £8,601 (13,845 – 5,244) is deductible from the company's trading profits and so there will be a corporation tax saving of £1,634 (£8,601 @ 19%) on the increased NIC.

Annual Tax on Enveloped Dwellings (ATED)

The company's interest is within the charge to ATED as the value of the residential property exceeded £2 million on 1 April 2017. The annual charge is £24,250 as paid by the company, but because the property was sold on 30 June 2018, this can be reduced to 3/12 of this amount. An amended ATED return should be submitted to recover £18,188 (9/12 of £24,250).

Tax treatment of the gain on the disposal of the property

As the residential property was subject to the ATED charge, and has been disposed of for more than £500,000, capital gains tax is payable by the company.

The CGT is calculated using a cost equal to the market value of the property on 5 April 2013 (ie, approximately £3,112,000 here).

	£
Proceeds	3,718,000
Cost (MV at 5 April 2013)	(3,112,000)
Taxable gain	606,000
CGT at 28%	169,680

The element of gain prior to 5 April 2013 is charged to corporation tax:

	£
Proceeds (MV at 5 April 2013)	3,112,000
Cost	(2,568,000)
	544,000
Indexation allowance (249.5 – 234.4)/234.4 = 0.064	(164,352)
	379,648
CT at 19%	72,133

Therefore the total tax on the gain on disposal of the property = £169,680 + £72,133 = £241,813.

Foreign currency loan

The loan would have been initially recognised in the accounts using the rate on 1 April 2018 but revalued at 31 March 2019 for the accounts, with the difference reflected in the income statement.

	Loan value	Exchange difference
1 April 2018	500,000/1.24 = 403,226	
31 March 2019	500,000/1.12 = 446,429	43,203 loss
30 April 2019	500,000/1.08 = 462,963	16,534 loss

As the loan was used for trading purposes, the exchange loss of £43,203 at 31 March 2019 should have been deducted from trading income ie, not added back to the accounting profits figure. Therefore, this amount should be deducted from the figure used in the CT computation for the year ended 31 March 2019.

The remaining exchange loss of £16,534 will be deducted in the following year, with no adjustment required to accounting profits.

Sale of machinery

The financial controller was correct to deduct the disposal value of the machinery from the main pool. However, the disposal value is restricted to the lower of cost and proceeds. The cost of the machinery was £150,000. Provided Fastmole Ltd had given its VAT registration number to the vendor, the supply from the EU would have been zero-rated ie, the amount paid equals the cost to the company. This adjustment will increase the capital allowances available, and will affect the tax written down values brought forward at 1 April 2019.

Additionally, because the machinery is sold for a profit, a chargeable gain arises. The sale should have included VAT of £40,000 (£240,000 × 1/6), such that the proceeds were £200,000. Indexation runs to December 2017.

	£
Proceeds	200,000
Cost	(150,000)
	50,000
Indexation allowance (278.1 – 252.6)/252.6 = 0.101	(15,150)
	34,850
CT at 19%	6,622

(b) **Summary of additional taxes if treatment of these transactions is corrected**

	£	£
Residential property:		
Increase in class 1A NIC (13,845 – 5,244)	8,601	
Decrease in CT (19%) as a result of increased NIC	(1,634)	
	6,967	
7.25 years of error (Note)		50,511
Refund of ATED		(18,188)
Increase in tax (CGT and CT) on gains (241,813 – 127,747)		114,066
Foreign currency loan		
Decrease in CT due to taxation of foreign currency loss		
£43,203 at 19%		(8,209)
Decrease in CT due to increase in WDA		
(18% × (240,000 – 150,000) × 19%)		(3,078)
Increase in CT due to gain on sale of machinery		6,622
		141,724

Note: It is likely that the class 1A NIC in respect of the director's use of the property has been calculated incorrectly since 2011/12, such that there will be additional tax (NIC less CT saving) in the region of £6,967 for since that time (although varying for changes in corporation tax rates and the official rate of interest).

(c) **Other implications and actions to take**

In respect of the accommodation benefit, for each incorrect P11d submitted, there could be a £3,000 penalty and interest will be charged on underpaid class 1A NIC. The director's personal self assessment tax returns will also be incorrect and the director should inform HMRC.

The corporation tax return for the year ended 31 March 2019 is within the time limit for amendment and so this should be amended for the increased class 1A NIC deduction, for the changes to the corporation tax treatment of the residential property gain, for the increased capital allowances and for the deduction of the foreign currency loss.

There may be penalties for errors if the corporation tax return is not amended. These are reduced for disclosure, especially if unprompted.

The company pays corporation tax by instalments, but in fact the overall corporation tax charge decreases and so no additional payments are made.

A tax return must be submitted by 31 January 2020, including the part of the gain on the residential property that is chargeable to capital gains tax.

14 Unele Ltd

Marking guide

		Technical	Skills	Marks
14.1	Funds available for distribution	1	2	
	Pre-liquidation dividend	1	2	
	Post-liquidation distribution	1	4	
	Conclusions	1	1	
		4	9	
	Max			10
14.2	Costs of lease and equipment	1	-	
	VAT treatment of costs	1	2	
	SDLT	-	3	
	CT treatment of costs	1	2	
	Freelancer hours	1	1	
		4	8	
	Max			10

	Technical	Skills	Marks
14.3 Employee status argument	2	4	
Personal service company	1	2	
	3	6	
Max			7
14.4 Net relevant earnings	1	1	
High-income individuals	1	3	
Annual allowance charge	1	2	
	3	6	
Max			8
			35

14.1 Liquidation of Unele Ltd

Funds available for distribution

	£
Trading profits	98,000
Less redundancy payment (restricted to statutory amount plus 3 times that)	(20,000)
Less balancing allowance (24,000 – 8,000)	(16,000)
	62,000
Non-trade loan relationship credits	7,500
Taxable total profits	69,500
Corporation tax at 19%	13,205

Therefore, the cash available for distribution will be £380,000 + £8,000 – £13,205 = £374,795.

Pre-liquidation dividend

Cash received by each shareholder if distribution made prior to liquidation:

	Samantha £	Ian £	RK Ltd £
Dividend £374,795 80%/10%/10%	299,836	37,480	37,479
Less income tax 38.1%/W/nil	(114,238)	(1,574)	–
Net after tax receipt	185,598	35,906	37,479

There would be no corporation tax on the dividend received by RK Ltd. Samantha already receives other dividends from quoted company investments and so the dividend nil rate band will have already been used.

WORKING

Ian's income tax on dividend

	£
Dividend income	37,480
Less personal allowance	(11,850)
	25,630
Income tax:	
£2,000 at 0%	0
£(25,630 – 2,000) at 7.5%	1,772

Post-liquidation distribution

If the distribution is made after the liquidation has commenced, then it will be treated as a capital disposal of the shares.

	Samantha £	Ian £	RK Ltd £
Proceeds	299,836	37,480	37,479
Less cost	(8,000)	(1,000)	(1,000)
Gain	291,836	36,480	36,479
Annual exempt amount	(11,700)	(11,700)	
Taxable gain	280,136	24,780	Nil
CGT at 10%	28,014	2,478	

Samantha has owned more than 5% of a trading company, and has been a director of the company, for more than one year, and so entrepreneurs' relief will be available on the gain. Therefore, it is taxed at 10%.

Ian is also taxed at 10% on the gain but because he has no other income and so the gain falls fully within the basic rate band.

The gain for RK Ltd is exempt because RK Ltd has owned a substantial shareholding (10%) for at least 12 months in the last six years, and Unele Ltd is a trading company. Therefore, the substantial shareholdings exemption is available.

The net proceeds received from a post-liquidation distribution are:

	Samantha £	Ian £	RK Ltd £
Proceeds	299,836	37,480	37,479
Tax	(28,014)	(2,478)	
Net after tax cash	271,822	35,002	37,479

In conclusion, Samantha would prefer the post-liquidation distribution, receiving £86,224 (£271,822 – £185,598) more than if she were to receive a pre-liquidation dividend. Ian, however, would prefer the pre-liquidation dividend as he would receive £904 (£35,906 – £35,002) more than if he received the post-liquidation distribution. Samantha could gift Ian this difference from her much larger net proceeds.

It makes no difference to RK Ltd whether the distribution is pre or post liquidation as no tax is due in either case.

14.2 Costs in the first year of the expansion

	Cost £	CT deductible cost £
Lease premium (£20,000 + (£20,000 × 20% × 23%)) (W1)	20,920	960
Annual rent (£12,000 + (£12,000 × 20% × 23%))	12,552	12,552
Equipment (£30,000 + (£30,000 × 20% × 23%))	31,380	31,380
Plus SDLT on lease (W2)	660	–
	65,512	44,892
Less CT deduction £44,892 × 19%	(8,529)	
Costs in the first year of the expansion	56,983	

Notes and assumptions:

The proportion of taxable supplies to total supplies is 260,000/340,000 = 77% (rounded up). Therefore 23% of the VAT incurred on expenditure to make both supplies is irrecoverable and is a cost to the company.

Duote Ltd uses the leased property in its trade, and so an element of the lease premium payment is deductible, being 1/15 of the landlord's property income assessment (W1).

Assuming that Duote Ltd has not already used the whole annual investment allowance, the cost of the equipment can be fully relieved by the AIA.

WORKINGS

(1) **Deductible element of lease premium**

Property income assessable on landlord = £20,000 × (51 – 15)/50 = £14,400

Annual deduction = £14,400/15 = £960

(2) **SDLT on lease**

The annual rent is charged with standard-rated VAT as the landlord has exercised the option to tax ie, annual rent is £12,000 × 1.2 = £14,400.

The NPV of the lease rentals is 15 × £14,400 = £216,000.

SDLT on the lease rentals = (216,000 – 150,000) × 1% = £660.

There is no SDLT on the lease premium as the amount is less than £150,000 (and so 0% SDLT).

Calculation of freelancer hours

Funds available in first year to pay freelancers = £150,000 – £56,983 = £93,017.

Freelancer hours cost £50 per hour or £40.50 after CT deduction at 19%. This means £93,017/40.5 = 2,296 hours can be purchased.

14.3 Tax risks of engaging freelancers – employment status issues

Duote Ltd is able to engage up to five freelancers with total annual hours of 2,296 between them ie, each freelancer may provide approximately 460 hours per year, or more than one full day's work per week. Duote Ltd may use fewer freelancers and give them more hours.

Duote Ltd will provide equipment for the freelancers.

The company will also provide a place for the freelancers to work suggesting that the company will control the work.

The work also seems to be ongoing over time, rather than a single defined project, although limited in terms of the hours that could be offered.

It follows that the freelancers may actually be employees rather than self-employed. If this were the case, Duote Ltd would have to pay class 1 secondary national insurance contributions, and operate a PAYE system for paying the workers. Although the NIC would be an allowable deduction for corporation tax purposes, the overall costs of the workers would increase.

Whether the freelancers would be considered employees depends on other factors such as the wording of the contract. A contract for services is made between the company and a genuine freelancer. A contract of services is made with an employee.

The contract can determine whether the freelancer can decide whether to accept more work, and whether Duote Ltd will agree always to provide a set number of hours of work (mutuality of obligations). One factor which would help argue against employee status would be if the freelancer could send a substitute to do the work instead of themselves. A self-employed person is not entitled to sick pay or holiday pay. Equally if the freelancer has to rectify any defective work in their own time and at their own cost, this would suggest they are not acting as an employee.

Working for other clients would help but would not necessarily indicate that an employee relationship does not exist.

If the freelancer is engaged through a company but would be deemed an employee if engaged directly, then the personal service company rules would apply. That company would be deemed to make a salary payment to the freelancer on 5 April each year, and would have to pay class 1 secondary national insurance on this. The freelancer would also have to pay class 1 primary national insurance and income tax on this. This would be a similar situation to that of the freelancer being treated as an employee except that the personal service company bears the NIC costs rather than Duote Ltd.

15.4 Personal pension contribution

Gross contribution = £30,000 × 100/80 = £37,500.

Even without considering any salary from Unele Ltd, Samantha has net relevant earnings in 2019/20 of £100,000 because of the income from furnished holiday lettings. Therefore, she can make the contribution of £37,500 in 2019/20 and receive income tax relief.

If a gross pension contribution exceeds the annual allowance, an annual allowance charge is due. The annual allowance for 2019/20 is £40,000 (assumed to be the same as 2018/19). However, this is reduced for high-income individuals.

Samantha is a high-income individual if both:

- her adjusted income exceeds £150,000; and
- her threshold income exceeds £110,000.

Assuming the distribution of funds from Unele Ltd takes place after the liquidation commences, Samantha's adjusted income (net income) will be £200,000 in 2019/20. Her threshold income will be £200,000 less £37,500 pension contribution ie, £162,500. Both the adjusted income and threshold income limits are exceeded and Samantha is therefore a high-income individual. Samantha's annual allowance for 2019/20 will be:

	£
Annual allowance 2019/20	40,000
Less ½ (200,000 – 150,000)	(25,000)
	15,000
Excess contributions = gross contribution less annual allowance	22,500
Annual allowance charge = £22,500 × 45%	10,125

The higher rate limit will be increased by £37,500 to £187,500 and so Samantha will save a further 25% tax relief on her gross contribution of £37,500 ie, £9,375 in addition to the £7,500 paid into her pension fund by HMRC. This gives total tax relief of £16,875 (£9,375 + £7,500). However, Samantha will still be an additional rate taxpayer, so the annual allowance charge is taxed at 45% and consequently £10,125 of this relief is clawed back. Net tax relief is reduced to £6,750 (being her annual allowance of £15,000 at her marginal rate of 45%).

15 Raffles Ltd (December 2015)

Scenario

This question built on a question set in the first sample exam produced for the new BP:T exam, and not examined in detail before December 2015; the topic of close companies and the consequences of close company loans to participators. The questions ranged across corporation tax anti-avoidance rules and income tax and national insurance contributions.

	Technical	Skills	Marks
Why company is close	1	1	
Qualifying interest	2	2	
	3	3	
Loans to participators			
Notional tax on loans to participators			
• Charge	1	–	
• Marion	1	1	
• Penalty charge	1	1	
• Write off	–	1 ½	
• Income tax	–	1 ½	
	3	5	
Notional tax on loans via director loan accounts			
• Kate	1	1	
• Laura	1	2	
	2	3	
Benefit of loan at cheap rate			
• Marion	1	–	
• Kate and Laura	1	3	
	2	3	
Benefits to participators			
• Laura	1	1	
• Company	–	2	
• Penelope	1	3	
	2	6	
Total marks	12	20	32
Maximum			25

Tutorial note

The examiners will not allocate marks for the report format of the answer.

Raffles Ltd is controlled by five or fewer participators/its directors (Kate and Laura own 80% of the company).

This makes Raffles Ltd a close company.

As a close company there are a number of transactions with the participators (shareholders) that need to be reported to HMRC and have tax consequences.

LAURA'S LOAN TO BUY HER SHARES IN RAFFLES LTD

A shareholder owning at least 5% of the share capital of a close company, who takes out a loan to buy shares in a close company can obtain tax relief for the interest paid on this loan, provided the shares in the company do not qualify for EIS relief.

For 2017/18 Laura was able to deduct interest of £11,250 (£150,000 × 15% × 6/12) from her total income in her income tax computation.

For 2018/19 this increased to £22,500 pa.

There should be no restriction on this deduction, under the rules concerning the restriction on income tax reliefs deductible against total income – given the deduction is the higher of £50,000 and 25% of adjusted total income.

LOANS TO PARTICIPATORS

There are two potential charges to tax on a loan to a participator:

- notional tax on the loan under s.455 CTA 2010; and
- a benefit if the participator is also an employee and paying a cheap rate of interest.

Notional tax – loans to participators

When a close company makes a loan to a participator, it must make a payment of notional tax to HMRC under s.455 CTA 2010.

The notional tax is 32.5% of the loan, and is payable 9 months and 1 day after the end of the accounting period in which the loan is made.

A loan to a director or employee is excluded from these rules if total loans to the participator do not exceed £15,000, the borrower works full-time for the company and the borrower does not have a material interest (over 5%) in the company.

Marion Miller's loan is therefore excluded from the s.455 charge, as her loan is less than £15,000, Marion works full-time for the company and her interest in the company is only 4%.

Penelope Phillips however does not work full-time for the company, so her loan is subject to the s.455 charge. The charge is £10,000 × 32.5% = £3,250 and is payable to HMRC on 1 July 2019.

Penelope's loan is to be written off in June 2019. As this date is before the s.455 tax has been paid, the s.455 tax will not be payable. However, the £10,000 written off will be treated as a distribution to Penelope.

Penelope will then pay tax of 32.5% on the distribution to the extent that it exceeds the dividend nil rate band. If Penelope has not used her dividend nil rate band she will have tax on the dividend of £2,600 ((£10,000 – £2,000) × 32.5%).

Notional tax – loans to the directors through their directors' loan accounts

Balances on directors' loan accounts are also potentially subject to a s.455 tax charge.

The directors' loan account balance for Kate Kendall is again, under £15,000 and Kate works full-time for the company. However, Kate has a material interest in the company and so s.455 tax is payable on her loan of £12,000. This will be 32.5% × £12,000 = £3,900, due on 1 July 2019, provided the loan account has not been repaid by this date.

The directors' loan account balance for Laura Lark of £25,000 gives rise to penalty tax of £8,125 (£25,000 × 32.5%). Her plan to repay the loan on 30 June 2019 and then take out a larger loan on 2 July 2019 is seen as an attempt to avoid the s.455 charge. The repayment of £25,000, will therefore be allocated as a repayment of the new loan and the s.455 penalty tax will still be due on 1 July 2019.

Benefit of a loan at a cheap rate of interest to a participator also an employee

If a participator is also an employee and receives a cheap or interest free loan, there is an additional tax charge on the benefit of the cheap interest.

Therefore Marion's loan of £10,000 could have given rise to an additional benefit. However, the beneficial loan rules require an employee loan to be over £10,000 for beneficial interest to be taxable.

The directors' loan account balances were interest free. As the balances were both in excess of £10,000, there is a benefit taxable on the directors as follows for 2018/19:

Kate £12,000 × 2.5% × 11/12 = £275
Laura £25,000 × 2.5% × 10/12 = £521

BENEFITS TO PARTICIPATORS

Benefits to participators who are employees or directors are taxed as benefits and therefore as employment income.

Therefore the car benefit taxable on Laura Lark is taxed as an employment income benefit, calculated as follows.

As Laura is a basic rate taxpayer, she pays tax at 20% on the value of the benefit of £990 = £198.

Raffles Ltd is able to claim a deduction against its taxable profits for the cost of providing the car. Class 1A National insurance Contributions are payable on the value of the benefit by the company at 13.8%. These NICs are also be tax deductible for corporation tax purposes.

Benefits to participators who are not employees are taxed as distributions by the company.

Therefore the car provided to Penelope Phillips gives rise to a distribution to be taxed on Penelope.

The value of the distribution is the value of the car benefit that would have been taxed on Penelope if she had been an employee. As Penelope is a higher-rate taxpayer she is taxed at 32.5% on the distribution to the extent that she exceeds the dividend nil rate band.

The distribution is £2,700.

So the maximum tax payable (assuming she has used her dividend nil rate band) is:

£2,700 × 32.5% = £878.

Examiner's comments

This question produced the poorest performance on the exam, which was a surprise to the examining team, marking teams and the tutors, who all considered it to be a discrete topic, where a well-planned answer could have scored well on straight forward issues.

This question was often attempted first or second and there appeared to be no correlation of poor performance with time pressure, given the positioning of answering the question and also given the large volume of most answers.

The problem lay in unravelling the strands of the question and identifying that there were different categories of individuals in the question, who, in each situation had a subtly different tax treatment.

Those who analysed the question before attempting it and used a methodical approach scored very well.

As a team we are still mystified as to why some candidates thought the company should be using 'opening year rules' (not relevant and an income tax concept) or why many candidates considered EIS and SEIS investment rules in great detail. The poorer answers failed to recognise that the close company rules were relevant and instead focussed on extraction of profits from the company by the shareholders and CGT reliefs on future disposal of shares. This demonstrated a lack of application skills and the habit of reverting to the LMs and copying out copious amounts of irrelevant rules.

Groups and consortia

16 Zesst plc (March 2014)

Scenario

The candidate is in the role of an assistant in the finance department at Zesst plc. This is a group scenario in which the candidate is required to consider the tax implications of the acquisition of a subsidiary on the group; the implications of financing transactions; and advise on the placing of debt finance to produce effective tax relief of losses to prevent NTLR deficits from being stranded. Assuming the proposed acquisition and financing transactions take place on 1 April 2019, the candidate is required to prepare a working paper for the finance director that includes:

16.1 An explanation of the tax implications for the Zesst group of the proposed acquisition of the shares of Hairctz Ltd by Zesst plc. (Ignore the proposed financing transactions for this requirement.)

16.2 Explanations and calculations of the tax implications for the Zesst group of the financing transactions identified by the board (Exhibit 2). Include your recommendation as to which company (Zesst plc or Mall Ltd) would be best placed to take on the £30 million bank loan in order to maximise tax relief for the group.

16.3 A calculation of the taxable total profits for Zesst plc, VHotels Ltd, Mall Ltd and Vrange Ltd for the years ending 31 March 2019, 2020 and 2021 and Hairtctz Ltd for the years ending 31 March 2020 and 2021. Use your calculations and recommendations from part 16.2 and assume that all relevant claims for group relief are made.

Marking guide

	Technical	Skills
16.1 Tax implications of share acquisition		
Group formation	1	1
Degrouping	-	2
Due diligence	1	2
Stamp duty/VAT	1	2
	3	7
16.2 Tax implications of financing transactions		
Debenture sale		
• Gain	1	2
• NTLR	1	1
• When and where charged	1	1
Share sale		
• SSE conditions	1	2
• SSE history	1	2
Loan		
• NTLR deficit	3	1
• Loss groups	-	2
Recommendations		
• Zesst plc	-	2
• Mall Ltd	-	3
	8	16

	Technical	Skills	Marks
16.3 TTP for group companies			
Additional items included	–	4	
Y/e 31 March 2019			
• Loss relief	–	1	
• Taxable total profits	1	–	
Y/e 31 March 2020			
• Loss relief	–	2½	
• Taxable total profits	2	–	
Y/e 31 March 2021			
• Loss relief	–	2½	
• Taxable total profits	2	–	
	5	10	
Total marks	16	33	49
Maximum			40

16.1 Tax implications of share acquisition

The 100% shareholding in Hairctz Ltd will establish a group relief group and a chargeable gains group relationship with Zesst plc, VHotels Ltd and Mall Ltd (and Vrange Ltd for gains only). This will enable Hairctz to be included in group planning in respect of trading losses, NTLR deficits and chargeable gains and losses.

The chargeable assets of Hairctz Ltd will remain at their historical cost. There will in any case be no de-grouping charge issues in respect of the London salon since it was transferred to Hairctz Ltd more than six years before the shares in Hairctz Ltd are to be sold.

There appear to be no trading losses in Hairctz Ltd to carry forward as these have been group relieved to Softsope plc group companies. There may however be chargeable gains rolled over against its assets which would crystallise on the future disposal of these assets. Therefore tax due diligence work should be performed before the acquisition is finalised.

Stamp duty at 0.5% will be payable on the consideration paid for the shares; ie, £200,000.

16.2 Tax implications of financing transactions

Sale of debentures by Zesst plc

The sale of the debentures results in two tax implications for Zesst plc:

The gain deferred on the takeover will now crystallise. This is calculated as the difference between the market value at the takeover date and the cost allocated to the debentures as follows:

	MV at takeover £m	Cost £m
25,000 × 15 shares × £12	4.5	2.4
25,000 £100 debentures × £120	3.0	1.6
	7.5	4.0

Chargeable gain on sale of debentures is therefore £1.4 million (£3m – £1.6m).

The second tax implication for Zesst plc of selling the debentures is that a NTLR profit arises being the difference between the consideration and the market value of the debentures at the time of the takeover. The debentures would have been recorded at fair value at 31 March 2019 (£130) however as it is an available for sale (AFS) financial asset, profits and losses are taken to reserves. Therefore the gain is taxed on disposal as follows:

	£m
Consideration for 25,000 £100 debentures @ £130	3.25
Market value of 25,000 £100 debentures @ £120	3.00
NTLR profit	0.25

This NTLR profit will be included in the taxable total profits for Zesst plc in the year ending 31 March 2020 as the disposal is assumed to take place on 1 April 2019.

The chargeable gain could be treated as arising in another 75% subsidiary to use group capital losses.

Sale of shares in EG Ltd by Zesst plc

The substantial shareholding exemption applies to certain disposals by companies of shares in trading companies. The disposal here is of shares in a trading company, EG Ltd.

The shares must be sold out of a substantial shareholding which is a shareholding which entitles the holder to 10% of the distributable profits and 10% of the assets on winding up. These conditions must be satisfied for a continuous 12-month period during the six years prior to the sale. To determine whether this applies to the disposal of EG Ltd shares, the shareholding history needs to be examined as follows:

Shareholding history

	%
Shares in EG Ltd acquired in January 2000	20
1,200 shares sold in October 2018	(12)
	8
Proposed sale of 300 shares	(3)
Remaining shareholding	5

Although Zesst plc will be selling shares out of an 8% shareholding, the ownership requirement of 10% in 12 months out of the six years before sale is satisfied and therefore the gain will be exempt.

Loan from the bank for £30 million

Interest payments associated with raising debt finance are allowable deductions for tax purposes, provided the group net interest expense is below £2 million. It would appear to be so in this situation but further clarification is required. As the loan is for the purpose of acquiring a subsidiary, the costs will be allowable as NTLR deficits and not as deductions from trading income. The amount available will be the same as the costs recorded in the profit and loss account therefore the £1.2 million interest cost will be allowable as a NTLR deficit.

The decision to be made is which company is best placed to hold the debt to ensure tax relief is obtained for the NTLR deficit since the application of tax rules may result in the NTLR being stranded and unrelieved.

A NTLR deficit can be set off wholly or partly against any profits of the same accounting period.

Alternatively the deficit can be wholly or partly group relieved which is an option in this group scenario.

Or the deficit can be set off against NTLR profits of the previous 12 months. Otherwise if no claim is made under these previous provision, the deficit is carried forward, and as the deficit is post-1 April 2017 it can be relieved against total profits of future accounting periods, subject to possible restriction for the relevant maximum.

The companies in the group relief group are Zesst plc, VHotels Ltd, Mall Ltd and Hairctz Ltd from 1 April 2019. Zesst plc's effective shareholding in Vrange Ltd is 72% (90% × 80%) which is insufficient to establish a group relief relationship. However Mall Ltd and Vrange

Ltd form a separate group. This means that losses arising in Mall Ltd can be group relieved to Vrange Ltd.

Recommendations regarding the placing of the £30 million

It is not advisable for the loan to be placed with Zesst plc as its only income on an ongoing basis is non-taxable dividends and Zesst plc already has excess management expenses.

The additional interest payable may also impact on its distributable profits and affect the group's ability to pay dividends.

The loan would be better placed in Mall Ltd, since this would enable the deficit to be group relieved to Vrange Ltd which is making taxable profits.

Zesst plc is to buy the shares in Hairctz Ltd. Therefore if the loan is raised in Mall Ltd, the cash needs to be transferred to Zesst plc. There are sufficient reserves in Mall Ltd to enable a dividend to be paid to Zesst plc. The directors should consider the minority shareholders in Mall Ltd – any group relief claims should be made considering the minority shareholders and appropriate financial consideration should be made to Mall Ltd for losses used by the group.

16.3 **Taxable total profits for group companies**

The projected profits and losses have been adjusted for the following calculations:

(1)   Zesst plc – debenture interest received for 2019 of £200,000
(2)   Zesst plc – NTLR profit on disposal of debentures of £250,000 in 2020
(3)   Zesst plc – Chargeable gain crystallising on disposal of debentures of £1.4 million in 2020
(4)   Mall Ltd – finance costs on loan £1.2 million in 2020 and £1.2 million in 2021

Year ending 31 March 2019	Zesst plc £m	VHotels Ltd £m	Mall Ltd £m	Vrange Ltd £m	Hairctz Ltd £m
Trading loss for the period	(2.00)	(14.00)			
Taxable trading profit			1.80	20.00	
NTLR – debenture interest	0.20				
Relief against total profits	(0.20)				
Group relief from Zesst plc to Mall Ltd			(1.80)		
Taxable profit	Nil	Nil	Nil	20.00	N/A
Loss carried forward	Nil	(14.00)	Nil	Nil	N/A

It may be possible to carry back the loss in VHotels to the prior year to obtain a repayment of tax but further information would be required to confirm this.

2020

	Zesst plc	VHotels Ltd	Mall Ltd	Vrange Ltd	Hairctz Ltd
Trading loss for the period	(2.00)	(8.00)			(2.00)
NTLR deficit for the period			(1.20)		
Taxable trading profit			1.00	32.00	
NTLR Profit on sale of debentures in Digital plc	0.25				
Crystallising of deferred gain on debentures in Digital plc	1.40				
Group relief to Mall from Zesst			(0.35)		
Group relief to Mall from VHotels			(0.65)		
Relief against total profits	(1.65)				
Group rel NTLR defic Mall to Vrange	-			(1.20)	
Taxable total profits	Nil	Nil	Nil	30.80	Nil
Loss brought forward	Nil	(14.00)	Nil	Nil	Nil
Loss carried forward (0.65 used)	Nil	(21.35)	Nil	Nil	(2.00)

2021

Trading loss for the period	(2.00)				
NTLR deficit for the period			(1.2)		
Taxable trading profit		1.50	1.0	45.0	3.2
Brought forward loss offset against total profits		(1.50)			(2.0)
Group relief NTLRD Mall to Vrange				(1.2)	
Group relief Zesst to Mall and Hairctz			(1.0)		(1.0)
Group relief (c/fwd losses) VHotels to Haircutz					(0.2)
Taxable profit	Nil	Nil	Nil	43.8	Nil
Loss brought forward		(21.35)			(2.0)
Loss carried forward	Nil	(19.85)	Nil	Nil	Nil

The total relief by group companies for brought forward losses is under £5 million so there is no restriction in respect of the relevant maxima of the group companies.

Conclusion

If the loan had been placed with Zesst plc, the use of the NTLR deficit would be delayed. It could not be used in the current periods but would be carried forward for use against future total profits of Zesst plc, or future total profits of Zesst plc's group companies.

Examiner's comments

16.1 Most candidates identified a reasonable number of issues associated with the acquisition of the new company, although many commented on a potential degrouping charge and commented incorrectly that it would apply. Weaker candidates took the opportunity here to 'knowledge dump'. However, the exam is open book and marks were not awarded for knowledge which was not related to the scenario. Good candidates were selective in their approach and focussed on the issues relevant to the scenario.

16.2 The question specifically asked for the implication of the purchase of the shares and hence no credit was available for a discussion of the effects of a trade and assets acquisition. Only very good candidates fully appreciated the implications of the earlier 'paper for paper' transaction. However, many considered that a chargeable gain of £250,000 arose on the disposal of the debentures which enabled marks to be awarded for this issue. Some candidates then treated this transaction (and the share disposal) as occurring in the year ended 31 March 2019 although the question stated that all transactions would occur on 1 April 2019.

Those candidates who understood that the SSE would apply to the share disposal and clearly stated the reasons earned good marks. It was disappointing to see that many candidates made the specific statement that SSE wouldn't apply as 10% of the share capital hadn't been held for 12 months in the previous six years, thus exhibiting a failure to apply their knowledge to the scenario.

16.3 Candidates generally scored well on the calculation of the taxable profits especially those that have had good preparation – full follow through marks were again awarded where relevant.

17 ICee plc (June 2014)

Scenario

The candidate is in the role of a newly appointed financial controller at ICee plc, a UK trading company and a parent company of a UK group. The candidate is reporting to a fellow professional, the finance director, and therefore is required to communicate in an appropriate manner by producing a working paper. Exhibits were provided which included background information; a tax computation prepared by the former financial controller which was incorrect; and three tax planning proposals suggested by the former financial controller.

	Technical	Skills	Marks
Explanation of errors or omissions	–	1	
R&D			
• Incorrect adjustment	1	–	
• SME relief	1	2	
• Qualifying expenditure/depreciation	–	2	
• Adjustment	1	1	
Patent			
• Incorrect adjustment	1	1	
• Goodwill in accounts	–	1	
• Amortisation	1	1	
Rollover of IFA gain			
• Identifying ROR	–	1	
• Amount of relief	1	½	
• Effect of claim	1	1	
Interest on loan	1	2	
Revised adjustment to profits			
• Add backs	1	1	
• Deductions	1	2	
Use of ICee plc's trading loss			
R&D tax credit			
• Adjusted loss	–	1	
• Surrender of loss	2	2	
Use of loss by ICee plc	1	1	
Use loss as group relief			
• Group/consortium	1	1	
• Use of loss	1	1	
• Tax savings	–	1	
• Comparison/recommendation	–	1	
Evaluation of tax planning proposals			
VAT group	1	3	
Patent income	1	1	
Share option scheme	1	2	
Total marks	18	30½	48½
Maximum			40

An explanation of any errors or omissions made by the former Financial Controller

My predecessor identified three areas of uncertainty and it is clearly concerning that the computation has been submitted without appropriate review and without the issues being resolved. Although the group is not large enough to require the appointment of a senior accounting officer, the directors should ensure that appropriate controls over tax compliance issues are in place.

As the company tax return has already been submitted to HMRC, it will need to be amended. This can be done at any time up to 12 months after the filing deadline.

Research and development costs

There are errors in the adjustment to profit computation; for example costs have been incorrectly added back to profit.

As an SME, ICee plc will be able to claim an additional 130% deduction from trading profits (subject to a cap of €7.5 million). Of the costs identified by the financial controller, the staff costs and consumable materials appear to qualify, and are therefore deductible.

However, I recommend that an in-depth review should be performed to ensure that all relevant costs have been identified. This review may not be fully possible and will depend on the detail recorded in the accounting systems. On the basis of the review, recommendations could be made to assist in identifying R&D costs for future claims.

For example, qualifying R&D expenditure includes revenue expenditure on software, power and training costs and there appear therefore to be some obvious omissions.

The depreciation costs should be added back. However, I would like to review the capital allowances computation to ensure that 100% capital allowance has been claimed for all relevant research and development expenditure.

Therefore at the very minimum an additional deduction from profit of £4.16 million is available.

Patent costs

The patent costs are potentially being amortised correctly in the statement of profit or loss. Tax relief for intellectual property follows the accounting treatment.

Therefore the adjustment to add this cost back to profit is incorrect.

Relief is not available for amortisation of goodwill ie, it is not deductible from trading profits for tax purposes. Relief will only be available on realisation of the goodwill.

Rollover of gain on sale of brand name – Eris Ltd

Eris Ltd has sold an intangible fixed asset (IFA) and realised a taxable profit of £160,000. As Eris Ltd and ICee plc are part of the same chargeable gains group, a claim for rollover relief to ICee plc of this profit is possible as ICee plc has invested in new IFAs – the trade and assets of Oogle Ltd.

If a company makes a profit on realisation of an IFA and reinvests in a new IFA, a claim for rollover relief may be made. The relief is the excess of the proceeds on realisation over the original cost.

The amount of £160,000 represents the accounting profit on the IFA which is the difference between the sale proceeds less TWDV (original cost less amortisation charges taken to the statement of profit or loss).

Therefore in order to make a claim for the relief, further information is required concerning the original cost of the patent sold by Eris Ltd.

The relief could be against either the patent cost of £1,920,000 or the goodwill of £500,000 in Oogle Ltd.

The claim would result in only part of the profit being taxable in Eris Ltd and would result in a restriction of the relief for ICee plc on the subsequent amortisation of the patent.

Interest on loan

The financial controller has incorrectly added this interest cost back to profit as the loan is in respect of the purchase of the trade and assets of Oogle Ltd and therefore the loan interest is a trading expense.

Therefore, no add back is required in the tax computation.

Interest received has been correctly deducted but should be taxed as a non-trading loan relationship (NTLR) credit.

A revised adjustment of profit

	£'000
Profit per the statement of profit or loss	353
Add back:	
Depreciation included in research and development	200
Other disallowable expenses	550
Less:	
Interest receivable	(82)
Capital allowances	(720)
R&D additional relief £3,200,000 × 130%	(4,160)
Trading loss	(3,859)

Use of ICee plc's trading loss

ICee plc has a number of options for the use of the trading loss.

Claim an R&D tax credit

As an SME, ICee plc can convert all or part of its trading loss into a R&D tax credit.

	£'000
Trading loss	(3,859)
Less:	
Possible s.37 claim for NTLR credit	
Interest receivable	82
Adjusted trading loss	(3,777)
Surrenderable loss is lower of:	
Adjusted trading loss	(3,777)
and	
230% of R&D expenditure	
£3,200,000 × 230%	7,360

Therefore the credit available is 14.5% of £3,777,000 = £547,665. As ICee plc is a member of a group for group relief purposes, it is more advantageous to consider using the trading loss within the group.

Use of loss by ICee plc

The loss could be set off against the NTLR profit or against previous year total profit. This would save tax of £15,580 (£82,000 × 19%).

The loss could also be carried forward against future total profits, however, this would be uncertain and not useful for cash flow purposes.

Use loss as group relief

The group structure is as follows:

ICee plc	→ 100% →	Auge GmbH
↓ ↓		↓
Optical Ltd MedEquip Ltd		Eris Ltd
100% 70%		80%

ICee plc could use its loss as group relief by transferring its trading loss to companies within the 75% group relief group.

The group companies who are part of the group relief group are Optical Ltd and Eris Ltd because ICee plc has a direct or indirect shareholding of more than 75% in Eris Ltd.

The 70% shareholding in MedEquip Ltd is insufficient and MedEquip is not part of the group for loss relief. Therefore, the £63,000 loss arising in MedEquip Ltd cannot be utilised by any of the ICee group companies. The directors should consider restructuring the shareholdings to enable this loss to be used. MedEquip is also not a consortium company, as its other shares are owned by individuals.

Auge GmbH has a small loss and potentially this could be used by Eris Ltd. However, it is likely that this loss can be used under German loss relief provisions and this should be investigated – therefore the loss is unlikely to be available for group relief in the UK.

Both Optical Ltd and Eris Ltd have made taxable profits.

	Optical Ltd £'000	Eris Ltd £'000
Trading profit	225	3,645
Rental income	25	
	250	

It would be more tax efficient for the ICee group to use ICee plc's loss for group relief than for ICee plc to claim an R&D tax credit since this would save at 19% compared to 14.5%.

Assuming ICee plc uses some of its loss against its NTLR credit (£3,859,000 – £82,000), £3,777,000 is available for group relief. The loss could be surrendered to either company and save tax at 19%. Therefore allocate £250,000 to Optical (100% subsidiary) and the remainder to Eris (80% effective interest).

	Optical Ltd £'000	Eris Ltd £'000	Total £'000
Total profits	250	3,645	
Less group relief from ICee plc	(250)	(3,527)	3,777
Taxable profits	0	118	

Tax savings:

Optical Ltd

£250,000 × 19% = £47,500

Eris Ltd

£3,527,000 × 19% = £670,130

Total saving = £47,500 + £670,130 = £717,630

Compared to an R&D tax credit of £547,665

Brief evaluation of the tax planning proposals

VAT Group

The tax rules for forming a VAT group require control - shareholdings more than 50%

ICee plc makes standard rated supplies; it could potentially form a VAT group with Optical Ltd, MedEquip Ltd and Eris Ltd as they are all under control and have a fixed establishment in the UK. Auge GmbH could not form part of the VAT group.

It is important that those companies which are in a repayment situation or that could potentially create a problem with partial exemption are not included in this group.

MedEquip Ltd should be excluded as this would result in a cash flow disadvantage as all supplies are zero rated.

Similarly, Eris Ltd should be excluded as all supplies are exempt from VAT and so the group would become partially exempt if it was included.

Patent income year end 31 March 2020

ICee plc could elect for the profits arising from the eye activated technology to arise within a patent box which would be eligible for a lower rate of corporation tax.

Patents must be dealt with on a patent by patent basis - as a new substream. This requires a detailed level of record keeping, but depending on the accounting records system this may not be too onerous.

There are additional administration costs in determining the appropriate profits and adjustments. However, this should be investigated further to determine whether it is beneficial.

Share option scheme

The company could issue share options under a number of tax advantaged schemes - a CSOP may be appropriate in this case.

As long as the shares were not issued at a discount there would be no income tax or NIC to pay on the grant or exercise of the option. There are certain conditions which must be considered regarding the size of the company for some schemes but not the CSOP.

Potentially a 10% capital gains tax rate is achievable on disposal. In the case of a CSOP scheme the shareholding must be over 5% in order for it to qualify for entrepreneurs' relief and be eligible for capital gains tax at the reduced rate of 10%. However, even without achieving this requirement, the managers would have a 20% tax rate on the disposal of the shares which represents a saving on the income tax rate. My recommendation would be to investigate this further.

Examiner's comments

Generally a well completed question with most candidates showing a reasonable understanding of most of the principles being examined. The question provided a well-prepared candidate to distinguish themselves and to achieve a high mark.

The requirement to review and recalculate caused some confusion and many candidates effectively double-counted the relief available in connection with the R&D expenditure. As a result there was a significant loss available for relief and they did not all therefore exhibit the decision-making skills associated with the most tax effective relief of this loss. However full follow-through marks were awarded. Candidates who explained the alternatives available and recognised that use within the group was more effective than the 14.5% tax credit scored well.

Many candidates mistakenly concluded that a consortium existed, failing to appreciate that ownership of 30% of the share capital by individuals meant the conditions were not satisfied.

Adjustment of profit

The majority of candidates correctly identified the need to explain, rather than just calculate the adjustments to profit, arising from computational errors.

The R&D amendment was recognised by the majority of candidates, with the most common error being a failure to understand how the original and further deductions for R&D would affect the computation of taxable profits. A handful of candidates identified ICee plc as a large company, despite the question stating that ICee was an SME (the learning materials stipulate that questions will identify the size of the company for R&D relief purposes). Another common error was the inclusion of depreciation as a qualifying cost.

The explanation of the tax treatment of patent costs was handled well by the best candidates, although many candidates were vague about how the cost of the patent or the goodwill should be treated in the computation. Some candidates failed to recognise that the tax treatment followed the accounting treatment [for patents] and thought that these were disallowable for tax purposes.

Candidates were usually aware that the tax treatment of the interest cost on the loan to buy an investment in the trade and assets of Oogle was dependent on the trading or investment purpose of the investment. However, judgement about whether this investment was trading or investment was not always well exercised.

For the actual computation, some candidates did not start with the correct figure from the statement of profit or loss and often deducted disallowed items rather than adding them back. On the whole though, this part caused very few problems.

The best candidates produced good answers in respect of the rollover of the gain on the sale of the brand name. Candidates intelligently considered that the gain could actually be rolled over from Eris Ltd against the cost of new 'Oogle' intangibles purchased by ICee plc and correctly described how rollover relief would operate and the fact that more information would be needed to calculate the amount of the relief available. The ability to apply professional scepticism and think about what further information is needed in a real life situation to reach a conclusion is a key skill in BP:T. It was also noted that candidates questioned whether the capital allowances and costs associated with R&D were correct in the first place, which again displayed excellent skills.

Group relief

The explanation of the options available for the use of the revised loss arising in ICee plc was handled well by the majority of candidates. It was good to see how many candidates recognised the need to explain the options for the use of the loss. In the December 2013 exam, the question on the use of losses clearly asked for these explanations and candidates have taken on board the message from the examining team that numbers alone are insufficient to demonstrate the skills required in the BP:T exam. The option to use losses to obtain a repayment via an R&D tax credit was considered by the better candidates and, again, acted as a good way to identify those candidates who had fully grasped and understood the syllabus.

There was some confusion around which companies actually could be included in the group for loss relief purposes, with some candidates including MedEquip Ltd in the loss group, despite ICee plc only holding a 70% stake. Whilst the majority of answers recognised that Auge GmBH's loss could not be used in the UK as the potential probably existed for loss relief in Germany, some answers both used and surrendered part of ICee plc's loss to Auge GmgH.

The actual calculations for loss relief were of a good standard, with the majority of candidates correctly concluding that the most efficient use of the loss was to surrender it to group companies.

Tax planning proposals

Answers to this part often scored full marks. Candidates were very well prepared for the VAT group part of the question and showed a detailed understanding of the rules, the consequences of VAT groups and the ability to apply to the scenario. Weaker candidates tended to state the VAT group rules without any application of the rules to the facts of the question. The answers in relation to patent income and the rules on 'patent box' were of a high standard showing that candidates were aware of the rules and had understood the operation of the regime. The answers to the proposals on the share option scheme were often quite brief with no real discussion on CSOP, just an acknowledgement of the fact that there were some benefits to be gained from setting up a tax advantaged scheme.

18 Splite Ltd

Marking guide

		Technical	Skills	Marks
18.1 (a)	VAT on purchase and CGS	1	2	
	Sale and transfer of going concern	1	2	
	Gains and losses	1	2	
	Loss relief and payments	1	3	
		4	9	
	Max			10
(b)	No tax relief on purchase of shares	1	–	
	Ongoing taxation if purchase shares	1	2	
	CFC	1	1	
	Related 51% group company	1	–	
	Relief for purchase of trade and assets	–	4	
	Ongoing taxation of PE	1	5	
		5	12	
	Max			14
(c)	SRT and split year treatment	1	2	
	Income tax implications	–	2	
	Expenses met by employer	–	2	
	Further information	1	–	
	Sale of shares	1	1	
		3	7	
	Max			8
18.2	Tax implications	1	1	
	Error on tax return	1	1	
	Criminal prosecution and tax evasion	1	–	
	Conflict with clients	–	1	
	Cease to act, inform HMRC, do not give reasons	–	2	
	Money laundering and SAR	1	1	
		4	6	
	Max			8
	Total marks	16	34	50
	Maximum			40

18.1 Meeting notes

(a) Capital transactions – VAT

Yogi Ltd ceased using the factory to make taxable supplies during the year. As the property was newly-constructed when purchased in 2014, the purchase price of £1,800,000 would have included standard-rated VAT of £300,000 (£1,800,000 × 1/6). Yogi Ltd initially used the factory to make standard-rated supplies and so was able to recover £300,000 as input VAT.

The use of the factory changed within the first 10 years of ownership, and the rental of the factory is an exempt supply. Therefore, under the capital goods scheme, some of the initial VAT recovered has to be repaid during the year ended 31 December 2018 ie, £30,000 (£300,000 × 1/10 × 100%).

As the building was sold with the tenants in situ it will probably be a transfer of a going concern for VAT purposes. As the building is now more than three years old and no option to tax was made by Yogi Ltd, no option to tax is required from the purchaser for it to be included with a transfer of a going concern. This means that it is outside the scope of VAT. The £2,400,000 received does not include VAT.

As the sale is part of a transfer of a going concern no adjustment on sale is required by Yogi Ltd. However, the purchaser takes over the remaining years of the capital goods scheme.

Capital transactions – chargeable gains

Qusi Ltd is in a gains group with Yogi Ltd (and some of the other group companies) following its acquisition by Poppie Ltd on 1 October 2018, because direct holdings are each 75% or more, and the effective holding by Splite Ltd is 64% (80% × 80%). Chargeable gains and losses can be transferred within gains groups to offset against each other.

Yogi Ltd has a chargeable gain on the sale of the factory of £715,470 (W). Qusi Ltd has a loss of £300,000 (£500,000 – £800,000) on the sale of the office building. The loss of Qusi Ltd is a realised pre-entry capital loss which can only be used for certain purposes; offsetting it against Yogi Ltd's gain is not a permitted use of a realised pre-entry capital loss.

Relief for trading loss

Lilts Ltd is a consortium company as two companies (Splite Ltd and Rile Ltd) ie, 20 or fewer companies, each own at least 5% and jointly own at least 75% (80%) of the ordinary share capital of another UK resident company.

Splite Ltd is therefore able to claim 40% of the loss of Lilts Ltd ie, 40% × £2,800,000 = £1,120,000. However, Splite Ltd only has taxable total profits of £100,000. Splite Ltd is a link company and the remaining (or all of the) loss can be group relieved to any other group in Splite Ltd's loss relief group. Yogi Ltd and Poppie Ltd are both in Splite Ltd's loss group. Qusi Ltd is not, as the effective ownership by Splite Ltd is less than 75% (64%).

Whichever group company claims the losses, the corporation tax saving will be at 19% ie, £1,120,000 × 19% = £212,800. The claimant company will have to pay Lilts Ltd £106,400 (£212,800 × 50p) for the loss and this payment will not be deductible for corporation tax purposes (nor taxable for Lilts Ltd).

After loss relief, corporation tax will be payable by each company at 19% on their taxable total profits (trading profits plus chargeable gains plus property income where appropriate).

WORKING

Chargeable gains

Yogi Ltd £

	£
Sale proceeds	2,400,000
Less cost (£1,800,000 – 300,000 + 30,000)	(1,530,000)
	870,000
Indexation allowance	
$(278.1 - 252.6)/252.6 = 0.101 \times £1,530,000$	(154,530)
	715,470

(b) **Trubo business**

Purchase of shares

There is no tax relief for Splite Ltd on the purchase of shares.

Trubo Inc is incorporated in Ritopia and as the local management will still be in place it will not be centrally managed and controlled from the UK if purchased by Splite Ltd. Therefore Trubo Inc will not be UK resident, so its profits will be subject to Ritopian tax at 12%, but not UK corporation tax.

Dividends received by Splite Ltd from Trubo Inc will be exempt, and there will be no relief for the withholding tax suffered in Ritopia.

If losses do arise in Trubo Inc in future, they could not be surrendered to the Splite group, but this should not be an issue as Trubo Inc appears to be profitable.

Trubo Inc will be a controlled foreign company (CFC) as it is a non-UK resident company owned more than 50% by a UK resident person (Splite Ltd). However, if the level of profits remain the same (ie, less than £500,000), the company meets the profit exemption and no CFC charge arises.

Trubo Inc will be a related 51% group company in future years, taken into account in determining whether group companies need to pay corporation tax by instalments. However, from the level of taxable total profits for the year ended 31 December 2018, it appears that most companies are already large for these purposes, and so an additional related 51% group company would have no effect.

Purchase of the trade and assets of Trubo Inc by Splite Ltd

Relief on purchase

Splite Ltd and Yogi Ltd are in the same gains group. On purchase of the assets of Trubo Inc, it may be possible to claim rollover relief for the gain generated by Yogi Ltd in October 2018. The purchase will take place within the qualifying time limit of three years of the disposal by Yogi Ltd. Trubo Inc has buildings used for business purposes, which Split Ltd would be purchasing. However, the rollover relief would be limited because Yogi Ltd's building was not used for business purposes throughout the period of ownership by Yogi Ltd. More importantly, the investment in buildings on the purchase of the Trubo Inc assets is small (maximum £150,000 by 2019) compared to the proceeds on the Yogi Ltd disposal. Any proceeds not reinvested would immediately become chargeable, and so significant other investment in qualifying assets would be necessary to roll over the gain.

A claim could only be made for relief in respect of the purchase of plant, if this was classed as fixed plant. Instead, Splite Ltd could claim capital allowances upon the initial purchase of the plant.

The purchase price of £1 million suggests significant goodwill, given the level of other assets. There would be no corporation tax relief for the purchase of goodwill.

Ongoing taxation of the Trubo business

The purchase of trade and assets means that Splite Ltd will have a permanent establishment in Ritopia. There is not an additional related 51% group company.

Splite Ltd is taxed at 19% on its worldwide income, including that of any permanent establishments. For UK corporation tax purposes, the taxable trading profits will be higher by at least £300,000 (£250,000 + £50,000), there being no deduction from trading profits for capital purchases of buildings. Additionally, the annual investment allowance may have been used by other group companies, such that relief for plant purchases is given more slowly (18% reducing balance each year).

Trading profits of £250,000 will also be taxed in Ritopia at 12%. Double tax relief is available for this, being lower than the UK corporation tax.

If the permanent establishment did make losses, it is likely that they could only be used against its own future trading profits. This is because it would be a separate overseas trade as it could not be part of an existing trade of Splite Ltd as it does not have an existing trade.

Alternatively, Splite Ltd could elect to exempt the overseas profits from UK corporation tax. The election is irrevocable and would have to apply to all future permanent establishments of Splite Ltd wherever located. This means that any losses generated by such entities in the future would not be relieved by the UK companies. Anti-diversion rules do not apply to prevent the exemption, as the Trubo business meets the profit exemption (as for the CFC rules).

(c) **Secondment**

2020/21

As Frank will work full-time overseas, he will meet the automatic overseas test of the statutory residence test, if:

- he works an average of 35 hours per week overseas;
- there are no significant breaks of more than 30 days in his overseas work;
- he has less than 31 UK work days;
- he spends no more than 90 days in the UK.

Provided these conditions are met, Frank will be non-UK resident in 2020/21.

2019/20

This is the year of Frank's departure. It is assumed Frank was UK resident in the previous year, 2018/19. He will not be UK resident in the following year, 2020/21. Therefore Frank will qualify for the split year treatment, provided the full-time work overseas test conditions are met from 1 July 2019 (pro-rated for the period from 1 July 2019 to 5 April 2020).

The split year treatment means that Frank is non-resident from the day on which he starts work in Ritopia (1 July 2019) but would remain UK resident in June 2019, whilst travelling.

Income tax implications

For the period to 30 June 2019, Frank will be UK resident and as such he will be subject to UK income tax on his worldwide income being his salary and any rental income for June 2019. From 1 July 2019, and throughout 2020/21, Frank will only be charged to UK income tax on his UK income ie, his rental income. As he is currently a citizen of the EEA, he will still be entitled to his personal allowance which may cover this amount.

The payment of accommodation for Frank while in Ritopia, is not taxable on Frank. However, the expenses for the visits of his parents, would be taxable.

Sale of shares

If Frank sells his shares while on secondment, he will still be liable to capital gains tax even if the sale takes place while he is non-UK resident as he will not be absent from the UK for more than 5 years. The gain would be chargeable on his return to the UK.

Further information required

Confirmation that Frank was UK resident in 2018/19. Also confirmation that Frank will not return to the UK, or at least, for short times which do not fail the full-time work overseas tests, and for example, he has no (or fewer than 31) UK work days.

18.2 File note

Tax and ethical implications of share award

The shares have not been awarded as part of a tax-advantaged scheme. Therefore, the finance director is treated as receiving employment income of the value of the shares when received, less any amount paid for them. This is liable to income tax, but as the shares do not appear to be readily convertible assets (not a listed company), no national insurance contributions will be due.

If the finance director has submitted his tax return for 2018/19 without showing this amount, then there is an error on this return which is both deliberate and concealed, because he changed documentation to show a different date. This carries a penalty of 100% of the potential loss revenue (income tax) and would be liable to interest.

It is also tax evasion as it is deliberately providing HMRC with false information. The finance director could face criminal prosecution and fines.

We should tell the finance director to disclose this to HMRC. He is within the time limit for amending his tax return if he has already submitted it.

If the finance director does not correct his tax return, we should consider whether we must cease to act for him. We must also consider if there is a conflict and whether we should also cease to act for the group. We would notify HMRC if we cease to act but not give the reason why.

We should report the matter to the firm's money laundering reporting officer (MLRO) as tax evasion represents the proceeds of crime. The MLRO would consider how we came to the knowledge of this – through tax compliance or through the director coming to us for legal advice. If the latter, there may be a defence of legal privilege and a report should not be made to the NCA. Otherwise, the MLRO will make a suspicious activity report (SAR) to the NCA. This is unlikely to constitute legal privilege.

19 Principia Ltd

Scenario

In this question candidates were working as an ICAEW Chartered Accountant in industry providing a report to one of the directors regarding the disposal of two group companies.

The first disposal is a sale of shares but requires consideration of a depreciatory transaction.

The second disposal was either by way of a share sale or a sale of trade and assets.

Candidates then had to consider the tax considerations for the vendor company, but also needed to be able to consider the impact on the total amount to be paid by the purchasers. Candidates also had to propose an alternative disposal method – ie, a hive down.

Finally the ICAEW Chartered Accountant has an ethical dilemma to consider.

Marks

	Technical	Skills	
19.1 **Sale of Opticks Ltd**			
Substantial shareholding and commercial loss	1	1	
Depreciatory transaction	1	2	
SDLT	2	1	
Scritti Ltd: Sale of trade and assets – option 1			
Gains on disposal (Appendix 1)	1	2	
• Use of loss	1	1	
• Use of rollover relief	–	2	
Plant and machinery	1	1	
Other assets	–	1	
Scritti Ltd cash available	–	2	
Distributions on liquidation	1	2	
Principia Ltd cash available	–	1	
Scritti Ltd: Sale of shares – option 2			
SSE	1	1	
Degrouping charge	1	2	
Use of trading losses	1	1	
Amount paid by Plato (incl SDLT – Appendix)	1	3	
Principia Ltd cash available (incl SDRT)	–	2	
Alternative method			
Hive down	–	3	
Clean company	–	1	
Trading losses	1	1	
Degrouping, SSE and SDRT	2	1	
SDLT	1	1	
	16	32	48
19.2 **Ethics**			
Confidentiality and intimidation threat	–	2	
Objectivity and self-interest threat	–	2	
Safeguards	–	2	
	–	6	6
Total marks	16	38	54
Maximum			40

19.1 Report to Johannes Newton on the disposal of two group businesses

Opticks Ltd

The disposal of Opticks Ltd is not subject to the substantial shareholding exemption as Opticks Ltd is not a trading company. As a result there is an allowable loss available.

Opticks Ltd will realise a commercial loss of £1.3 million (£2.2m – £3.5m), but only a part of this is due to the decline in value of the company's assets due to external factors ie, due to the landfill site. Of the total loss, £350,000 (£500,000 – £850,000) arises from the depreciatory transaction when Principia Ltd extracted value from the company ie, paid only £500,000 for a building worth £850,000.

This element of the capital loss is not allowed, and so the allowable loss on disposal of the Opticks Ltd shares is reduced on a 'just and reasonable' basis to £950,000 (£1,300,000 – £350,000).

Assuming there is no option to tax on the office building, Principia Ltd is due to pay stamp duty land tax of £32,000 ((£150,000 × 0%) + (£100,000 × 2%) + (£600,000 × 5%)) based on the market value of the asset transferred within 30 days of the August 2019 transfer. The SDLT is based on the market value as the two companies were connected at the time of the transfer. The transfer is not eligible for group relief as at the time of the disposal there are arrangements for the two companies to cease to be members of the same group.

Scritti Ltd: Option1 - sale of trade and assets

Scritti Ltd will have gains on disposal of the freehold factory and the goodwill totalling £1,541,049 (Appendix). This will result in corporation tax at 19% of £292,799. However, this could be mitigated as follows:

- As Scritti Ltd and Principia Ltd are in a gains group, Principia Ltd's allowable capital loss on disposal of Opticks Ltd can be transferred to Scritti Ltd and set-off against the gains, so reducing the taxable gains to £591,049 (£1,541,049 – £950,000).

- If another group company invests in qualifying assets between October 2018 and October 2022 then the gains can be rolled over against the base cost of the new assets. However as the group is restructuring and reducing in size, this may not be possible.

In addition to the gains, the disposal of the plant and machinery will result in a balancing charge of £320,000 (£400,000 – £80,000), changing the company from a break-even position to having a trading profit for period. The brought-forward trading losses of £410,000 can be set off against the total profits of £911,049 (£591,049 + £320,000), reducing the corporation tax liability to £95,199 (£501,049 × 19%).

It is assumed that the receivables and inventory are valued at their cost and so no trading profits or losses will arise. This needs to be confirmed.

Assuming that Scritti Ltd is able to make use of the Principia Ltd allowable capital losses (but that no rollover relief is possible) and that a claim is made to relieve the carried forward trading losses the total tax payable by Scritti Ltd is £95,199.

This results in cash available for distribution to Principia Ltd under option 1 of £3,114,801 (£3,210,000 – £95,199).

As Scritti Ltd is to be liquidated there are two possible methods for extraction of the net proceeds: pre-liquidation as an income distribution; or post-liquidation as a capital distribution.

A pre-liquidation income distribution ie, as a dividend is likely to be treated as an exempt dividend and so no tax would be payable. However, if such an arrangement created a capital loss it would be treated as a depreciatory transaction and so any capital losses would be disallowed. Therefore only proceeds in excess of £450,000 (the original cost of the shares to Principia Ltd) should be subject to an exempt pre-liquidation dividend strip. The remaining proceeds are then extracted by Principia Ltd post liquidation as a capital disposal. As the remaining proceeds of £450,000 equal the cost then the chargeable gain is nil.

Tutorial note

The above discussion regarding a capital distribution could be replaced by a statement that the substantial shareholding exemption would apply in any event, and so no tax would be payable on a post-liquidation distribution.

Therefore the cash available to Principia Ltd on a sale of trade and assets is £3,114,801, although this will also be reduced by substantial legal costs relating to the liquidation of Scritti Ltd.

Scritti Ltd: Option 2 – sale of shares

The sale of the shares in Scritti Ltd will be a disposal of a substantial shareholding as Scritti Ltd is a trading company, and Principia Ltd will have held a shareholding of at least 10% for a period of 12 months in the previous six years. Therefore the gain on disposal will be exempt.

There is a degrouping charge relating to the freehold factory that was transferred at nil gain/nil loss from Principia Ltd to Scritti Ltd in June 2014 ie, less than six years before Scritti Ltd leaves the group. However, as this is a qualifying share disposal, the degrouping charge is added to the sale proceeds of the share disposal. As the share disposal is exempt as a substantial shareholding, so the degrouping charge is also exempt.

No tax is payable by Principia Ltd on a share disposal.

The brought forward trading losses of £410,000 within Scritti Ltd will be preserved for future use unless the company undergoes a major change in the nature or conduct of the trade between October 2016 and October 2024 ie, within a five-year period of the change in ownership (starting not more than three years before the change in ownership).

The board of Plato Ltd have stated that they will pay no more than would be paid under option 1. The total cost of option 1 to Plato Ltd is the purchase price of the trade and assets plus the stamp duty land tax (SDLT) payable by Plato Ltd on the freehold factory ie, a total of £3,299,500 (£3,210,000 + £89,500 (Appendix)).

The purchase of the shares by Plato Ltd will be subject to stamp duty reserve tax at 0.5%, and so the price to be paid to Principia Ltd on the sale of the Scritti Ltd shares is £3,283,085 (£3,299,500 × 100/100.5).

The preferred method for the Principia Ltd group is therefore the share disposal route as this leaves more cash available.

Alternative method of disposal

An alternative method of disposal of Scritti Ltd is a hive down. This involves the transfer of trade and assets of Scritti Ltd to a new subsidiary (Newco) in which it has beneficial ownership, prior to a sale of Newco to Plato Ltd. The cash paid to Scritti Ltd will be available for distribution to Principia Ltd as in option 1 above, and the company can then be liquidated.

The major advantage of this method for Plato Ltd compared to a purchase of Scritti Ltd shares is the acquisition of a 'clean' company ie, free from tax and commercial history and any contingent liabilities.

The trading losses are able to pass from Scritti Ltd to Newco as at the time of the asset transfer they are under the same 75% beneficial ownership. So provided there is no major change in the nature or conduct of the trade now within Newco the losses are available.

Degrouping charges will arise on the assets transferred to Newco. However, as they were held and used in the trade of Scritti Ltd for 12 months before the transfer, and will be used in the trade of Newco at the time of the share sale, the shares in Newco will be treated as having been held for 12 months and it will be treated as having traded for the previous 12 months. The share sale will be a sale of a substantial shareholding and so the gain on share sale and the degrouping charge will be exempt.

The only major disadvantage of this method is that the exemption from SDLT on the freehold factory in respect of transfers between companies in the same 75% group will not be available due to the sale of Newco within three years of the transfer. This will therefore reduce the cash available for distribution to Principia Ltd.

Appendix

Scritti Ltd – option 1

Gains on disposal of assets

	Freehold factory £	Goodwill £
Proceeds	2,000,000	500,000
Less cost (W)	(882,200)	-
	1,117,800	500,000
Less indexation allowance (Jun 2014 – December 2017)		
(278.1 – 255.9)/255.9 = 0.087 × £882,200	(76,751)	-
Gain	1,041,049	500,000
Total gains	1,541,049	

WORKING

June 2014 Deemed cost on nil gain/nil loss transfer

	£
Original cost (January 1998)	550,000
Indexation allowance (January 1998 – June 2014)	
(255.9 – 159.5)/159.5 = 0.604 × £550,000	332,200
Deemed cost	882,200

SDLT payable by Plato Ltd

Non-residential property costing £2 million

Assuming that no option to tax has been exercised over the commercial property Plato Ltd will be required to pay SDLT of:

	£
£150,000 × 0%	-
(£250,000 – £150,000) × 2%	2,000
(£2,000,000 – £250,000) × 5%	87,500
SDLT payable is	89,500

19.2 I am being asked by Johannes, a person to whom I directly report, to pass on information about another party to a transaction based on my previous knowledge of that party.

I have been asked to breach the fundamental principle of confidentiality, as Plato Ltd would be unlikely to give authority to disclose information regarding their specific negotiation methods. As such I may be subject to an intimidation threat.

In addition, the fundamental principle of objectivity may be under threat as the influence of the potential bonus could override my professional judgement, and I am subject to a self-interest threat.

In order to mitigate these threats I should firstly discuss these issues with Johannes which may be sufficient to remove the threats to the fundamental principles. If he does not understand my difficulty then I may need to consider resigning my position.

20 Expandit plc (December 2015)

Scenario

This question asked candidates to consider the corporation tax implications of five different scenarios affecting a corporate client and to quantify the corporation tax due for the period, after adjusting for these items. The scenarios considered issues relevant to the topic of corporation tax at BP:T level, such as overseas taxation of companies, chargeable gains groups and degrouping charges, the substantial shareholding exemption and a small element of group and brought forward losses anti-avoidance.

The second part of the question considered the possibility of a VAT group and advice about whether this would be advantageous, or not, the correction of a VAT error and the ethical consequences of not reporting the error.

Marking guide

	Technical	Skills	Marks
20.1 Computation			
• TTP	1	1	
• CT payable	1	1	
Issue 1			
• Related 51% group companies	–	1	
• Loss group	1	2	
• Loss brought forward	1	3	
Issue 2			
• SSE exemption	1	1	
• Degrouping	1	3	
Issue 3			
• Tax and DTR	1	1	
• Branch exemption	1	2	
Issue 4	1	2	
Issue 5	1	1	
	10	18	
Max			21
20.2 VAT groups			
• Potential group companies incl. Holdit Ltd	1	2	
• Foldit Ltd	1	2	
Office building			
VAT			
• Initial VAT recovery	1	1	
• Exempt use	1	2	
Ethics			
• Disclosure of error by client	1	1	
• Consequences of non-disclosure	1	–	
• Confidentiality	1	½	
• Anti-money laundering and actions	–	1½	
	7	10	
Max			14
Total marks	17	28	45
Maximum			35

20.1 Expandit plc

Estimated corporation tax computation for the year ending 31 December 2018

	Issue	£
Taxable trading profits		3,800,000
Less adjustment for transfer pricing	5	-
Profits of overseas PE (gross)	3	140,000
Non-trading loan relationship income	4	18,750
Total profits		3,958,750
Less group relief (Foldit Ltd)	1	(210,000)
Adjusted total profits		3,748,750
CT:		
£3,748,750 × 19%		712,263
Less DTR:		
Faraway interest		
Lower of foreign tax £18,750 × 15% = £2,813		(2,813)
UK tax £18,750 × 19% £3,563		
Beregenian PE		
Lower of foreign tax £140,000 × 40% = £56,000		
UK tax £140,000 × 19% = £26,600		(26,600)
CT Due		682,850

Issue 1

The purchase of Foldit Ltd will bring an additional related 51% group company into the group from year ended 31 December 2019 (ie, the next accounting period). This will have no impact on instalment payments for Expandit plc, as it is already a large company.

Foldit Ltd is also a member of Expandit plc's 75% loss relief group. The losses brought forward from previous years cannot yet be used by the group. However, any unrelieved part of the brought forward loss that is a post-1 April 2017 loss will be available for group loss relief from five years after the end of the accounting period of the change in ownership (assuming no major change in nature or conduct of the trade during that period) ie, against profits arising after 31 December 2023. The trading losses of the year ending 31 December 2018 can be time apportioned into pre and post-acquisition amounts. The pre-acquisition loss cannot be group loss relieved in the current accounting period and is subject to the same five year rule as other brought forward losses. The post-acquisition loss of £210,000 (£360,000 × 7/12) can be offset against profits of other companies in the 75% group in the current accounting period. As the only other group company still owned by Expandit plc is situated overseas in the country of Faraway, this loss can be used by Expandit plc only.

Tutorial note

The question asks for a calculation of the CT payable by Expandit plc, but also explanations of how each of the five outstanding issues in the question would be dealt with. The anti-avoidance rules below will not impact on Expandit plc's current CT comp, but they are related to explaining the implications of the issue in the question.

Expandit plc should review the trade of Foldit Ltd to ensure that the losses brought forward in the company at acquisition (£150,000 + £360,000 × 5/12 = £300,000) are not lost, because of a major change in the nature or conduct of the trade. The £300,000 of losses brought forward at acquisition can be carried forward in Foldit Ltd and used against Foldit Ltd's total profits (if arising post-1 April 2017, otherwise against future trading profits) and any remaining post-1 April 2017 amounts group relieved after five years, provided these anti-avoidance rules do not apply. If the anti-avoidance rules are applied losses will not be available to carry forward beyond the date of the change in ownership.

Issue 2

The sale of a substantial shareholding is an exempt gain – the investing company has held 10% or more of the shares of a company for a continuous period of 12 months, during the six years preceding disposal. For this exemption to apply the company being sold must be a trading company or a member of a trading group. The gain of £1,450,000 is therefore exempt from tax under the substantial shareholding exemption, because Holdit Ltd is a trading company.

On the sale of a 75% group company, if assets have been transferred to that company on a no gain/no loss basis, within six years of the date of sale of the shares in the company, a degrouping charge would become chargeable – ie, the gain that would have been taxable on the earlier no gain/no loss transfer, had the no gain/no loss rules not applied. The degrouping charge, if applicable, would be added to the proceeds of sale and so increase the gain on sale for Expandit plc.

As the substantial shareholding exemption applies to the disposal of Holdit Ltd, the exemption will also apply to any degrouping charge.

Issue 3

The profits of an overseas permanent establishment are subject to UK corporation tax on Expandit plc. The profits will be added to the taxable profits of Expandit plc. In this case the gross profits of £140,000 are added to the taxable profits of the company and the double tax relief will be available on the lower of the overseas corporation tax paid in Beregenia of £56,000 (£140,000 × 40%) or the UK tax. This is deductible from the corporation tax liability of Expandit plc.

Expandit plc can make an election to exempt the profits (and losses) of overseas permanent establishments from UK tax. However, this election only applies for accounting periods after the period in which the election is made and applies to all overseas permanent establishments and is irrevocable. As Expandit plc may be unsure about its future expansion strategy, it may be worthwhile reflecting on possible future permanent establishments, before making such an election, to make sure there will not be any disadvantage in making the election for Expandit plc. Any election made before the end of December 2018 would not have removed the £140,000 profits from the corporation tax computation of the year ending 31 December 2018.

Issue 4

The profits of an overseas subsidiary company will be taxed in the overseas country.

Grabbit Inc remits two sources of profit to the UK.

Interest – for the year ending 31 December 2018, the gross interest remitted to the UK is £18,750. This is taxable in the UK as non-trading loan relationship income. The gross amount is taxable, however the tax withheld in Faraway will be deductible form the UK corporation tax due for the year ending 31 December 2018, using the DTR rules.

The interest payable is at a market rate and so is not subject to adjustment for any anti-avoidance rules.

The dividend should be exempt from corporation tax.

Issue 5

The goods transferred from Expandit plc to Grabbit Ltd were transferred at a non-arm's length price. Expandit plc is a large company (over 249 employees) and so is subject to the transfer pricing legislation. It is possible that Expandit plc will need to restate its profits for corporation tax purposes, by reducing profits by £200,000. Expandit plc could enter into an advance pricing agreement (APA). However, this may not apply as there is no apparent UK tax advantage. Therefore no adjustment has been made for this issue. However more information may be required to confirm this.

20.2 File note: VAT issues for the Expandit plc group

VAT Groups

To be a member of a VAT group, a company need both control and a fixed establishment in the UK. Only two controlled companies have a UK fixed establishment, Holdit Ltd and Foldit Ltd. Holdit Ltd is no longer part of the group and so we do not need to consider this company any further.

Foldit Ltd prints and sells newspapers and journals. The supplies it makes are therefore zero-rated for VAT purposes, whereas Expandit plc makes standard rated supplies.

If a VAT group were to be established between Foldit Ltd and Expandit plc, it is likely that this would provide a cash flow disadvantage to the group. Currently, as a zero-rated trader, Foldit Ltd receives regular repayments of input VAT. These VAT repayments can be arranged on a monthly basis. If it were to be included in a VAT group with Expandit plc, the group would produce one quarterly VAT return and the input VAT deductions from Foldit Ltd would simply be absorbed within that VAT return. From a cash flow perspective keeping Foldit Ltd as a separate company outside a VAT group may be advantageous.

Office building

On purchase of a new commercial building input VAT of £100,000 would have been charged. As the building was being used 100% for the purposes of your standard rated VAT registered trade, all of this VAT would have been recoverable on purchase.

However, for the return period to 31 December 2017 onwards, the building has only been used 50% for taxable purposes and 50% for exempt purposes ie, rent of a building where there has been no option to tax.

Therefore for the periods ended 31 December 2017 and ending 31 December 2018, a payment of £5,000 for each period should have been repaid to HMRC. This is a clawback of the original input VAT recovered on the building on purchase. Under the capital goods scheme property costing £250,000 or more requires an adjustment to the initial input tax recovery, if the proportion of standard/zero or exempt use changes over the initial 10-year period.

Although this amount of money is small, and, so far, only the £5,000 for the 31 December 2017 and 2018 adjustment periods are overdue, we need to advise the client about the ethical approach to communicating errors to HMRC.

We should advise the client to make a voluntary disclosure of the error and pay the VAT due.

The client should also be advised of the consequences of non-disclosure:

(1)   penalties
(2)   possibility of committing a civil fraud
(3)   interest due on overdue VAT

This advice must be confirmed in writing.

If the client refuses to disclose the information we should consider if they are an appropriate client for the firm.

We may or may not be able to inform HMRC of the error ourselves (it depends on the terms of our engagement letter). We should not disclose information to HMRC unless we have the authority to do so.

We need to consider the money laundering implications of tax evasion.

We should consider a report to our MLRO, who will consider whether a report to NCA is necessary.

We should document all steps taken in writing in our files.

We should avoid informing our client of our actions in relation to money laundering, to ensure we are not 'tipping off' the client.

Examiner's comments

20.1 This part produced the best answers on the exam. However, candidates need to be aware that when they are asked to provide explanations about how things are treated in a computation, it is not sufficient to regurgitate technical knowledge without relating it to the facts of the question. A good example of this is determining if a company is a related 51% group company or not. A comment that a company is group company will be worth very little credit, in isolation. The candidate needs to go on to comment on whether this has any impact on the corporation tax computation and if not, why not. The importance of this part has diminished since the exam due to changes in legislation.

Candidates did seem confused about when overseas profits would be taxed in the UK and about the operation of double tax relief. There was also significant discussion on the rules relating to CFCs, which was not relevant. Candidates need to carefully read the facts in each question and consider if issues are relevant, given the particular scenario.

On the other hand the issue of the substantial shareholding exemptions and the knock on effect onto the degrouping charge was really well dealt with in many cases.

20.2 This part contained a simple decision and commentary on the suitability of a VAT group and an ethical issue concerning a VAT error and disclosure to HMRC.

As is often the case, the ethical issue was poorly answered. There was no evidence of time pressure, but a lot of candidates wrote one or two sentences on the disclosure of the VAT error. Given that the syllabus states that there will be a minimum of five marks on an ethical issue, candidates must have been aware that this was not enough. Performance on the ethical issues remains a concern.

Overseas aspects of corporation tax

21 Scandipop AB (December 2014)

Scenario

In this question the candidate is a tax adviser in a firm of ICAEW Chartered Accountants providing advice to an offshore client. The client aims to set up in business in the UK and second staff to the UK operation. The aim of the question was to consider both the income tax and the corporation tax issues for the same client in this scenario. The question also considered the ethical issues arising from a comment made by an officer of the client company.

Marking guide

		Technical	Skills	Marks
21.1 (a)	**Income tax consequences of UK secondment**			
	2019/20			
	• Automatic overseas tests	1	1	
	• Automatic UK tests	1	3	
	• Full-time work	1	2	
	Split year			
	• Basic test	1	1	
	• Sufficient ties	1	1	
	2020/21			
	• Automatic tests	1	2	
	• PAYE/NIC	2	1	
	• PA and benefits	2	2	
		10	13	
(b)	**Response to chief operating officer**			
	• Evidence	1	1	
	• Contact client	–	1	
	• Engagement letter/cessation	–	2	
	• Tax evasion/anti-money laundering	2	2	
		3	6	
21.2	**Briefing note on UK tax implications of setting up Scandipop UK Ltd, financing arrangements and supply of raw materials**			
	• UK residence	–	1	
	• Diverted profits tax	1	2	
	• Transfer pricing	1	3	
	• APA	–	½	
	• Thin capitalisation	1	3	
		3	9½	
	Total marks	16	28½	44½
	Maximum			35

21.1 (a) Guide for Scandipop AB employees on the UK income tax implications of proposed secondments to the UK

The residence and domicile status of an employee and the location in which he carries out his duties determine the tax treatment of his earnings.

Residence

The residence of an individual is determined by the statutory residence tests. This status usually applies for whole tax years, however, in certain circumstance the tax year can be split and an individual can be treated as UK resident for only part of the tax year.

To identify if an individual is classified as UK resident, we must first see if that individual satisfies any of the automatic overseas tests. If the individual satisfies any of these tests he will be classified as non-UK resident.

For 2019/20 the secondees will spend more than 46 days in the UK and they will therefore not satisfy the automatic overseas residence test.

If none of the automatic overseas tests are met, we then look to see if an individual can be classified as UK resident by either satisfying one of the automatic UK tests or the sufficient ties test.

For 2019/20 secondees are unlikely to spend at least 183 days in the tax year in the UK or a period of 91 consecutive days, where they have a home in the UK and no home overseas. However, they are likely to satisfy the full-time UK work test. This is satisfied if all the conditions are met.

Secondees will spend a period of 365 days (the secondment is from 1 January 2020 to 30 June 2021), all or part of which falls within the tax year, when the taxpayer works an average of 35 hours a week in the UK (the secondment stipulates 37 hours' work a week in the UK).

Within the 365-day period, there are no significant breaks of more than 30 days when he does not work in the UK (ignoring annual and sick leave).

Within the 365-day period the individual is working 100% in the UK, this satisfies the test that at least 75% of the individual's working days must be in the UK and there is at least one day where the secondees will work, in the UK, for 3 hours.

There will be no need to apply the sufficient ties test, as the full-time UK work test has been satisfied.

Split-year treatment

Normally UK residence applies for a whole tax year, however, if the individual was not resident in the previous tax year and is arriving in the UK, they will only be treated as UK resident for part of the tax year in certain, limited circumstances.

Our secondees were not resident in the UK in 2018/19 and as they arrive to work in the UK for a 365 day period starting in 2019/20, a tax year in which they satisfy the UK full-time work criteria and do not have sufficient UK ties before they start work in the UK, the individual will only be UK resident from 1 January 2020, the date they start to work in the UK.

The number of days used in applying the sufficient ties tests is reduced to 8/12 of the numbers for a full year, because there are 8 whole months from 6 April 2019 to 31 December 2019. In the period before 1 January 2020, if the secondees have spent minimal time in the UK, they would not have to determine if they met any of the sufficient ties tests and would be classified as UK resident from 1 January 2020 onwards. If the number of days spent in the UK in 2019/20, prior to 1 January 2020, exceeded 30, (46 days × 8/12) then the employees would have to consider if they satisfied at least four of the sufficient ties tests. This is unlikely.

For 2020/21, the employees will not meet any of the automatic overseas tests and are likely to meet the automatic UK tests, because they will spend at least 183 days in the UK and because they should (as in 2019/20), satisfy the full-time UK work test. The secondees should cease to be UK resident from 1 July 2021, when they cease to work in the UK, using the split year treatment.

In being taxed as a UK resident, the secondees will be taxed on their UK employment income on an arising basis under the PAYE scheme, which deducts income tax and national insurance contributions at source, from gross pay. Employees then receive their pay net of income tax and national insurance contributions.

Personal allowance and taxation of benefits

If the secondees are classified as UK resident for the duration of their secondment, they should be entitled to a full UK personal allowance for each tax year of residence. The UK personal allowance is the amount of income that can be received tax free in a tax year and amounts to £11,850. The personal allowance varies from tax year to tax year, and is likely to increase in future years – we will advise secondees of the tax free amounts for future years once they are finalised.

Tutorial note

The personal allowance given is that for 2018/19 and assumes that rates and allowances for 2018/19 continue into the future.

Provision of benefits in relation to UK employment is usually regarded as taxable. In the case of the secondees, they are provided with rent-free accommodation and with travelling expenses.

Because their employment in Norwen continues, their secondment to the UK will be treated as a temporary workplace, therefore rent-free accommodation and travel expenses will be tax free benefits.

(b) Scandipop AB's chief operating officer has suggested that complying with UK legislation in terms of employment and tax obligations is unnecessary when setting up a subsidiary in the UK.

Firstly, we need to ascertain if this is his attitude to UK law and regulations. We should request further evidence from the client to determine their attitude to complying with the law and regulations in the UK and research the attitude of the parent company to legal and governmental compliance in Norwen.

If we find that the client's COO believes that it is acceptable to fail to comply with UK law in respect of the legal status of employees seconded to the UK, we should write to the client and make it clear that we are unable to support actions by the client, which we know to be unlawful. We should advise the client to comply with the law and advise the client of the consequences in terms of fines and other penalties for non-compliance with the law.

We should review the terms of our engagement letter with the client to discover if we have the right to disclose any illegal acts of the client to the authorities.

If the client goes ahead and fails to satisfy their legal obligations in relation to the seconded employees in the UK, we should cease to act for the client.

A failure to register the seconded employees with HMRC as UK taxpayers could be classified as tax evasion. In these circumstances we may need to consider reporting the offence to the MLRO within our firm, who would then consider if a report needed to be made to the National Crime Agency (NCA). We should be careful not to alert the client to the fact that we have reported them to NCA. If we do tip-off the client, we may have committed the offence of tipping-off the client and be subject to sanctions as a firm.

21.2 If a company is resident in the UK it will pay tax in the UK on its worldwide profits. Scandipop UK Ltd is incorporated under UK law and is therefore resident in the UK. The company has been established to manufacture and sell Scandipop in the UK. The company should, therefore only have UK profits.

A Norwen based professional tax adviser should be consulted to advise on the tax payable by Scandipop UK Ltd in Norwen, if any.

Scandipop UK Ltd will pay tax on its UK profits at the rate of 19% which is higher than the current rate of corporation tax in Norwen of 16%.

Scandipop AB appears to be a large company (having more than 249 employees) and also appears to be entering into transactions designed to divert profits from the UK and into Norwen, in order to take advantage of the lower corporation tax rate in Norwen.

The transactions may be caught by the diverted profits tax legislation, where transactions lack economic substance. However, it may escape a charge as there may not be an 'effective tax mismatch outcome' ie, the tax paid by one party may be at least 80% of the tax reduction in the other party. The tax rate of 16% in Norwen is more than 80% of the UK tax rate of 19%. However, this needs to be investigated further if the method of calculating taxable profits differs in the two countries. Even if there is an effective tax mismatch the taxable diverted profits will be nil provided a transfer pricing adjustment is made (see below).

These transactions will be caught by the transfer pricing legislation, which states that where connected large companies (Scandipop AB is a large company having more than 249 employees) enter into transactions at other than arm's length, such that one company gains a tax advantage, the transfer pricing rules may apply.

The company gaining a tax advantage (in this case Scandipop UK Ltd) is required to adjust its corporation tax self-assessment by substituting an arm's length price for the original price.

There are two transactions to be restated under the transfer pricing rules:

Interest charged on the loan from Scandipop AB

£1,350,000 × (15% – 7%) = £108,000

The transfer price charged for the lingonberries

500 tonnes × £400 (£500 – £100) per tonne = £200,000

The transfer pricing adjustment required is to increase profits in the UK by £308,000, to remove the effect of excessive costs being charged in the UK accounts.

An Advance Pricing Agreement (APA) could be entered into with HMRC which would set out how the above transactions will be treated before a return in submitted.

In addition, it appears that Scandipop UK Ltd is thinly capitalised (that is, more funds have been lent to the company by a connected company than would have been lent by unconnected third parties). As a result of this the interest on the excessive amount of loan is not treated as tax deductible.

The interest on the excessive amount of the loans made to Scandipop UK Ltd of £850,000 (£2,850,000 – £2,000,000) would be disallowed for corporation tax purposes.

Therefore, the interest of 7% × £850,000 = £59,500 would be disallowed.

In total £367,500 (£308,000 + £59,500) of adjustments would be made to increase the profits/decrease the losses made by Scandipop UK Ltd in the first year of its trade.

The statutory residence tests, and their application in a split year scenario, should have been a 'hot topic' and well understood by candidates. In a fully-open book exam, these rules are also available in all the materials taken into the exam by candidates. Coverage on this straightforward part of the question was disappointing, with a lot of candidates proving unable to explain the rules underpinning the statutory residence test and also unable to apply them to the facts of the question.

There was evidence that candidates are, at last, starting to get to grips with the ethical requirements, which have often been poorly answered in previous exams. There was less tendency to assume that the client is a criminal and more answers tried to evaluate the merits of the ethical dilemma and form a professional judgement as to the outcome.

Part 2 was very well answered. Most candidates spotted the effect of the anti-avoidance, thin capitalisation, rules and were able to apply them to the facts of the question.

Candidates produced full answers, but many just seemed unaware of how the statutory residence rules worked in practice.

22 Staplit plc

Scenario

This question asked candidates to consider the tax implications of a number of overseas scenarios affecting a corporate client. The scenarios considered issues relevant to the topic of diverted profits tax, VAT and corporation tax at BP:T level.

The second part of the question tested excessive interest (thin capitalisation) in relation to a loan guarantee.

Marking guide

	Technical	Skills	Marks
22.1 Overseas issues			
Issue 1			
• DPT – lack economic substance	–	1	
• Conditions	2	–	
• Effective tax mismatch calculations	–	3	
• Insufficient economic substance explanation	–	2	
• Payment of DPT	1	1	
• HMRC administration	2	–	
Issue 2			
• E-commerce place of supply (including special rule)	1	3	
• Reverse charge procedure	1	1	
• Error correction	–	1	

Issue 3

• Deferral of gains on incorporation	1	1	
• CT after deferral of gains	–	2	
• CT on disposal of shares to directors	1	2	
• CT on disposal of factory	1	1	
	10	18	28

22.2 Thin capitalisation		1	
Terms to consider	3	2	
Calculation of excessive interest		3	
Relief in Staplit plc	1	2	
	4	8	12
Total marks			40
Maximum			35

22.1 Staplit plc

Issue 1 – Pancras Ltd

Pancras Ltd is deemed to have taxable diverted profits as a result of a series of transactions which 'lack economic substance'. This applies because:

- Pancras Ltd is UK resident;

- it has entered into an arrangement with Templehof Inc;

- at the time both parties are controlled by Staplit plc; and

- the transaction causes an 'effective tax mismatch outcome' as:

  - the operating lease rentals of £6 million are deductible in calculating Pancras Ltd's trading profits, and so UK corporation tax is reduced by £1.14 million;

  - the resulting reduction exceeds the resulting increase of £480,000 (£6m × 8%) in the tax liability of Templehof Inc; and

  - the resulting increase of £480,000 is less than 80% of the £1.14 million decrease in UK corporation tax (£1.14m × 80% = £912,000).

The transaction has 'insufficient economic substance' as it is reasonable to assume that the operating lease and the involvement of Templehof Inc are designed to secure a tax reduction, and the non-tax financial benefits do not appear to be a consideration.

Furthermore the involvement of the Templehof Inc staff is insufficient to have much of an impact on the financial benefits.

Pancras Ltd will be required to pay diverted profits tax (DPT) equal to 25% of the taxable diverted profits. For these purposes they will need to consider the 'relevant alternative provision' ie, what would the UK corporation tax position have been if Pancras Ltd had purchased the machinery directly. Further information is required regarding the purchase price of the machinery and the capital allowances available to Pancras Ltd.

Tutorial note

The question was deliberately silent on the purchase price of the machinery to avoid the need to make detailed calculations of the DPT.

DPT is not self-assessed. Pancras Ltd must notify HMRC by 30 June 2019 ie, within three months of the end of the accounting period, that it is within the scope of DPT.

HMRC will issue the company with an estimate of the taxable diverted profits, following which the company has 30 days to make representations if it disagrees. HMRC will then issue a charging notice and the DPT must then be paid within 30 days.

Issue 2 – online distance learning

The supply of online distance learning training is a service supplied by e-commerce and has special rules about the place of supply.

The place of supply of services to Staplit plc would usually be in the UK (ie, where Staplit plc is established). However, additional rules apply where the services are effectively used and enjoyed outside of the UK – they are treated as supplied in that place.

So the supply of training to:

- the 50 UK employees and 40 EU employees in the EU is treated as supplied in the UK;

- the remaining 70 employees is treated as supplied in Erehwon ie, no UK VAT implications.

The VAT on 90 employees is accounted for using the reverse charge procedure ie, VAT of £9,000 (£80,000 × 20% × 90/160) should have been included as output tax on the VAT return to 31 March 2019 and also reclaimed as input tax subject to the partial exemption rules applying.

The details supplied suggest that VAT has been dealt with using this procedure but on the whole cost of £80,000 ie, VAT of £16,000 included on the return. This matter will need to be investigated further and may require HMRC to be notified of an error on the return.

Issue 3 – incorporation of a permanent establishment

The capital assets of the Ruritanian permanent establishment (PE) are treated as disposed of and reacquired at market value.

As the transfer is at least partly in exchange for shares in Hermy SA and Staplit plc will own at least 25% of the shares in the new non-UK resident company, a claim to postpone the gains can be made.

The gain that is initially postponed is

total gains × market value of the shares at transfer/market value of the total consideration

£(500,000 + 100,000) × 1.8m/2m = £540,000.

Hence £60,000 will remain in the charge to UK corporation tax, giving tax payable at 19% of £11,400.

There will be two charges to corporation tax when the Hermy SA shares are sold to the local directors:

- **A gain on the disposal of the shares**

	£
Sale proceeds of the 25% disposal	550,000
Cost of the shares (25% × £1.8m)	(450,000)
Gain chargeable	100,000

  However, if Staplit plc considered delaying the sale of the shares to the local directors by another six months then this gain may be exempt as a substantial shareholding.

- **Part of the deferred gain**

  £540,000 × 25% = £135,000

There will be a remaining deferred gain of £405,000 (£540,000 – £135,000), and additional corporation tax of £44,650 (£(100,000 + 135,000) × 19%).

When Hermy SA disposes of the factory within six years of incorporation there is a further charge to corporation tax for Staplit plc based on the remaining deferred gains:

Balance of deferred gains × gain on factory on incorporation/gross gains on incorporation

ie, £405,000 × 500,000/600,000 = £337,500.

Assuming the corporation tax remains at 19% there will be an additional tax charge of £64,125.

22.2 Briefing notes (continued)

Felisk Ltd loan

Thin capitalisation rules apply to the bank loan guaranteed by Staplit plc, such that interest on a 'real' bank loan is disallowed for Felisk Ltd.

This requires Felisk Ltd's own borrowing capacity to be considered on a standalone basis, without taking into account the guarantee provided by Staplit plc ie:

*   the loan would only have been £10 million;
*   the interest would have been at 9%; and
*   the loan would only have been for five years.

Without the guarantee, Felisk Ltd would have had interest payable of £900,000 per annum (£10m × 9%) for five years until year ended 31 March 2023.

With the guarantee, the company has interest payable of £1.4 million per annum (£20m × 7%) for 10 years until year ended 31 March 2028.

The excess interest of £500,000 is disallowed in Felisk Ltd for each of the first five years. In the final five years the loan would not have been available and so the whole £1.4 million per annum will be disallowed in Felisk Ltd.

However, it may be possible for Staplit plc, as the guarantor, to claim a deduction for the excessive interest ie, £500,000 in the first five years and £1.4 million in each of the final five years. This will only be possible if Staplit plc would have been able to borrow the £20 million on the same terms.

Corporate interest restrictions are not likely to be an issue as after the adjustments for thin capitalisation net interest is likely to be less than £2 million. However there is a need to confirm whether there are other loans in the company and the group that may cause group net interest to exceed £2 million.

Changing business structures

23 Poachers Products plc

	Technical	Skills	Marks
23.1 R&D tax credit			
• RDEC tax credit	2	2	
• Use of credit	1	3	
• Qualifying expenditure	1	2	
Patent box			
• Calculation of profit	1	1	
• Nexus fraction	1	2	
• Calculation of tax	1	1	
Other features of the UK tax system			
• CT rate	-	1	
• Dividends	-	1	
• Double taxation	-	1	
• Loss surrender	-	2	
	7	16	
23.2 Analysis of reorganisation			
• Step 1	2	1	
• Step 2	1½	1	
• Step 3	1½	1	
• Step 4	1	1	
	6	4	
Total marks	13	20	33
Maximum			30

23.1 UK as a location for Research and Development activities: draft tax section for report

There are two important UK tax incentives which would apply to the European research and development (R&D) activities and the related manufacturing if they were located in the UK. These are the Research and Development Expenditure Credit (RDEC), and the patent box rules.

R&D tax credit

Newco will be a 'large' company for the purposes of the UK R&D tax credit rules. Where a large company incurs expenditure on qualifying R&D, it can claim a credit of 12% of the expenditure. The credit on expenditure of £5 million would therefore be £600,000. From an accounting perspective the credit is intended to be reflected 'above the line' as a reduction in operating costs, although you would need to take US GAAP advice on how it will be treated in the consolidated accounts.

The credit is taxable, so at the 19% corporation tax rate the net credit on expenditure of £5 million is (£5m × 12%) × (100% - 19%) = £486,000.

There are detailed rules on how the credit is used: where the company has no corporation tax liabilities, the credit can be repaid to the company by the UK tax authorities. The amount which is repayable is always capped at the lower of the after-tax value of the credit (ie, £486,000 here) and the amount of income tax and national insurance contributions paid over via PAYE in relation to workers working on R&D activities. Any excess over the cap is carried forward and available in future periods. However, amounts which are unused by the company itself can be surrendered to other UK resident group members. If there are taxable profits in the UK group, it should therefore be possible for the full value of the credit to be realised each year.

Expenditure is only 'qualifying' if it is of an 'income' nature (ie, expenditure which is not expected to create an enduring benefit). Capital expenditure on R&D activities is fully deductible in the year in which it is incurred, but with no additional credit.

Expenditure is also only 'qualifying R&D expenditure' if it falls within guidelines set out by the UK Department for Business, Energy and Industrial Strategy. It must therefore seek to advance knowledge in a particular field. Consideration would therefore need to be given to each element of the company's work to determine whether it would qualify. Developing a version of the patented technology which can be used at very low temperatures is likely to qualify on the basis that it represents an overall increase in knowledge in this field. The work to develop a large-scale manufacturing process would only qualify if it represented an appreciable improvement on the existing process, although expenditure on trial production can qualify for the relief in cases where it is needed to resolve technological uncertainty.

Patent box

The 'patent box' rules apply a reduced rate of corporation tax of 10% to that part of a company's profits which relates to patents, or products incorporating patents. Newco should qualify as it will own a patent, and will develop products incorporating the patent.

The rules require a number of adjustments to be made to identify the patent box profits. However, in this case the calculation is likely to be simplified because all of the company's products will incorporate the patent (no apportionment is needed if the patent is incorporated into a product: all of the profit from the product is eligible), and the company will make arm's length payments for the use of all marketing intangibles.

The main adjustment will therefore be to modify the patent profit figure by applying the 'nexus fraction'. As the company has not subcontracted any R&D, the nexus fraction (N) is the lower of 1 and $D \times 1.3/(D + A)$. D is the in-house direct expenditure on R&D and A is the expenditure on the purchase of intellectual property. (Note there is no subcontracted R&D expenditure.)

The nexus fraction in year one is $(£5m \times 1.3)/(£5m + £10m) = 0.433$ ie, 43.3% for this patent.

So the profit within the patent box rules is $£8m \times 43.3\%$ ie, £3.464 million and so the tax charge would be £346,400.

Other features of the UK tax regime

A flat main rate of corporation tax (currently 19%) usually applies regardless of a company's profits, subject to the patent box reduction noted above.

The UK does not impose any withholding tax on dividends. If you were to repatriate profits from Newco to the US by way of dividend, there would therefore be no additional tax cost.

The UK has an extensive double tax treaty network. This should minimise any withholding tax on royalty payments paid to Newco for the use of the patent.

Losses can be surrendered between UK resident members (and UK trading permanent establishments) of a 75% corporate group, meaning that immediate relief should be available for losses which Newco realises in its first few years of trading. This is subject to the caveat that no loss is treated as arising until a company starts to trade. This is likely to be when it is first in a position to make sales, which may not be until late in 2021. Costs incurred before it starts to trade will be treated as incurred on the first day of trading, so there should be no overall loss of relief. There is, however, likely to be a delay in obtaining relief for the costs incurred in the first year in which the facility is operational.

23.2 Tax consequences of reorganisation

(1) Share buy back

A purchase of own shares from a corporate shareholder is treated as a capital disposal. Therefore this will be treated as a part disposal of Poachers Products plc's shareholding in Poachers Trading Ltd. However, as it is a disposal of shares in a trading company, and at least a 10% shareholding has been held for more than 12 months, the substantial shareholding exemption should apply so that no tax charge results.

The loan from Poachers Products plc to Poachers Trading Ltd should fall under the loan relationship rules, and will be a non-trading loan relationship for both parties. Interest received and paid would normally be taxed and deducted on an accounts basis.

However, further information on the terms of the loan, the borrowing capacity of Poachers Trading Ltd, and the reasons for the transaction would be needed, to confirm whether the position could be challenged either under the thin capitalisation/ transfer pricing rules (on the basis that the interest rate on the loan was not at arm's length, or that the amount of the loan was greater than an arm's length lender would have been willing to provide), or the rules relating to loans for unallowable purposes (which apply where a loan is taken out for tax avoidance purposes). If an adjustment arises under the transfer pricing rules on a transaction between two UK companies, the other party to the transaction should be able to claim a corresponding adjustment. This is not the case if a disallowance arises under the unallowable purposes rules.

(2) Transfer of Poachers Finance Ltd to PHUK

The transfer of the Poachers Finance Ltd shares to PHUK should fall within the paper for paper rules (which take priority over both the intra group transfer rules and the substantial shareholding exemption). There will therefore be no taxable disposal, and the shares issued by PHUK will be treated as acquired by Poachers Products plc at the same time and for the same cost as the Poachers Finance Ltd shares. PHUK will be treated as having acquired the Poachers Finance Ltd shares for their market value at the date of transfer.

(3) Transfer of Poachers Trading Ltd to Outdoors Holdings Luxembourg SA

In this case, the substantial shareholding exemption takes priority over the paper for paper rules. The conditions for the exemption should be met (the analysis is the same as for transaction (1) above), so there should be no corporation tax charge. Poachers Products plc is treated as acquiring the Outdoors Holdings Luxembourg SA shares for the value of the consideration given to acquire them, which is the same as their market value.

Tutorial note

The treatment is different for each of (2) and (3). In (2) the companies are in a gains group so nil gain nil loss (NGNL) treatment would apply. As NGNL would apply the substantial shareholding exemption (SSE) does not apply, and so paper for paper rules take priority. In (3) one of the companies is non-UK resident and so NGNL treatment cannot apply, so SSE takes priority.

(4) Distribution of the Outdoors Holdings Luxembourg SA shares by Poachers Products plc

This is a taxable disposal of the shares in Outdoors Holdings Luxembourg SA. It is a non-arm's length disposal, and a disposal to a connected party, so the disposal will be treated as made for consideration equal to the market value of the shares.

As the shares were distributed on the same day as they were received, the market value at distribution should be the same as that when they were acquired, and therefore no gain will arise.

24   CFR (March 2014)

Scenario

The candidate is in the role of a tax assistant working for a firm of ICAEW Chartered Accountants. The scenario involves a business which is expanding and the sole trader is first incorporating and will then issue shares to a relative who is willing to invest in her business.

The candidate's firm advises both clients. The candidate is required to consider the ethical implications of this in particular the issue of when one client wishes to withhold information from the other. Therefore this question requires a high level of professional skills from the candidate in their need to consider both the clients' perspectives and the firm's perspective too.

The candidate is required to prepare notes for the manager which include tax planning recommendations and advice on opportunities to save tax where relevant.

Marking guide

		Marks
	Technical	Skills
24.1 Tax implications of incorporation		
• Two periods – closing year rules	1	1
• Loss relief	1	2
• Long closing period	1	2
• Incorporation relief	1	1
• Disclaiming IR	1	2
• SDLT	–	1
• Retain building	1	2
• Goodwill in company	–	1
• VAT	1	1
• Dividends	–	1
• R&D	1	1
	8	15

		Marks
	Technical	Skills
24.2 £600,000 investment		
• EIS relief	1	1
• 30% of shares	–	1
• IT relief	1	3
• CGT reinvestment relief	1	2
	3	7
24.3 Gift of shares		
• CGT	–	2
• IHT	1	2
	1	4

24.4 Ethics

• Conflict of interest	–	2
• Notify both parties	1	1
• Safeguards	2	2
	3	5

Total marks	15	31	46
Maximum			35

24.1 Tax implications of incorporation

When Fiona incorporates her sole trader business the tax implications are as follows:

The closing year rules will apply to her business profits. As an election will be made to transfer assets at TWDV to Fiona Mare Ltd, no capital allowances are claimed in the final year of trading.

If Fiona prepares accounts to 31 December 2018 and for the period to 30 April 2019, the following trading loss and profit would arise:

	Trading(loss)/profit £
2018/19 £20,000 – £50,000	(30,000)
2019/20	10,000

No capital allowances are claimed in the final period and the company will take over the plant pool and the special rate pool at their 1 January 2019 TWDV.

As there is no appropriate income available for a terminal loss claim, the loss in 2018/19 can be carried forward against the profit in 2019/20 and the remaining loss of £20,000 can be carried forward under s.86 which provides that the loss can be set off against income received from the company by the former owner as if such income were trading income. As a result no tax arises on her sole trader business profit for 2019/20 and a loss of £20,000 is carried forward.

Alternatively Fiona could prepare a long final account for the period from 1 January 2018 to 30 April 2019. This is not beneficial in terms of cash flow since no claim for capital allowances would be made leaving Fiona with taxable income in 2018/19.

However this does enable her to use her personal allowance in 2018/19 (as she has no other income in that tax year). In addition the value of the assets going into the capital allowances pool in the company is £50,000 higher, which will save tax for the company in the future. Overall therefore the decision is a balance between overall saving and immediate cash flow.

Incorporation

A chargeable gain will arise on the disposal of the chargeable assets in Fiona's business to Fiona Mare Ltd (ie, on the disposal of the goodwill and the freehold factory unit to the company). Incorporation relief automatically applies to roll over the gain against the base cost of the shares provided all assets other than cash are transferred.

Therefore no chargeable gain arises to be taxed in 2019/20.

Alternatively Fiona could disclaim incorporation relief and would pay CGT. In doing so the base cost of the shares would be equal to the market value of the assets transferred which would reduce any gain arising on the subsequent disposal of the shares. Since the new company is a close company, Fiona can only claim entrepreneurs' relief (ER) at 10% on the gain relating to the factory unit, giving CGT of £16,000 and the gain relating to the goodwill will be taxable at 20% after the deduction of her annual exempt amount, giving tax of £17,660 ((£100,000 – £11,700) × 20%). The capital gains tax payable of £33,660 (£16,000 +

£17,660) may outweight the benefit of a higher base cost for future share disposals, especially if the shares qualify for entrepreneurs' relief in the future.

SDLT of £17,500 will be payable on the market value of the freehold factory unit ((£250,000 – £150,000) × 2% + (£560,000 – £250,000) × 5%).

Fiona has a number of tax planning opportunities in connection with the incorporation.

She could retain the building personally and therefore save SDLT of £17,500 (and also an effective double charge to tax if the building is sold at a later date in the company and the proceeds extracted).

However, retaining the building personally means that incorporation relief would not apply although Fiona could claim business asset gift relief for the goodwill which defers the gain against the base cost of the asset. For gift relief to be claimed in full, the goodwill would have to be gifted for nil consideration ie, not transferred in return for shares, although the other assets could be so transferred.

Using gift relief means the chargeable gain is rolled over against the cost of the asset (goodwill). If the goodwill is sold in the future an increased profit would arise in the company, where it would be taxed at the corporation tax rate (currently 19%).

Alternatively she could crystallise the gain on the goodwill as above, using her annual exempt amount and giving CGT at 20% of £17,660.

Owning the building personally means that Fiona could charge the company a rent. The company would receive a tax deduction for the rent and Fiona would pay income tax on the rental income received. However, charging a market rent would result in entrepreneurs' relief not being available on the future disposal of the building.

A further tax liability will arise for Fiona in connection with her car. Fiona has previously claimed 90% business use on her company car. After incorporation she becomes an employee and the car is an asset of the company. She would therefore be taxed on a benefit on the car which will be in the region of £75,000 × 37% = £27,750 which would be taxed at her marginal rate of tax (likely to be at least 40%). The company will also pay class 1A NIC on the benefit. She should consider owning the car personally and charging a business mileage rate to the company.

Fiona Mare Ltd

There is no relief (ie, as amortisation) for the goodwill. The company should be eligible for capital allowances on plant and machinery transferred.

VAT

The transfer of the assets to Fiona Mare Ltd is not treated as a supply of goods and services and no VAT is payable on the assets transferred since the business is a going concern (this would also be the case if the premises were not transferred).

Fiona Mare Ltd should be registered for VAT as its turnover will exceed the registration limit within the first month assuming the limited company continues to have the same level of revenue achieved by the sole trader business which was £2 million for the year ended 31 December 2018.

Corporation tax and profit extraction

Fiona Mare Ltd will pay corporation tax on its adjusted profits.

Any salary paid to Fiona, and the associated employer's national insurance, will be deducted before corporation tax is calculated and she will pay income tax and national insurance on the salary drawn from the business.

As Fred is receiving a dividend of £45,000, Fiona will receive a dividend of £135,000 (assuming that all shares issued are of the same class and have the same dividend rights).

She would need to ensure that the company has sufficient distributable reserves to pay the dividends. She will also be subject to income tax (not national insurance contributions) on any dividends received.

Research & Development (R&D) tax relief

As Fiona Mare Ltd is likely to be an SME at least in the initial years of trading, it would qualify for an R&D tax deduction which would not have been available to Fiona as a sole trader. An SME may take an additional 130% deduction from trading profits for revenue expenditure. The amount of expenditure Fiona has planned is less than €7.5 million and therefore will not be subject to capping.

To the extent that the expenditure on R&D is capital expenditure the total expenditure will be allowed ie, 100% capital allowances in the year of purchase.

24.2 Fred's investment in Fiona Mare Ltd

The investment in Fiona Mare Ltd presents a tax planning opportunity for Fred.

Tax relief for an individual under the EIS is available if he subscribes for new fully paid up shares in a qualifying company. Fiona Mare Ltd would appear to qualify as it will be an unquoted company with a permanent establishment in the UK and meets the size criteria. Fred has no intention to be involved in the day-to-day business of Fiona Mare Ltd.

Fred and his associates must not own more than 30% of the shares. Fiona as his niece is not an associate for EIS purposes.

Income tax relief can be given in the year of the investment and/or in the previous year. If the shares are sold/gifted within three years, the relief will be clawed back. There is no point therefore in claiming more relief than necessary.

The amount of deduction is equal to the lower of:

- 30% × the amount invested in the scheme = 30% × £600,000 = £180,000; and
- the amount that reduces his tax liability to nil.

Therefore the tax liabilities of both years will be eliminated by EIS relief.

	2018/19 £	2019/20 £
Tax liability (per the scenario)	20,260	
2019/20 reworked to include dividend from Fiona Mare Ltd and loss of personal allowance due to level of income		
34,500 × 20%		6,900
45,500 × 40%		18,200
80,000		
Interest (500 × 0%) + (3,250 × 40%)		1,300
Dividends (10,000 + 45,000) = 55,000		
2,000 × 0%		-
53,000 × 32.5%		17,225
		43,625
Tax liability prior to EIS claim	20,260	43,625

Tutorial note

The level of detail given in the answer is more than would have been required, because the tax reducer is sufficient to relieve Fred's income tax liabilities in 2019/20 and 2018/19 in full. Full credit would be given for a less detailed answer, provided the answer clearly illustrated why less detailed computations were in point.

CGT reinvestment relief

Tax on the gain on disposal of his business in June 2018 could be deferred provided the investment is made before June 2021. To qualify for reinvestment relief, Fred would need to be UK resident at the time the gain was realised and when the shares are purchased.

Fred can restrict the claim so that he can use his annual exempt amount.

Entrepreneurs' relief will be available on the deferred gain when it becomes chargeable as presumably the original disposal qualified for entrepreneurs' relief ie, he had an ownership period of more than one year.

24.3 Gift of shares

CGT implications

If Fred gives his shares to Fiona after three years, any deferred gain arising from the sale of his sole trader business will crystallise but any increase in the value of the shares will not be taxed under the current rules, although the future tax rules could change this.

IHT implications

The gift of the shares would be a potentially exempt transfer and an IHT charge could arise if Fred were to die within seven years of the gift. However gifting his Fiona Mare Ltd shares should qualify for BPR since he would be gifting shares in an unquoted company provided he has owned the shares for at least two years.

BPR reduces the value of the transfer by 100% subject to there being no excepted assets to reduce the amount of relief at the date of transfer. However, the relief would be withdrawn if Fiona did not still hold the shares at the date of Fred's death.

24.4 Ethics

Without considering Fred's comment about not revealing to Fiona his intended gift of the Fiona Mare Ltd shares, there is a clear conflict of interest arising for CFR working for both Fred and Fiona (and Fiona Mare Ltd) which the firm must address.

CFR must check that they have engagement letters for all parties and that these do not exclude working for the other parties.

CFR must notify both Fred and Fiona that the firm acts for them both and ensure that this is reflected in the respective engagement letters and if necessary that the engagement letters are revised.

Appropriate safeguards should be set up to ensure that client's confidentiality is maintained and the independence of CFR's advice is preserved.

These safeguards should include informing the clients of the potential conflict of interest; using separate teams within the firm; or indeed deciding that working for both clients is not possible if the quality of advice and confidentiality is to be assured.

Although CFR could advise Fred to be transparent in his relationship with Fiona, he has a right to confidentiality.

Examiner's comments

24.1 Marks were available for a wide range of points associated with the incorporation of the sole trader business and few candidates scored particularly well on this part. Some spent a significant amount of time discussing loss reliefs failing to identify that the absence of previous taxable income necessitated the carry forward of the loss. Several candidates suggested that the transfer at tax WDV impacted on the CGT position and it was concerning to see discussion of a chargeable gain arising on the cash balance. Although few candidates considered the possibility of retaining the property to save SDLT, many candidates discussed the possibility of disapplying incorporation relief and benefitting from the entrepreneurs' relief thus gaining much needed marks.

24.2 and 24.3 Those candidates who failed to identify the opportunity of EIS relief struggled to achieve good marks in the context of Fred's position and those who did identify it did not necessarily follow through as to the impact of this on the gift. However, credit was given in these situations for discussion of gift relief on the gift to Fiona.

24.4 Most candidates achieved good marks on the ethics issue with sensible discussion of the issues and alternatives available. It was very pleasing to see that candidates adopted a structured approach to answer this section – the better candidates considered the issues from both perspectives: client and firm.

25 Shandy Ltd (September 2014)

Scenario

The candidate is a tax adviser in a firm of ICAEW Chartered Accountants and is asked to prepare a briefing note for use in a meeting with the client.

The client is a management buy-out team who intend to buy the trade and assets of Shandy Ltd, with or without the company. Shandy Ltd has current and brought forward trading losses.

The question presented candidates with three options for the management buy-out: a sale of shares, a sale of trade and assets and a hive down.

The candidates were expected to evaluate the tax implications of each of the three options for the management buy-out. By asking for the tax implications the examiner was expecting a discussion of all of the tax issues for the purchasing team. Answers confined to corporation tax implications would have missed out the marks for income tax, stamp duty and VAT.

Candidates were also expected to provide a reasoned recommendation to the client about the best option for the MBO from a tax perspective.

This question involves the candidate in making decisions in the face of some ambiguous and uncertain information and deliberately tests their skills in sifting information to determine its relative importance and identifying the further information needed to provide a final answer.

The final part of the question considered the failure by the vendor company to report a VAT error to HMRC, the ethical implications of this and the impact of this error on the validity of the information being provided by the vendor to the MBO team.

Marking guide

	Technical	Skills
		Marks
25.1 Explanation for the MBO team of: Purchase of shares		
• Carry forward losses	–	2
• Group relief	1	2
• Major change	1	2
• Future savings	1	1
• VAT	–	1
• Contingent liabilities	–	1

	Technical	Skills
• Stamp taxes	-	½
• IT relief	1	1½
Purchase of the trade and assets		
• Corporation tax	1	2
• VAT	1	1
• Stamp taxes	-	1
• Tax relief	1	1
• Contingent liabilities	-	1
Hive down		
• Corporation tax	1	1
• VAT	-	1
• Stamp taxes	1	1
• Contingent liabilities	-	1
	9	21

	Technical	Skills	
25.2 Recommendations to the MBO team of the method to adopt	-	2	
25.3 List of further information required	-	3	
25.4 Response to email re: ethical issue of errors in VAT returns			
• Engagement	1	1	
• Consequences	1	1	
• Due diligence	1	1	
• Anti-money laundering	1	2	
	4	5	
Total marks	13	31	44
Maximum			35

Briefing note:

Prepared for a meeting with the MBO Team

The MBO team intend to purchase the trade and assets of Shandy Ltd (Shandy) and must decide which of the three proposed methods of acquisition they will use.

This briefing note looks at the transaction from the perspective of the purchasing team.

25.1 **Tax implications for the MBO team, of each of the three different options**

Option 1: Purchase the share capital of Shandy for £2 million

Corporation tax

Because the MBO team are buying the entire share capital of an existing company, the company continues for legal and tax purposes, and there would be no cessation of trade.

Initially, the unused trading losses of Shandy, at the date of the MBO, would be carried forward within the company. The trading losses of £30,000 (£60,000 × 6/12) from pre-1 April 2017 are carried forward for use against the first available trading profits of the same trade; the unused post-1 April 2017 trading losses of up to £409,000 (including the £250,000 loss of the current year ended 30 September 2019) are carried forward for use against total profits.

Pickle plc (Pickle) is profitable and in a 75% group with Shandy up to the date of sale. Pickle could claim some of Shandy's current year trading loss and some of the post-1 April 2017 trading losses brought forward at 1 October 2018 as group loss relief and so the loss available to be carried forward in Shandy at 1 October 2019 may be reduced by a group relief claim made by Pickle.

If the shares in Shandy are to be sold, there will be a point at which group relief will be denied to Pickle, due to the existence of 'arrangements' for Shandy to leave the group. The loss carried forward is therefore likely to be between £30,000 (pre-1 April 2017 loss brought forward) if group relief is available until 30 September 2019, and £234,500 (£30,000 + £79,500 (159,000 × 6/12) + £125,000 (250,000 × 6/12)) assuming group relief is available for six months to 31 March 2019.

However, as the Shandy MBO team intend to diversify in order to bring the company back to profitability, there is a risk that the changes the MBO team intend to make to the trade would be classified by HMRC as a major change in the nature or conduct of the Shandy trade. If a change in trade which occurs within five years of the change in ownership is considered to be a major change (and the diversification of products and change from trade to retail customers appear to be major changes). It is possible that the unused trading losses would not be available to carry forward beyond the change in ownership of Shandy (beyond 30 September 2019).

If value is being attributed to losses as part of the negotiation of the purchase price, we could consider further the likely availability of the loss and the maximum value of these to the company. Assuming Shandy is able to carry forward its losses this will reduce the corporation tax liability of Shandy in future periods by a maximum of £44,555 (£234,500 × 19%).

VAT

The VAT registration of Shandy would continue and the company would retain its VAT registration number. A share sale is exempt from VAT.

Contingent liabilities

These stay with Shandy and given the VAT irregularities uncovered in discussions with the Finance Controller, the new owners of Shandy would be liable for the repayment of underpaid VAT to HMRC and also for any penalties or interest due on the mis-reporting of VAT liabilities.

Stamp taxes

The MBO team would pay stamp duty at 0.5% on the purchase of the shares. On a purchase price of £2 million, this would amount to £10,000.

Income tax relief on the purchase of shares

The MBO team will be purchasing the shares in Shandy using finance. If Shandy is a close company the MBO team would be able to claim income tax relief for any interest paid on a loan to purchase the shares in Shandy.

For this relief to be available the managers must hold more than 5% of the ordinary share capital or be full-time working officers or employees involved in the management of the company and own some shares.

Income tax relief under the enterprise investment scheme would not be available as an alternative method of gaining tax relief for the costs of investing in the shares of Shandy, given the MBO team were connected to Shandy prior to acquiring the shares ie, as employees of the company.

Option 2: Purchase the trade and assets of Shandy for £2 million

Corporation tax

The MBO team will need to set up a new company. Assets eligible for capital allowances will be added to the capital allowance computation of this company at market value on purchase and the base cost of the assets will be based on the market value of the assets.

The carried forward trading losses would stay with Shandy, the vendor company, and would not be available to carry forward in the new company.

The purchase price paid for Shandy's trade and assets may include a payment for the goodwill of the Shandy trade. There will be no relief, ie, in the form of amortisation, for the new company on the purchased goodwill.

VAT

The sale of the trade and assets of Shandy would probably be classified as the transfer of a going concern (TOGC) and if so there would be no VAT payable on the transaction because it would not be a taxable supply for VAT. There are conditions to be satisfied in order to be classified as a TOGC.

In addition, if any land and buildings are transferred as part of the TOGC the TOGC does not cover buildings under three years old or land and buildings which the transferor has opted to tax. The transferee needs to opt to tax these buildings, otherwise VAT at 20% will be chargeable on the transfer of these assets. This input VAT will be recoverable if the transferee occupies the building for trade purposes. This could affect cash flow for the MBO team, because the additional cost of any VAT payable on purchase would have to be financed by the MBO team, even if it was recoverable by the company in the first VAT quarter, should the building be occupied for the purposes of the trade.

Stamp taxes

If the company has any land and buildings, stamp duty land tax will be payable on the market value of non-residential land and buildings at a maximum rate of 5% (in tranches). This would be an additional cost to the company to be financed by the MBO team.

Tax relief for the MBO team on financing the purchase of the trade and assets

The purchase of the trade and assets would be by the MBO team's new company and any finance raised by the MBO team would be to buy shares in that company and be subject to the same comments on tax relief for the costs of that finance, as raised under option 1. If finance was raised directly by the company, tax relief would be available as part of the calculation of the company's taxable profits.

Contingent liabilities

Liabilities for past actions of Shandy remain with the vendor company. This means that liabilities like the underpayment of VAT and consequent interest and penalties will not be suffered by the MBO team.

Commercially, it would be necessary to arrange for the transfer of all relevant contracts etc.

Option 3: Hive down of trade and assets to NewShandy Ltd (NewShandy) and purchase of the shares in NewShandy by the MBO team for £2 million

Corporation tax

Assets will have been transferred to NewShandy from Shandy at tax written down value, because the companies were in the same 75% group.

The capital allowance and corporation tax accounting periods will continue on sale of the shares to the MBO team.

Trading losses would have been transferred to NewShandy, from Shandy, however, on the change in ownership of NewShandy the major change in the nature or conduct of the trade restriction, as discussed under Option 1, could still apply. It would be unlikely that these losses could be carried forward beyond the change in ownership of the NewShandy Ltd shares on 30 September 2019.

VAT

The purchase of shares is exempt from VAT. The VAT registration of NewShandy would continue on purchase.

Stamp taxes

Stamp duty will be payable at 0.5% on the purchase price of the shares in NewShandy.

SDLT was not payable on the transfer of assets from Shandy to NewShandy as the companies were in a 75% group. However, as NewShandy has now left the 75% group, within three years of the earlier transfer, SDLT will be payable on any land and buildings that were transferred from Shandy to NewShandy at a maximum of 5%.

Degrouping charges may be chargeable on NewShandy, as it is being sold outside a 75% CGT group, within six years of a no gain/no loss transfer of assets. However, as the sale of shares by Pickle is a qualifying share disposal and the degrouping charge is added to Pickle's proceeds on disposal then the degrouping charge is not taxed. So this does not affect the MBO team or NewShandy.

Contingent liabilities

As NewShandy is a new, 'clean', company; the MBO team should not be responsible for past actions and liabilities of Shandy.

25.2 Recommendation

It is likely that trading losses will not be available for use in any entity purchased, because of the major change in nature or conduct of the trade.

Therefore the main criterion to take into account as a purchaser would be the effect of contingent liabilities on the future liabilities of the company. In the light of the VAT irregularities uncovered, this may indicate that there could be other financial irregularities to uncover and also as Shandy is a chemical company, there could have been other, past issues, such as contamination of land or water courses, which might result in liabilities payable by Shandy in the future.

I would recommend either the purchase of the trade and assets of Shandy (Option 2) or the purchase of NewShandy (Option 3) assuming trading losses could not be carried forward under any of the options. Therefore the main disadvantage to a purchaser of the purchase of trade and assets would not be an issue. The MBO team would also avoid liabilities for the past acts of Shandy and the value of assets for capital allowances and the CGT base cost of assets would be maximised at current market value.

If the anticipated changes to the nature of the trade are anticipated to occur beyond the five-year period and there is therefore a potential benefit to retaining the losses, the hive down route would still give the purchasers the protection from past liabilities of Shandy.

25.3 Further information required

- A list of the assets to be transferred from Shandy – to determine:
  - the type of assets transferred and their market value at purchase for the calculation of capital allowances and goodwill;
  - the stamp duty land tax payable on the value of any land and buildings purchased.
- Will any new company be registered for VAT and satisfy the other conditions to be classified as a TOGC under Option 2?
- Will the transfer of trade in option 2 be regarded as a going concern (an issue as the trade has been in decline)?
- Details of any group relief claims to be made by Pickle in respect of Shandy's post-1 April 2017 and current period losses and whether the claim is to be restricted due to the existence of negotiations for the sale of Shandy.
- Is the sale of NewShandy a qualifying share disposal?
- A determination from HMRC about whether the change from trade to retail customers and the diversification of products constitutes a major change in the nature or conduct of the trade?

25.4 VAT Irregularities

VAT irregularities have been admitted by the financial controller of Shandy and Pickle.

We would need to independently review and check that the error had indeed been made in the VAT returns and calculate the effect of these errors.

We should ensure that all discussions in connection with this matter are appropriately documented.

Our engagement is with the MBO team. If the MBO team were to acquire Shandy and its contingent liabilities we would discuss this issue with the client and advise them to disclose the error to HMRC.

However, we do not have an engagement letter with Shandy. Therefore, although we could advise the financial controller to inform HMRC of the error, we do not have any contractual rights to report the error to HMRC under the terms of an engagement. We do not act for Shandy and so could not resign from an existing engagement.

The consequences of not reporting the VAT error, for Shandy would be that:

- this would constitute tax evasion by Shandy;

- should HMRC discover the error, there would be penalties for the submission of incorrect returns and this penalty may be greater if the error has been deliberately concealed;

- having knowledge of the error and not acting upon it could be classified as a criminal offence or a civil fraud;

- interest will accrue on any underpaid VAT, until it has been paid.

Shandy appears to have an inappropriate attitude to compliance with the tax law and we may need to safeguard our clients, the MBO team. We may also need to carry out extra due diligence work on the books and records of Shandy, if we intend to take over their contingent liabilities, in order to satisfy ourselves that our clients are not going to be liable for inappropriate actions by the Financial Controller.

Although we cannot report the inaccuracies to HMRC, if we have reasonable grounds for knowledge or suspicion that a money laundering offence has been committed, we could make a report to the firm's MLRO, who, in turn, could report this issue to the National Crime Agency in a suspicious activities report. In this case, given our client is the management team of Shandy, we might need to be careful not to tip off the MBO team concerning our report to the National Crime Agency, because they are currently colleagues of the alleged money launderer.

Examiner's comments

Although this question concerned an area of the syllabus which has been trailed in the sample papers for BP:T (sale of shares in a company v sale of trade and assets), the use of a management buy-out as the vehicle for the transaction and the emphasis on the position of the purchaser and not the vendor added a new slant to the scenario. Candidates had clearly not encountered this scenario before and so answers were very mixed. The stronger candidates did adopt the correct approach and discussed the difference between purchase of shares, purchase of trade and assets and a hive down, which is covered extensively in the learning materials. For this reason, this question was a good discriminator between the stronger and the weaker candidates.

Specific comments on sections of the question:

25.1 The stronger candidates scored very well and recognised that the key advantage with the purchase of shares was that the losses could potentially be carried forward. The discussion of whether the 'changes' would constitute a major change in nature or conduct of trade was very encouraging. Candidates also thought about the VAT, Stamp duty and Income tax consequences of each option. Better marks were displayed for logical answers, which discussed each option in turn. The weaker candidates scored quite poorly as they did not know how to approach the question. Answers tended to be quite unstructured and whilst at times did discuss some relevant points, such as ability to use losses in the future, it was clear that candidates struggled to apply basic knowledge when faced with a scenario which was slightly different to some of the questions in the learning materials.

25.2 and 25.3 Candidates sometimes failed to make recommendations, which was very surprising given how well set out the question was and how clear the requirements were. Those who made sensible recommendations and discussed the availability of information in terms of valuation of assets, group relief etc scored well on this part.

25.4 This was the ethical scenario and, as usual, this was answered quite poorly. The hint in the question about failure to disclose an error should have given candidates ample material to work with and it was very apparent that to not report the VAT error was tantamount to fraud. However, instead of working with the facts presented, candidates went down the route of discussing every fundamental ethical principle they knew, without really applying them to the question. A future approach for candidates should be to identify the problem, discuss the implications of the problem and then the action which should be taken. The better answers did adopt this approach and also discussed what discovery of an error may do the valuation of the company overall for the MBO which produced some very good, intelligent answers. Ethics needs to be given more prevalence when candidates are studying for this exam, given, that for the weaker candidates this should be a source of relatively easy marks.

26 Upten plc (June 2015)

Scenario

This is a business start-up question in a corporate environment. The candidate is presented with two alternative ownership structures: one which creates a group relationship for group relief purposes; and the other which creates a consortium relationship. The candidate must identify that the transfer of a building as part consideration creates in the first structure a nil gain/nil loss transfer and in the second structure a disposal and hence a chargeable gain as the building is now leaving the group. The candidate must also identify and explain a tax advantaged share option scheme to motivate the managers of the parent company.

	Technical	Skills	Marks
Briefing note			
Share option scheme			
• EMI recommendation	1	1	
• Advantages	2	2	
• Size of company	–	1	
• After tax cash	2	2	
	5	6	
Tax implications of alternative structures			
Structure 1			
• Group relationship	1	3	
• Gains on warehouse	1	3	
• VAT on warehouse	1	2	
• SDLT	1	2	
	4	10	
Structure 2			
• Gains	1	3	
• Unused trading loss	–	2	
• VAT/SDLT	1	2	
• Consortium relief	2	2	
• Link company	1	2	
• Calculation	1	3	
	6	14	
Total marks	15	30	45
Maximum			30

Briefing note to finance director
Prepared by: Tina Yarn

Share option scheme

The most appropriate scheme for Upten plc would be an EMI scheme.

The options granted will be less than £250,000 per employee and the employees are full-time.

The advantage of an EMI scheme is that it is a tax-advantaged scheme and no income tax or NIC are payable at grant or on exercise. Gains are taxable when the shares are sold. This is an advantage for the employee and the employer. Also other tax-advantaged schemes normally require a minimum period of three years before vesting.

Another advantage is that gains on EMI shares qualify for entrepreneurs' relief, potentially leading to a 10% rate of CGT on gains.

I would need to check the size of Upten plc and Upten plc cannot have more than £3 million of options in issue at any one time.

Assuming the employee sells the shares on 30 June 2021 for £6 each, the after tax cash receivable for one employee under the share option scheme would be as follows:

	£
Proceeds 40,000 × £6	240,000
Cost 40,000 × £2.50	100,000
Gain	140,000
Annual exempt amount (assuming not used elsewhere)	(11,700)
	128,300
Capital gains tax at 10%	12,830

As the option was granted more than a year before disposal and the employee works full-time for the company, entrepreneurs' relief is available.

After tax cash receipt is £240,000 – £12,830 = £227,170 less £100,000 (cost of shares) = £127,170.

Tax implications of alternative structures

Structure 1

Upten plc will own 75% and Wohnung GmbH will own 25% of the ordinary shares in DLP Ltd.

Structure 1 creates a group relationship between Upten plc, Woren Ltd and DLP Ltd both for chargeable gains purposes and trading loss purposes. As Upten plc will own 75% or more of the DLP Ltd shares, a group relief claim is possible from DLP Ltd.

Therefore, all of the DLP Ltd loss is available for group relief to either Upten plc or Woren Ltd.

As Upten plc has brought forward trading losses, it must use its own loss first therefore the group relief of DLP Ltd's loss should be to Woren Ltd. In addition, the post-1 April 2017 loss brought forward in Upten plc is also available for group loss relief to Woren Ltd. The losses relieved within Upten plc itself are £1.5 million of the £1.9 million (£2.5m – £0.6m) pre-1 April 2017 losses which are automatically set against the first available trading profits of the same trade. The remaining pre-1 April 2017 losses of £400,000 (£1.9m – £1.5m) are carried forward for relief against future trading profits of the same trade within Upten plc.

	Upten plc £'000	Woren Ltd £'000
Trading profit	1,500	4,500
Brought forward loss	(1,500)	
	Nil	
		4,500
Group relief (current period) from DLP Ltd		(3,600)
Group relief (brought forward losses) from Upten plc		(600)
Taxable profits	Nil	300

Disposal of warehouse

Where one group company transfers a chargeable asset to another group company it is deemed for tax purposes to take place at such a price as gives no gain and no loss to the transferor company ie, deemed proceeds = allowable expenditure plus indexation allowance up to the date of the transfer (or to December 2017, if earlier).

Tutorial note

Indexation allowance is ignored for this question, so reference to indexation allowance is not required.

Under Structure 1 the warehouse is not leaving the chargeable gains group and therefore the transfer is made at no gain/no loss basis. The no gain/no loss treatment applies if both the transferor and transferee company are part of the same group at the time of transfer, and are either both UK resident or the asset is chargeable both before and after the transfer.

It is likely a VAT group will exist and that DLP Ltd will join it. If so then no VAT will arise on the transfer of the warehouse. A VAT group can normally include companies with a shareholding of greater than 50%.

Since the transferee is in the same 75% group, SDLT group relief will be due, though an SDLT 'degrouping' charge would apply if DLP Ltd were to leave the group whilst owning the warehouse within three years of the transfer.

Structure 2

Upten plc will own 65% and Home Ltd will own 35% of the ordinary shares in DLP Ltd.

Under Structure 2 a chargeable gain will arise in Upten plc, as the warehouse is now being disposed of outside the group. Upten plc's shareholding in DLP Ltd is 65% and is not sufficient to create the 75% relationship required for an intra-group transfer.

The cost used when calculating a gain is by reference to the original cost of acquisition by the group ie, by Woren Ltd.

Tutorial note

Should indexation be calculated, although not required in this question, this is taken as the cost plus indexation allowance to the date of transfer, or to December 2017 if earlier. This cost is then indexed as appropriate to December 2017.

A chargeable gain arises of £5m – (£4m – £0.3m) = £1.3m. This is reduced by the capital loss brought forward of £550,000 resulting in a chargeable gain of £750,000 for Upten plc.

Upten plc cannot offset the pre-1 April 2017 brought forward trading loss against the chargeable gain, only against trading profits. However the post-1 April 2017 trading loss can be relieved against total profits ie, against the gain reducing it further to £150,000 (£750,000 – £600,000).

It is likely a VAT group will exist and that DLP will join it. If so then no VAT will arise on the transfer of the warehouse. A VAT group can normally include companies with a shareholding of greater than 50%.

Stamp Duty Land Tax of up to 5% (in tranches) would be due on transfer of the warehouse.

Relief for DLP Ltd's loss

A consortium relationship will exist between Upten plc and Home Ltd ('consortium members'); they will each own at least 5% and jointly own at least 75% of the ordinary share capital of another UK resident company, DLP Ltd ('consortium company').

Losses may be surrendered, in either direction, between a consortium member and the consortium company.

Under this structure DLP Ltd's loss can be surrendered to Upten plc and Home Ltd. The maximum surrender is the lower of:

- available loss = consortium member's % holding in the consortium company × consortium company loss; and

- available profits = all of the taxable total profits of the consortium member.

Upten plc is also a 'link company' as it is both a consortium member and a member of a group. Consortium relief can also be surrendered via Upten plc, the 'link company', to Woren Ltd. Any UK related member of the consortium member's group can claim consortium relief on behalf of the link company and can surrender its losses to a UK related company owned by the link company's consortium.

Under this structure DLP Ltd's loss can flow through Upten plc to its profitable subsidiary Woren Ltd. Woren Ltd is a related company as it is a UK resident company.

The effect of these rules is that if the link company has insufficient profits to absorb a loss made by the consortium company, it can be used by a fellow group company. Indeed a fellow group company can claim these losses in preference to the link company.

As all companies pay corporation tax at the same rate, it does not matter which qualifying company the losses pass to. Therefore up to £150,000 can be used by Upten plc with the balance to Woren Ltd.

Subject to the consortium members agreeing, a claim for consortium relief can be made for 65% of DLP Ltd's loss by Upten plc.

	Upten plc £'000	Woren Ltd £'000
Trading profit	1,500	4,500
Brought forward loss	(1,500)	
Chargeable gain	150	
Total profits	150	4,500
Consortium relief from DLP Ltd – 65% × £3,600,000 = £2,340,000	(150)	(2,190)
Taxable profits	Nil	2,310

Examiner's comments

The quality of responses to this question varied significantly. Poor time management was often evident in weaker candidates, with the second part barely attempted in some cases. Poorer quality answers sometimes failed to distinguish properly between Structure 1 and Structure 2, or alternated between them in a confusing fashion demonstrating weak skills in assimilating information from the scenario. This question differentiated candidates who were able to step back and use their time wisely to interpret the scenario.

Specific comments on sections of the question:

Tax advantaged share option scheme

Most candidates scored well on the share options issue with clear explanations as to why an EMI scheme was most appropriate in the scenario. Disappointingly many candidates stated that the options were to be granted at a discount although the question clearly stated that the grant would be at market value. Once again candidates struggled to identify after tax proceeds with many deducting the CGT annual exempt amount or simply deducting the tax from the gross proceeds and failing to recognise the cost associated with exercising the options.

Alternative ownership structures

The majority of candidates identified that the alternative structures represent a group and a consortium respectively, but many failed to understand the effect on the transfer of the property – and even some of those who had referred to the gains group, then included the gain in the calculation of taxable profits in Structure 1.

27 Montgomery Ltd (September 2015)

Scenario

In this question candidates were working as an in-house tax adviser for a UK-based company going through a rapid period of expansion. The candidate was expected to advise on:

27.1 The tax consequences of an acquisition of the trade and assets of another company, that had already happened; and

27.2 The tax consequences, including anti-avoidance rules, of expansion into international markets through a proposed business venture.

Marking guide

Marks

	Technical	Skills	
27.1 Acquisition of trade and assets of Romulus Ltd			
• Capital and trade losses	–	2	
• Fever Ltd commencement	2	2	
• Purchase of assets	1	2	
• Capital allowances	–	4	
• Amortisation	1	1	
VAT on sale of property			
• TOGC	2	2	
• Property and TOGC	1	2	
• CGS	1	1	
• Adjustments	2	2	
SDLT on property	2	2	
	12	20	
27.2 Separate Asiatic registered subsidiary v PE			
• Overseas subsidiary	1	2	
• Central management and control	1	1	
• PE	1	2	
• Conclusions	1	1	
Transfer pricing/CFC			
• Transfer pricing	1	2	
• CFC definition	1	2	
• Exemptions	1	2	
• Tax treatment	–	1	
• Overseas PE exemption	1	1	
• Disadvantages	1	1	
• Conclusions	1	1	
	10	16	
Total marks	22	36	58
Maximum			40

27.1 The acquisition was of the trade and assets of Romulus Ltd (Romulus), rather than the shares.

As there was no common ownership of Romulus and Fever Ltd (Fever), at the time of the transfer, both capital and trading losses will remain with Romulus.

Fever will start trading and must notify HMRC that it is within the charge to corporation tax.

The company will be required to complete corporation tax returns. The returns will be based on the accounting dates of the company so if these are coterminous with those of Montgomery Ltd (Montgomery), the first return will be for the 9 month period ended 31 March 2020, due to be filed by 31 March 2021.

It is likely that the corporation tax for the period ended 31 March 2020 will be due on 1 January 2021 and the dates of future payments will depend on the level of the taxable profits of the company.

A group payment arrangement could be set up for future years whereby one of the companies is responsible for making payment in respect of the group liability.

Fever will acquire assets in accordance with the purchase agreement. In the absence of an alternative attribution of the consideration, the total consideration is likely to be attributed based on market values with the balance attributable to purchased goodwill as follows:

	£
Property	300,000
Plant and machinery	75,000
Net current assets	25,000
Goodwill	200,000
	600,000

Tax relief will be available in respect of the expenditure as follows.

Property – the price paid of £300,000 will be the base cost of the asset on any future disposal, for the purposes of capital gains tax.

In addition, if the property includes eligible fixtures (eg, air conditioning units) capital allowances may be available. These allowances will only be available if Romulus has previously claimed allowances in respect of the fixtures and a joint election is signed agreeing the value to be attributed to the fixtures. Relief will therefore be available at either 18% or 8% depending upon the nature of the assets.

The plant and machinery acquisitions of £75,000 may qualify for the annual investment allowance (100% capital allowances would be available in the accounting period ended 31 March 2020). Otherwise the additions would be added to the main pool.

No succession election would be available to transfer assets at tax written down value, because there was no common ownership between Fever and Romulus.

Relief is not available for amortisation of goodwill ie, it is not deductible from trading profits for tax purposes. Relief will only be available on realisation of the goodwill.

The sale of the property will have both VAT and stamp duty implications.

It is likely that the transfer of the trade and assets from Romulus to Fever will be a transfer of a going concern (TOGC). If so, the transaction will be outside the scope of VAT, meaning that Fever will not be charged VAT on the purchase of the trade and assets by Romulus.

For the transaction to be a TOGC, certain conditions will need to be satisfied:

(1) The whole of the business needs to be transferred. This appears to be the case here.

(2) The assets are to be used in the same kind of business in the future. This also appears to be the case here.

(3) The transferor is VAT registered. We have confirmed that this is the case here.

(4) There is no significant break in trading. This also appears to be the case here.

In the case of items (1), (2) and (4) above we would need to confirm that these conditions have been satisfied.

As the property is more than three years old at the date of transfer and Romulus did not opt to tax, the property is covered by the TOGC rules and no VAT charge will arise provided that the conditions were satisfied.

At present Fever has not exercised the option to tax in respect of the property. As Fever makes mainly taxable supplies (sales of clothing) and a very small amount of exempt supplies (rent of the factory third floor with no option to tax), the business will be partially exempt. The impact of this partial exemption will depend upon the level of input tax attributed to exempt activities, which could result in a restriction on the recovery of input tax.

As the property is still within the first 10 years of its life, and originally cost more than £250,000, it is within the capital goods scheme.

If the property was covered by the TOGC rules, there would have been no adjustment on sale required by the vendor (Romulus) and the purchaser (Fever) assumed responsibility for the remaining tax adjustment period.

Therefore Fever will need to make adjustments at the end of each annual adjustment period, if the building is not used for fully taxable purposes.

With effect from 1 July 2019, the taxable use will only be 66% of the building as Fever is to rent one floor of the building to other businesses. If no VAT is charged on the rent, as the option to tax has not been exercised, the clawback of VAT each annual VAT period would be:

(£275,000 (original VAT exclusive price) × 20% = £55,000/10) = 5,500 × (66% – 100%) = £1,870 pa VAT clawback.

This VAT will be clawed back from Fever for each remaining period of the 10-year capital goods scheme period. As the capital goods scheme first applied for the year ended 31 March 2015, including the year ended 31 March 2020, there will be five remaining periods of clawback.

Alternatively Fever could exercise the option to tax to retain fully taxable use of the property. This would result in an increased effective rental cost to the non-VAT registered small businesses who are to be the tenants. However, there would be no adjustments in respect of the Capital Goods Scheme and the business would make 100% fully taxable supplies so no partial exemption restrictions would apply to the recovery of input VAT.

As a result Fever should consider carefully the impact of exercising the option to tax on the level of the rents that could be charged to tenants before making the final decision on this matter.

Stamp duty land tax is payable by the purchaser (Fever) at the rates for non-residential property. The stamp duty land tax payable on the purchase of the land and buildings would be £4,500 (((£250,000 – £150,000) × 2%) + (£50,000 × 5%)) assuming that the TOGC conditions are met and hence no VAT was charged on the acquisition.

Tutorial note

Any other relevant and correct observations on the impact of the purchase of trade and assets of Romulus Ltd on Montgomery Ltd and Fever Ltd would have received credit from the examiners.

27.2 In setting up the overseas factory in Asiatica, Montgomery must decide whether the factory is to be:

- a separate Asiatic registered subsidiary company; or
- a permanent establishment (PE).

The tax consequences of a separate Asiatica subsidiary would be, prima facie, that the profits of the Asiatica subsidiary would be taxed at the rate of 5% in Asiatica only.

This would give rise to Asiatic corporation tax (CT) of £10,000 for the period ending 31 March 2020 and £50,000 for the year ending 31 March 2021.

If the profits were then sent to the UK in the form of dividends, these are likely to be exempt from CT in the hands of the UK parent.

If it were considered that the company was centrally managed and controlled in the UK the company would be liable to UK corporation tax. The extent of management exercised in the UK should therefore be carefully reviewed.

The UK tax consequences of a PE would be that the profits of the Asiatica PE would usually be included within the profits of the UK parent company and taxed in the UK at the UK CT rate. This would give rise to corporation tax at 19% on those profits. This would mean a tax liability of £38,000 for the period ended 31 March 2020 and £190,000 for the year ended 31 March 2021.

If any tax is suffered on these profits in Asiatica (for example if the PE is taxed at the 5% rate) this tax will be deductible from the UK CT due.

Based on these facts alone, the incorporation of a foreign subsidiary company would seem to be the most tax efficient structure for the Asiatic factory operation.

However, we would also need to consider anti-avoidance legislation, which might amend the tax consequences noted above.

If the overseas factory is incorporated as a subsidiary:

Transfer pricing

As all sales are made from the overseas factory operation to Montgomery in the UK we will need to ensure that the transfer prices charged are at arm's length. The group is large (employs at least 250 people) and so the transfer pricing rules are relevant. If non-arm's length prices are being charged, in order to transfer profits from the higher tax jurisdiction of the UK to the lower tax jurisdiction of Asiatica, then profits would need to be restated in the UK, to ensure that the correct amount of profit is taxed in the UK.

An advance pricing agreement can be reached with HMRC and the Asiatic tax authorities to ensure that the prices being charged between the UK and Asiatica are at arm's length.

Controlled foreign company

Given that the subsidiary would be a non-UK resident company, controlled by UK residents it would be a controlled foreign company (CFC).

A CFC charge applies if none of the exemptions apply and chargeable profits arising, pass through one of the 'gateways' to bring them into the charge to UK tax.

The possible exemptions are:

- exempt period – only relevant to existing businesses coming under the control of UK residents;

- excluded territories list – Asiatica is not on this list;

- low profits – given the anticipated annual profits of £1 million, the exempt limit of £500,000 would be exceeded;

- tax exemption – this requires local tax to be at least 75% of the UK tax that would have arisen on the profits. The 5% tax rate in Asiatica means that this would not apply.

Any profits deemed to pass through a gateway would therefore be assessable at the main rate of CT on Montgomery, in the UK. This would negate the tax advantage of the subsidiary being set up, as all profits would be subject to UK CT at the rate of 19%, rather than Asiatica CT at 5%. Any Asiatica CT paid would be deductible from the UK CT due.

Profits considered attributable to UK activities will pass through the gateway unless they meet an exemption. As incorporating the subsidiary could be seen to be an arrangement, one of the purposes of which is to reduce or eliminate a charge to UK tax the profits would be attributed, unless there is considered to be a commercial capacity for the business to continue if no UK management or there are no assets or risks managed or controlled from the UK. The level of involvement of the UK management should therefore be considered carefully to decide if the rules will apply.

Overseas PE exemption election

If the overseas operation were a PE in Asiatica, we could consider whether to make the election to exempt the income and losses of overseas PEs from UK tax.

This election applies to all overseas PEs and is effective from the start of the accounting period after the one in which the election is made and is irrevocable. Therefore, if the election were made now, it would only be in force from 1 April 2020 and so profits of the period to 31 March 2020 would still be taxable in the UK.

The disadvantage of this election is that although it might appear to be advantageous in this case, it might be disadvantageous when applied to PEs set up by Montgomery in the future.

As the foreign operation is likely to be treated as a CFC if it were to be incorporated, there is also an anti-diversion rule, which means that profits of a PE to which an exemption applies are not exempt if the CFC rules would have applied if the PE had been incorporated.

Because of this anti-diversion rule, the use of a PE, rather than a subsidiary would not be a tax advantage if the CFC regime applied to the Asiatica operation.

Examiner's comments

The tax impact of the purchase of trade and assets from another company has been examined in previous BP:T examinations; however, in previous questions, the purchase has been prospective and a decision had to be made about whether to buy trade and assets or shares. In this question, the purchase had already been made and so part 1 of the question was not asking for advice about how to structure the acquisition, but, instead about the tax implications of a deal that had already happened. The danger for candidates was that they would simply list a checklist of factors to consider from their study materials, whereas, the marking guide was structured to look for application of the knowledge to the particular scenario set.

Candidates should appreciate that it is not enough to refer to the names in the question and regurgitate the contents of the study text. Information given in an answer needs to be relevant to the scenario set and applied to the facts of the question.

Part 2 of the question concerned a decision about the structure of an overseas expansion vehicle (separate subsidiary company or branch of the UK parent company). The relative tax treatments had to be considered and also the anti-avoidance legislation which exists to prevent abuse of the global marketplace.

This anti-avoidance legislation is topical and increasing in volume and it is a good way of determining whether candidates understand the impact of the UK as a jurisdiction on the global marketplace for goods and services and the ethical considerations surrounding 'jurisdiction-shopping'.

A large number of answers were too limited to rote-learned facts and lists. The better candidates applied the anti-avoidance rules to the scenario set and drew conclusions about the impact of anti-avoidance legislation on the decisions the company was trying to take.

March 2016 exam answers

28   Delia, Chris and Ella

Scenario

The candidate is a trainee ICAEW Chartered Accountant at a firm which specialises in advising start-up businesses. The candidate is preparing briefing notes for a manager on: whether each business should start as a company or sole trader, and in respect of the business structured as a corporate entity, the most favourable tax implications for a third party investor. Projections for the two new businesses are provided, as are details of investor's past and projected future income and gain. Technical issues included the consideration of personal service companies (IR35), R&D, use of trade losses, residence and the Enterprise Investment Scheme.

Marking guide

		Technical	Skills	Marks
(a)	**Tax efficient business structure**			
	Sole trader v company	1	2	
	Loss relief	-	2	
	Delia	1	2	
	Pre-trading expenditure	-	1	
	R&D costs	1½	3	
	Patent costs	1	-	
	Patent box	2	2	
	Recommendations	-	3	
	Chris opening year losses	2	3½	
	Recommendations	-	3	
		8½	21½	
	Max			24
(b)	**Extraction of profits**			
	Limited company options	1	-	
	Dividend	1	1½	
	Salary	1	1½	
	Pension	-	1	
	Chris	½	1	
		3½	5	
	Max			6
(c)	**Investment**			
	EIS conditions	3	-	
	EIS relief	-	2	
	UK residence	1	2	
	Tax liabilities	2	1	
	CGT	1	2	
		7	7	
	Max			10
	Total marks	19	33½	52½
	Maximum			40

(a) **Tax efficient business structure for Delia and Chris**

Tax is only one consideration and there are other non-tax considerations to consider when deciding upon an appropriate business structure.

Both Delia and Chris have a choice between a sole trader and a limited company as a means of structure for their business.

The main difference in terms of tax liabilities for the two alternative structures is that as a sole trader, the individual would be taxed on all of the profits regardless of the level of drawings. Operating through a limited company would mean that the company pays tax on its profits. However, Delia or Chris would be an employee of the company and receive employment income. A limited company structure also enables profit to be extracted by means of a dividend which potentially could save NIC. However, unlike a salary, dividends are appropriations and are not deducted in arriving at the company's taxable profits.

An important consideration is whether the business will make a profit in the opening years. The use of losses is more flexible for a sole trader as losses in the first four years of trade can be set off against total income of the previous three years (subject to an overall cap on deductions).

Losses in a new limited company can only be set off against current period income and/or carried forward against future total profits. Losses therefore can remain unrelieved if the company does not make taxable profits in the near future at a time when the business could benefit from the cash flow effect of a tax refund. To determine whether the business has a tax loss, the potential additional deductions available to the business must be identified and the taxable profit adjusted.

Delia

There are a number of factors from the scenario which would suggest that Delia's business should be structured as a limited company for tax reasons. These include:

- research and development expenditure
- patent

For both of these a limited company structure would give reliefs not available for a sole trader. In addition start-up losses, which favour treatment as a sole trader, are not projected here. Therefore a company is likely to be a more appropriate way in which to carry on the business. However, there is a potential issue with the provision of her services as a dietician to private clinic which may increase tax liabilities (see below).

Pre-trading expenditure

Capital expenditure incurred before a business starts is eligible for capital allowances.

In general, the capital expenditure is treated as incurred on the first day of trading and so included in the capital allowances computation for the first accounting period.

However, the rate of allowances available is determined by the actual date of the expenditure. Assuming that AIA is available a deduction from the trading profit of £45,000 for the computer equipment purchased on 1 March 2019 would therefore be made.

Research and development costs

As a limited company making qualifying R&D expenditure, it would qualify for an additional deduction of 130% of the actual qualifying expenditure incurred on R&D. Assuming the company is a small/medium-sized enterprise (SME), an additional 130% deduction from trading profits could be made. Of the costs, the staff costs and power water and materials would appear to qualify for the additional revenue deduction. The expenditure on plant and machinery would qualify for a 100% capital allowance.

As none of these costs have been included in the calculation of taxable profits, the following further deduction would be available:

	2020 £	2021 £
Power water and materials	23,000	8,000
Salary costs of research staff	45,000	45,000
	68,000	53,000
130%	88,400	68,900
	156,400	121,900
100% capital allowances for P&M	19,000	-
Additional deduction from profit	175,400	121,900

Patent costs

Delia intends to patent the new product and although no details of these costs are given, the patent costs will be treated as intangible fixed assets and amortised in the statement of profit or loss. Tax relief for intangible fixed assets follows the accounting treatment.

Patent box

Potentially as a limited company, the business could elect for the profits arising from the Luzit patent to arise within a patent box which would be eligible for a lower rate of corporation tax.

There is a requirement to extract income and expenditure of the patent separately and this may add to the burden of administration.

There will be some additional administration costs in determining the appropriate profits and adjustments. However, this should be investigated further.

Revised taxable trading profits

	2020 £	2021 £	2022 £
Taxable trading profit before capital allowances	260,000	360,000	425,000
Less capital allowances:			
Computer equipment (1 March 2019)	(45,000)		-
Plant and machinery	(19,000)		-
Website revenue costs	(8,000)	(5,000)	(5,000)
R&D	(156,400)	(121,900)	
Adjusted taxable profit	31,600	233,100	420,000

Recommendations

Given the availability of R&D relief and the potential to use of the patent box, the advice would be that the business should be structured as a limited company.

One concern however is the treatment of the income from the supply of Delia's services as a dietician to the private clinic. Potentially the contract could come within the personal service company legislation (IR35). IR35 applies where an individual provides services to a client through an intermediary, and would be treated as an employee but for the existence of the intermediary.

To determine whether the contract would come within the IR35 legislation, the terms of the contract would need to be examined by applying the self-employed/employed tests of control and case law. On the basis of the information given, it is possible that Delia is treated as an employee of the clinic as she works on the clinic's premises, to their given hours and advises their clients. Appointments are booked in for her, and she is paid an hourly rate.

If the contract comes within IR35 additional national insurance will become due and this will fall as a liability on Delia's company. PAYE and NIC will be due on the deemed payment although the company will receive tax relief for these payments.

If she is a sole trader, she would probably be treated as an employee of the clinic and PAYE and NIC applied.

Chris

Chris's business appears to be making trading losses in the opening years and therefore it would be most appropriate to set up as a sole trader. This would have the advantage of generating a tax refund for Chris of £9,300.

	2020 £	2021 £	2022 £
Taxable trading (loss)/profit before capital allowances	(36,000)	15,000	185,000
Less capital allowances: equipment	(22,000)	(5,000)	(5,000)
Adjusted taxable (loss)/profit	(58,000)	10,000	180,000

Loss memorandum 2019/20	Loss £	Tax refund £
Basis period (Actual)	58,000	
Less s.72 claim in 2017/18	(35,000)	4,700
Less s.72 claim in 2018/19	(23,000)	4,600
	Nil	9,300

	2017/18 £	2018/19 £
Employment income	35,000	40,000
s.72	(35,000)	(23,000)
		17,000
Less personal allowance		(11,850)
	Nil	5,150
Tax payable		1,030

Before claim		
Employment income	35,000	40,000
Less personal allowance	(11,500)	(11,850)
	23,500	28,150
Tax @ 20%	4,700	5,630
Tax refund	4,700	4,600

The statutory redundancy payment will be exempt and the remaining payment will be covered in the first £30,000 exemption as it is a discretionary termination payment.

Recommendations

Initially Chris should establish his business as a sole trader to take advantage of tax relief for the opening year losses. If the predicted expansion and profits happens in the third year, Chris should consider incorporating his business. Alternative recommendations may also be valid – for example the benefit of loss relief is not huge and Chris could incorporate from the start of his business. This would have the downside of not making early year loss relief claims but the benefits of wasting less losses on amounts covered by personal allowances.

Incorporation would ensure that the profits of the year ending 5 April 2022 would be taxed at 19% instead of partially at 45%. Only profits extracted would be subject to higher rates should these exceed the higher rate band. Incorporation would lead to gains becoming chargeable on the workshop and goodwill. Reliefs are available to defer the gains under incorporation relief or gift relief.

(b) **Tax implications for Delia and Chris of extracting an after tax amount of £20,000 from their business profits in the year ending 5 April 2020**

Delia - Limited company

As an employee and shareholder Delia could extract profits as either a dividend, salary or pension contribution.

In 2019/20 she will be a higher rate tax payer as she will be receiving a salary from Nisty Foods plc. It would save national insurance if she extracted the £20,000 as a dividend. The company would, however, not receive tax relief for the dividend as it is an appropriation. (The company would also need to ensure that it has distributable profits available to pay not only a dividend to Delia but also to Ella should she take a 20% equity stake in the business.)

Payment of a dividend

	£
Payment required	20,000
Tax for a higher rate payer ie, (£20,000 – £2,000) × 32.5/67.5	8,667
Cash dividend to be paid by the company	28,667

Tutorial note

Delia has the £2,000 of dividend nil rate band, so only the excess dividends are subject to tax at 32.5%.

Payment of a salary

	£
Gross salary required = £20,000 × 100/58	34,483
Less income tax at 40%	(13,793)
Less NIC at 2% (since earnings from Nisty exceed the upper earnings limit)	(690)
	20,000
Payments to be made by the company	
Gross salary	34,483
Employers' NIC (£34,483 – 8,424) × 13.8%	3,596
	38,079
Less corporation tax saving at 19%	(7,235)
Cash cost to company	30,844

Tutorial note

The calculation of the national insurance computations should strictly have a deduction of the primary threshold before multiplying the balance by 2%. However the examiners allowed this simplified calculation in the exam.

Pension contribution

A pension contribution may be appropriate for Delia if she has sufficient funds for her living costs. A pension contribution would attract tax relief for the company at 19% and would therefore only cost the company £16,200. No additional tax or national insurance would be due.

Chris - sole trader

Extracting £20,000 from the sole trader business has no tax consequences for Chris if he operates as a sole trader. Tax is calculated on the taxable profits of the business irrespective of the level of drawings. As the business has not made a profit, no tax would be payable.

(c) **Tax savings arising from the investment for Ella for the tax years 2018/19 and 2019/20**

Recommendation

As Ella wishes to make a tax efficient investment she should be looking to make use of the reliefs available under the EIS scheme. Seed EIS (SEIS) is not appropriate as the investment limit is £100,000, whereas Ella plans to invest £250,000.

Tax relief under the EIS is available if Ella subscribes for new fully paid up shares in a qualifying company. Delia's company would appear to qualify as it will be an unquoted company trading in the UK, it meets the size criteria and there is a risk to capital. We would need to confirm that Ella has no intention to be involved in the day-to-day business of the company but given that she is a surgeon then this would seem unlikely.

Ella must not own more than 30% of the shares – and as her requirement is for a 20% share in the business this would seem to be met.

Income tax relief is given in the year of the investment and/or in the previous year. If the shares are sold/gifted within three years, the relief will be clawed back. There is no point therefore in claiming more relief than necessary.

The amount of deduction is equal to the lower of:

- 30% of the amount invested in the scheme = 30% × £250,000 = £75,000; and
- the amount that reduces her tax liability to nil – £80,100 (see below).

Ella will be treated as resident from the date of arrival in the UK for the following reasons:

- In 2018/19 she will not meet any of the automatic overseas tests because although she appears to have been non-resident in the previous three tax years, she will be spending more than 46 days in the UK.

- For 2019/20 it is probable that she will meet both the 91-day UK home and no foreign home test although this would need to be confirmed and the automatic UK test for full-time work in the UK (because she intends to be here working for full-time for more than 365 days, working a 35-hour week). If any of these tests are passed she would be UK resident for 2019/20.

Split year treatment should apply to 2018/19 ie, she will be UK resident from 1 November 2018 provided that she has not established sufficient 'ties' in the period before coming to the UK.

As she appears not to have been resident in the previous three years and has no days in the UK in the period before 1 November 2018 (ie, less than 46 days prorated for the number of whole months in the period 6 April 2018 to 31 October 2018 ie, 6 months) she meets the automatic overseas test for this period.

Should split year treatment be appropriate, Ella would be liable to capital gains tax on her worldwide assets once she is UK resident. Therefore, the gain on the sale the property in Poland will be taxable in the UK as the split year also applies to capital gains tax. She may have tax liabilities in Poland and should take advice from a tax adviser in Poland.

Ella's tax liabilities for 2018/19 and 2019/20 are projected to be as follows:

Income	2018/19 £	2019/20 £
Employment income/taxable income		
1 November 2018 to 5 April 2019 – in London	124,000	
6 April 2019 to 5 April 2020		210,000
34,500 @ 20%	6,900	6,900
(124,000 – 34,500) × 40%	35,800	
(150,000 – 34,500) × 40%		46,200
(210,000 – 150,000) × 45%		27,000
	42,700	80,100
Less EIS relief		(75,000)
Income tax liability		5,100

Capital gains tax EIS reinvestment relief is available where an investment is made under EIS scheme. To qualify for the reinvestment relief, the individual must be UK tax resident both at the time the gain is realised and when the shares are purchased. As the gain on the disposal of the property was realised in February 2019 when Ella was UK tax resident, it will qualify for reinvestment relief provided that the reinvestment happens within 12 months before or up to 36 months after. The maximum amount of relief is the lower of:

- the amount of the gain – £55,000; and
- the subscription cost of the new shares – £250,000

Partial claims are possible to take advantage of the annual exempt amount. The claim therefore should be for £43,300, as the CGT annual exempt amount is £11,700.

The gain will crystallise if Ella sells the shares, or, within three years, becomes non-UK resident or the company or shares cease to be eligible for EIS.

Examiner's comments

Candidates answered part (a) of this question very well providing accurate calculations for research and development, adjusted trading profits for both businesses and clear advice regarding business structure. Weaker candidates allowed themselves to be sidetracked into writing out lists of points without considering whether these points were relevant or not and, if relevant, without making their commentary specific to the situation in the question.

Better candidates identified quickly the key issues of treatment of losses; R&D expenditure; the different marginal rates of the two taxpayers; the potential for the application of patent box; and made appropriate recommendations.

A surprising number of candidates were under the impression that sole traders do not qualify for AIA.

Candidates who were unsuccessful typically did not use the numbers given in this question to inform their recommendations.

Part (b) The extraction of profit from a company in the form of dividend or salary was generally understood although it was rare to see accurate calculations for the salary extraction. Other methods such as a loan, were also given credit. The discussion of the tax implications for the sole trader were less well done. Many candidates happily discussed the distinction between sole trader and limited company structures in part (a) but failed to apply the theory to the practice in respect of part (b). A large number wasted time in calculating PAYE and NIC for the 'sole trader' salary extracted by Chris – many even went so far as to say this would increase his loss. Marks were not lost for this. Candidates effectively penalised themselves as time wasted could have earned them marks later in the exam.

Part (c) was generally well answered, although many candidates concluded, incorrectly, that SEIS relief was the most appropriate form of venture capital investment relief available. The size of the investment would have restricted this to EIS. Full follow through marks were awarded both for this and for the advice given in part (a).

Many candidates failed to make the link between EIS reinvestment relief, the capital gain in Poland and her residence status.

29 ZD Holdings plc

Scenario

The candidate works for a firm of ICAEW Chartered Accountants engaged by ZD Holdings plc which owns 100% of the Homewize Ltd shares. The candidates firm is assisting with the sale of Homewize Ltd to Anacim Ltd, a private equity firm.

The candidate is required to explain the tax implications of three outstanding issues in the subsidiary's tax computation which include the tax treatment of the sale and lease back of the company's freehold stores, a forex issue and the company's brought forward trade loss. The candidate then has to prepare a revised projected trading loss and explain the use of this loss and finally evaluate the tax implication of the two ways of selling the business.

ZD Holdings plc is proposing two possible ways to sell the Homewize business; a sale of the shares in Homewize Ltd or a hive down of the trade and assets to a new company followed by a share sale.

In addition, the CEO of ZD Holdings plc has complained to the candidate about comments made by and the aggressive behaviour of the firm's manager on the assignment. The candidate is required to evaluate the ethical issues arising for the candidate and the candidate's firm and the actions to be taken.

Marking guide

	Technical	Skills	Marks
29.1 Briefing notes			
Factory gain	1	1	
VAT	-	1	
SDLT	1	2½	
Lease rentals	1	2½	
Issue 2	1	1	
Issue 3	-	2	
	4	10	
Max			11
Revised calculations			
Summary calculation	1	2	
Recommendations	-	3	
	1	5	
Max			5
Shares v trade and assets			
Shares			
ZD Holdings plc	1	2	
Homewize Ltd	1	1	
Anacim Ltd	-	2	
VAT	-	2	
Hive down			
ZD Holdings plc	-	1	
Homewize Ltd	-	1½	
Office building	½	1	
Anacim Ltd	-	1	
Recommendation	-	1	
	2½	12½	
Max			13

	Technical	Skills	Marks
29.2 Ethics			
Fundamental principles and threats	2	2	
Actions	–	3	
	2	5	
Max			6
Total marks	9½	32½	42
Maximum			35

29.1 Briefing notes for Bernie Styl

Issue 1

The disposal of the freehold stores will give rise to a chargeable gain of £21.8 million which will be chargeable to corporation tax.

> **Tutorial note**
>
> The following working assumes that the transaction costs are deductible against the chargeable gain. Alternative assumptions regarding the split of the costs are also valid.

	£m
Proceeds	73.0
Less disposal costs (£50m + £1.2m)	(51.2)
Chargeable gain	21.8

The sale of the stores should be exempt from VAT as they are old commercial property and no option to tax has been made. It is also outside of the 10-year period for the capital goods scheme.

SDLT

Homewize Ltd as lessee, will pay SDLT on the £5 million lease premium therefore SDLT on the premium will be:

As there appears to be no option to tax by either party, no VAT is charged on the premium.

	£
£150,000 × 0%	–
£100,000 × 2%	2,000
£4,750,000 × 5%	237,500
	239,500

Homewize Ltd will also pay SDLT at 1% on the net present value of lease rentals payable to the landlord in excess of £150,000, and 2% in excess of £5 million. For exam purposes the net present value is the total rent payable over the term of the lease, £40 million (10 × £4m). This results in further SDLT of £748,500 payable calculated as follows:

((£5m – £150,000) × 1%) + ((£40m – £5m) × 2%) = £748,500

Given the inexperience of the team at Homewize Ltd, we would need to confirm that these additional SDLT payments have been made and also how these costs have been presented in the statement of profit or loss and ensure that they are disallowed in the tax computation.

> **Tutorial note**
>
> The SDLT payable on the lease back may be exempt under s.57A of Finance Act 2003. However, the facts given are insufficient to determine whether the exemption is available. This is also beyond the scope of the syllabus. Credit was available where a candidate made reference to this exemption.

Some of the lease premium will be treated as rental income for the property company and will therefore be allowed as additional rent deduction for Homewize Ltd.

£5 million (51 – 10)/50 = £4.1 million divided by the number of years of the lease (10 years) gives an annual deduction of £410,000.

In the year ending 31 March 2019 tax deductions in respect of the lease will be:

	£m	
Rental charge	4.00	Already charged to profit or loss – no further adjustment required
Deemed rent	0.41	

The lease premium of £5 million and the £1.2 million transaction costs are disallowable costs and must be removed from the loss for the year per the statement of profit or loss. The £35.2 million accounting profit in respect of the disposal of the stores is not taxable and therefore is removed and increases the loss for the year per the statement of profit or loss.

Issue 2

Forex gains and losses on monetary items such as loans are dealt with under the loan relationship rules.

At 1 May 2018 the loan was valued at a sterling equivalent of £769,231 ($1m/1.30). However, at 31 March 2019 the exchange rate will have changed and so the loan is at a sterling equivalent of £729,927 ($1m/1.37). At the accounting period end there is a net credit (gain) on loan relationships of £39,304 (£769,231 – £729,927). However as no adjustment has been made in the financial statements no adjustment is required in the calculation of the tax adjusted trading loss for the year ended 31 March 2019.

Issue 3

The pre-1 April 2017 trading loss of £2 million cannot be used in the current year (year ended 31 March 2019) as it must be set off against Homewize Ltd's trading profits of which there are none, and so this loss is carried forward in Homewize Ltd. The trading loss of £17 million brought forward from post-1 April 2017 is available for carried forward group relief, subject to the relevant maximum restriction. Homewize Ltd has also made a further loss in the current year (recalculated below). See further notes below on the implications of the sale of Homewize Ltd on carried forward loss relief.

Revised calculation of Homewize Ltd's tax trading loss for the year ending 31 March 2019 and a recommendation of how Homewize Ltd could use the loss.

	£m
Tax trading loss (before adjusting for outstanding issues 1-3 – see below)	(76.00)
Less profit on disposal	(35.20)
Add lease premium and transaction costs (£5m + £1.2m)	6.20
Less deduction for deemed rent	(0.41)
Revised tax trading loss	(105.41)

Recommendation for use of trading loss for year ended 31 March 2019

Homewize Ltd has no subsidiaries but is owned 100% by a UK tax-resident company. There may therefore be a possibility of using the loss by means of group relief to ZD Holdings plc and members of the ZD Holdings group.

Tutorial note

This part of the question specifically excludes discussion of the proposed sale. However, where arrangements are in place for a company to leave the group it is no longer possible to surrender losses. Therefore, the potential sale of Homewize Ltd may limit the availability of group relief.

The loss can be set off against other profits in the year – ie, the chargeable gain of £21.8 million leaving trading losses of £83.61 million to be carried forward against future total profits or group relieved. In total therefore there are trading losses of £102.61 million to carry forward (£83.61m + £19m).

Evaluation of the tax implications for ZD Holdings plc, Homewize Ltd and Anacim Ltd of the two alternative methods for the sale of the Homewize Ltd business

Sale of shares

Implications for ZD Holdings plc

ZD Holdings plc is a corporate shareholder and owns 100% of the shares in Homewize Ltd. It has owned the shares for more than 12 months in the last six years. Therefore, the substantial shareholding exemption (SSE) would apply which means that the chargeable gain on the disposal of the shares in Homewize Ltd is exempt from corporation tax.

Group relief for current period losses – this is only relevant if ZD Holdings plc has the capacity to use relief by making taxable profits and will only be available up to the date when 'arrangements' are in place to sell the company.

Implications for Homewize Ltd

The brought forward trading losses will continue to be available to be set against future trading profits from the same trade for the £2 million of pre-1 April 2017 trading losses and against total profits for the post-1 April 2017 trading losses, subject to the relevant maximum restriction. However, there is a possibility that the carry forward of the losses may be denied if there is a major change in the nature of the trade within a period of five years of the change in ownership (starting not more than three years before the change in ownership).

Implications for Anacim Ltd

Anacim Ltd will pay stamp duty at 0.5% on the transfer of the shares of £13.75m × 0.5% = £68,750.

Current period group relief will be available for Anacim Ltd and its 75% subsidiaries after the purchase of the shares in Homewize Ltd.

Group relief for the post-1 April 2017 carried forward losses of Homewize Ltd is not available until five years after the end of the accounting period of the change in ownership.

VAT implications on office building

The office building falls within the capital goods scheme as input VAT was payable when it was newly constructed for Homewize Ltd and it originally cost more than £250,000.

Therefore, if the business use of the office building changes within 10 years of the recovery of the input VAT, an adjustment is required. For Homewize Ltd, no adjustments were required up to 1 April 2019, as the usage was 100% taxable. However, if Anacim Ltd carries out its plans to let part of the building to the financial services company and does not 'opt to tax', an adjustment for change of use will apply for each of the remaining intervals as follows:

Homewize Ltd recovered VAT at 20%

£2.85m × 1/6 = £0.475m

$$\frac{£475,000}{10} \times (60\% - 100\%) = £19,000 \text{ per annum repayable to HMRC.}$$

Hive down

A hive-down involving the transfer of the trade and certain assets of Homewize Ltd to a newly incorporated company, NewCo Ltd, followed by the sale of the NewCo Ltd shares to Anacim Ltd for £11 million. The assets transferred would exclude the office building.

Implications for ZD Holdings plc

As the trade and assets transferred to NewCo Ltd were held and used in the trade of another group company (Homewize Ltd) for 12 months before transfer, and the assets are used in the trade of NewCo Ltd at the time of the transfer, the shares will be treated as having been held for 12 months. Consequently, the sale of NewCo Ltd's shares will be exempt under SSE rules.

Implications for Homewize Ltd/NewCo Ltd

The assets of Homewize Ltd are transferred to NewCo Ltd at a no gain/no loss basis as the companies are in a gains group.

However, it is possible that the trading losses will not be transferred to NewCo Ltd as the suggestion of a hive down comes from Anacim Ltd. This would be taken as evidence that the sale of NewCo Ltd has been agreed prior to the hive down.

Trading losses can be passed from Homewize Ltd to NewCo Ltd as the companies have common 75% ownership immediately before and after the transfer of trade and assets. The trading loss transferred is restricted to the extent that Homewize Ltd becomes technically insolvent (ie, relevant liabilities exceed relevant assets). When NewCo Ltd leaves the group, the remaining carried forward post-1 April 2017 trading losses cannot be group relieved to Anacim Ltd group companies for five years from the end of the accounting period of change in ownership. Loss relief is not available at all if the change in ownership is also accompanied by a major change in the nature or conduct of the trade, originally carried on by Homewize Ltd, within five years of the change in ownership.

Office building

Homewize Ltd is letting the office building and will therefore no longer be using the building for its trade. An adjustment of use will be required for each of the remaining intervals as follows:

$$\frac{£475,000}{10} \times (0\% - 100\%) = £47,500 \text{ per annum repayable to HMRC.}$$

Implications for Anacim Ltd

Anacim Ltd acquires NewCo Ltd without the asset it no longer needs but as noted above, the trading losses may not be available.

Anacim Ltd will pay stamp duty on the shares of £11m × 0.5% = £55,000

Recommendation

If Anacim Ltd is concerned about the use of Homewize Ltd's tax loss, the purchase of shares would be the preferred route.

29.2 Ethical issues

There is an intimidation threat both for Sam and for YG arising from the telephone call from the CEO. Potentially YG may not be able to continue with the engagement.

There is also a self-interest threat for Sam arising from the fact that the complaint is against her manager and potentially therefore she may be jeopardising her own position at YG.

This would also give rise to a threat to objectivity and integrity which may impact on the quality of work that is performed by YG staff.

Actions

Sam should bring the matter to her manager's attention and seek to ascertain the facts. Depending on the results of her initial investigation she should consider bringing the matter to the attention of the client partner. YG should meet with the client before continuing with the assignment.

The firm's quality control partner should also be consulted in respect of the threat to the quality of work.

Examiner's comments

Issue 1, the sale and lease back; this was answered very well by many candidates. The treatment of the foreign currency contract in issue 2 is different to that in the real exam due to a syllabus deletion. Issue 3 highlighted gaps in some candidate's knowledge and it was not uncommon for candidates to suggest that the [pre 1-April 2017] brought forward loss could be group relieved.

The revised computation and treatment of the current year loss was often missed out by weaker candidates. Full follow through marks were given.

The evaluation of the alternative methods of sale: This section was answered well by many candidates. Weaker candidates produced lists of points which were not always relevant to the scenario given. However, the embedded point regarding the capital goods scheme implications was picked up by many candidates although the calculations were less frequently correct.

A persistent problem even with better candidates was basic maths – it was not uncommon to see calculations where the decimal point was in the wrong place in the calculation of the stamp duty on the lease premium and lease rentals making the calculations incorrect by a factor of 10 – a significant amount when calculating tax payments.

Information about the use of trading losses in all parts of the question was sometimes poor and often vague. Candidates were too fond of vaguely mentioning the acronym MCINOCOT, without any explanation of what it meant or the consequences in this situation. Candidates seem to consider that this acronym is all they need to mention when considering a change of ownership and losses.

In part 2 some candidates immediately jumped to the conclusion that Bernie was completely at fault and that being aggressive with clients was not professional and that the candidate should remove him (Bernie, her manager) from the assignment. Better answers looked at the problem from both perspectives and discussed the potential intimidation and self-interest threats from the allegations made by the CEO and the need for objectivity in dealing with the difficult situation. Weak answers were, vague, formulaic and inconclusive.

30   Elexi plc

Scenario

The candidate works in the technical advisory department of a firm of ICAEW Chartered Accountants. The clients are a quoted company Elexi plc and a shareholder, Peter May. Peter May had been gifted shares in Delby Ltd by his grandfather. Peter and his grandfather accepted an offer from Elexi plc for all of their shares in Delby Ltd in exchange for shares in Elexi plc which Peter now intends to sell.

The candidate is asked to advise on the capital gains tax implications of the paper for paper takeover which includes the possibility of disapplying the rules to take advantage of entrepreneurs' relief. The second requirement asks the candidate to consider the IHT consequences of the death of Peter's grandfather in respect of the gift of his Delby Ltd shares to Peter. Finally, the candidate is asked to advise the directors of Elexi plc on the recent acquisition by a company resident in a lower-tax jurisdiction followed by a change in pricing policy and a newly-established branch in Germany.

		Technical	Skills	Marks
30.1 Paper for paper				
Paper for paper and entrepreneurs' relief		1	2	
Disapply paper for paper		1	2	
Calculation		–	2	
Additional information		1	1	
		3	7	
	Max			8
30.2 Other implications				
IHT and PET		1	2	
BPR		1	1	
Additional tax		–	1	
		2	4	
	Max			5
30.3 Overseas transactions				
CFC		1	1	
Dividend from Crea Inc		–	1	
Transfer pricing		2	3	
PE		1	2½	
DTR		1	1½	
Calculations		–	1½	
		5	10½	
	Max			12
Total marks		10	21½	31½
Maximum				25

30.1 The financial controller is incorrect in saying that there "will be a tax liability" arising for Peter – the issue needs careful consideration of Peter's circumstances and future plans.

The Delby Ltd shares were exchanged for shares in Elexi plc. This is a 'paper for paper' exchange and no gain is chargeable to capital gains tax at the time.

The disposal of Peter's shares in Delby Ltd would qualify for entrepreneurs' relief. However, as he now holds less than 5% of the shares in Elexi plc, his new shares will not qualify for entrepreneurs' relief when he sells them in the future.

I would recommend that he disapply the 'paper for paper' rules and take advantage of the 10% entrepreneurs' tax rate, particularly if he sells the shares in July 2019. The rate of CGT he would pay in the future would be higher as the 10% rate would not be available. , although there is uncertainty about the availability of future reliefs and rates.

Therefore, if he wishes to crystallise his gain and take advantage of entrepreneurs' relief, he would pay chargeable gains tax of:

	£'000
Disposal proceeds	
15 × 11,000 × £10 =	1,650.0
Less cost (market value at date of gift)	(900.0)
	750.0
Less annual exempt amount (assumed not already utilised)	(11.7)
	738.3
Tax @ 10%	73,830

Additional information required to make a recommendation

The calculation of the gain above assumes that Peter's grandfather did not claim gift relief at the time of the gift of the Delby Ltd shares – this would require confirmation and further information regarding the cost of the shares.

Does Peter have the cash available to pay the CGT now?

Does Peter have any brought-forward capital losses?

Has Peter made previous disposals and used his lifetime limit of £10 million for entrepreneurs' relief?

30.2 As your grandfather was domiciled in England, his worldwide assets will be liable to inheritance tax (IHT) at 40%.

The gift of the shares to you of the Delby Ltd shares is a potentially exempt transfer (PET) which, as he has unfortunately passed away within seven years of the date of the gift, may now be liable to IHT (subject to taper relief). The amount payable may be reduced by taper relief.

Had you held on to the shares, they may have qualified for business property relief (BPR) at 100%. This would have reduced the IHT liability to £nil. However, you have reinvested the proceeds in a non-controlling interest in quoted shares and therefore BPR is probably not available.

The fact that the executor is contacting you suggests that the additional tax due will be your responsibility and would suggest that your grandfather has not made any provision for the tax to be met by the estate.

30.3 Crea Inc is a controlled foreign company as it is resident overseas and controlled from the UK. Provided one of the exemptions apply, no CFC charge will arise. For example, the tax rate of 16% in Erewhon seems to suggest that tax paid overseas is at least 75% of the UK corporation tax, assuming taxable profits are calculated in a similar way.

As Crea Inc is tax resident in Erewhon it will pay tax on its profits in Erewhon and its profits will be taxed at 16%. Its profits will not be taxed in the UK.

However, there are a number of other ways the investment may or may not affect the taxable profits for Elexi plc for the year ended 31 December 2018:

Dividend from Crea Inc

The dividend received from Crea Inc in September 2018 will be exempt from corporation tax if it falls within the list of exemptions in UK tax legislation. The list of exemptions available for dividends is wide ranging and in almost all cases therefore foreign dividends received will be exempt dividends.

Transfer pricing

From the summary of the facts it appears Elexi plc sold goods to Crea Inc in Erewhon at a lower than market price which results in a tax advantage for Elexi plc in the UK – this transaction would come within the transfer pricing legislation.

Elexi plc appears to be a large company for transfer pricing purposes as it employs more than 250 employees. Where large connected companies enter into transactions other than at arm's length, such that one company gains a tax advantage, transfer pricing rules may apply. The company which gains a tax advantage (ie, lower profits or higher losses) is required to adjust its corporation tax self-assessment by substituting an arm's length price for the original price.

The reason for the favourable selling price offered to Crea Inc, a group internal pricing agreement, is irrelevant as the transfer pricing legislation applies where such a transaction results in a tax advantage to one of the parties.

The legislation requires the income, expenditure, profits and losses of the advantaged party to be adjusted where prices are not at arm's length.

Therefore, Elexi plc's taxable profits would increase by £1.5 million.

However, Elexi plc may wish to consider a justifiable management charge to the subsidiary.

Manufacturing operation in Germany

The operation in Germany is a permanent establishment (PE) of Elexi plc and its profits will be taxed in the UK as Elexi plc is tax resident in the UK and is, therefore, liable to UK corporation tax on its worldwide income.

In addition, in common with most countries, the German tax authorities have charged tax on the trading profits of Elexi plc's German PE.

Companies have an option to make an irrevocable election for foreign PEs, located anywhere in the world, to be exempt from UK corporation tax on their profits.

It needs to be confirmed whether this election has been made.

Assuming not, the election is only effective from the start of the accounting period after the one in which the election is made and, therefore, it is too late for Elexi plc to make this election for the year ended 31 December 2018.

The client should be made aware of this election, which would apply to all PEs established by Elexi plc. The decision to make this election will depend upon factors such as the future locations and tax rates of the jurisdictions. Also if losses may arise in the PEs then a branch exemption election is less likely to be appropriate.

Therefore, Elexi plc will suffer double taxation on trading profits accruing to its PE in Germany.

However, double tax relief (DTR) either in the form of treaty relief or unilateral DTR should apply to prevent Elexi plc suffering tax twice on this income. The details of the German DT treaty should be reviewed since treaties will take precedence over UK tax law.

Assuming DTR is available, either under the treaty or unilaterally, the OECD standard model which allows foreign tax as a credit against a UK corporation tax liability is likely to apply. DTR is allowed up to the UK corporation tax attributable to the German branch profits.

As the tax on the German branch profits is higher than the UK tax, there would be no point in electing to exempt PE profits.

Relevant calculations

The impact on the UK corporation tax liability would be as follows:

Year ended 31 December 2018

	£m
Trading income	4.2
Transfer pricing adjustment	1.5
Profits from PE in Germany	1.2
Taxable total trading profits	6.9

Examiner's comments

Part 1 was answered very well by most candidates who identified the potential higher tax liabilities if Peter sells his shares in the future. Answers were well structured showing good analysis of the scenario. This part of the question was a good discriminator between weak and excellent candidates – as understanding of the structure of the transaction was required.

The IHT implications were also answered very well with many candidates discussing the implications for the estate at death and the availability for BPR. Credit was also given for candidates who discussed the value of the shares.

The final part of the question, concerning overseas tax issues for a company was well answered, although, again, students often failed to be analytical enough and relate their knowledge to the facts of the question.

In particular, consideration of the election to exempt profits of PEs from UK taxation was rarely considered in anything other than very brief terms.

It was, however, pleasing to see many candidates adjusting the taxable total profits correctly for the impact of the transactions.

June 2016 exam answers

31 Marmalade Ltd

Scenario

In this question candidates were working as an ICAEW Chartered Accountant in a tax practice providing advice to both a corporate and individual shareholders on the tax consequences of a company repurchase of shares and a sale of shares between shareholders. The structure of the share sale was prescribed in the question and students were asked to advise within the parameters of a given scenario. The company purchase of own shares was constructed to ensure that students had to analyse the scenario and determine what the treatment of the share sale proceeds would be under income tax rules. A more usual question scenario would be to plan a transaction to avoid income tax treatment. This question discriminated well between those who had rote-learned that a company purchase of own shares is more tax efficient if the proceeds are treated as capital and those who understood the rules sufficiently to apply them to a scenario and make a recommendation arising from the facts of the actual question, rather than from a rote-learned formula.

Candidates were then presented with an ethical dilemma, advising on a tax saving scheme, which was clearly tax avoidance that could be attacked by HMRC under the GAAR, DOTAS and Ramsay principle as abusive tax arrangements.

ICAEW Chartered Accountants should be able to identify the impact of abusive, if legal, tax avoidance on the economy and understand their obligations in advising clients of the legal and ethical threats of such arrangements.

Marking guide

		Technical	Skills	Marks
31.1 (a)	**Purchase of own shares**			
	Allocation of distributable profits	–	1	
	Treatment of each repurchase	1	2	
	Substantial shareholding	1	1	
	Capital conditions	2	2	
	Income treatment	1	2	
	Calculation	1	2	
		6	10	
	Max			15
(b)	**Lucy's loan**			
	Loan amount/shareholding	1	1	
	Close company income tax relief	2	2	
	Limit on relief	1	3	
		4	6	
	Max			8
(c)	**Share disposal**			
	Gain calculation	2	1	
	Entrepreneurs' relief	1	1	
	CGT payable	1	1	
		4	3	7

	Technical	Skills	Marks
31.2 Email re scheme			
Tax evasion v tax avoidance	1	2	
Ramsay doctrine	–	3	
DOTAS regime	1	2	
Promoters	–	2	
GAAR	1	3	
Conclusion/integrity	–	2	
	3	14	
Max			10
Total marks	17	33	50
Maximum			40

31.1 (a)   Marmalade Ltd intend to repurchase shares from both Cooper Ltd and Paddy.

The distributable reserves of £2 million will allow the company to buy back all of Cooper Ltd's shares for £1.65 million (£50 × 33,000).

This leaves £350,000 of reserves available for the repurchase of Paddy's shares.

This will mean that Marmalade Ltd can buy back 7,000 of Paddy's shares (£50 × 7,000 = £350,000).

> **Tutorial note**
>
> The repurchase would also require stamp duty at 0.5%. Stamp duty was not considered in the original mark plan, but it is likely that credit would be given.

The share repurchase from Cooper Ltd will always be treated as a capital repurchase.

As a capital repurchase, Cooper Ltd will be able to claim the substantial shareholding exemption because it has owned at least 10% of the shares in Marmalade Ltd for 12 months out of the last 6 years and Marmalade Ltd is a trading company. The gain on repurchase of the shares is therefore exempt.

The repurchase of shares from Paddy could be treated as either an income or a capital distribution. In order for the mandatory capital distribution route to be applied to the repurchase, the repurchase needs to satisfy certain conditions:

(1)   The repurchase should be for the benefit of the trade. A dissenting shareholder being removed could be seen to be of benefit to the trade.

(2)   The vendor must not hold more than 30% of the shares in the company after the repurchase. Paddy will own 26,000 out of the 59,000 shares in issue after the repurchase. This is 44% of the shares in the company.

(3)   The vendor is UK resident and has held the shares for at least five years.

(4)   The vendor should have substantially reduced his shareholding, such that he holds 75% or less of the pre-sale holding. As the repurchase of the Cooper Ltd shares happens first, the shares in issue in Marmalade Ltd, just before Paddy's shares are repurchased will be 66,000.

(5)   Paddy will own 50% of those shares before the repurchase. If he is to reduce his after sale holding substantially he would need to hold 37.5% of the shares or less after repurchase.

(6) He would hold 26,000 shares out of 59,000 in issue = 44%.

As a result he does not satisfy the conditions for mandatory capital treatment and he would be treated as receiving an income distribution on the share repurchase, which would be taxed as follows (assuming Paddy has not used his dividend nil rate band):

Dividend of 7,000 × (£50 – £1) = £343,000

Income tax due:	£
£2,000 × 0%	0
£18,000 × 32.5%	5,850
£323,000 × 38.1%	123,063
Total	128,913

(b) The remaining 26,000 shares are worth £50 each and so Lucy would need a loan of £1,300,000 to buy Paddy's remaining shares.

At this point Lucy would own 59,000 shares out of the 59,000 shares still in issue, which would be a 100% stake in the company.

Marmalade Ltd is a close company (control in the hands of five or fewer participators or any number of directors).

Interest on loans taken out to purchase shares in close companies, by a participator, who owns at least 5% of the share capital of the close company, is tax deductible from total income of the shareholder in the income tax computation.

The amount deductible is however limited to a maximum of the higher of £50,000 and 25% of the adjusted total income of the tax year. As the interest rate on the loan is 8%, the interest payable amounts to £104,000 per annum, it is likely that not all of this interest will be deductible for tax purposes. Adjusted total income would need to amount to £416,000 for the interest to be fully deductible. We would need more information about Lucy's taxable income to be able to confirm the amount of tax relief available.

(c) The sale of shares to Lucy is a capital disposal.

The gain will be £1,274,000 (£1,300,000 – £26,000).

As Paddy has never had capital gains, he has owned the shares for many years and works full-time for the company; he will be eligible to claim entrepreneurs' relief. Paddy will not have exceeded the lifetime limit for gains eligible for entrepreneurs' relief of £10 million.

This relief means that the gains are taxed at 10%, instead of 20%.

The capital gains tax payable on the disposal will be £126,230 [(1,274,000 – 11,700) × 10%].

31.2 Email

To: Lucy, Marmalade Ltd
From: A Tax Adviser Brown and Co
Subject: Advice on the legal and ethical consequences of the scheme to save UK corporation tax payable on Marmalade Ltd's profits

Dear Lucy,

Tax evasion is illegal and involves deliberately misstating tax liabilities, suppressing information or providing false information to HMRC. In the circumstances described in your email, it does not appear that the tax-saving scheme described is tax evasion.

Tax avoidance is legal and involves reducing tax liabilities by legal means. However, HMRC separately consider tax planning and tax avoidance. The latter may be challenged by HMRC if it involves the use of artificial steps to use loopholes in the legislation (see below).

The tax saving scheme described may be considered by HMRC to be tax avoidance, given the consultants claim it is legal and, as a result, this could be seen as a legitimate way to reduce Marmalade Ltd's tax liability.

However, the Ramsay doctrine has for some years given the courts the power to ignore elements of a transaction, which have no commercial purpose or effect. The tax consultants promoting the scheme claim that UK anti-avoidance legislation does not apply to the steps inserted into the transaction. Under the Ramsay doctrine, it may be that these steps would be ignored and the anti-avoidance rules could then apply to the transaction, negating the tax advantages gained by routing profits through the tax haven of Unterbourg.

If the Ramsay doctrine were not applicable, it is still possible that HMRC would have an interest in the tax-saving scheme.

The disclosure of tax avoidance schemes (DOTAS) regime gives HMRC early warning of tax-avoidance schemes, which then allows HMRC to close the loopholes that render such schemes attractive. If a tax-saving scheme falls within the DOTAS regime and the scheme is not notified to HMRC, there are penalties, but these are mainly aimed at the promoters of such schemes, not the users. If the main benefit of an arrangement is obtaining a tax advantage, it is likely that the scheme would need to be registered with HMRC, by the promoter of the scheme, under the DOTAS regime. If a scheme is registered under the DOTAS regime, the promoter should provide you with a scheme reference number, which should be used on your tax return.

The general anti-abuse rule (GAAR) is intended to counter tax advantages from complex planning schemes. It applies if gaining a tax advantage was one of the main purposes of arrangements and the arrangements are abusive. Arrangements are abusive if they cannot be regarded as a reasonable course of action. There is little precedent in respect of the GAAR and so a level of uncertainty, but you would need to be aware that it is possible that this scheme could be covered by the GAAR, and, if so the tax advantages gained by the use of the scheme would be negated as just and reasonable adjustments would be required to counteract the tax advantages gained.

In conclusion, for the reasons stated above I would advise not investing in this scheme, given that any tax advantage gained may be challenged by HMRC.

I would also be concerned about the threats to the fundamental principles of integrity posed by this scheme.

Best wishes

A Tax Adviser

Examiner's comments

Part 1(a) was very clear, with unambiguous requirements, and success or failure in answering the question hinged on thinking through the problem before answering. Candidates often realised that a corporate shareholder would always have a capital disposal and then recognised the availability of the substantial shareholding exemption. The analysis of the impact of the company purchase of own shares on the individual was often incomplete, and many candidates assumed that the, crucial, substantial reduction text would be satisfied, without actually testing and therefore finding that it was not satisfied. The failure of candidates to adopt a logical approach to the question led to incorrect conclusions and therefore marks were lost.

Part 1(b) required candidates to think across to the impact on purchasing shares in a close company, for a shareholder/director. The poorer candidates did not assimilate the information in the question to recognise that this was a close company and that there were income tax deductions available for qualifying loan interest. A fundamental misunderstanding of the rules caused candidates to conclude that for Lucy, the loan could be treated under the non-trading loan relationship rules, which scored no marks.

Part 1(c) focused on capital gains tax planning for the sale of the shares. Some candidates had already considered this in their earlier calculations in parts (a) and (b). Marks were awarded wherever candidates considered the issues. This question demonstrated some candidates' lack of ability to plan their answers properly and often markers had to unpick very messy and confused calculations.

Part 2 was a complex and unusual tax saving scheme. Candidates who actually analysed the issues and thought through the scenario identified the relevance of GAAR, DOTAS and the Ramsay principle. Candidates who simply applied a formulaic approach to the ethical scenario often scored very poorly on this part of the question, mentioning issues that were not relevant, such as money laundering.

32 Kamran Siddiqi

Scenario

The changes to the taxation of dividends received from companies means the corporate structure is not as beneficial as it once was, so many small company owners may consider disincorporation to become an unincorporated business.

This question asked candidates to consider the tax implications of a company disincorporating and the business reverting to a sole trader.

The question was split into four parts, which were deliberately constructed to guide students through the scenario in a logical order. Disincorporation is firmly within the syllabus and the learning materials cover it in full, however, it has not been examined before.

The legislation has changed since this question was set, and so the answer has changed and the mark allocation reduced.

Marking guide

	Technical	Skills	Marks
32.1 Taxable total profit for SRL			
Computation and use of losses	2	4	
Working 1			
• Final period allowances	2	1	
• Succession election	2	2	
Working 2			
• Gain	2	1	
Working 3	1	1	
	9	9	18
32.2 Amount of distribution to Kamran	1	1	2
32.3 Tax treatment of distribution			
Capital distribution	–	2	
Calculation	2	2	
Entrepreneurs' relief	1	1	
	3	5	8

	Technical	Skills	Marks
32.4 VAT on disincorporation			
TOGC	2	2	
VAT registration	-	1	
	2	3	5
Total marks	15	18	33
Maximum			30

32.1 Siddiqi Restaurant Ltd (SRL)

Taxable total profit for the period ending 31 July 2019

	£
Draft taxable trading loss	(115,000)
Capital allowances (W1)	Nil
Taxable trading loss	(115,000)
Relieved against: gain on disposal of pre-2002 goodwill (W2)	95,000
Remaining tax adjusted trading loss	(20,000)

The trading loss of £115,000 cannot be carried forward, because trade has ceased and there is no provision to carry forward company losses on disincorporation to the successor sole trader business. The loss could be relieved against the gain on disposal of the goodwill under s.37(3)(a) and then carried back to the previous accounting period under s.37(3)(b). This would reduce taxable total profits of the period ending 31 July 2019 to nil and generate a reduction in the taxable total profits of SRL for the year ended 31 December 2018 of £20,000. In that period a tax repayment of £20,000 × 19% = £3,800 would be generated.

WORKINGS

(1) **Capital allowances**

In the final period of trade the company is not entitled to a WDA, as the assets are all sold on the last day of trade. However, there would be a calculation of a balancing charge or allowance on disposal.

	£
TWDV at 1 January 2019	50,000
Less proceeds = market value	65,000
	(15,000)
Balancing charge	15,000
TWDV at 31 July 2019	0

This balancing charge would be added to profits in the final period of trade and charged to corporation tax. However, the trade is being transferred to Kamran, who is sole shareholder of the company and owner of the sole trader business. Therefore SRL and the sole trader business are connected and an election can be made to transfer the assets at TWDV. In this case there would be no balancing charge to add to profits.

As this will reduce the tax payable now, I will assume that a succession election is made and that the balancing charge does not occur.

The succession election should be made by 31 July 2021.

(2) **Chargeable gains**

The disposal of the goodwill to Kamran would give rise to a taxable gain in SRL.

As the business commenced trade in 2001 and was then transferred by a related party to the company, the goodwill is treated as pre-2002 goodwill and so within the chargeable gains rules.

On disposal a gain is calculated as follows:

	£
Proceeds	95,000
Less cost (W3)	(0)
Chargeable gain	95,000

This gain is added to the taxable profits of the company for the 31 July 2019 accounting period and taxed on SRL, subject to loss relief.

(3) **Base cost of goodwill**

On incorporation the goodwill was gifted to the company at its market value of £45,000. Gift relief was claimed and so the base cost would have been reduced to nil by the gift relief claim.

32.2 Total amount available for distribution to Kamran by SRL as at 31 July 2019

	£
Total assets of SRL at 31 July 2019	200,000
Add tax repayment on carry back of losses to y/e 31.12.18	3,800
Total amount for distribution	203,800

32.3 The distribution of the company's assets to Kamran on 31 July 2019 will be treated as a capital distribution, because it takes place after the appointment of a liquidator.

The £203,800 distributed will be the proceeds for the disposal of Kamran's shares in SRL.

	£
Proceeds of sale	203,800
Less cost (nominal value of shares)	(200)
Gain	203,600
Less annual exempt amount	(11,700)
Taxable gain	191,900
CGT at 10%	19,190

Note: As Kamran has owned the shares for over a year and the company is a personal trading company, assuming he has not used his lifetime limit, he will be entitled to entrepreneurs' relief on the gain on disposal. His gain will therefore be taxed at 10%.

32.4 VAT consequences of the transfer of the SRL restaurant business to Kamran Siddiqi

VAT will not be charged on the transfer of assets from SRL to Kamran, provided the transfer satisfies the conditions to qualify as the transfer of a business as a going concern (TOGC).

The conditions for a TOGC appear to be satisfied, because the restaurant is a going concern. However, Kamran will need to register for VAT in respect of his new sole trader business to satisfy the TOGC conditions.

SRL's VAT registration number can be transferred to Kamran's sole trader business, however, this also transfers the VAT history of SRL to the new business.

Examiner's comments

Part 1 was the most challenging part of this question for candidates with some candidates failing to deal with the problem analytically and so failing to consider the planning options available in the scenario. Candidates also need to be aware that when they are asked to provide explanations about how things are treated in a computation, it is not sufficient to regurgitate technical knowledge without relating it to the facts of the question.

Part 2 was designed to form a logical bridge between parts 1 and 3 of the requirements, to ensure that candidates could appreciate the link between disincorporation and distribution of the assets of the company to the shareholder. The requirement clearly asked for a calculation. Some of the poorer candidates failed to answer this part of the question, despite the requirement being very specific. Again, some candidates answered elements of 1 in this part of their answers. Marks were awarded for relevant points but again, markers had to work their way through very mixed up answers allocating marks where appropriate.

Part 3 looked at the tax implications of a post-liquidation distribution. This required candidates to identify that the distribution was post liquidation, identify the tax implications for the distribution and consider the tax reliefs available to mitigate the tax liability.

Part 4 considered the VAT implications of the disincorporation. This part of the question was very well answered.

33 John

Scenario

This question considers issues related to personal taxation and the taxation of employment income, in particular.

The candidate is asked to identify the income tax and national insurance treatment of termination payments.

The candidate is then asked to compare the net spendable income arising from each of two possible employment income packages. This aims to relate the taxation of employment income to the practical necessity of determining the difference between cash and benefits, not only for tax purposes, but also in terms of cashflow.

Finally the candidate is asked to evaluate the suitability of investments in venture capital for the small investor.

	Technical	Skills	Marks
33.1 **Termination payment**			
1 mark for each item in the redundancy package	5	–	5
33.2 **Net spendable income**			
Summary calculation – package 1	1	2	
Summary calculation – package 2	1	2	
Conclusion	–	2	
Working 1	1	2	
Working 2	1	1	
Working 3	–	1	
Working 4	1	–	
	5	10	
Max			13

		Technical	Skills	Marks
33.3 **Venture capital schemes**				
	Income tax relief only	–	1	
	Three schemes	1	2	
	Tax reducer/dividends	1	1½	
	Conclusions	–	1½	
	Withdrawal of relief	1	1½	
		3	7½	
	Max			7
Total marks		13	17½	30½
Maximum				25

33.1 Termination payments can be fully or partially exempt from tax or fully taxable.

The termination payment package is taxable as follows:

	IT Status	Explanation	Employee's NIC status
Salary in lieu of notice	Fully taxable	Payments in lieu of notice are fully taxable	Employee's NIC due on salary as normal
Statutory redundancy pay	Exempt from income tax	Not taxable, but counts as part of the maximum of £30,000 not taxable for discretionary payments	No Employee's NIC
IT equipment	Fully taxable	Taxable because this is not a discretionary payment, given the expectation created ie, all other senior staff receiving this as part of redundancy packages	No Employee's NIC because this is a benefit, not cash
Contribution to pension scheme	Fully exempt	Employer contributions to pension schemes are non-taxable	No Employee's NIC
Non-contractual goodwill payment	Partially taxable (exempt in this case as within the limit)	Up to £30,000 can be received free of tax. This £30,000 is reduced by statutory redundancy pay	No Employee's NIC

33.2 Net spendable income from the two job offers are as follows:

	Employment Package 1 Net Spendable Income £	Employment Package 2 Net Spendable Income £
Salary	75,000	60,000
Less income tax on package (W1)	(18,360)	(19,052)
Less employee's NIC (W2)	(5,124)	(4,824)
Add cash from share options (W3)		6,000
Less cost of own car pa	(5,700)	
Net spendable income	45,816	42,124

Based on these figures, Employment Package 1 would produce more spendable income and if this is your main criterion for making the judgement, you should accept Employment Package 1.

Tutorial notes

These calculations could have been done on apportioned figures for 2019/20 (given the new job will start on 1.7.19) however, the comparison on full year figures is easier and also more realistic as the ongoing pay from the job is more important to the decision than just the position for the current tax year. In marking, no additional credit was given for time apportioning the figures, although time-apportioned figures were marked the same as full-year figures.

WORKINGS

(1) **Calculation of income tax (2018/19 rates used)**

	Employment Package 1 £	Employment Package 2 £
Salary	75,000	60,000
Car benefit (W4)		10,730
Non tax-advantaged share scheme		6,000
Personal allowance	(11,850)	(11,850)
Taxable Income	63,150	64,880
Tax		
34,500 × 20%	6,900	6,900
28,650/30,380 × 40%	11,460	12,152
	18,360	19,052

(2) **Employee's NIC**

NIC 2018/19 rates used.

Employment package 1:

	£
£46,350 – £8,424 × 12%	4,551
£75,000 – £46,350 × 2%	573
	5,124

Note: No employee's NIC on employer pension contributions.

Employment package 2:

	£
£46,350 – £8,424 × 12%	4,551
£60,000 – £46,350 × 2%	273
	£4,824

No employee's NIC on car benefit and also none on the share scheme shares, assuming the shares in the share scheme are not readily-convertible assets.

(3) **Share Option Scheme**

As the shares are in a non tax-advantaged share scheme, the exercise of the share options will give rise to employment income on the difference between the market value of the share and what you pay for them. As you pays nothing for the shares this gives rise to a taxable amount of £6,000 (3,000 × £2). On immediate disposal of the shares for market value, there would be no capital gains tax due, as the cost of the shares would be deemed to be the value charged as employment income, which is equal to the market value, so there would be no capital gain on the disposal of the shares.

(4) **Car Benefit**

37% × £29,000 = £10,730

> **Tutorial note**
>
> In marking this question credit was given for the use of any appropriate rates and allowances. This part of the question was set in 2019/20, but use of the 2018/19 rates and allowances was given equal credit.

33.3 **Subject: Investing £25,000 in venture capital share schemes**

There are three venture capital share schemes to choose from.

All three schemes require investment in unquoted company shares, which carry a greater risk that the investor may lose their capital invested if the company fails.

Given the amount you have to invest, all three schemes would be open to you.

You have no capital gain requiring shelter, so you will be interested in the amount of income tax relief you could receive for your investment. The three schemes would give the following amount of relief in 2019/20:

EIS	SEIS	VCT
30%	50%	30%
£7,500	£12,500	£7,500

All reliefs are given as tax reducers to reduce your income tax payable and you will have sufficient income tax liability in 2019/20 to absorb this tax relief.

In addition, investment in a VCT would allow you to receive dividends from the VCT company, tax free.

If you wish to maximise your income tax relief, investment in the SEIS scheme would be the most advantageous. However, if you are concerned about the riskiness of your investment, you might consider a VCT investment less risky, as this invests in a portfolio of unquoted company shares, rather than in one single SEIS company.

In all three cases, income tax relief will be withdrawn if the investment is disposed of too quickly. For EIS and SEIS, the minimum holding period is three years. For VCT the minimum holding period is five years. You need to consider how long you intend to invest for, to determine if the tax advantages of this investment are going to be worthwhile.

Examiner's comments

This question produced the best performance on the exam. It was a discrete topic, where a well-planned answer scored well on straight forward issues.

Those who analysed the question before attempting it and used a methodical approach scored very well.

The biggest failing was that candidates did not consider national insurance contributions, as part of the tax implications. This was surprising as questions on the after tax cash position have been set before and there are examples in the learning materials.

September 2016 exam answers

34 Fragmarb plc

Scenario

The candidate was in the role of a tax adviser for a firm of ICAEW Chartered Accountants, acting for a company, Fragmarb plc and also an employee of Fragmarb plc in personal tax affairs.

The question covers a range of corporation tax issues and also includes a short income tax issue. With the flat rate of corporation tax now in place questions covering a range of technical corporation tax issues should be expected by students.

Marking guide

	Technical	Skills	Marks
34.1 Corporation tax payable for Fragmarb plc			
Revised computation	1	2½	
Issue 1			
• Gains on incorporation conditions	1	2	
• Postponement	–	2	
• Calculations	2	2½	
• Share consideration and disposal of shares/factory	–	2	
• Gain on factory	2	2	
• Deferred gain/profit on share sale	2	2	
• Gain on share sale	1	1	
Issue 2			
• Patent box	1½	2	
Issue 3			
• Share for share exchange	2	2	
	12½	20	
Max			23
34.2 Overseas issues			
Residence status	–	1	
CFC status	1	3	
Diverted profit tax	1	1	
Avoided PE	2	2	
Conclusions	–	3	
	4	10	
Max			8
34.3 Email			
UK resident	1	–	
Full time work overseas	3	2	
Split year rules	1	1	
Delayed secondment	–	2	
Conclusion	–	1	
	5	6	
Max			9
Total marks	21½	36	57½
Maximum			40

34.1 Revised CT computation

	Non-patented £'000	Patented £'000
Tax adjusted trading profit	2,600.0	4,250.0
Trading profit on stock (issue 1)	250.0	
Chargeable gains (issue 1)	399.7	
Profit on goodwill (issue 1)	289.9	
Patent box reduced by nexus fraction (issue 2)		3,262.5
Remaining patent box profits (4,250 – 3,262.5)	987.5	
Revised TTP	4,527.1	3,262.5
CT payable at 19%/10%	860.1	326.3
Total CT payable = £1,186,400		

Issue 1

On incorporation of Toka SARL, the PE will cease to trade.

Incorporation will result in balancing adjustments arising on branch assets transferred to the non UK company.

Incorporation will result in chargeable gains/losses in the hands of the UK company (Fragmarb plc).

Relief exists for chargeable gains on incorporation to be postponed where:

- the trade of a foreign PE is transferred to a non-UK resident company with all the assets used for trade except cash;

- the consideration for the transfer is wholly or partly securities;

- the transferring company owns at least 25% of the ordinary share capital of the non-UK resident company;

- a claim for relief is made.

Therefore, the conditions appear to have been met and the gains on the factory, warehouse, the gain on the fixed plant and machinery and the accounting profit on the 'new' goodwill are eligible to be postponed.

Gains are as follows:

Factory

	£
MV	600,000
Cost	(150,000)
IA (£150,000 × 0.438)	(65,700)
Gain	384,300

Warehouse

Loss	(50,000)

Fixed P&M

MV	150,000
Cost	(100,000)
IA (£100,000 × 0.087)	(8,700)
Gain	41,300

Goodwill and stock

As the business started in 2006 the goodwill and stock represent trading assets and realise profits of £1,000,000 and £250,000 respectively. The gain on the goodwill can be deferred on the same grounds as the capital assets.

Net chargeable gains to be postponed = £375,600 and intangible profit £1,000,000.

As the entire consideration was in the form of shares then the whole gain can be postponed.

However, as Fragmarb plc has now disposed of some of the shares in Toka SARL and in addition, Toka SARL has disposed of the factory within six years of the transfer, the gains will become chargeable on the UK company and will be calculated as follows:

$$\text{Remaining balance of net gain deferred} \times \frac{\text{Gain on asset at incorporation}}{\text{Gross gains at incorporation}}$$

On sale of the factory the following gain will become chargeable:

$$£375,600 \times \frac{384,300}{425,600} = £339,152$$

The balance of the postponed gain carried forward is therefore £36,448 (£375,600 – £339,152).

In terms of the disposal of securities, the gains previously deferred are chargeable in addition to any gain arising on the disposal of the securities themselves. The disposal of the shares will not meet the conditions for SSE because the securities have not been held for the required period. Therefore a chargeable gain will arise on Fragmarb plc as follows:

Balance of chargeable gain × A/B where A = MV of securities disposed of and B is total MV of securities held immediately before disposal:

$$£36,448 \times \frac{£800,000}{£2,760,000} = £10,565$$

Crystallisation of intangible profit

$$£1,000,000 \times \frac{£800,000}{£2,760,000} = £289,855$$

In addition, the disposal of the securities themselves will realise a chargeable gain and in this situation, the SSE does not apply. The gain will be £50,000 (£800,000 – £750,000).

Total chargeable gains are therefore £399,717 (£339,152 + £10,565 + £50,000).

Issue 2

As Fragmarb plc owns patents, there may be a possibility for an election to be made for profits from patents to arise within a patent box.

We would need further information on whether Fragmarb plc is carrying on qualifying development. If this is the case then the post-BEPS version of the patent box can apply:

	£'000
Patent box streamed profits	4,250.0
Less 10% return on cost (10% × £2,750)	(275.0)
Less marketing royalty (5% × £7,000)	(350.0)
Patent box profit	3,625.0
Nexus fraction: £3,625 × 90%	3,262.5

Issue 3

As Fragmarb plc has received shares in Wemble plc in exchange for shares in Mokle Ltd, then these are treated as being acquired at the same price and on the same date as the original shares in Mokle Ltd. However, if Fragmarb plc had sold the shares for cash the SSE would have applied. As the SSE takes precedence, Fragmarb plc is treated as having sold its shares in Mokle Ltd giving rise to an exempt gain or loss and having acquired the shares in Wemble plc for their market value of £600,000.

34.2 Gobo Inc transactions

Whilst as a non-resident entity, Gobo Inc would not usually be liable to UK tax, there are a number of anti-avoidance rules that could result in a UK tax charge arising in connection with the profits of Gobo Inc. Firstly, if Gobo Inc were considered to be centrally managed and controlled in the UK the company would be deemed UK resident for tax purposes.

Assuming that there is independent management in Glubeck, it is then necessary to consider whether the Controlled Foreign Company rules could result in a tax charge arising for Fragmarb plc. The rules apply to overseas companies controlled by UK companies (as Gobo Inc is) where none of the exemptions apply and profits are deemed to pass through one of the identified gateways. There is a tax exemption when the tax paid in the overseas country is at least 75% of the UK tax charge. A tax rate of 15% (ie, £750,000/£5m) may mean that this exemption is applicable, but more details of the rate of tax and basis of charge in Glubeck would be needed to confirm this.

If the tax exemption does not apply, profits will be taxable on Fragmarb plc if they pass through one of the gateways. This could be the case if the incorporation of Gobo Inc were considered to be an arrangement designed with the main purpose of reducing UK tax and it was concluded that the company could not run its business without UK management input.

Further details of the operation of the company would be required to conclude on this matter.

Additionally anti-avoidance legislation exists to prevent companies from diverting profits away from the UK without paying tax in the UK or overseas. Diverted profits tax (DPT) applies when either arrangements exist to avoid having a UK PE or transactions lack economic substance. DPT is 25% of taxable diverted profits and companies must notify HMRC if they expect to be within the scope of DPT.

It appears that the arrangements in place with Gobo Inc are an attempt to avoid having a UK PE. Fragmarb plc is taking on the role of an 'avoided PE' by carrying on an activity in the UK in connection with supplies of goods by a non-resident UK company.

It is reasonable to assume that the activity of Fragmarb plc is designed to ensure that the Gobo Inc does not carry out a trade in the UK for tax purposes. The 'tax avoidance' condition appears to have been met and possibly the 'mismatch condition' as Fragmarb plc and Gobo Inc are connected. There appears to be an effective tax mismatch outcome and insufficient economic substance.

Therefore Gobo Inc will have to pay DPT on 25% of taxable diverted profits. This will be based on notional PE profits. Further information will be needed on the amount of profits attributable to the 'avoided PE'.

DPT is not self-assessed and Gobo Inc will need to notify HMRC within three months of the relevant accounting period.

Additional taxable profits could also arise in the UK if adjustments are considered necessary to the transfer pricing of services between Fragmarb plc and Gobo Inc. If the fees paid by Gobo Inc to Fragmarb plc or the after sales service are considered below the arm's length value for such services, an adjustment must be made as part of the self-assessment to recognise the appropriate level of additional income.

34.3 Response to marketing director email

As you have always been UK resident, you have been liable to tax on your worldwide income and gains.

If you meet the full-time work overseas criteria for a whole tax year, you will be treated as a non-UK resident for income tax and capital gains purposes from the day on which you start working overseas. This treatment should apply if the secondment starts on 1 January as you will be working overseas for the whole of 2020/21. Conditions to qualify as full-time work overseas for an entire tax year include:

- working overseas for an average of 35 hours per week
- no breaks from overseas work of more than 30 days
- no more than 30 days working in the UK
- no more than 90 days in the UK

The split year rules may apply in the tax year in which you return to the UK, subject to the UK ties test being satisfied in the part of the tax year in which you are working overseas. You would be treated as UK resident from the day after the last day working overseas.

If you delay the secondment and you work in the UK both in the part of 2020/21 before you leave and the part of 2021/22 after your return, you are likely to be regarded as UK resident throughout the whole of both tax years as a result of the full-time UK work test. In this case income may be subject to both UK and overseas tax.

Regardless of when you take up employment, all UK sources of income will continue to be subject to UK income tax. If the tax rate in Faraway is lower, then it may be that the 1 January 2020 start date is preferable so that your overseas salary of £135,000 is not subject to UK tax in 2020/21 and possibly parts of 2019/20. Further information would be needed on this.

Examiner's comments

Whilst some candidates performed very well on the first part of this question, many failed to appreciate the implications of the incorporation of a permanent establishment with some considering that the subsidiary would form part of a 'No Gain No Loss' group thus allowing a tax free transfer of assets. In addition, candidates produced very general answers which focussed on the transfer of trade and assets and therefore considered VAT, SDLT and use of any losses. This showed an inability to answer the question actually set. Instead, candidates seemed to regurgitate answers to similar questions which had been set in the past on this area and displayed a 'rote learning approach' to answering this question.

Those who discussed the operation of incorporation relief generally scored well, although it was disappointing to see how many candidates used indexation to increase a capital loss and the references to the company claiming Entrepreneurs' Relief were concerning. This showed a complete lack of understanding of the differences between corporation tax and capital gains tax for individuals.

The majority of the candidates identified the opportunity to benefit from the Patent Box regime, although only the best candidates scored the extra marks by explaining the need to consider activities etc. This was encouraging as whilst patent box has featured in previous exams, this question developed the concept further and required candidates to perform computations.

Candidates had the opportunity to score well on the second part of the question and most identified the potential application of anti-avoidance legislation although it was surprising that not all candidates identified the potential application of the DPT. This area is new and therefore candidates should have been expecting it. Nonetheless good discussion of CFCs and transfer pricing also scored well.

The weaker students adopted a scattergun approach to this question and merely copied out the rules on CFC's and the operation of the transfer pricing regime from the Learning Materials. This showed a lack of skill in spotting the relevant issue; which is a key factor in being able to do well in this exam.

Most candidates showed a basic understanding of the residency rules, although many did not seem clear on the distinction between residence and non-residence – ie, that UK residents are taxable on worldwide income whilst non-residents are only liable to UK income tax on their UK income. Many candidates identified the potential application of the split year rules, but generally failed to appreciate the distinction between the departure dates. Better marks were scored by those who clearly set out the conditions for the full time work overseas test and applied these to the scenario.

Again this question displayed that candidates are comfortable stating the relevant conditions when looking at technical rules, but seem to disregard the information in the question which if applied, would have led to many more candidates scoring full marks on this question.

35 Derek Woodhouse

Scenario

In this question the candidate is a tax adviser in a firm of ICAEW Chartered Accountants providing advice to a client (Derek Woodhouse) who runs an unincorporated business. The client for many years and is transferring the trade and assets of the business to his son. The client also wishes to transfer shares in a quoted company to his grandchildren and is seeking advice on the most effective method in order to minimise overall tax liability.

The question also focussed on the ethical implications of misclassification of a payment made to a new employee. In addition, Veronica, Derek's wife, is also a client of the firm and is seeking advice on the maximum amount of contribution she can make to a personal pension scheme.

Marking guide

		Technical	Skills	Marks
35.1 (a)	**Email re retiring from business**			
	CGT	1	2	
	Gift relief	2	3	
	Entrepreneurs' relief and gift relief	2	2	
	Entrepreneurs' relief only	–	2	
	IHT – PET	1	1	
	BPR	1	2	
	Left in will and conclusion	1	2	
		8	14	
	Max			17
(b)	**Grandchildren**			
	BPR	–	1	
	Alternative 1	1	3½	
	Alternative 2	1	2½	
	Alternative 3	1	2	
		3	9	
	Max			10

		Technical	Skills	Marks
(c)	**Payment to employee**			
	Restraint of trade v bonus	1	2	
	Ethics for employee/client	–	2	
	Ethics for accountant	$\frac{1}{2}$	$\frac{1}{5}$	
	Max			6
35.2	**Pension contributions**			
	Tapered annual allowance	2	–	2
	Total marks	15	28	43
	Maximum			35

35.1 (a) **Response to email**

Retiring from business – Capital gains tax (CGT)

If you dispose of your business during your lifetime to Andrew, then despite the fact that you are selling the premises at less than the market value and gifting the other business assets, for CGT purposes you will be treated as disposing of the assets for market value.

Therefore, during your lifetime, there will be capital gains tax payable as follows:

Premises – (£625,000 – £225,000) = £400,000

Goodwill – (£500,000 – Nil) = £500,000

The plant and machinery will be exempt from capital gains tax as there have market values costs of less than £6,000 and the inventory is not a chargeable asset.

This would result in £900,000 of total gains.

If you have not already used it, this gain can be reduced by your annual exempt amount of £11,700. In addition there are some reliefs available which would allow you to mitigate your CGT liability.

Gift relief

If you and Andrew make a joint election, then gift relief will allow part of the gain on the disposal to be deferred and deducted from the base cost of the assets disposed to Andrew.

As you have received some sales proceeds in respect of the premises, the entire gain is not eligible for deferral. The excess of proceeds received less original cost are subject to CGT immediately and the balance of the gain can then be deferred. Therefore £375,000 (£600,000 – £225,000) of the gain will be taxed immediately and only £25,000 can be deferred. The gain on the goodwill of £500,000 could also be deferred. However, the gain will become chargeable if Andrew disposes of the business in the future as his base cost will be lower (nil for the goodwill and £600,000 for the building).

Entrepreneurs' relief (ER)

If a joint election for gift relief was made then the gain arising on you in relation to the premises would qualify for ER and the gain would be taxed at 10% so capital gains tax payable would be £37,500, assuming the annual exempt amount is already used. ER is available in respect of gains on disposals by individuals of all or part of a trading business carried on by an individual provided the business property has been owned for a period of a least one year ending with the date of disposal. This is providing you have not used your lifetime limit of £10 million. Any gains in excess of your lifetime limit would be charged to CGT at the rate of 10% or 20%.

Alternatively, if gift relief was not claimed by yourself and Andrew then you could claim ER on the entire gain of £900,000 resulting in a capital gains tax liability of £90,000. Hence the immediate liability would be £52,500 higher, but Andrew would benefit from full base cost on the assets (goodwill £500,000 and premises £625,000) – an increase of £525,000.

Inheritance tax (IHT)

The disposal of the business to Andrew could also potentially be liable to IHT.

At the time of the transfer of the business, the gift would be a Potentially Exempt Transfer (PET), meaning no tax would be payable in your lifetime.

However, if you were to die within seven years of the date of the PET, the value transferred would be in charge to IHT on your death.

Given that you are unwell, this is a consideration.

However, as the assets transferred are the assets of your unincorporated business, which you have owned for more than two years, 100% Business Property Relief (BPR) should be available which effectively removes the value of this transfer from the inheritance tax calculation. This will only be available if Andrew still owns the assets at the date of your death.

Leaving the business to Andrew in your will

If you hold on to your business and transfer it under the terms of your will, on death, there will be no capital gains tax liability on assets transferred on death.

If your business forms part of your death estate, there should also be no inheritance tax liability, because BPR at the rate of 100% should exempt your business assets from tax.

The capital tax cost of transferring the business to Andrew on your death, is potentially £Nil.

Therefore this option appears the most tax efficient and no tax is immediately payable and Andrew will benefit from the higher base cost as the value of the assets at the time of his inheritance will represent his base cost for future disposals. However, other non-tax factors will of course also be relevant to your decision.

(b) **Providing for your grandchildren**

Unfortunately although you paid IHT when you inherited the shares, any transfer you make is considered separately from this and further inheritance tax may arise as explained below.

BPR will not apply as the shares are quoted shares and the holding is not a controlling holding.

Alternative 1

If you make a gift to your grandchildren during your lifetime then this will be treated as a PET for IHT purposes. No IHT will be payable during your lifetime but if you were to die within seven years then the PET would become chargeable. The transfer of value could be reduced by the annual exemption of £3,000 and any annual exemption you have brought forward from the previous tax year, potentially reducing the value of the gift to £494,000. Your nil rate band of £325,000 could also then be used, providing you have made no other lifetime gifts, resulting in IHT at 40% on £169,000. This would, however, reduce the amount of the nil rate band available on your death.

The inheritance tax liability could be reduced by taper relief if you survive at least three years from the date of the gift.

Alternative 2

If you make a gift to a trust, then this constitutes a chargeable lifetime transfer (CLT) for IHT purposes. Tax will be payable at the time of the transfer at the rate of either 20% if the trustees agree to pay the tax or 25% if you pay the tax. As noted above, the transfer of value will be reduced by any nil rate band and annual exemptions you have available. If you do not survive for seven years from the date of the gift then further IHT will become payable but this would be reduced by the amount of lifetime tax already paid and, if you survive for more than three years, taper relief.

Alternative 3

If you leave the shares in your will then they will form part of your death estate and the excess of the total market value of your estate on death over your nil rate band will be subject to IHT at 40%. However, as you inherited the shares, then quick succession relief (QSR) could apply.

This applies where there are two charges to IHT within five years. Given that you inherited the shares initially and paid IHT on them then QSR could potentially apply and will be calculated as:

$$\text{Tax paid on first transfer} \times \frac{\text{net transfer}}{\text{gross transfer}} \times \text{relevant percentage}$$

This would reduce the IHT payable on the death estate.

(c) **Restraint of trade payment**

Any bonus paid to an employee is taxable and subject to PAYE and NICs in the normal way. A restraint of trade payment paid by an employer to an employee in return for not competing with the employer on termination of employment is generally treated as capital and subject to capital gains tax rules. However, this is not the case here.

You are potentially asking an employee to share confidential information with you which is not acceptable. You should consider carefully exactly what the suggested payment is for and assess whether such a payment should be made.

In addition you are proposing mis-classifying the actual nature of the payment.

As an ICAEW Chartered Accountant I must act with honesty and integrity and urge you to treat the payment as a bonus and disclose to HMRC. I am able to do so with your authorisation – and will review my engagement letter to see if I am already authorised to do so.

Tutorial note

This cannot be divulged to the client but there may be concerns that this could constitute money laundering and if the client treats the payment incorrectly, then disclosure should be made to the MLRO in order to comply with the ethical and technical requirements of the profession.

35.2 Advice for Veronica

As you are aware the annual allowance is a restriction as to the amount of contributions to pension schemes which is eligible for tax relief. The limit is currently £40,000 pa. Although this annual allowance limit can be increased by unused annual allowance from the previous three years, I understand that you have fully used your allowances in previous years.

In addition the allowance is tapered if you are deemed to be high-income. The annual allowance will be tapered if both:

- 'adjusted income' for the tax year exceeds £150,000; and

- 'threshold income' for the tax year exceeds £110,000 (ie, £150,000 – the full annual allowance).

'Adjusted income' is calculated as net income but adding back your own pension contributions (only if deducted from employment income under net pay arrangements) plus contributions made by your employer.

'Threshold income' is net income less gross pension contributions into a personal pension scheme by you.

Therefore if the level of your future salary and contributions are such that you exceed both of these limits, the annual allowance of £40,000 is reduced by £1 for every £2 that your adjusted income exceeds £150,000, down to a minimum of £10,000.

Examiner's comments

Most candidates scored well on the first part of this question with a reasonable explanation of the CGT and IHT positions. Whilst candidates generally identified the opportunity to claim gift and entrepreneurs' reliefs, explanations sometimes showed a lack of understanding as to the business structure with many references to shares and companies. Whilst less candidates focused on IHT it was pleasing to see that many of those who identified the possibility of BPR explained this well and appreciated that need for Andrew to retain the assets. A number of candidates showed an awareness of the rules concerning goodwill and entrepreneurs' relief, but did not appreciate that this applies only to a gain arising on incorporation. This was not relevant to the question.

In Part 1 (b) many candidates spent time discussing the CGT implications, which were very similar to those in the first part of the question failing to appreciate that the question specifically asked for consideration of the IHT implications only. This wasted time. Nonetheless the IHT was generally discussed well by those who focused on this area. Candidates showed a good understanding of the different between PETs, CLTs and gifts on death. QSR was also relevant on this question which is brought forward knowledge from Tax Compliance. A number of candidates discussed its relevance and therefore produced some excellent answers.

In Part 1 (c) the quality of the discussion on the 'bonus' varied significantly. Those who identified that concerns arose from both the nature of the payment and the tax treatment thereof scored well. The actions that should be taken were also very sensible and candidates followed a logical approach. This is an improvement from previous answers to ethical scenarios which conveys more of a focus by candidates on the approach to this type of question.

Some candidates ignored the requirement altogether and instead interpreted the question as they wanted to see it, with lots of detailed income tax calculations on the liability of the bonus. This was irrelevant and candidates should be encouraged to fully digest the requirements, plan their answer and not waste time producing calculations which were not required.

The final part of the question has changed since it was set by the examiners.

36 Baluga Ltd

Scenario

In this question the candidate worked in a firm of ICAEW Chartered Accountants but had been seconded to the finance department of a client, Baluga Ltd. The scenario was divided into three distinct areas on which the candidate needed to advise:

(1) Loss relief options for a consortium company where Baluga Ltd is a consortium member
(2) Tax implications of a potential management buyout (MBO) of Baluga Ltd
(3) VAT implications of retail sales and online sales to Germany

Marking guide

		Technical	Skills	Marks
36.1 Loss relief				
Consortium relief		2	1	
Amount of loss relief/restrictions		1	3	
Use of PS Ltd loss – group relief		–	3	
Use of PS Ltd loss – no group relief		1	2	
		4	9	
	Max			11
36.2 MBO				
Hivedown		–	1	
Corporation tax – transfer of assets		1	1	
Loss relief		1	2	
VAT		1	1	
SDLT		1	2	
Finance		1	1	
		5	8	
	Max			11
36.3 VAT overseas aspects				
Retail sales		–	2	
Ecommerce transactions		1	1	
Direct sales		–	1	
		1	4	
	Max			3
Total marks		10	21	31
Maximum				25

36.1 Cosmo plc is a consortium company as it is a UK company of which corporate entities, Baluga Ltd and Actifirm Ltd, each at least own 5% and jointly own 75%.

Overseas companies can be consortium members.

Losses within Cosmo plc can be surrendered to UK resident consortium members.

The amount of loss available for surrender is for the loss of the corresponding accounting period and the consortium member's percentage holding in the consortium company.

The loss to surrender from Cosmo plc will be restricted by the amount of any possible current year loss claim in Cosmo plc. As Cosmo plc is also a member of a group, the loss available for surrender to member companies will be further restricted by a notional group surrender claim to companies in the group/consortium companies group.

Therefore, the loss in Cosmo plc will be reduced by £30,000 in respect of a current year claim giving £745,000.

The amount available for consortium relief will then depend on whether Perfect Skin Ltd's loss is group relieved and to what extent. The amount of Perfect Skin Ltd's loss available for group relief, after relieving first against its own profits, is £27,500 (£35,000 – £7,500). If this was fully relieved against Clarouge Ltd's profits of £380,000 then the balance of £352,500 would be available for relieving Cosmo plc's loss.

This would then leave £392,500 (£745,000 – £352,500) available for relief to consortium members. Of this, Baluga Ltd can claim 6/12 × 60%, so £117,750.

If no claim was made to relieve the loss of Perfect Skin Ltd in Clarouge Ltd then the potential group relief claim by Clarouge Ltd would be £380,000 and Baluga Ltd would then claim 6/12 × 60% of £365,000 (£745,000 – £380,000), so £109,500.

However, before any claims are made the budgeted results for the current period should be reviewed. If Cosmo plc is expected to make a taxable profit and will be able to utilise the loss, it may be better to leave the loss in Cosmo plc and carry back the current period loss in Baluga Ltd.

36.2 MBO

The proposed transaction is a hive down, allowing the management team to acquire the business, but through a clean company with no historical liabilities.

Corporation tax

On setting up the new company, Maxxi Ltd, the assets will have been transferred from Baluga Ltd at tax written down value as both companies were in the same 75% group. The accounting period from 1 October 2019 to 31 March 2020 will continue on the sale of the shares to the MBO team.

There is a change in ownership and so any brought forward losses would not be available for group loss relief for five years from the end of the accounting period of the change ie, first relief against profits of the year ended 31 March 2026. However this may not be available as it seems there may also be a change in the nature of trade, given the management team's plans for an intended return of the company to profitability. Therefore, the losses of the trading period to 30 September 2019 may not to be available to carry forward and set off either in future accounting periods of Maxxi Ltd or via group relief.

VAT

The purchase of shares is exempt from VAT and the transfer of the trade and assets will be outside the scope of VAT as a transfer of a going concern (TOGC).

SDLT

The exemption from stamp duty land tax on any land and buildings in respect of transfers between companies in the same 75% group will not be available due to the sale of Maxxi Ltd within three years of the transfer. Therefore SDLT will be payable on the building.

Finance

As the managers are acquiring finance to fund the acquisition then there may be some income tax relief available for them, if Maxxi Ltd is a close company and the managers own at least 5% of the shares and continue to work for the company.

36.3 VAT

When Maxxi Ltd sells goods to the retail outlets in Germany, this constitutes a dispatch of goods to another EU state. As the retail outlets are likely to have to register for VAT in Germany then zero rating will apply to the dispatch of the goods.

The sale of goods to individual customers by Maxxi Ltd will be via the internet. Therefore as this is an e commerce transaction, involving physical goods over the internet then tax arises in the country to which the goods are delivered.

If Maxxi Ltd sells directly to individual customers and not via the website, then this will be subject to VAT in the member state of origin and so the dispatch from the UK will be taxable at the standard rate of VAT. VAT will be added to the invoice by Maxxi Ltd.

Examiner's comments

Disappointingly many candidates failed to identify that a consortium existed in the first part of the question, or indeed argued that it did not, thus reducing the opportunities for loss relief. This again, shows a lack of ability to apply the rules to the scenario in the question. As there were some individual shareholders, candidates immediately concluded that the company could not be a consortium, instead of working through the consortium criteria step by step; in which case they would have clearly noted that the company in the question was in fact a consortium as the corporate shareholding met the conditions.

Many of those who did identify the consortium failed to appreciate that whilst a shareholding by an overseas company can be taken into account when establishing a consortium, the overseas company will not be in the charge to UK tax and will not therefore claim a proportion of the losses. This is fundamental knowledge and there are examples of this in the learning materials.

Many candidates answered the second part of the question well identifying the key implications of a hive down with the best answers focusing as asked on the implications for the management team.

The weaker candidates merely copied from the learning materials and did not focus on the implications for the management team as the question specified. Whilst some marks could have been picked up with this approach, this exam is a skills based exam where a significant proportion of the marks are allocated for applying knowledge to the scenario. Answers to this part again demonstrated the technique of using the learning materials and previous questions to produce answers to fit the previous questions asked and not the one being asked in the exam. Candidates need to be very careful as whilst this exam did focus on some areas which have been tested before, the scenarios and indeed the tax implications were not from the same perspective as previous questions.

Candidates generally did well on the third part and recognised the distinction between dealing with VAT registered traders, individual customers and online sales. The Learning materials are very clear in this area and it was apparent that a high number of candidates had consulted them for this part of the question.

December 2016 exam answers

37 Ant plc

Scenario

The scenario considers corporation tax for a group of companies and the tax treatment (corporation tax, VAT and stamp duty implications) of a number of transactions undertaken during the year. The question tests a candidate's ability to deal with a number of more complex corporation tax issues, many of which are new at the Business Planning: Taxation syllabus, such as consortium companies, credit on realisation of intangibles and the rollover of intangibles by indirect reinvestment. The second part of the question considers the ethical dilemma for the company and the Senior Accounting Officer of the discovery of a large error in previous corporation tax returns.

Marking guide

	Technical	Skills	Marks
37.1 Group relationships	1	–	
Ant plc			
Sale of shares – SSE	1	2	
Sale of shares – deferred gain	–	2	
Sale of patent – realisation gain	1	3	
Sale of patent – rollover relief	2	3½	
Cod Ltd			
Gain on warehouse	1	1½	
Capital goods scheme – purchase	1	1½	
Rollover relief	2	2	
Allocation of group gains		1½	
Capital goods scheme – future	1	1	
SDLT	1	2½	
Option to tax	2	2	
Dog Ltd			
Consortium loss	2	3	
RDEC	2	3	
	17	28½	
Max			33
37.2 Gift in lifetime			
Penalties	–	1	
Mitigation	1½	2½	
Interest	–	1	
SAO	1	3	
	2½	7½	
Max			7
Total marks	19½	36	55½
Maximum			40

37.1 Report to the finance director

Corporation tax issues for the group – year ended 30 September 2018

Explanation of group relationships

Ant plc

Sale of shares in Elk GmbH

On disposal of the 20% holding in Elk GmbH, the substantial shareholding exemption (SSE) will apply, and no gain on the sale will be chargeable to corporation tax.

The SSE applies because Elk GmbH is a trading company and Ant plc has held at least 10% of the shares in Elk GmbH for 12 months out of the past 6 years.

However, a proportion of the gain deferred on the incorporation of Elk GmbH will be chargeable on Ant plc on disposal of the shares. As 20% of the shares were sold then the gain chargeable is:

£550,595 × 20% = £110,119. SSE will not apply to this gain.

Sale of patent

On disposal of the patent a profit on realisation will be taxable.

The profit is calculated by comparing the disposal proceeds to the TWDV of the patent after the 4% WDA deductions have been made.

	£	£
Disposal proceeds		750,000
Less cost	250,000	
4% WDA (250,000 × 4% × 6)	(60,000)	
TWDV		(190,000)
Realisation gain/credit		560,000

This credit would be added to Ant plc's taxable profits for the year ended 30 September 2018.

The purchase of a new group company by Bat Ltd, which includes an intangible fixed asset (IFA) would allow Ant plc to claim group rollover relief to reduce the amount of the profit on realisation in charge to tax.

	£
Ant plc realisation gain/credit	560,000
Less rollover relief (Note)	(394,000)
Realisation gain/credit	166,000

Note: The TWDV of the underlying IFA in Rag Ltd (£644,000) is less than the cost of the shares in Rag Ltd of £800,000. This TWDV is therefore the deemed cost of the new IFA. Full rollover relief is therefore not possible as the disposal proceeds of Ant plc's patents (£750,000) exceeds this. Relief is restricted to the excess of the TWDV of Rag Ltd's IFA over the original cost of the patent sold by Ant plc: £394,000 (£644,000 – £250,000).

The TWDV of the underlying intangible fixed assets in Rag Ltd will be reduced by the rollover relief claimed (644,000 – 394,000 = £250,000) This will reduce the tax deduction available on these assets in Rag Ltd for future accounting periods and may increase the amount of gain/credit on realisation when the assets are sold in the future.

Cod Ltd

The sale of the warehouse will give rise to a chargeable gain.

The gain is calculated as follows:

	£
Proceeds	1,000,000
Less cost (Note)	(583,333)
Less SDLT on purchase on VAT inclusive amount	
4% × £700,000	(28,000)
Less indexation allowance	
278.1 – 240.8/240.8 = 0.155 × 611,333	(94,757)
Net gain	293,910

Note: On purchase, VAT of 20% would have been charged by the developer on the supply of a new commercial building. Cod Ltd is registered for VAT and would have reclaimed the VAT of £116,667 (£700,000 × 1/6).

On the sale of a building with a cost £250,000 or more, within the first 10 years of ownership, there could be a claw-back of VAT recovered on purchases under the capital goods scheme. An adjustment on sale for the complete intervals following the year of sale will also be required assuming 0% taxable use if the sale itself is exempt. As it is sold within the 10 intervals of acquisition it will be subject to a clawback of input tax on the original purchase price.

When sold, as the building was more than three years old and there had been no election to tax the building, the proceeds of sale would have been exempt from VAT.

The purchase of the new warehouse would be an opportunity to rollover the gain on the sale of the old warehouse. The new warehouse cost £1.5 million gross of VAT. Net of VAT this would be a cost of £1,250,000. Of this, two thirds of the building are used for trading purposes ie, £833,333.

Therefore, full rollover relief is not possible. Proceeds of £166,667 are not reinvested (£1m – £833,333). As a result, a gain of £166,667 would be chargeable and £127,243 (£293,910 – £166,667) of the gain could be rolled over. This chargeable gain could potentially be allocated to other companies within the group if there are capital losses available. The rollover relief will be deducted from the base cost of the new warehouse.

Two-thirds of the VAT charged on the acquisition of the new building would be recovered by Cod Ltd. The building would be under the capital goods scheme, because the buildings cost £250,000 or more. The input tax recovery could be amended over the course of the next 10 years should the taxable use of the building change.

Cod Ltd would have paid SDLT on the purchase price of the new commercial building. This tax will be charged on £1.5 million of chargeable consideration, at a cost of £64,500 ((£150,000 × 0%) + (£100,000 × 2%) + (£1,250,000 × 5%)).

The decision on whether to opt to tax the building or not will depend on the future plans for the building. Cod Ltd currently rents out a third of the building and without an option to tax rental income will be an exempt supply. However, the rental is only expected to be for the first five years of the building's life. After this the building should be used 100% for Cod Ltd's trade. Under the capital goods scheme a change in the percentage of taxable use will mean that more of the initial input VAT is recovered.

If we opt to tax the building we will have to charge VAT on the rent charged to our tenant. As they make zero rated supplies and they would be able to recover any VAT charged on rent.

The decision to opt to tax, or not, will be affected by the plans Cod has for eventual sale of the warehouse and whether charging VAT on the sale would deter any potential purchasers.

SDLT will be payable by the charity on the lease of £11,000 (($250,000 × 5) - £150,000) × 1%. This will not affect Cod Ltd.

Dog Ltd

Dog Ltd is a consortium company. The company is at least 75% owned by Ant plc and Monkey Ltd, and no one company owns 75% of the company's shares.

Dog Ltd has made a tax adjusted loss for the year ended 30 September 2018.

This loss needs to be adjusted for R&D expenditure.

	£
Adjusted loss	(450,395)
Add RDEC 12% × £412,500	49,500
Trading deduction for capital expenditure on laboratory buildings	(750,000)
Revised adjusted loss	(1,150,895)

In the current period this loss could be used by the consortium members as consortium loss relief or carried forward and used in future accounting periods.

The consortium loss relief available to Ant plc would be 40% × £(1,150,895) = £460,358.

Dog Ltd is entitled to a tax credit (RDEC). As the company has no tax liability in the current year, the first cap is applied and the tax credit in year ended 30 September 2018 is restricted to £40,095 (£49,500 - (19% × £49,500)). This is recoverable as it is less than the PAYE/NIC liability for R&D staff. The remaining RDEC of £9,405 (£49,500 - £40,095) is carried forward to the following year for relief.

37.2 Errors in previous year's computations

HMRC will charge penalties, based on the potential lost revenue (which in this case is large at £1,200,000), the type of the error and when the error was reported to HMRC.

The errors, once identified and quantified must be reported to HMRC as soon as possible. The speed with which we inform HMRC of the error can help mitigate any penalties HMRC may charge. The penalty charged will be less if we inform HMRC about the error before they find out about it (unprompted disclosure). We should also make full disclosure of the facts surrounding the error.

We need to identify why these errors occurred. Were they deliberate errors, or careless mistakes?

If we can be seen to have taken 'reasonable care' but still made a mistake, HMRC will not charge a penalty.

The penalty ranges for unprompted disclosure are as follows:

Type of error	Penalty range for unprompted disclosure
Careless	0% to 30%
Deliberate but not concealed	20% to 70%
Deliberate and concealed	30% to 100%

Reductions in penalties are given for 'telling', 'helping' and 'giving access'. Therefore, to minimise the penalties to be charged, we need to co-operate fully with HMRC and make as full disclosure as possible. For a careless error, the maximum penalty would be £360,000 and the minimum £0.

Interest will also be payable on any outstanding liability and so any outstanding tax should be paid without delay.

As you are the Senior Accounting Officer (SAO) of Ant plc, you are required to take reasonable steps to establish and monitor accounting systems within your company, that are adequate for the purposes of accurate tax reporting.

Once we have established the cause of the errors in last year's returns, we will be able to determine whether any of the errors were caused by failures of the accounting systems. The penalty for the failure to establish and maintain appropriate tax accounting arrangements is £5,000. This penalty will be your personal liability and not the company's.

The broader issue is understanding the breakdown in controls, which allowed this error to happen. HMRC may wish to investigate the company, as the error is so large and we need to be able to satisfy them and also the board of directors that we have identified the reasons behind the error and made arrangements to ensure that similar errors cannot happen in the future.

Examiner's comments

Candidates had to deal with a number of transactions by the companies in the group and they needed to identify the tax implications of each transaction, not just in terms of corporation tax, but also any other relevant taxes, such as VAT and stamp taxes.

Ant plc had sold shares in Elk GmbH and also an intangible asset. Both sales had wider reaching consequences than just calculating taxable profits or gains. The sale of the Elk shares required candidates to link the sale to the original incorporation of Elk, listed in a later part of the same Exhibit, and identify and calculate the crystallisation of a gain deferred on incorporation. The sale of the intangible required links to the purchase of another intangible in a newly acquired group company and the impact, availability and calculations around a group rollover of the taxable profit on the disposal of the intangible.

Cod Ltd sold a building and purchased a new building. The obvious part of this transaction was the calculation of a gain and the consideration of rollover relief on the purchase of the new building. However, in addition, there were wide ranging stamp tax and VAT consequences to be brought into consideration.

Dog Ltd had research and development expenditure to consider and the consideration of R&D relief for a large company was a slight change from the consideration of an SME's in previous exams.

Successful candidates were those who analysed the transactions in detail and considered all angles of each transaction. Weaker candidates tended to have only a surface interpretation of the items to be considered and did not look at the more complex, planning aspects of the transactions or question the alternative tax treatments available for each transaction.

As tax rates have harmonised between small and large companies, the impact of tax groups is shifting to aspects of groups other than losses and candidates need to be aware of the areas in which groups are still relevant to tax.

Candidates should also be wary of spending too much time drawing group structure diagrams and commenting on the basics of group structure. Although marks are awarded for drawing relevant conclusions about group relationships, the emphasis should be on the word 'relevant'. Far too many candidates gave long narratives on all the possible group relationships between the Ant plc group companies, when those relationships were irrelevant to the transactions in the question. These candidates had insufficient knowledge and understanding to be able to discriminate between the areas of their technical knowledge that were relevant or irrelevant.

Part 2 considered the impact of errors in corporation tax computations already submitted to HMRC, the action to be taken and the impact on the Senior Accounting Officer of Ant plc. This should have been a relatively straightforward area of the question. However, given that it had an ethical element, weaker candidates failed to analyse the actual situation posed and instead produced formulaic answers, concentrating on money laundering. Although, at its ultimate conclusion, there could be money laundering aspects to the situation described, they certainly would not be the first issue to consider, or the most important. Weaker candidates could improve their answers by making sure that their answers are related to the question actually set and by considering the relevance of points made to the scenario, using judgement to consider what the most important aspects of a scenario might be.

38 Jolene and Kenton

Scenario

The scenario requires candidates to consider the tax implications on dissolution of a partnership under two alternative methods. Candidates needed to consider a range of taxes including income tax, VAT, CGT and stamp taxes. The question tests the application of rules introduced in FA2015 in relation to eligibility of entrepreneurs' relief on goodwill and also the application of the GAAR.

Marking guide

	Technical	Skills	Marks
38.1 **Tax consequences**			
Income tax			
• Trading losses on cessation	1	2	
• Losses on incorporation	1	2	
VAT			
• Transfer of registration	½	½	
• TOGC	1	2	
SDLT	–	1	
Stamp duty	–	1	
Recommendation	–	2	
Appendix 1			
• Assessments	1	1	
• Losses	1	1	
Appendix 2			
• Gains	2	1	
• Entrepreneurs' relief – partnership share	½	1½	
• Incorporation relief	2	3	
• Entrepreneurs' relief – goodwill	½	1	
Appendix 3			
• Gains on incorporation (inc ER)	–	2	
• Incorporation relief	1	3	
• CGT calculation	2	1	
• Sale of shares	–	2	
	13½	27	
Max			32
38.2 **Ethics**			
• GAAR	1	2	
• Tax advantage	–	1	
Client communication	–	2	
	1	5	
Max			3
Total marks	14½	32	46½
Maximum			35

38.1 Advise Jolene and Kenton of the tax consequences of the dissolution of the partnership and the incorporation of the business on 31 December 2019

Income Tax

The partnership will cease to trade on 31 December 2019.

As at 31 December 2019, we estimate that the partners will each carry forward losses, from the start of trade, of £67,500 (Appendix 1).

On cessation of trade, trading losses cannot be carried forward, because there are no future profits from the same trade.

Jolene and Kenton have no scope to carry back losses under terminal loss relief or use losses under s.72 opening year loss relief.

On incorporation, unrelieved trading losses can be carried forward against income from the company under s.86. This loss relief could apply as consideration is solely shares. However, only Jolene would benefit, because the losses can only be used if the shareholder owns the shares throughout the year in which loss relief is given. If Kenton does not receive any shares, or if he sells his shares within six months, he will not be eligible for s.86 loss relief and his £67,500 of brought forward losses will be lost.

Jolene could therefore carry forward her £67,500 of losses against income from Jolene Ltd under s.86. Kenton would lose his losses.

VAT

The partnership is registered for VAT.

The VAT registration can be transferred to Jolene Ltd.

The transfer of the business to the company will be classed as a transfer of a going concern (TOGC), assuming Jolene Ltd registers for VAT, there is no significant break in trading and the whole of the business is transferred.

If the transfer is a TOGC, there is no taxable supply and no VAT is charged on the transfer.

The land and buildings can be transferred as part of the TOGC as they are more than three years old and there has been no option to tax.

Stamp duty land tax

On incorporation, Jolene Ltd would pay stamp duty land tax on the purchase of the commercial land and buildings of £7,000 ((£250,000 – £150,000) × 2% + (£350,000 – £250,000) × 5%).

Capital gains tax and stamp duty

Alternative 1

When Kenton sells his 50% share in the partnership to Jolene, he will incur capital gains tax of £32,580 and Jolene will have no tax to pay on incorporation of Jolene Ltd, although the base cost of the shares will be reduced by the gains on incorporation, so tax payable when the shares are sold in future will be higher (Appendix 2). However, entrepreneurs' relief should be available on a sale of her Jolene Ltd shares if this takes place after at least one year.

Alternative 2

If Kenton acquires shares in Jolene Ltd, stamp duty will be payable by Jolene when she buys Kenton's shares of £2,375 (£475,000 × 0.5%).

Kenton would incur capital gains tax of £57,660, on incorporation of Jolene Ltd because entrepreneurs' relief would not be available on the gain on goodwill.

Jolene's base cost of the shares in Jolene Ltd will be the same as under alternative 1.

Recommendation

Kenton would pay less capital gains tax if he sold his partnership share to Jolene before incorporation (57,660 – 32,580 = £25,080). There would also be £2,375 less stamp duty for Jolene to pay on the purchase of Kenton's shares.

Jolene should, therefore buy Kenton's partnership share and then incorporate the whole business as a second step.

Appendix 1
Income tax assessments Jolene and Kenton

Trading Income Assessments	Jolene £	Kenton £
2015/16		
y/e 31.12.16		
1.1.16 to 5.4.16		
3/12 × £(150,000)/2	(18,750)	(18,750)
2016/17		
y/e 31.12.16		
1.1.16 to 31.12.16		
£(150,000) – £(37,500) (used in 2015/16)/2	(56,250)	(56,250)
2017/18		
y/e 31.12.17		
£(55,000)/2	(27,500)	(27,500)
2018/19		
y/e 31.12.18		
£20,000/2	10,000	10,000
2019/20		
y/e 31.12.19		
£50,000/2	25,000	25,000

Use of losses:

Total trading losses cfwd:

	£
2015/16	18,750
2016/17	56,250
2017/18	27,500
Total losses each partner	102,500

Losses used:

	£
Losses per partner b/fwd	102,500
Used 2018/19	(10,000)
Used 2019/20	(25,000)
c/fwd at 1 January 2020	67,500

Appendix 2

Capital gains tax – Alternative 1

Gain on Kenton in 2019/20:

	Land and Buildings £	Goodwill £
Proceeds	175,000	262,500
Less cost	(100,000)	–
Gain	75,000	262,500

Note: no gains on plant and machinery as each item cost <£6,000.

	£
Total gains	337,500
Less annual exempt amount 2019/20 (assume unchanged)	(11,700)
Net gains	325,800
Tax at 10% (Note)	32,580

Note: Tax is at 10%, because Kenton qualifies for entrepreneurs' relief on the disposal of his partnership share, because he has owned it for at least one year and he is selling his entire interest in the partnership. The restriction on sale to a limited company does not apply here, because Kenton is not selling his goodwill to a company in which he has an interest.

Jolene will also have a gain on incorporation of the partnership on 31.12.19 (in the 2019/20 tax year).

	Land and buildings £	Goodwill £
Market value at 31.12.19	350,000	525,000
Less cost	(275,000)	(262,500)
Gain	75,000	262,500
Total gains		337,500
Less incorporation relief		(337,500)
Taxable gains		Nil

Jolene will accept the incorporation relief available (automatic relief if the whole business is transferred in exchange for shares). If she has no intention of selling the shares in the immediate future, she should be able to claim entrepreneurs' relief on some of the gain in the future, when the shares are sold.

If incorporation relief were disapplied, entrepreneurs' relief would not have been available on the gain on the goodwill, because it was transferred to a related (ie, close) company. Entrepreneurs' relief could have been claimed on the gain on the land and buildings. By not having any chargeable gain, due to incorporation relief, Jolene will lose her annual exempt amount for 2019/20.

	£
Base cost of Jolene Ltd shares	
Market value of assets	950,000
Less incorporation relief	(337,500)
Reduced base cost	612,500

Appendix 3

Capital gains tax – Alternative 2

Jolene and Kenton will have a gain on incorporation of the partnership:

	Land and Buildings £	Goodwill £
Proceeds	350,000	525,000
Less cost	(200,000)	–
Gain	150,000	525,000

These gains will be split between Jolene and Kenton (50% each).

	Jolene £	Kenton £
Gain on Land and Buildings 50:50	75,000	75,000
Gain on goodwill 50:50	262,500	262,500
Total gains each partner	337,500	337,500

Neither partner will be eligible for entrepreneurs' relief on the gain on the goodwill, because of the anti-avoidance rule which prevents this relief being available if goodwill is transferred to a related (ie, close) company.

However, there is no advantage to Kenton in accepting incorporation relief on the gains, because he will be selling the shares, immediately, to Jolene and there will be no ER.

So, the best course of action would be for Jolene to accept the incorporation relief available on her gains – for the same reasons as in scenario 1 above and for Kenton to dis-apply incorporation relief and to be taxed on his gains, but claim entrepreneurs' relief on the gain on the land and buildings.

	Jolene £	Kenton £
Total gains	337,500	337,500
Less incorporation relief	(337,500)	
Less annual exempt amount		(11,700)
Taxable gains	Nil	325,800
CGT		
Gains eligible for ERs' relief 75,000 × 10%		7,500
Gains not eligible for ERs' relief 262,500 – 11,700 × 20%		50,160
Total CGT payable		57,660

Gain on sale of Kenton's shares to Jolene

Kenton will incur a gain when he sells his shares to Jolene.

However, as the proceeds will equal the cost of the shares the gain will be nil.

Jolene's base cost

The base cost of Jolene's shares in Jolene Ltd will be:	£
Cost of shares (475,000 + 475,000)	950,000
Less incorporation relief	(337,500)
	612,500

38.2 Ethical considerations

The General Anti-Abuse Rule (GAAR) is effective for all arrangements entered into on or after 17 July 2013.

This rule applies to most taxes and is intended to counter tax advantages sought from aggressive tax avoidance arrangements.

In order to apply, it must be:

- reasonable to conclude that obtaining a tax advantage was one of the main purposes for the arrangements.

- such that the arrangements are abusive.

In this situation the specific order in which the retirement of Kenton and the incorporation of the partnership take place could be concluded to be being determined in order to seek a tax advantage.

The effect of changing the order of these events results in a tax advantage.

Although it is not clear if the GAAR will apply in this situation, we should make our clients aware of the legislation and caveat our tax advice with language that informs our clients that the GAAR may apply to the tax advice given. If the GAAR does apply then the tax advice given may be ineffective for tax purposes.

Part 1 was the most challenging part of this question, with some candidates failing to deal with the problem analytically and so failing to consider the planning options available in the scenario.

It was disappointing that some answers concentrated solely on the capital tax elements of the question and ignored the income tax implications of the cessation of trade and the use of brought forward trading losses, particularly on incorporation. However, the majority of candidates showed a great deal of skill in terms of applying knowledge to the scenario and identifying appropriate conclusions.

Part 2 was designed to get students to consider the appropriateness of common tax planning scenarios in the context of the changing landscape of tax planning in the UK; in particular in the context of the general anti-abuse legislation. It is unrealistic to test tax planning in a vacuum, assuming that the landscape in which tax planning is carried on in the UK has been unaffected by recent legislative and public opinion changes. Part 2 tested this issue in line with the material within the learning materials on this area.

39 Royston Clark

Scenario

This question requires candidates to explore the implications of the difference between lifetime and death gifts for both IHT and CGT purposes and the interaction of each tax. The candidate is required to perform calculations and give advice on alternative actions and take into consideration the practicalities for Royston of giving away his assets and the resulting implications for his lifestyle.

Marking guide

	Technical	Skills	Marks
39.1 Tax consequences			
IHT and CGT	1	3	
Appendix 1			
• May 2014	1	–	
• August 2016			
Lifetime IHT	2	3½	
IHT on death	1	1½	
CGT	1	3	
• November 2016	1½	3	
	7½	14	21½
39.2 Asset gifting			
Gifts on death	–	1	
Spouse planning	1	1	
Lifetime gifts	–	2	
GWROB	–	2	
PPR	1	1	
Gift of cash	–	1	
Other assets	1	2	
Recommendation	–	3	
	3	13	16
Total marks	10½	27	37½
Maximum			25

39.1 Tax on lifetime gifts

You wish to consider a strategy to gift your assets to your immediate family (wife, children and grandchildren) either in lifetime or on death, with the minimum tax liability.

Gifts in lifetime may attract both inheritance tax and capital gains tax.

Gifts on death will only incur inheritance tax.

You have already made some lifetime gifts. In Appendix 1 I have calculated the tax liabilities arising on these gifts and identified the impact these gifts will have on later gifts.

The lifetime gifts will use up the nil rate band against the gift made on 12 August 2016. Therefore any lifetime gifts of assets or gifts of assets on death, up to 11 August 2023 could be fully chargeable to IHT.

Consideration of gift of assets

If you are going to make any more lifetime gifts, you need to consider the dual tax implications of lifetime gifts.

Gifts on death will only incur IHT.

If you give away no further assets, and your death estate is fully chargeable, you will incur IHT of £1,834,000, being 40% of the value of your death estate of £4,585,000 (ignoring the half of the net value of the family home belonging to your wife).

Tutorial note

The residence nil rate band is not available as the death estate is in excess of £2.25 million.

IHT on the death estate would be reduced by £220,000 (£550,000 at 40%) if Royston dies after 1 June 2019, because BPR would be available on the Morrell Ltd shares (owned for more than two years).

Tax planning could therefore save you a substantial amount of tax.

Tax planning measures

You and your wife should take advantage of standard IHT tax planning measures:

(1) You both should each gift £3,000 each tax year. Over 10 years from 2018/19 to 2027/28 this could save tax each year of £2,400 and up to £24,000, in total.

(2) You both should take advantage of the small gifts exemption. Each of you can gift up to £250 in total to an individual each tax year. If you were to make three gifts of £250 each, for the next 10 tax years, you would save £6,000 of tax.

In addition, in general terms, gifts made to other individuals in lifetime could be exempt from inheritance tax, if you survive 7 years from the date of the gift, or the inheritance tax due could be reduced by 20% for every year you survive beyond 3 years from the date of the gift. It would therefore appear to be beneficial to give assets away as soon as possible in order for you to maximise your opportunity to save tax.

However, it should be borne in mind that:

(a) You will need certain practical assets to live your life, such as a house and a car. If you give away the house in which you live, this would not qualify as a valid gift, if you continue to live there. It would be classified as a gift with reservation of benefit (GWROB). As a GWROB the asset would remain part of your death estate and so the tax advantage of making a lifetime gift would be lost.

(b) The gift of your own home in lifetime is advantageous, because of the CGT principal private residence exemption, however, you would then need somewhere else to live. So, you and your wife, could give away your current family home, claim the PPR exemption and then buy the purpose built house you require for your illness with some of your cash reserves. This new home would still be an asset subject to IHT, but it could be in Margaret's sole name, so that no part of the dwelling came into your death estate.

(c) You will also need some cash to maintain your lifestyle and to provide a lifestyle for your wife, after your death, so it would not be practical for you to give away all of your cash. Cash can, however, be given away in lifetime with no CGT liability on the gift. So you should assess your cash needs and make gifts of surplus cash as soon as possible.

(d) Certain assets can be given away without the need to pay CGT in lifetime. In your case this would be:

- cash – although we should bear in mind the living expenses of you and Margaret – see above.

- cars – although we should bear in mind your need for an ongoing means of transport.

  (Although you could give away your vintage Rolls Royce and keep the Range Rover for practical use.)

- chattels – furniture and jewellery, with a value and a cost of £6,000 or less can be gifted without any CGT.

Shares in unquoted companies, may be eligible for gift relief if they are shares in trading companies meaning that any gain is deferred until the recipient sells the shares. The shares in Clark Ltd will qualify for gift relief, because it is a company trading in shares not an investment company.

The shares in Morrell Ltd can be given away free of CGT from 1 June 2020 onwards. Because they were subscribed for as part of an enterprise investment scheme investment, any disposal in the first three years of ownership would trigger a potential CGT charge on the profit made on disposal (subject to gift relief) and would also result in a claw back of the income tax relief given of £120,000 (30% × £400,000).

39.2 Recommendations

I would therefore advise you to gift the following assets to your children/grandchildren, immediately:

- gift the vintage car;
- as much cash as you consider you can afford;
- any items of antique furniture with a value and a cost of £6,000 or less.

Because these assets can be given away with no CGT cost and the longer you survive the greater the likelihood that no IHT will be due on the gift.

On 1 June 2020, I would gift the shares in Morrell Ltd. This gift will then be CGT free and will not trigger a claw-back of the EIS income tax relief. BPR is likely to be available on these shares in any event.

You could then gift other assets to your spouse, taking advantage of the spouse exemption. Although this will not remove these assets from the charge to IHT, your wife has her own £325,000 nil rate band to use, and, as she is not ill she will have longer to dispose of the value of the assets in order to avoid the charge to IHT.

If any assets are to be left in your will, after 11 August 2023, you will have another £325,000 nil rate band to use. You could use this to leave assets to your grandchildren in your will.

You might choose to do this in order to skip a generation of IHT charge, by missing out your children assuming they will be wealthy in their own right.

Appendix 1: Lifetime gifts

8 May 2014: was a gift to spouse and so exempt from IHT. It will also be treated as a transfer at NGNL for CGT.

12 August 2016 was a gift to a discretionary trust and so a chargeable lifetime transfer (CLT).

	£
Value of Clark Ltd Holding before gift (Note 1) £35 × 40,000	1,400,000
Value of Clark Ltd holding after gift (Note 2) £25 × 20,000	(500,000)
Diminution in value	900,000

Notes

1 Value before gift is of a 50% holding (including related property held by Mrs Clark).

2 Value after the gift is of a 30% holding (including related property held by Mrs Clark).

3 Even though Clark Ltd is an unquoted company, there is no BPR available, because it is a company that deals in shares.

	£
CLT	900,000
Less annual exemption:	
2016/17	(3,000)
2015/16	(3,000)
Net gift	894,000
First £325,000 × 0%	0
Next £569,000 × 25% (Note)	142,250

Note: Assumption made that donor paid the lifetime tax due.

If you die within seven years of 12 August 2016, so, by 11 August 2023, further IHT will be due on death.

Assuming that you paid the inheritance tax due on the creation of the trust, the tax due on death would be:

Gross chargeable transfer (142,250 + 894,000) £1,036,250

	£
£325,000 × 0%	0
£711,250 × 40%	284,500
Less lifetime tax paid	(142,250)
Tax due on death	142,250

However, taper relief will reduce the tax payable by 20% on each anniversary from 12 August 2019 onwards that you are still alive.

On creation of the trust, capital gains tax would also have been payable. The market value of a 20% holding on 12 August 2016 of £400,000 would have been the deemed proceeds, giving rise to a taxable gain. The gain would have been £380,000 (£400,000 – £20,000 nominal value).

This gain could have been deferred under s260 TCGA 1992 gift relief. In which case, you would have paid no CGT in August 2016, but the gain of £380,000 would have been deducted from the CGT base cost of the shares. The base cost of the shares to the trust would have been £20,000 (£400,000 – £380,000).

The gift on 21 November 2016 to your son Brian on the occasion of his marriage would not have been chargeable to CGT, because it was a gift of cash. For IHT, it would have been a potentially exempt transfer.

The annual exemptions for 2016/17 and 2015/16 had already been used against the gift on 12 August 2016. The marriage exemption of £5,000 would be deductible – leaving

£395,000 as the value of the PET. The nil rate band has already been used by the previous lifetime gift on 12 August 2016.

If you were to die within seven years of 21 November 2016 – that is by 20 November 2023 – inheritance tax would be payable on the £395,000 of PET at the rate of 40%. This tax (£158,000) would be reduced by 20% for every year you survive from 21 November 2019 onwards.

Examiner's comments

This question produced the best performance on the exam. It was a discrete topic, where a well-planned answer scored well on straightforward issues.

Those who analysed the question before attempting it and used a methodical approach scored very well.

Weaker candidates failed to identify that two taxes were in point – both CGT and IHT – and, if they did identify the two taxes, muddled up the rules between them. Candidates needed to be very secure in their technical knowledge of both taxes to be able to consider the interaction of the taxes and plan to mitigate the client's ultimate tax liability.

March 2017 exam answers

40 Taul plc

Scenario

The candidate is a trainee ICAEW Chartered Accountant working for the finance department of Taul plc, a UK tax resident company which is owned by a US parent. Taul plc is buying an optician's business and is considering alternative methods either by purchase of shares or the trade and assets. The optician business owner Val Howey who owns 100% of the share capital, will be continuing to work in the business and is being offered a remuneration package which includes share options in Taul plc.

		Technical	Skills	Marks
(a)	**Buying HG**			
	Method 1			
	Share for share exchange	1	1	
	Contingent consideration	-	2	
	Gain on cash	1	2	
	Entrepreneurs' relief	-	2	
	Disapply share for share	1	1	
	Other tax implications	-	2	
	Method 2			
	Disposal of assets/impact on loss	1	1	
	IFAs	2	2	
	Equipment	1	1	
	Inventory	1	1	
	Adjusted loss	-	2	
	Val – double taxation	-	1	
	Distribution pre winding up	1	3	
		9	21	
	Max			22
(b)	**Corporate interest restriction**			
	Rules and impact	3	1	
	Purchase of shares	-	2	
	Purchase of trade and assets	-	1	
	Current position	-	1	
		3	5	
	Max			6
(c)	**Other tax factors**			
	VAT – TOGC/CGS	1	3	
	VAT – shares v trade and assets	1	1	
	Corporation tax	-	1	
	Stamp duty	-	1	
		2	6	
	Max			6

		Technical	Skills	Marks
(d)	**Share options**			
	Grant	1	1	
	Exercise	1	3	
	Gain	–	1	
	NIC	–	1	
	Taul plc	–	1	
		2	7	
	Max			6
Total marks		16	39	55
Maximum				40

(a) **Tax implications for Val and HG Ltd**

Method 1 - Share purchase

Implications for Val

The share element of the consideration would be treated as a share for share exchange with no capital gains tax arising now. A gain will only be taxable when Val sells her shares in Taul plc. At that point, the base cost for Val would be the base cost of the share in HG Ltd allocated in proportion to the consideration.

£100,000 × £4m/£5m = £80,000

The cash element will be taxable now even though it is deferred until April 2020.

This is because the future payment is contingent on performance but the amount is known in advance. Therefore, this is treated as a single disposal. If the contingency is not met, then the computation may subsequently be amended.

The cash consideration on the sale of Val's shares will give rise to a chargeable gain and if she has not used her lifetime limit, entrepreneurs' relief should be available and the gain taxed at 10% as follows:

	£'000
Proceeds	1,000.00
Less cost	(20.00)
	980.00
Less annual exempt amount	(11.70)
	968.30
CGT @ 10%	96.83

I am not advising Val and we do not know her intentions in respect of her Taul plc shareholding. She would exchange her shares in HG Ltd for a 3% shareholding in Taul plc. There is uncertainty as to whether entrepreneurs' relief (ER) will be available to Val on the future disposal of her shares in Taul plc.

To create certainty for Val, subject to her having the cashflow to pay the tax, Val could disapply the paper for paper rules on the takeover to ensure that she qualifies for entrepreneurs' relief. Val should be advised to seek independent tax advice.

For HG Ltd the sale of its shares to Taul plc means that trade continues. No balancing adjustments will occur as assets remain at TWDV. There are no VAT implications – see later, part (c). The loss for the year can be carried forward to the following accounting period or carried back to the previous accounting period as HG Ltd has made taxable profits in the previous accounting period. Any loss carried forward cannot be group relieved until five years after the end of the accounting period of change in ownership. Loss relief within HG Ltd and group relief for brought forward losses are not available if there is a major change in conduct of the trade and a change in ownership.

Method 2 – Sale of trade and assets

Implications for HG Ltd

For HG Ltd the tax implications are that the sale of the trade and assets of HG Ltd will result in disposals of its assets which give rise to tax liabilities subject to corporation tax.

The tax loss for the accounting period to 31 March 2019 will be increased and decreased by the disposal of the company's trade and assets.

Intangible fixed asset (IFA)

The tax treatment of intangible assets follows the accounting treatment ie, debits and credits. HG Ltd could have elected to claim a 4% writing down as an alternative to allowing debits and credits and I would need to check that this election has not been made.

Assuming this election has not been made and the carrying amount represents the TWDV, then additional taxable income would arise in respect of the sale of the trademarks of £3.4 million calculated as follows:

	£'000
Proceeds	9,700
Less TWDV = Carrying amount	6,300
Taxable credit	3,400

Equipment

The sale of the equipment would give rise to a balancing allowance of £500,000 calculated as follows:

	£'000
Proceeds	1,500
Less TWDV = Carrying amount	2,000
Balancing allowance	(500)

The balancing allowance will increase the taxable loss for the year.

We would need to check the amount of the allowances claimed to date to ensure the balancing allowance figure is correct and the TWDV does not include a writing down allowance claimed for the accounting period in which the assets were transferred.

Inventory

The inventory would be sold at less than its carrying amount and there will therefore be an increase in the tax trading loss for the year by £700,000 as follows:

	£'000
Proceeds	1,800
Less carrying amount	2,500
Tax loss	(700)

Therefore, the tax trading loss of £1.2 million becomes a taxable profit of £1 million calculated as follows:

	£'000
Tax trading loss	(1,200)
IFA credit	3,400
Balancing allowance on equipment	(500)
Inventory loss	(700)
Taxable trading profit	1,000

Corporation tax payable will be £1 million × 19% = £190,000

The tax implications for Val will be that she effectively suffers double taxation, once at the company level and again on extraction of the cash from HG Ltd.

Implications for Val

Val would probably be advised to wind up her company. Distributions made before the winding up of the company would normally be income distributions and taxed as dividends. Distributions made after the appointment of a liquidator are capital distributions.

The advantage for Val is that, subject to her life time limit for entrepreneurs' relief purposes, the tax rate on the capital distribution is lower than the income distribution. She should therefore seek independent tax advice concerning the appointment of a liquidator to wind up the company.

Distributions made in anticipation of striking off a company without the appointment of a liquidator which are less than £25,000 (and certain conditions are met), can be treated as a capital distribution. However, after collecting receivables and paying off the creditors, Val is likely to have more than £25,000 distribution to make on winding up.

(b) **Impact of the two alternative methods for the acquisition of HG Ltd's business on the ability of Taul plc to receive tax deductions for interest in the UK**

The corporate interest restriction rules only apply where the worldwide group's aggregate net tax-interest expense exceeds £2 million for a 12-month period.

The aggregate net tax-interest expense is the aggregate of the net interest income and the net interest expense amounts (as calculated for tax purposes) for all UK resident companies in the group.

If Taul plc buys Val's shares in HG Ltd, it acquires all the net assets which include its bank loan. This is likely to increase the fixed ratio debt cap of the group. The calculation of the 'aggregate tax-EDITDA' will also be affected by the purchase of HG Ltd.

Prior to the acquisition of HG Ltd the group's basic interest allowance is the lower of:

	£m
30% of aggregate tax-EBITDA (30% × £158m)	47.4
Fixed ratio debt cap (ANGIE)	103

ie, interest allowance is £47.4 million

As the aggregate net tax-interest expense of the group is £47.0 million there is currently no restriction. However following the acquisition of the shares in HG Ltd, the figures will vary to some extent, and as the interest allowance is close to the group interest expense this could lead to restriction of interest deduction for tax purposes in the UK.

Acquiring the trade and assets is likely not to result in a restriction as only an additional debt of £2 million is required to finance buying the trade and assets resulting in additional interest of £200,000. Taul plc will not take on the liabilities of HG Ltd.

(c) **Other tax related factors which Taul plc should consider**

VAT

As the business appears to be being transferred as a going concern (TOGC), there is no taxable supply and VAT is not charged by HG Ltd on the sale of its assets to Taul plc.

Within the equipment there could be single computer items costing £50,000 or more. Which may come within the capital goods scheme. If there were items within the capital goods scheme, as part of the TOGC, the supply is neither taxable not exempt so no adjustment is required. Instead, Taul plc would assume responsibility for any adjustments to input tax required under the scheme for the remainder of the adjustment period.

If the business is sold to Taul plc as a share sale, no VAT will be charged.

HG Ltd's business includes both standard/zero rated and exempt supplies. Therefore, acquiring the trade may result in restriction of the recovery of input tax in the future.

If the shares are acquired, Taul plc will need to consider whether HG Ltd should be part of any VAT group to prevent any potential restriction of input VAT.

Corporation tax

There are no tax losses to bring forward if the trade and assets are sold as the adjustments result in a trading profit.

Acquiring 100% of the shares of HG Ltd would mean HG Ltd would become a member of Taul plc group relief and gains groups.

Stamp duty

Stamp duty will be payable by Taul plc at 0.5% on the transfer of the shares – buying HG Ltd's trade and assets would result in no stamp duty liability for Taul plc.

(d) **Tax implications for Val and for Taul plc of the share options**

Implications for Val

As the scheme is not tax-advantaged, no tax will arise on grant but any increase in value in the period to exercise will be taxed as income and the increase in market value from exercise to disposal as a capital gain. Therefore, the grant of the option in April 2019 will not trigger a tax liability.

However, if Val exercises her option on 4 April 2020, the difference between the option price she pays and the exercise price will be deemed employment income as follows:

	£
Market value of shares on exercise 80,000 × £4.50	360,000
Cost of the option (price paid by Val) 80,000 × £2.50	200,000
Taxable as income	160,000
Income tax £160,000 × 45% (as she has other income and hence the 45% rate applies)	72,000

A chargeable gain will arise for Val on disposal of her shares in Taul plc as and when she sells them.

National insurance contributions (NIC) implications

If the shares are 'readily convertible assets' (ie, broadly, if there is a market in them) the income tax that arises on exercise is payable under PAYE, together with both employer's and employee's NIC.

Taul plc is not a listed company which means its shares are not quoted on a stock market and therefore it is questionable whether the shares are 'readily convertible' – further information is required.

Implications for Taul plc

The cost of providing shares may qualify for a corporation tax deduction for Taul plc. However, as Taul plc is under the control of another company, Taul plc's parent is in the US, tax relief for providing shares under the scheme may not be allowed. More tax efficient methods should be investigated for structuring this remuneration package for Val which secures the tax deduction for Taul plc.

Examiner's comments

(a) The more competent candidates dealt with the first part very well. Weaker candidates failed to distinguish that Val and HG Ltd were separate entities. Because of this fundamental misunderstanding, candidates attempted to apply SSE to Val's share disposal and sometimes recommended indexation allowance. They also treated the sale of trade and assets as a gain taxable on Val, being subject to entrepreneurs' relief.

For those who did compute tax implications correctly and recognised that there was a tax liability for HG Ltd, there was a noticeable failure to use all the information available and assimilate to arrive at a revised profit as opposed to a loss for corporation tax purposes. This led to candidates wasting time describing how the overall loss could then be used when in fact the result was a taxable trading profit. Candidates should use the information in the question and not just reiterate the answers they have seen in practice questions. There was a lot of explanation about group relief, chargeable gains groups and terminal loss relief which in the circumstances was mostly irrelevant as no information about the group was given in the question scenario.

The better candidates demonstrated very good application skills and the answers produced considered how Val could extract any cash from the business via liquidation routes and the consequences.

(b)   Due to a change in legislation this part is different to the original exam question.

(c)   The other tax related factors of acquisition did not prove too challenging to candidates, however, some candidates decided to repeat points both relevant and irrelevant relating to losses which they had already discussed. Some good answers were produced and considered stamp duty implications, possibility of rollover relief, VAT and TOGC together with a consideration of whether a VAT group should be formed. Although (a) refers to Val and HG Ltd and (c) to Taul plc, there is potential for some overlap. Marks were awarded for all relevant points, no matter where candidates identified them in their answers provided the comments related to the correct entity.

(d)   In terms of the tax implications of the remuneration package, most candidates identified that there would be an assessment on Val when her rights were exercised and whilst most candidates identified that £160,000 would be taxable as income; some calculated £100,000 by using the market value of the shares at grant date. Only the more able candidates discussed that Taul plc's status, as it was not quoted on a stock exchange, could impact the NIC liabilities. A significant minority of candidates did not use the information in the question and did not question the NIC position nor the tax deductibility of the cost of providing the scheme for Taul plc.

41   Marie Gao

Scenario

The candidate is an ICAEW Chartered Accountant and works as a tax assistant for a firm of ICAEW Chartered Accountants. Marie Gao is a new tax client who has previously completed her own tax affairs but has decided for 2018/19 to seek advice because her affairs have become more complicated. She is a non-domiciled, but UK tax resident and so the potential for using the remittance basis is available to her to keep her income and gains arising in Ozland out of UK tax charge.

The question includes an ethical issue for the candidate who comes across some information on the internet which alleges that Marie's husband has been evading tax in Ozland. Marie having a share in the Ozland business profits is therefore potentially also involved in evading tax.

	Technical	Skills	Marks
41.1 Claims and elections	2	2	
No claim			
• Income tax	2	3½	
• CGT	1	2	
Claim			
• Income tax	2	3	
• CGT	1	1	
Recommendation	–	1	
	8	12½	
Max			16
41.2 Transfer to trust			
CGT/RBU	1	1	
CLT	–	1	
IHT – variation/transfer to trust	1	3	
CGT – variation	–	1	
	2	6	
Max			6
41.3 Ethics			
Professional scepticism	–	2	
Engagement	–	2	
Marie	1	–	
Money laundering	–	1	
Integrity	1	1	
Actions	–	2	
	2	8	
Max			8
Total marks	12	26½	38½
Maximum			30

41.1 Explanation of claims and elections

Marie is tax resident in the UK but appears to be non-domiciled as she was born in Ozland. She is not a formerly-UK domiciled individual, nor has she been resident in the UK for long enough to be considered deemed UK-domiciled.

Therefore, she could apply to be a remittance basis user (RBU) in respect of her foreign income.

As Marie is already restricted in her entitlement to a personal allowance due to the level of her UK income, this is not a factor in the decision of whether to claim to be a RBU or not. Under a claim for remittance basis, Marie would not be entitled to the personal allowance.

Marie should be able to claim double tax relief (DTR) for tax suffered in Ozland. The following calculations assume DTR is given based on the lower of UK tax and overseas tax suffered.

Calculations

No claim for RB

			Non-savings £	Savings £
Trading profits			140,000	
Less trading loss brought forward			(60,000)	
			80,000	
Rental income			20,000	
Business profits in Ozland			200,000	
Interest in Ozland savings account 9,000 × 100/75				12,000
			300,000	12,000
No personal allowance – income high				
Basic rate	£34,500	20%		6,900
Higher rate (balance)	£115,500	40%		46,200
Additional rate	£150,000	45%		67,500
Savings income	£12,000	45%		5,400
Income tax liability				126,000
Less:				
DTR Ozland tax on business profits				(40,000)
Withholding tax on interest				(3,000)
Income tax payable				83,000

Capital gains tax

		Res property £	Other assets £
House in Ozland	50% × £75,000	37,500	
Quoted shares			15,000
Less capital loss brought forward		(5,760)	
Annual exempt amount		31,740	
Chargeable gain		(11,700)	
		20,040	15,000
Capital gains tax at 28%/ 20%		5,611	3,000
Total tax liabilities (£83,000 + £5,611 + £3,000)			91,611

With claim for RB

			Non-savings £	Savings £
Trading profits			140,000	
Less trading loss brought forward			(60,000)	
			80,000	
Rental income			20,000	
Business profits in Ozland remitted to UK			25,000	
			125,000	
No personal allowance – RBU			–	
Basic rate	£34,500	20%		6,900
Higher rate (balance)	£90,500	40%		36,200
Income tax liability				43,100
RBU charge based on residence of at least 7 out of last 9 years				30,000
Less DTR Ozland tax on business profits				(5,000)
Income tax payable				68,100

Capital gains tax

	Savings £
Quoted shares	15,000
	15,000
Less capital loss brought forward	(5,760)
Chargeable gain	9,240
Capital gains tax at 20%	1,848
Total tax liabilities (£68,100 + £1,848)	69,948

Recommendation

Marie should elect to be a remittance basis user in 2018/19.

41.2 Tax efficient method of transferring shares

The issue here is that as the value of the shares has increased since her mother's death then potentially there is a capital gains tax liability on the increase in value of £25,000.

If the transfer is made in the current tax year 2019/20 and Marie claims to be a RBU, there is no annual exempt amount available to reduce the gain and CGT would be payable at 20%. If she delays until 2020/21, potentially the same issue would arise if she again claims the remittance basis. There is no gift relief for business assets available to defer the chargeable gain as the shares are quoted shares and are not shares in Marie's personal company.

However, the transfer to a trust is also a chargeable lifetime transfer – which gives rise to an immediate IHT charge. However if Marie has not used her nil rate band there should be no IHT to pay now. However, the fact that this is a chargeable transfer for IHT (whether any actually arises) means that any capital gains arising on transfer may be deferred using a special form of gift relief. The asset does not need to be a business asset for this relief to operate.

As a beneficiary of an estate Marie can decide that she wishes her share of the estate should pass to her own children. This can be achieved by a variation of the terms of the will. This can be effective both for IHT purposes and for capital gains tax purposes. Marie would have to meet certain conditions. The variation must be made:

- by herself as the original beneficiary;
- within 2 years of the death;
- in writing;
- for no money nor money's worth; and
- contain a statement that the variation is to have an effect for CGT.

Provided the conditions are met then transferring the shares to a trust would not give rise to a capital gains tax liability as the assets are treated as passing direct to the beneficiary at probate value of £200,000 and the beneficiary making the variation ie, Marie is not treated as making a disposal.

Marie should make a variation of her mother's will by 27 February 2020 passing the shares in Lemion plc to the trust for her children. The variation should include a statement saying that the variation is to have effect for IHT purposes. This is tax neutral for her mother's estate as the transfer will be a chargeable transfer in the same way.

The variation should also include a statement that it is effective for CGT also to prevent the transfer at £225,000 and a potential charge to CGT.

41.3 Professional and ethical issues

I should first investigate the credibility of the source of information – was the website a respected news medium or could this story be speculation or fake news? I should read the information with professional scepticism.

In terms of the professional ethical position of the firm, I need to consider who the firm is acting for. The firm has an engagement with Marie and not with Jon.

However, Marie has become a partner in Jon's business and those profits are within the UK charge to taxation.

The firm would need to consider whether there are any potential money laundering issues.

Potentially there could be reputational issues for the firm of being associated with tax evasion and therefore a threat to integrity.

Actions: I should speak to Marie to find out information; report the matter to my manager and the firm's money laundering officer.

Examiner's comments

41.1 This section was answered well by many candidates who produced two alternative calculations for RBU and non RBU. Some candidates did not produce separate calculations to show Maria's tax liability (although the requirements clearly state that they were expected to 'calculate') and adopted instead an 'explain' approach. Marks were awarded for relevant points including identifying that there would be double tax relief, use of losses and a remittance basis charge of £30,000 and due credit was given when candidates structured arguments to arrive at an appropriate recommendation. Weaker candidates wasted significant time writing at length on the statutory residence test and the rules on domicile rather than applying the rules to the scenario.

Those that did produce computations generally scored very well.

41.2 Some candidates chose to produce an answer they wanted to write as opposed to the answer which the question required. It was apparent due to the facts given and the way the question was worded that for this part, candidates should have considered a deed of variation. The better candidates did this. However, the majority reiterated a prepared answer which discussed the different implications of a PET and CLT and the operation of trusts. Whilst some parts of this discussion are relevant in terms of using the annual exemptions and nil rate band to mitigate the liability, a lot of what was produced was irrelevant and therefore restricted the number of marks which could be awarded.

41.3 Candidates were required to question the validity of the information they had received to deal fully with the ethical issue. It was encouraging to see that many candidates did do this. However, weaker candidates did not adopt a logical approach to dealing with this element of the question and instead just jumped straight to the conclusion that Maria's husband's behaviour was tantamount to money laundering and should be reported. Those that did adopt a logical approach and showed professional scepticism tended to score full marks on this section. Candidates were not required to have detailed knowledge of penalties for offshore tax evasion to answer this ethics requirement.

42 Lyre Ltd

Scenario

The question requires the candidate to comment on the tax implications of three issues including a sale and lease back, the use of a company flat by a shareholder, and loans to participators and employees. To answer this question, the candidate needs to have the skills to consider different perspectives.

	Marks	
	Technical	Skills
Sale and leaseback		
• Gain	1	1
• Deemed rent	1	2
• SDLT on purchase	–	1
SDLT		
• Lease premium	1	–
• Lease rentals	1	1
• VAT effect	–	1
Use of flat		
• Close company	2	2
• Distribution – income tax	2	2
• Distribution – corporation tax	–	1
Loans to participators	1	2
Directors' loan accounts		
• Diane s.455 charge	1	3
• Dividend income	–	1
• Loan interest benefit	1	–
• Company NTLR and NIC	–	1
• Sam Bens	1	3
Employee loan	1	2
Total marks	13	23	36
Maximum			30

Notes for meeting with Mel Granger

Sale and lease back

The chargeable gain of £375,000 has been correctly included in the tax computation for the year ending 31 March 2019 and will be taxed as part of the total profits of Lyre Ltd for the year at 19%.

If Lyre Ltd invests in a qualifying asset there is a possibility of rollover relief to defer the gain.

An annual revenue deduction will be available to Lyre Ltd in respect of the lease premium based on the deemed rent as follows:

Deemed rent

£50,000 × ((50 – 6)/50) = £44,000

The annual deduction therefore is:

£44,000/7 years = £6,286

Also, Lyre Ltd will claim tax relief for the lease rentals as they are charged to profit or loss.

Although the purchaser of the factory, ie, the Bank, will pay stamp duty land tax (SDLT) on the purchase, Lyre Ltd will also pay SDLT on the lease premium and the lease rentals.

SDLT on lease

As the value of the lease premium is less than £150,000 there is no SDLT on the premium.

However, Lyre Ltd will pay SDLT on the rental.

The rental charge is based on the net present value of the rent payable to the landlord over the term of the lease. However, ignoring discounting, only the excess is chargeable over £150,000 at 1% (within the £5 million limit).

7 years × £66,250 = £463,750 - £150,000 = £313,750 × 1% = £3,138

> ### Tutorial note
>
> The SDLT payable on the lease back may be exempt under s.57A of Finance Act 2003. However, the facts given are insufficient to determine whether the exemption is available. This is also beyond the scope of the syllabus. Credit was available where a candidate made reference to this exemption.

As there is no option to tax there is no VAT charged on the sale as the building is a commercial building over three years old.

Use of flat by mother

Lyre Ltd is controlled by five or fewer participators/its directors. This makes Lyre Ltd a close company.

As a close company, there are a number of transactions with the participators (shareholders) that need to be reported to HMRC and have tax consequences.

Ann Bens is not a director nor an employee of the company; therefore, as Lyre Ltd has provided a benefit to her, it cannot be taxed as employment income and is instead treated as a distribution.

The amount of the distribution is the amount that would have been taxed as a benefit.

The distribution is calculated as follows:

	£
Annual value £62,000 × 11/12	56,833
Heat and light costs	7,500
Cleaning for 11 months	11,000
	75,333

There would also be a benefit because the property is likely to be an expensive property – I would need further information to calculate this.

It appears that Ann is a higher rate payer and she will therefore have tax to pay at 32.5% because of this transaction (with 0% paid on the first £2,000 if her dividend nil rate is available) – I would need further details about her income to determine this for her.

For Lyre Ltd the actual cost of providing the benefit will be a disallowable cost in its corporation tax computation and Mel must ensure that his predecessor has made the correct adjustment for this.

Loans

Loans to participators

There are two potential charges to tax on a loan to a participator:

(1) Notional 25% tax (pre 6 April 2016) on the loan under s.455 CTA 2010

When a close company makes a loan to a participator, it must make a payment of notional tax to HMRC under s.455 CTA 2010.

The notional tax is 25% of the loan, and is payable 9 months and 1 day after the end of the accounting period in which the loan is made.

(2) A benefit if the participator is also an employee and paying interest at a rate less than the official rate of interest.

A loan to a director or employee is excluded from these rules if total loans to the participator do not exceed £15,000, and the borrower works full-time for the company and the borrower does not have a material interest (over 5%) in the company.

Director's loan account balances

Balances on directors' loan accounts are also potentially subject to a s.455 tax charge.

Diane's loan

Loan made 1 May 2015 – £150,000 – this was advanced in the accounting period to 31 March 2016 – the normal due date for the corporation tax assuming this is not a large company would be 1 January 2017. However, Diane has repaid £42,000 on 1 May 2016 and therefore the s455 tax paid on 1 January 2017 should have been:

(£150,000 – £42,000) × 25% = £27,000

Loan waived in April 2019 which is in the accounting period to 31 March 2020 – tax will be recovered by Lyre on 1 January 2021 = £27,000

Diane is assessed on dividend income in 2019/20.

An employment benefit will also arise for Diane because the loan was interest free. For the tax year 2018/19, this would be £108,000 × 2.5% = £2,700.

Lyre Ltd cannot treat the loan write off as a non-trading loan relationship debit. This is specifically prohibited as a deduction.

However, Lyre Ltd is likely to be liable for class 1 NIC at 13.8% on the loan waiver and on the difference between the official rate of interest and the actual rate of interest. The NIC will be tax deductible for Lyre Ltd.

Sam Bens

The directors' loan account balance for Sam Bens is under £15,000 and Sam works full-time for the company. However, Sam has a material interest in the company and so s.455 tax at 32.5% (post 6 April 2016) is payable on his loan of £5,450. This will be 32.5% × £5,450 = £1,771

As the loan was outstanding at 31 March 2018, this tax was due on 1 January 2019 – Mel must be advised to pay this tax immediately if it has not already been paid.

As the loan is less than £10,000 no beneficial loan interest charge will be due for Sam.

Employee loan

John Smith's loan is excluded from the s.455 charge as his loan is less than £15,000, he works full-time for the company and his interest in the company is only 2.5%.

No benefit arises for John as he is paying interest on the loan at more than the official rate of interest.

Examiner's comments

The sale and leaseback was answered very well by many candidates who produced accurate calculations for the rental premiums and the stamp duty land tax. It was encouraging in the first part of the question that candidates demonstrated an ability to link taxes and the VAT implications of the sale and leaseback were also discussed.

The higher scoring candidates then dealt with each participator in turn and identified the tax liability on both the company and the individual. There was some confusion amongst the weaker candidates about both the technical rules and the difference between a shareholder and a director.

Weaker candidates did not recognise Lyre Ltd as a close company and often treated Ann Bens as an employee, despite the question explicitly stating that she was not. So, whilst candidates recognised that Ann needed to be taxed on her use of the flat, they then proceeded to tax her on a benefit on kind and treat Lyre Ltd as having to pay employer NIC. Answers which considered the possibility that HMRC could perhaps tax Diane and Sam on the benefit were awarded credit.

June 2017 exam answers

43 Tea Group

Scenario

The candidate is in the role of a corporate tax specialist within a company.

This question considers many different aspects of company tax residence and the tax implications of migration of a company from the UK tax jurisdiction, and the opportunities to mitigate the tax costs of migration by deferring any potential 'exit charges' on migration.

The potential migration to a 'low tax jurisdiction' also brings into question the application of the controlled foreign company tax regime.

Amendments to the transfer pricing regime between group companies and the implication of the anti-avoidance transfer pricing legislation are considered, in the context of understanding whether the transfer pricing changes being suggested have any commercial substance or not.

Marking guide

		Technical	Skills	Marks
43.1 (a)	**Tree Ltd**			
	Residence	1	–	
	Effective management	1	3	
	Ceasing to be UK resident	2	3	
	Calculation	1	3	
	CT accounting period	–	1	
	Deferral of gain	1	3	
	Other gains aspects	1	2	
	Advance notice	–	1	
	Trading profit	–	1	
	Cost of migration	–	2	
	Group aspects	–	1	
	Offshore	1	1	
	Trunk OOD			
	Residence	–	1	
	Migration	1	1½	
	Deferral	1	1	
	Profits taxed	–	1	
		10	25½	
	Max			24
(b)	CFC	1	1	
	Exemptions	2	1	
	Apportionment and tax	1	2	
		4	4	
	Max			6

	Technical	Skills	Marks
43.2 Transfer pricing	1	1	
Tax advantage	-	2	
Commercial/bonus	-	3	
Self-interest/integrity/whistleblowing	-	2	
Action	1	2	
Potential resignation	1	-	
	3	10	
Max			10
Total marks	17	39½	56½
Maximum			40

43.1 (a) Report to the CEO

Tax implications and tax costs of relocating the management of Tree Ltd and Trunk OOD

Tree Ltd

Tree Ltd is a UK registered company and considered to be resident for tax purposes where it is incorporated.

If the effective management of Tree Ltd is relocated to Estaban, it would normally be considered to remain UK resident, because of its incorporation in the UK. However, as Estaban has a double tax treaty with the UK, which allows companies regarded as resident in Estaban to be treated as non-resident in the UK, it is possible that the residence of the company will move to Estaban.

The relocation of the effective management of Tree Ltd to Estaban would need to be considered carefully, to ensure that the actions taken could be construed to be sufficient to move the central management and control of the company from the UK to Estaban. It is important that no decisions affecting the company are taken in the UK and the UK directors need to be aware that they should refrain from the use of telephone or email, when making decisions, whilst physically present in the UK. It is also important that the Estaban directors have the knowledge and expertise to run the business and make decisions and are not just 'straw men'. Tree Ltd would be expected to self-assess its residence status in the first instance and we must be confident that the management is indeed taking place in Estaban.

When a company ceases to be UK resident, it is deemed to have disposed of and re-acquired all of its assets at market value, immediately prior to becoming non-resident.

However, there is no deemed disposal of assets, situated in the UK immediately after the company becomes non-resident and which are used in a trade carried on in the UK through a permanent establishment.

In this case, this means that Tree Ltd will be deemed to have disposed of the investment property held in the UK and the headquarters building in Estaban.

These two deemed disposals will give rise to gains of:

	£
Investment property	930,000
Headquarters in Estaban [(1,250,000/2.5) - 100,000]	400,000

Becoming non-UK resident brings to an end the current corporation tax accounting period at the date of migration. The gains above would fall into the five-month period ended 31 August 2019.

The gain on the Estaban headquarters could be deferred, because Tree Ltd is at least 75% owned by Tea plc (a UK resident parent company) and the Estaban headquarters are used in the trade of the Tree Ltd outside the UK. The deferral requires an election. The gain would crystallise if the UK parent company ceased to own at least 75% of Tree Ltd or if the asset is sold within six years of the company migrating or if the UK parent company itself becomes non-UK resident. Given the CEO plans that Tea plc may become non-UK resident in the future, the cost of this would include the crystallisation of this gain of £400,000 on Tea plc. This would cost £76,000 of tax, assuming a corporation tax rate of 19%.

The gain on the investment property of £930,000 cannot be deferred.

In addition, a gain of £650,000 would arise on the disposal of the office building.

In total these gains would give rise to corporation tax of £300,200 ((£930,000 + £650,000) × 19%).

Tree Ltd will be required to provide HMRC with advance notice of its intended migration, and also provide a guarantee that any unpaid UK tax liabilities will be paid.

Given that the trade of Tree Ltd will continue to be carried on within the UK, the profits of the trade will probably continue to be taxed in the UK, as the trade will be a permanent establishment in the UK.

The tax cost of the proposals relating to Tree Ltd (including relocating the residence of the company to Estaban) of £300,200 may not therefore be cost effective.

There are various other tax implications to consider such as the impact on the group for loss relief and chargeable gains purposes. The plant and machinery will no longer be subject to capital allowances.

In order to ensure that profits are not taxed in the UK, the trade of Tree Ltd would need to move offshore. If this happened, gains of £2,750,000 (£1,250,000 + £1,500,000) would be incurred on the sale of the UK factory and the goodwill, in addition to the gains on the sale of the office building, investment property and Esteban headquarters building of £1,980,000 (£400,000 + £930,000 + £650,000). At the corporation tax rate of 19%, this would incur a cost of £898,700 to relocate the management and trade and a tax saving equal to this would need to be made, before the migration could be considered to be making a saving.

Trunk OOD

Trunk will cease to be UK resident.

On migration of the company from the UK to Bulgaria (brought about by changing the central management and control of the company from the UK to Bulgaria) the accounting period of Trunk OOD will come to an end. All assets of the company will be deemed to be sold and re-acquired just before migration at market value. This would give rise to a gain of £1 million on the warehouse and an IFA profit of £250,000 on the goodwill. This would give rise to corporation tax of £237,500 at 19%.

As Trunk OOD is migrating from the UK to another EU member state, it can choose to defer the corporation tax payable in relation to the migration under an exit charge payment plan.

There are two different deferral methods to choose from: the standard deferral method, under which the tax is payable in six, equal instalments; the first instalment would be due on 1 June 2020 and the next five instalments on the next five anniversaries of this date. Alternatively, the realisation method, where the tax on the warehouse would be due on the earlier of the disposal of the asset and 31 August 2029. The tax on the IFA profit would be due over 10 equal annual instalments of £4,750 (£250,000 × 19%/10) starting on 1 June 2020.

As Trunk OOD would then be trading from Bulgaria, profits would be taxed in Bulgaria, not the UK. The tax rates in Bulgaria would need to be more favourable than in the UK to compensate for the cost of company migration of £237,500.

(b) **Anti-avoidance legislation which may be relevant to the Tea Group**

Controlled foreign companies

Trunk OOD is situated in Bulgaria, outside the UK and is controlled by Tea plc, a company resident in the UK.

Bulgaria is not an excluded territory. Trunk OOD does not have low profits or appear to have a low profit margin. The tax rate in Bulgaria is 52.6% (10/19) of the tax rate in the UK and so it is likely to be classed as a low tax jurisdiction (tax paid in Bulgaria being less than 75% of the tax that would have been paid in the UK).

If Trunk OOD is deemed to be situated in a low tax jurisdiction, and there are no relevant exemptions, the overseas profits of these companies could be apportioned 100% to Tea plc and taxed at the UK main rate of corporation tax of 19%, less a tax credit of the Bulgarian tax paid at 10%.

43.2 Where large companies enter into a transaction at a non-arm's length price, such that one company gains a tax advantage, transfer pricing rules may apply.

The company which gains a tax advantage is required to adjust its corporation tax self-assessment by substituting an arm's length price for the original price.

The transfer pricing changes suggested by the CEO may have a commercial justification, however, in the light of his private conversation with me, I believe that they have been chosen in order to move or shift profits from one jurisdiction to another to save tax for the Tea group, by moving profits to Bulgaria and so reducing the group corporation tax charge.

I believe the CEO may be motivated by the desire to earn a large bonus.

There is a self-interest threat to my integrity in that the CEO has suggested that if I comply with his request he will also pay me a large bonus.

I should consider if there is an appropriate senior person I can confide in about the CEO's suggestion, perhaps by invoking the company's whistle-blowing policy.

I should not act as the CEO suggests if, as a professional, I evaluate that the transfer prices charged are not at arm's length, I should adjust these transfer prices to arm's length prices in calculating the profits for the self-assessment corporation tax returns. Failing to adjust for these transfer prices would be tax evasion. I could speak to HMRC about an advance pricing agreement, which would allow me to identify if the transfer prices being charged are at arm's length or not, before I complete the corporation tax returns.

If the CEO, and any other senior member of staff I report this matter to, refuse to allow me to act in line with my professional judgement I should resign from my position with the Tea plc group.

Examiner's comments

43.1 There were some very good answers to this part of the question, which linked the rules on company migration back to the scenario. Most candidates readily identified that, because Tree Ltd was incorporated in the UK, attempting to migrate company residence would ordinarily be very difficult; but the existence of the Estaban:UK tax treaty meant that, provided the process were to be managed carefully, migration could occur. Commonly, candidates failed to identify the implications of maintaining a trade in the UK on the deferral of the gains on migration. This showed a lack of understanding of the scenario as a key piece of information was that Tree Ltd was still operating a PE in the UK. It was encouraging to note that many candidates were familiar with the rules on deferral of the exit charge.

Weaker answers demonstrated an inability to apply their knowledge to the scenario and produced standard checklists, which could be copied from the study material, about companies ceasing to be part of loss and chargeable gains groups.

Candidates also dealt with the issues in relation to Trunk OOD well. The higher scoring answers identified the standard and realisation method of deferral which showed the application skills expected at this level. Answers relating to the anti-avoidance element tended to be quite general. The better answers had recognised that Trunk OOD was potentially a CFC and applied the rules to the scenario. The weaker answers discussed at great length the various anti-avoidance measures such as transfer pricing, GAAR, BEPS and DPT without considering the context of the information in the scenario and what was relevant.

Disappointingly, even though the question specifically asked candidates to consider the tax costs of moving abroad, very few candidates produced answers which considered the commerciality and actual costs to the companies of migration and evaluated if the migrations suggested were a good idea.

43.2 This part of the question was built around a scenario involving transfer pricing anti-avoidance legislation and ethics. The better answers adopted a logical approach, considered the applicability of the transfer pricing legislation and used the facts in the scenario to identify that there was an artificial diversion of profits, which was probably motivated by the promise of a bonus. These candidates then went on to consider the threats to integrity, self-interest and independence and accordingly recommended sensible actions. The weaker answers focussed primarily on tax evasion, money laundering and tipping off without using or applying the facts in the scenario to structure their answer. Ethics continues to be an area where weaker candidates rely on formulaic answers, which do not relate to the facts in the scenario.

44 Ben and Martha

Scenario

Partners in a farming business have asked for advice following an offer from a property developer to buy the farmhouse and land. The partners require capital gains tax and inheritance tax advice. One of the partners is going to reinvest in more farmland but will gift it to his daughter either during his lifetime or on death. He wants a recommendation for his best course of action. The potential inheritance tax liability is to be calculated in the event of the death of the other partner.

Marking guide

	Technical	Skills
		Marks
44.1 **CGT**		
Calculation	2	2
Rates and AEA	1	1
Rollover relief	2	1
Potential restrictions in relief	1	2
Entrepreneurs' relief	1	2

	Technical	Skills	Marks
Ben recommendation	–	1	
Martha's tax position	1	1	
	8	10	
Max			15

44.2 Gifting farmland
Lifetime gift
	Technical	Skills
• CGT	1	2
• IHT – lifetime	½	1
• IHT – death	1	1

Death gift
	Technical	Skills
• CGT	1	2
• IHT	–	1
Recommendation	–	1
	3½	8

Max			8

44.3 Sale of farmland and farmhouse
	Technical	Skills
APR and BPR	–	2
IHT calculation pre sale	1	2
IHT calculation post sale	1	2
	2	6

Max			7
Total marks	13½	24	37½
Maximum			30

44.1 The sale of the farmland and the farmhouse will give rise to capital gains as follows:

	Farmland: Ben £	Farmland: Martha £	Farmhouse: Martha £
Proceeds	1,000,000	1,000,000	750,000
Less cost (Note)	(450,000)	(12,500)	(201,250)
Gain	550,000		548,750
	550,000		
Less annual exempt amount	(11,700)		(11,700)
Taxable gains	538,300	987,500	537,050

Note: Martha's cost of the farmhouse is 50% of the £2,500 cost from 1983 plus 50% of the £400,000 market value on Phil's death in 2000.

Both Ben and Martha are normally higher rate taxpayers (£60,000 of profits are being taxed in the 2019/20 tax year – year ending 30 June 2019 accounts) and so would pay capital gains tax at 20% on the gains on the farmland and Martha would pay 28% on the gain on the farmhouse, because it is residential property. Martha would allocate her annual exempt amount against the gain on the farmhouse, in order to save tax at 28%, rather than 20%.

However, Ben would be eligible for replacement of business assets (rollover) relief, as he intends to reinvest his sale proceeds in more farmland.

Provided Ben reinvests all of the sale proceeds in new farmland he would be able to rollover all of the gain. The gain rolled over would be deducted from the CGT base cost of the new farmland, increasing any gain made in the future on the sale of that land. However, as Ben has no intention of selling the land and intends to leave it to his daughter, this would not impact on Ben immediately.

If Ben keeps back any of the proceeds, the amount of the proceeds not reinvested will be the amount of the gain chargeable immediately. If however, he keeps back proceeds to buy depreciating assets, such as farm plant and machinery, the gain will be deferred for a maximum of 10 years.

All reinvestment needs to take place within three years of the initial sale of the farmland.

Ben and Martha would also be eligible for entrepreneurs' relief on the sale of the farmland. They are selling an interest in a partnership and have owned the asset for at least a year.

The effect of entrepreneurs' relief is that any gains on the farmland would be taxed at 10%, rather than 20%.

In Ben's case a claim for rollover relief would be more beneficial than a claim for entrepreneurs' relief. In Martha's case, her only option is to claim for entrepreneurs' relief and pay tax at the reduced rate of 10%.

The farmhouse has never been used as a business asset and so entrepreneurs' relief would not be available, and the gain on the farmhouse would be taxed at 28%, because it is residential property. Martha's tax payable would be £249,124 (£537,050 × 28% + £987,500 × 10%).

44.2 Ben wants to determine whether it is more tax efficient to gift the farmland in lifetime to his daughter or whether he should wait till death.

Lifetime gift

If he gifts the land in his lifetime, CGT may be payable on the difference between the market value of the asset gifted and its CGT base cost. Given he claimed rollover relief on the sale of the farmland from Redmires Farm, the gain of £550,000 would effectively crystallise on the gift (with the annual exempt amount used against any further gain on disposal). However, as the land is business property, Ben and his daughter could jointly elect for holdover relief for gifts to apply to the gain. The gain would then be deferred against the base cost of the farmland and would crystallise in the future.

The gift of the land in lifetime would be a PET for IHT purposes and would attract 100% APR against the agricultural value of the property. If Ben buys land that has no development value, this would 100% of the land's value.

If Ben were to die within seven years of the gift of the land, the PET would come into charge to tax on Ben's death. The APR would still be available if the farmland were still in use for agricultural purposes at the date of Ben's death. If, however, Ben's daughter had sold the land or ceased to use it for agricultural purposes the APR would not be available to reduce the value of the gift on death. This means that the gift could be chargeable to IHT at 40%.

Taper relief could reduce the IHT payable if Ben were to survive for more than 3 years after making the gift

Death gift

If Ben were, instead, to gift the farmland under the terms of his will, on death, there would be no CGT on the gift. The farmland would pass to his daughter at its probate value on death and there would be a tax-free uplift in value, extinguishing the gain that was rolled over into the land on the sale of Redmires Farm.

There would also be no IHT due on death, because the farmland would be eligible for 100% agricultural property relief against the agricultural value of the property.

As Sharon has no interest in farming the land, it would be safer to wait until death and transfer the farmland under the terms of his will. In this case there would be no CGT payable and no IHT, due to the operation of APR.

44.3 As a partner in a farming partnership, before the farmland was sold Martha would have been able to claim 100% agricultural property relief to reduce the agricultural value of the farmland to nil for IHT purposes and 100% Business property relief to reduce the development value of the farmland to nil.

The IHT due before the sale of the farmland and the farmhouse would have been:

	£
Value of farmland	1,000,000
Less APR 100% of agricultural value	(600,000)
Less BPR on development value	(400,000)
Value of farmhouse	750,000
Own home	1,500,000
Other assets	500,000
Total estate	2,750,000
Less nil rate band	(325,000)
Less residence nil rate band (2019/20) – restricted	-
Chargeable estate	2,425,000
IHT at 40 %	970,000

Phil's nil rate band was fully used on his death by the gift of other assets totalling £400,000 to Ben. So none was transferred to Martha.

After the sale of the farmhouse and the farmland, Martha's estate would have included the net cash proceeds, after CGT, of the farmhouse and farmland as well as her own house and other assets.

The IHT now due would be:

	£
Proceeds of farmland net of CGT (1,000,000 – 98,750)	901,250
Proceeds of farmhouse net of CGT (750,000 – 150,374)	599,626
Own home	1,500,000
Other assets	500,000
Total estate	3,500,876
Less nil rate band	(325,000)
Less residence nil rate band (2019/20) – restricted	-
Chargeable estate	3,175,876
IHT at 40%	1,270,350

45 Stollen Ltd

Scenario

The scenario relates to a bakery company and its managing director who are both clients of a firm of ICAEW Chartered Accountants. The managing director intends to take additional remuneration from the company in the form of pension contributions and share schemes. In addition the company intends to purchase new larger premises via the pension fund. A calculation of the income tax computation of the managing director is required.

	Technical	Skills	Marks
45.1 Pension			
Earnings and annual allowance	1	2	
Calculation	1	1	
Annual allowance charge/tapering	2	3	
SSAS funds/mortgage	2	2	
Other tax advantages	-	3	
	6	11	
Max			13
45.2 Share scheme			
Choice of scheme	-	2	
CSOP v EMI	2	2	
Income tax	-	2	
CGT	1	2	
Corporation tax	1	1	
	4	9	
Max			12
45.3 Income tax			
Taxable income	½	1	
Tax rates	1½	1	
Annual allowance charge	-	2	
	2	4	
Max			5
Total marks	12	24	36
Maximum			30

45.1

> **Tutorial note**
>
> In determining the maximum tax deductible pension contributions, candidates had to decide who they believed was paying the pension contributions – Stollen Ltd or Amy herself?
>
> Marks were allocated for part 1 based on the approach taken by the candidate, that is, either a personal or a corporate pension contribution.

If Amy were paying the pension contribution, the maximum pension contribution payable into a pension scheme by an individual would be the higher of the total relevant earnings or £3,600. In Amy's case this would be £68,600.

In this case it is likely that Stollen Ltd would be making the pension contributions to the SSAS and any amount contributed by Stollen Ltd would be deductible for corporation tax purposes. Therefore, potentially, Stollen could contribute the entire £100,000 into the scheme, if it wished to maximise the deduction for corporation tax purposes.

However, the maximum pension input amount (total of employee and employer pension contributions) that can be paid into a pension scheme, without incurring an excess contributions charge on Amy, is subject to Amy's available annual allowance, currently £40,000. The annual allowance can be increased by unused annual allowance from the previous three tax years.

Amy has unused annual allowance brought forward from the three previous tax years of £10,000 (see below), making a total annual allowance for 2019/20 of £50,000.

 ICAEW 2019

Tax Year	Amount of contribution £	Annual Allowance £	Unused Annual Allowance c/fwd £
2015/16	30,000	40,000	More than 3 years ago
2016/17	45,000	40,000	0
2017/18	40,000	40,000	0
2018/19	30,000	40,000	10,000

Any contributions in excess of the annual allowance are subject to an excess contribution charge, which would be levied on Amy at her marginal rate of tax.

Therefore if a total pension contribution payment were to be made to the SSAS of £68,600, then Amy would have suffered an excess contribution charge on the £18,600 of the pension contribution, which exceeded her annual allowance of £50,000.

If Stollen Ltd wanted to maximise the deduction for corporation tax and pay the entire £100,000 into the scheme, then an excess contribution charge on £50,000 would be suffered by Amy.

Therefore, in order to avoid the excess contribution charge, the maximum total pension contributions which would be made should be equal to the annual allowance available of £50,000.

Tutorial note

Further information would be needed on Stollen Ltd's position given both Stollen and Amy are clients of our firm to ascertain whether it wishes to maximise the deductible amount for CT or whether it wishes Amy to be remunerated without an excess contribution charge arising. Reasonable assumptions made by candidates were accepted.

The annual allowance tapering provisions, which restrict the amount of annual allowance available, will only apply, if Amy has adjusted income in excess of £150,000.

Tutorial note

For this purpose pension contributions are added to taxable income:
68,600 + 2,000 = £70,600 + £(pension contribution)

The funds in a SSAS can be used to help Stollen Ltd fund the purchase of the industrial unit. The SSAS can lend up to 50% of the fund value to Stollen Ltd to help the company buy the property itself, or the SSAS could buy the commercial property itself and rent it to the company.

Stollen Ltd has contributed £145,000 to the SSAS on Amy's behalf, already and is now due to contribute an additional amount in 2019/20. Therefore, given the funds have also been invested, there should be sufficient capital within the SSAS to fund the purchase of an industrial unit for £200,000.

The SSAS could also raise a commercial mortgage to purchase the industrial unit, if necessary.

The main tax advantage of the SSAS purchasing the property, rather than Stollen Ltd, is that there would be no CGT on a subsequent sale of the property; any rent paid to the SSAS by Stollen Ltd would not be taxable on the SSAS; and the property would be protected from creditors, should Stollen Ltd become insolvent.

45.2 The share option scheme is limited to benefitting one employee, so SAYE and share incentive plan share option schemes are not available.

The choice would therefore be between setting up a company share ownership plan (CSOP) and an enterprise management incentive (EMI) scheme.

If £50,000 is invested in a pension then an additional £50,000 (£100,000 – £50,000) is to be the value of the share options granted.

Under a CSOP scheme up to £30,000 of options can be held at any one time. Under EMI the limit is £250,000. Amy owns 22% of the shares in the company and so less than the 30% limit. Therefore, Amy could set up an EMI scheme, or set up both a CSOP scheme and an EMI scheme and invest in both.

Stollen Ltd would qualify as a company eligible to set up an EMI tax-advantaged share, given it is a trading company and has less than 250 full-time employees and gross assets of less than £30 million.

Given the cost of setting up a scheme, I would suggest that Stollen Ltd only sets up an EMI scheme.

If the shares are not issued at a discount, there will be no income tax and no employers' or employee's national insurance contributions at the grant or exercise of the options.

Shares in a CSOP must be granted at market value, however shares in an EMI can be granted at a discount to market value. If EMI shares are granted at a discount, then the employee will pay income tax on the discount once the share options are exercised, however, there should be no national insurance contributions due on this income, because the shares are not quoted.

A gain will be taxed on sale at 20% (as Amy is a higher rate taxpayer), or at 10% if Amy is eligible, at disposal, to claim entrepreneurs' relief.

Stollen Ltd would be able to claim corporation tax relief for the costs of setting up the scheme and also, at exercise, for the difference between the market value of the shares and the exercise price.

45.3 Amy Crisp

Income Tax Computation 2019/20

> **Tutorial note**
>
> Assuming a pension contribution of £50,000 by Stollen Ltd and additional income of £50,000 to exercise EMI options and a consequent reduction of the annual allowance – this is only one of the possible routes that could have been taken by a student – and relies on assumptions. Marks were awarded for computations consistent with a candidate's own answers to parts 1 and 2.

	£	£
Salary from Stollen Ltd		68,600
Additional remuneration for EMI purchase (assuming this was paid in year)		50,000
Dividend from Stollen Ltd		2,000
		120,600
Less personal allowance (W1)		(1,550)
Taxable income		119,050

	£	£
Tax due:		
£		
34,500 × 20%	6,900	
82,550 × 40%	33,020	
	39,920	
117,050		
2,000 × 0%		
119,050		
Excess contributions charge (W2)		
£10,300 × 40%	4,120	
Total income tax due		44,040

WORKINGS

(1) **Personal allowance**

	£
Personal allowance	11,850
Reduced by (120,600 – 100,000)/2	(10,300)
Reduced personal allowance	1,550

(2) **Excess contribution charge**

Adjusted income will be £120,600 + £50,000 = £170,600

Threshold income is also greater than £110,000.

Reduction of annual allowance (½ (£170,600 - £150,000)) = £10,300

Annual allowance is therefore reduced from £50,000, by £10,300 to £39,700.

The annual allowance charge will be £10,300 × 40% based on a contribution of £50,000.

Examiner's comments

Candidates produced a variety of income tax computations, because the recommendations each individual student made in parts 1 and 2 varied, based upon the approach taken by individual students. Therefore there were alternative amounts contributed to the pension scheme which could have been recommended, depending on Stollen Ltd's position and the excess contribution charge which could be levied on Amy.

Credit was given for computations, which followed on from the candidates' own decisions in parts 1 and 2, including, if candidates presented alternative answers, which recommended a decreased amount to avoid the excess contribution charge. This question, overall, tested a candidate's ability to assimilate the information and consider the alternative amounts which could be contributed and the resulting tax implications from both the company and individual perspectives.

The investment in the EMI scheme could require Stollen Ltd, in practice, to have to pay Amy increased remuneration so she could then purchase the EMI options, depending on when the options were exercised. Therefore, an additional amount of remuneration could have been added into the income tax computation. This would also trigger the reduction of the annual allowance as the inclusion of the additional remuneration would result in Amy becoming a high income individual. However, full credit was given to candidates who did not include this as it was perfectly valid to assume that any such remuneration would have been paid as and when the options were exercised and not at grant, at some date in the future.

September 2017 exam answers

46 LM Ltd

Scenario

The student is in the role of a trainee ICAEW Chartered Accountant working in LM Ltd, a UK trading company and a parent company of a UK group. The student is reporting to the finance director. The scenario involves the liquidation of Fall Ltd a company in which LM Ltd has a 45% shareholding. The student is required to prepare a draft report for the LM Ltd board of directors explaining the tax implications of cessation at two alternative dates and to explain the tax implications for the shareholders. The ethics requirement involved the student considering the implications of an overheard conversation regarding a payment made to a customer of Fall Ltd. The ethical issue is that potentially this could be a bribe and therefore present legal issues and be regarded as tax evasion.

Marking guide

		Technical	Skills	Marks
46.1 (a)	**Cessation of trade**			
	Declaration of solvency	1	–	
	Accounting period end	1	–	
	Carry forward of loss	–	1	
	Cessation 30 September	1	2	
	Recommendation	–	3	
(b)	**Liquidation**			
	Capital allowances	½	1½	
	Brand	1	1	
	Gain	–	1	
	Revised adjusted loss	1	2	
	Loss relief group and carry back options	–	3	
	Terminal loss calculation	1	1	
	Remaining loss of y/e 31.3.2019	1	1	
	Use of terminal loss	1	2	
	Calculation	2	2	
	Tax refund	–	2	
	Capital distribution	–	3	
	Allocation to UK shareholders	–	2	
	Net cash to LM Ltd	–	3	
	Net cash to Ken	–	3	
		10½	33½	
	Max			32

		Technical	Skills	Marks
46.2 **Ethics**				
Facts and scepticism		–	3	
Tax evasion		1	2	
Limiting further liabilities		–	1	
Actions		–	3	
		1	9	
	Max			8
Total marks		11 ½	42 ½	54
Maximum				40

46.1 (a) Although Fall Ltd has made a loss, it is not insolvent and will have sufficient cash to pay its creditors and make a distribution to its shareholders. A resolution to wind the company up requires a declaration of solvency to be made by the directors. If the company is still trading, at the time of the resolution then trading losses can be carried forward. As this is a voluntary liquidation, Fall Ltd can control the date of cessation of trade and the timing of the appointment of the liquidator.

The commencement of winding up proceedings will result in the end of an accounting period and the beginning of the next.

Therefore, when Fall Ltd ceases to trade and a liquidator is appointed, the loss cannot be carried forward to a period after cessation under s.45A. Trade has ceased and so its trade loss cannot be carried forward against any chargeable gains in the final period. To advise on the timing of the cessation of trade, the timing of disposals and the ability to offset trade losses against chargeable gains needs to be considered.

Cessation on 30 September 2019

Assets on which capital allowances have been claimed and the brand name will give rise to balancing charges and allowances in the final period, therefore there is no advantage to either 30 September or 31 October 2019.

However, the sale of the holiday homes and land is to take place on 10 October 2019. If this happens after trade has ceased, the tax adjusted trading loss is not available to set off against the chargeable gain of £543,000 in the period to 30 September 2019.

If the company ceases to trade at 30 September 2019 and incurs expenses in October 2019, it will not have a trade to receive tax relief for these costs. If it earns any investment income, this will be taxed.

Recommendation

It appears that an additional loss will arise in the October 2019 of £26,000; however, it is not clear whether this loss is avoidable if trade were to cease at 30 September. Although this would need confirming, the amount in cash terms is potentially, after tax relief, considerably less than the potential tax payable on the chargeable gain.

Therefore, on an initial assessment, the company should cease to trade on 31 October 2019 and appoint the liquidator at that date.

(b) **The tax implications for Fall Ltd and LM Ltd if the liquidation of Fall Ltd takes place on 31 October 2019**

Before considering the use of the losses arising in Fall Ltd it is necessary to complete the adjustment of profits. At present no adjustments have been made for capital allowances.

Capital allowances

A balancing charge arises in respect of the main pool of £1,040,000 - £920,000 = £120,000. This will decrease the loss in the final period.

The brand is to be sold on 20 September 2019 for £280,000. Because Fall Ltd has claimed only a 4% writing down allowance each year, this will give rise to a deduction of £72,800 (£352,800 (£420,000 × 4% × 4) - £280,000). This will increase the loss in the final period.

The land and holiday homes will give rise to a chargeable gain of £543,000. This will be taxable. However, Fall Ltd will be able to use its trading loss against the chargeable gain.

Revised adjusted loss for the seven months to 31 October 2019

	£'000
Tax adjusted trading (loss)	(626)
Less allowable deduction for brand name	(73)
Add balancing charge on main pool	120
Adjusted loss	(579)

Loss relief options

Implications for LM Ltd

Fall Ltd is not a member of the LM Ltd group for group relief purposes as LM Ltd's shareholding in Fall Ltd is less than 75%. A consortium claim could be made by LM Ltd as together with RXX Inc it owns more than 75% of the shares. This is because two or more companies each own at least 5% of the share capital of Fall Ltd and together they hold at least 75%. However, there is scope for Fall Ltd itself to make a current and an extended carry back loss relief claim.

Fall Ltd could make a current year claim against the property income and the chargeable gain and then an extended carry back loss relief claim.

There is a strict order in which losses are dealt with and the losses of earlier years are dealt with first.

The loss of the last 12 months is available under s.39 CTA 2010 for an extended carry back period of three years.

There are two elements to the loss calculation for the final 12 months as follows:

		£'000
Loss in the last 12 months		
Part of year ended 31 March 2019	810,000 × 5/12	337
Period ending 31 October 2019 (see above)		579
Total loss over the two accounting periods		916

Part of the loss arising in the year ended 31 March 2019 is not eligible for terminal loss relief and this should therefore be dealt with first and set off against current year profits under s.37(3)(a) CTA 2010 and then carried back under s.37(3)(b).

The amount of the loss not eligible for extended carry back is:

£810,000 × 7/12 = £473,000

Therefore £47,000 will be used in year ended 31 March 2019 against property income and £424,000 carried back to 31 March 2018 leaving £2,000 of unrelieved loss.

The remainder of the loss (£337,000) is relieved under s.39 against the three years from the beginning of the accounting period (terminal loss relief), as noted above – 1 April 2015 on a last in first out basis.

Loss of £579,000 relating to the 7-month period to 31 October 2019 is dealt with next. The loss arising in the period to 31 October 2019 is eligible for carry back against profits arising from 1 April 2016. Included in the results for the 7-month period to 31 October 2019 is property income and a chargeable gain. The loss should be set off against the property income and the chargeable gain. This would leave no loss to relieve against profits arising from 1 April 2016 as the property income and chargeable gain of the seven month period total £579,000 (£36,000 + £543,000) which uses all of the loss available.

Years ended 31 March	2016 £'000	2017 £'000	2018 £'000	2019 £'000
Tax adjusted trading (loss)/profit	608	315	385	
Property income	42	34	39	47
	650	349	424	47
CY s.37(a) – Y/E 31.3.2019				(47)
CB s.37(b) – YE 31.3.2019			(424)	
TLR s.39 – Y/E 31.3.2019	Nil	(337)	Nil	

Calculation of tax refund arising on use of loss relief

FY	Loss relief claimed £'000	Tax rate %	Refund £'000
2018	47	19	9
2017	424	19	81
2016	337	20	67
			157

Cash receivable by LM Ltd and Ken Haw

Calculation of cash receivable by the shareholders

	£'000
Land and holiday home sale	4,160
Other assets (plant and machinery)	1,040
WhiteRide	280
Bank loan	(516)
Cash at bank	280
Net current liabilities	(300)
Add tax repayment (see above)	157
Cash available for distribution to shareholders	5,101

The distribution will be treated as a capital distribution.

	LM Ltd £'000	Ken £'000
Final distribution 45%/ 24%	2,295	1,224.0
Less cost		(120.0)
(Loss)/Gain		1,104.0
Less annual exempt amount		(11.7)
		1,092.3
Tax at 10%		£109,230

Net cash on final distribution

LM Ltd will not pay any tax on the distribution as it will qualify for the substantial shareholding exemption.

It has owned the shares since 2005 and Fall Ltd is a trading company.

Therefore, LM Ltd will receive net cash of £2,295,000.

Ken will qualify for entrepreneurs' relief, if he has not already used his lifetime limit, as he is an employee of the company, and has owned at least 5% of the share capital in a personal trading company for a period of one year.

Therefore, he will receive net cash of £1,224,000 - £109,230 = £1,114,770

46.2 I should remember that this is an overhead personal conversation and is potentially inaccurate.

I should be sceptical about the source and nature of the conversation.

I should attempt to establish the facts by enquiry and/or examining the accounting records of Fall Ltd.

If what I have overheard is true, then this payment could amount to tax evasion if it is not adjusted, as this cost is not allowable for tax relief; it is remote from the trade, possibly bribery, and therefore an illegal payment.

I should consider the possibility that Ken is winding the company down to limit further liabilities and to prevent further claims.

Actions

Speak to LM Ltd finance director. The matter should be raised with both the Fall Ltd and LM boards of director.

Fall Ltd should take legal advice regarding the potential legal implications of making this payment.

I should consider the subsequent actions taken by the board and as an ICAEW Chartered Accountant I cannot be associated with illegal activities and tax evasion. As a ICAEW Chartered Accountant I would ring the ethics helpline for advice and consider my future employment with LM Ltd.

Examiner's comments

46.1 (a) In responding to this question, students often muddled the responses to part a and b, providing calculations in part a where the requirement specifically stated that this was not required. Although these calculations were considered in the marking of part (b), it was often the weaker students who struggled to organise the information effectively.

Many students could successfully identify that the decision of liquidation date was in the control of management and that if the liquidation date was set in September, the gains arising on the disposal of the holiday home would not be sheltered by losses.

However, many then went on to make statements about what would happen on liquidation rather than applying that information to the decision of whether September or October was the most tax efficient liquidation date.

Common answers which recommended a cessation date of 30 September gave the saving on staff costs for one month as an explanation. However, the more competent and higher scoring answers appreciated the tax implications of ceasing to trade later and the impact on the utilisation of losses against gains on the sale of the holiday homes. This showed a good ability to use all of the information in the question and reach sensible conclusions.

Marks were awarded for a reasonable conclusion based on the arguments presented and for demonstrating good commercial awareness.

(b) Answers to this question polarised between being exceptionally detailed and dealing with the requirement fully or being very general and brief displaying an inability of students to assimilate information from different sources.

Once the liquidation of 31 October had been set, students generally were able to identify the implications for the company, including the need to compute balancing allowance/charges on the plant and machinery and brand, and the availability of terminal loss relief.

In relation to the brand, most made a good attempt at the calculation, sometimes failing to get the correct numerical answer by incorrectly calculating the time over which allowances had already been given.

The majority could correctly calculate the adjusted tax loss; however, they often factored in the current year offset against the gain on the holiday home and the property income before calculation of the terminal loss.

Students achieved many of the marks available for demonstrating the use of the terminal loss and the current year loss, using their own figures. Marks were lost where students did not identify the loss for the year ended 31 March 2019 that was not available for terminal loss relief or for making the claims in the wrong order.

The requirement in relation to the distribution to shareholders was well answered. Almost all correctly identified that this would be a capital distribution and that the substantial shareholdings exemption would be available to LM Ltd to exempt the gain arising and entrepreneurs' relief available to Ken to reduce his tax liability.

Most then went on to correctly calculate the tax liability and a cash receivable based on their own figures.

Weaker students produced 'practice' answers which were very general and discussed cessation of trade implications generally but showed some confusion, particularly where TOGC principles were discussed. These answers tended to adopt the approach of discussing the various loss relief options, the fact that there would be balancing allowances and charges and capital gains for Ken. Often there was a failure to produce any calculations or computations on how the loss could be utilised. A common error was for the balancing charge on the plant and machinery to be calculated as £1,040,000 being forecast carrying amount less proceeds. There were also errors in the calculation of the profit on the intangible.

A significant number of students discussed the availability of entrepreneurs' relief on the gain made by the company and the availability of the substantial shareholding exemption to Ken. This is a common misunderstanding which has been displayed in numerous sittings where students seem to be mixing up corporation tax and capital gains tax for individuals.

There was quite a bit of discussion in some scripts on how a pre-liquidation distribution would be treated for tax. This just wasted time as the question very specifically stated that the distribution would be made post liquidation. Students need to be encouraged to answer the question set as no credit was given for irrelevant points.

46.2 Ethics requirement

Whilst the approach to ethics has improved in previous sittings, the answers to this part of the question were generally quite disappointing. The main problem was that students had not fully understood the scenario which clearly indicated that the student worked in the finance department at LM Ltd. Therefore, issues discussed which were not relevant were that client confidentiality had been breached and actions to take were to check the engagement letter, report to the MLRO and resign from the advisory relationship.

Students need to be encouraged to consider the scenario presented as the general answers showed a distinct lack of understanding of what was being asked in the question.

The higher scoring students had read and understood the scenario and appreciated the implications of bribery and the possibility of tax evasion. Many students did not identify the risk from the fact that the information had been overheard in a social setting and the need to find out more details before forming any conclusions. There was a lack of professional scepticism and most students took the overheard conversation to be a presentation of facts without thinking of the need to first validate the statement. As with all weaker answers to ethics questions, this conveys a lack of assimilation skills.

47 Aldo, Zeta and Greg

Scenario

A shareholder of a close company has decided to retire and sell her shares. There are three alternative methods of selling her shares:

Method 1:   Bella plc, an unconnected company, will purchase all of Zeta's shares.

Method 2:   Greg will purchase all Zeta's shares

Method 3:   Luca Ltd will repurchase some of Zeta's shares on 1 October 2019 and the remainder of her shares on 1 October 2020.

Zeta suggests a further method - to gift her shares to her son as she is in ill-health.

The company has insufficient distributable reserves to buy back all her shares in one tranche.

To answer this question, the student must demonstrate both a technical understanding of the tax implications of the purchase of the shares for different parties and the skills to identify, mediate and recommend a course of action.

Marking guide

		Technical	Skills	Marks
47.1(a)	**Purchase of shares**			
	Income tax and capital gains tax	-	1	
	Method 1			
	• Sale of shares to Bella - ER and tax rate	1	2	
	• Calculation	-	2	
	• Other implications	-	1	
	Method 2			
	• Capital transaction and gift relief	1	2	
	• Calculation	1	1	
	• IHT implications	1	1½	
	• Other implications	-	1	
	• Implications for Greg	-	2	
	Method 3			
	• Capital treatment and main conditions	1	2	
	• Distributable reserves and dividend payment	-	1½	
	• Substantial reduction	1	3	
	• Tax calculations	1	2½	
(b)	**Summary**			
	Summary table	-	3	
	Key points	-	2	
		7	27½	
	Max			24
47.2	**Gift of shares to Greg**			
	CGT	1	1	
	IHT - PET	1	-	
	GWROB	1	3	
	Recommendation	-	2	
		3	6	
	Max			6
	Total marks	10	33½	43½
	Maximum			30

Email

Dear Aldo, Zeta and Greg

Depending on the method chosen there will be either an income tax or a capital gains tax liability for Zeta.

47.1(a) **Method 1: Sale of 50,000 shares to Bella plc**

Zeta will have a straightforward capital gain if she sells her shares to Bella plc – the consideration she will receive will be £400,000. This will result in after tax cash received of £366,170 (£400,000 – £33,830).

Zeta should qualify for entrepreneurs' relief if she has not used her life time limit – she is an employee of the company and has owned at least 5% of the share capital in a personal trading company for a period of one year.

	£
Proceeds	400,000
Less cost	(50,000)
	350,000
Less annual exempt amount	(11,700)
Chargeable gain	338,300
Tax at 10%	33,830

Unless there are implications arising from the loss of close company status, there will be no tax implications for Aldo, Greg or Luca Ltd.

Method 2: Sale of 50,000 shares to Greg, Zeta and Aldo's son

Tax implications for Zeta

For Zeta, the sale will be treated as a capital transaction. As Greg is Zeta's son, they are connected persons. The market value must be used regardless of the actual amount paid by Greg.

The agreed market price for the shares is £8 per share. Therefore, the taxable consideration is £400,000.

Zeta and Greg could elect to make a joint election for gift relief under s.165 TCGA 1992 in relation to the undervalue payment for the shares.

Gift relief would reduce Zeta's gain to the amount by which actual proceeds exceed the base cost ie, £250,000 ((£6 – £1) × 50,000).

	£
Proceeds	400,000
Less cost	(50,000)
	350,000
Less gift relief β	(100,000)
Chargeable gain	250,000
Less annual exempt amount	(11,700)
Chargeable gain	238,300
Tax at 10%	23,830

The 'undervalue' on the sale of shares to Greg is also a potentially exempt transfer (PET) for IHT purposes. This will be subject to taper relief provided Zeta survives at least three years.

This should be covered by business property relief if Greg still holds the shares at Zeta's death, otherwise by exemptions and the nil rate band, providing there have been no other transfers of value.

There will be no tax implications for Aldo or Luca Ltd.

Tax implications for Greg

The base cost for Greg would be £300,000 (£400,000 – £100,000) if gift relief is claimed. Both parties must agree to the gift relief election.

Stamp Duty for Greg is £1,500 (0.5% × £300,000). There are no VAT implications.

Method 3: Sale of shares Luca Ltd as a purchase of own shares

From Zeta's point of view the sale of her shares to Luca Ltd will automatically be treated as a capital transaction unless the conditions for it to be treated as such are breached. This would mean that the sale would be treated as a distribution and taxed to income tax.

It appears that most of the conditions are met:

- Luca Ltd is an unquoted trading company;

- the buyback would appear to benefit the trade as Zeta and Aldo are now divorced and the potential breakdown in the relationship could be bad for the trade; and

- Zeta has owned the shares for at least 5 years.

- Zeta also needs to be UK resident and there is no information to indicate that this is not the case but would need to be confirmed.

Luca Ltd has distributable reserves of £120,000, which would mean that only 15,000 shares (£120,000/£8) could be bought back at 30 September 2019.

If Luca Ltd does not pay a dividend on 20 September 2019, sufficient reserves would be available. However this may not be acceptable to Aldo.

There is a requirement that Zeta's shareholding must be substantially reduced and therefore selling only 15,000 shares to Luca Ltd would not pass the substantial reduction test. This test involves comparing the relative shareholdings (including associates and for this purpose Greg, assuming he is over 18, is not an associate) before and after the buyback as follows:

	Zeta No. of shares	Aldo No. of shares	Total No. of shares
Before the buy back	50,000	50,000	100,000
Buy back of 15,000	(15,000)		(15,000)
	35,000	50,000	85,000

Percentage before	50.0%
Percentage after 35/85 =	41.1%
75% of the percentage before	37.5%

As the post-sale percentage is more than 75% of the pre-sale percentage, the test is not met and the income distribution treatment will apply. In addition, Zeta's shareholding has not been reduced below 30%.

As Zeta is the original subscriber of the shares, the income tax liability is as follows:

Income = 15,000 × (£8 – £1) = £105,000

Zeta is an additional rate tax payer and as the dividend nil rate band has been used, the tax liability on this would be:

38.1% × £105,000 = £40,005

Subject to an increase in Luca Ltd's distributable reserves in the future, the second sale of shares should qualify for capital gains tax treatment as Zeta would be selling all her remaining shares.

	£
Proceeds (35,000 × £8)	280,000
Less cost	(35,000)
	245,000
Less annual exempt amount	(11,700)
Chargeable gain	233,300
Tax at 10% or 20%	23,330/46,660

Entrepreneurs' relief is available if Zeta is still an employee/officer of the company – this should be confirmed.

(b) Summary and key points to consider

	Method 1	Method 2	Method 3
Income tax liability	–	–	£40,005
Capital gains tax liability	£33,830	£23,830	£23,330/£46,660
Total tax	£33,830	£23,830	£63,335/86,665
Effective tax rate	8.46%	7.94%	15.8%/21.7%
After tax cash received	£366,170	£276,170	£336,665/313,335

As a family, you need to decide whether you would like to see the shares in the company sold to a third party, Bella plc. Clearly if the company did not pay a dividend on 20 September 2019, distributable reserves would be available to buy back all of Zeta's shares assuming the company had enough cash to do this. This would result in the same tax liability for Zeta as if she had sold the shares to Bella plc as she would satisfy the conditions for the repurchase to be treated as a capital transaction. Aldo would then effectively control 100% of the shares in Luca Ltd. It would be possible then to issue shares to Greg without the held over gain and provide a clean break for Zeta.

Once you have considered the calculations relating to the methods of selling Zeta's shares which are included in this email, I think it would be a good idea for us to all have a meeting to come to an amicable solution. Please contact me at your convenience.

Kind regards

Tax adviser

47.2 **Advice for Zeta of the tax implications of a gift of her shares in Luca Ltd to Greg**

Capital Gains Tax

The gift of your shares for capital gains tax purposes would be covered by gift relief as described in my email to the directors and no tax would be payable on the transfer. However, the gain would crystallise when and if Greg came to sell the shares.

Inheritance Tax

Normally, the transfer of the shares themselves is a potentially exempt transfer.

However, given your serious illness you need to consider the IHT consequences. There are special rules which apply when you as transferor make a transfer of value but continue to enjoy some of the benefits from the gifted asset.

If you continue to receive dividends from the shares, then you are receiving a benefit and the gift is known as a gift with reservation of benefit.

If you retain the benefit in the asset transferred ie, receiving dividends until death, the value of the shares will be treated as being part of the death estate and charged to IHT.

If the asset ceases to be subject to the benefit, the transferor is treated as making a PET at the date of cessation.

If the asset could be charged twice to IHT, two calculations will be required but only the treatment which generates the higher tax liability will be payable – for an appreciating asset this will normally be by treating this as part of the death estate.

If Zeta still needs the income from the shares, my recommendation would be to retain the shares and continue to receive income. The shares will pass to her son as part of her estate.

Examiner's comments

47.1 (a)   Students generally found this question the most straightforward on the exam and very accurate calculations were produced showing a good understanding of the tax implications of the various scenarios. A common error by the weaker students was to treat the sale to an unconnected third party as a company purchase of own shares. Also, in computing the gift relief, students often did not consider the actual proceeds received.

Whilst the higher scoring answers correctly concluded that the company purchase of own shares would resulted in an income distribution as the sale of shares had not resulted in a substantial reduction, a high number of answers concluded that the capital route would be applicable as students had failed to use the information on the distributable reserves of the company. Follow through calculation marks were awarded where the incorrect route had been applied. Marks were lost where students did not conclude which approach would be followed and provided both an income route and capital route calculation for the same transaction. (To be distinguished from the situation where students correctly identified that the income route would apply to the first tranche of the buyback and the capital route to the second tranche.)

It was very encouraging to see that students had also considered the IHT implications in scenario 2, with very good answers on the implications of the sale being a PET and the availability of BPR being discussed.

(b)   A common error in this section was for students merely to produce the resulting tax liability under each scenario without thinking about the net cash received. However, many students did deal with this part very well appreciating that proceeds less tax liability led to the net cash position and hence scored full marks.

47.2 Most answers to this part discussed the general IHT implications of making a gift in terms of the gift being a PET, the availability of the NRB and taper relief and BPR. Some students started to discuss the use and operation of trusts and thus CLTs which was irrelevant as there was nothing in the question to indicate that there would be any gift to a trust.

The answers which scored full marks could interpret from the question that retention of the right to receive dividends constituted a gift with reservation of benefit and discussed accurately the potential two charges to tax and how this would be treated.

The CGT elements were dealt with well, with most students discussing the availability and operation of gift relief.

48 Gig plc

Scenario

In this scenario, the student provides advice to the CEO on the tax implications of complex transactions for research and development; a sale in a foreign currency and the disposal and acquisition of an intangible. The second requirement is to give feedback to the CEO on the tax risks of a proposal to replace IT employees by self-employed contractors.

Marking guide

		Technical	Skills	Marks
48.1 Report to CEO				
(1) R&D				
	Calculation of RDEC	2	2	
	Relief for RDEC	-	1	
	Other R&D costs review	-	1	
	Capital allowances	½	1	
(2) Ruritanian customer				
	Recording in the financial statements	1	2	
	Tax treatment	-	2	
(3) Sale of patent				
	Gain	1	1	
	Rollover relief	1	2	
		5½	12	
	Max			16
48.2 Revised taxable profit				
	Adjusted profit	-	3	
	CT liability	1	1	
		1	4	
	Max			4
48.3 Redundancy payments				
	IT employees	-	1	
	Frances	1	1	
	Taxable amount	1	2	
	Tax relief	-	1	
		2	5	
	Max			6
48.4 Risks of contracts				
	Employment status tests/control	1	2	
	PAYE/NIC implications	1	1	
		2	3	
	Max			4
Total marks		10 ½	24	34 ½
Maximum				30

48.1 Report to CEO: An explanation of the tax implications for Gig plc of the three outstanding matters in Issue 1

(1) Research and development

As a large company undertaking qualifying research and development, Gig plc can claim a taxable 'above the line' research and development expenditure credit (RDEC).

The above the line credit is 12% of qualifying expenditure. The qualifying expenditure is £4.5m + £0.52m (65% × £0.8m) = £5.02m as the amount of qualifying expenditure for externally provided workers is restricted.

This gives as credit of £602,400 (12% × £5.02m).

As far as possible this credit is treated as paying the current year's corporation tax liability.

As all the credit is recovered against the current year's corporation tax liability, there is no need to consider any further steps to cap the credit.

The list of research and development (R&D) costs does not appear to include other costs which could potentially be permitted such as computer software, power, heat and light, etc. Further information should be obtained to see if the company can identify any further relevant costs.

In addition, assets used for R&D are eligible for 100% capital allowances if they qualify as plant and machinery – this would lead to a further deduction of £2.2 million.

(2) Ruritanian customer

The receivables were recorded in the financial statements using the exchange rate at the date of the sale ie, a value of £2.16 million (R$3m/1.39).

Gig plc must be assessed to tax on the exchange gain or loss even though the amount is unrealised at 30 June 2019. As this relates to a trading transaction the gain/loss must be recorded in trading profits.

At 30 June 2019 the R$3 million balance is valued at £2.26 million (R$3m/1.33) and so there is an exchange gain of £0.1 million (£2.26m – £2.16m). The forex gain of £0.1 million should be added to trading profit as this is a trading transaction.

A further adjustment will be required at the date the company receives payment from the customer when the monies are converted into sterling.

(3) Sale of patent

Gig plc has sold an intangible fixed asset (IFA) and realised a taxable gain of £13 million. As Gig plc and Techo Ltd become part of the same capital gains group on the share purchase, a claim for rollover relief of this gain is possible as Gig plc has invested in new IFAs by buying the shares of Techo Ltd, a company where the value reflects IFAs held by that company.

If a company makes a gain on realisation of an IFA and reinvests in a new IFA, a claim for rollover relief may be made.

The taxable gain of £13 million (£21m – £8m (£14m – £2m × 3 years)) represents the accounting profit on the IFA which is the difference between the sale proceeds less TWDV (original cost less amortisation charges taken to the statement of profit or loss). The accounting profit is also the taxable profit.

The rollover relief is the excess of the proceeds on realisation over the original cost. This is calculated as follows:

£21m (proceeds) – £14m (original cost) = £7m.

If the full £21 million had been reinvested the full £7 million could be rolled over and therefore only £6 million (£13m – £7m) would be taxed.

However, as the full proceeds have not been reinvested, the rollover relief is restricted by the amount not reinvested of £4 million, ie, proceeds less the carrying amount (£21m – £17m).

The rollover relief of £7 million is restricted by the amount not reinvested of £4 million – ie, £3 million is the amount of rollover relief available.

The taxable amount is the accounting profit of £13 million minus the rolled over gain £3 million = £10 million.

As the accounting profit already includes £13 million profit, a deduction of £3 million should be made for the gain rolled over.

48.2 Calculation of the revised taxable profit for Gig plc for the year ended 30 June 2019

	£m
Tax-adjusted trading profit	45.0
Less capital allowances	(2.2)
Add: RDEC	0.6
Forex gain	0.1
Less IFA rolled over gain	(3.0)
Taxable total profits	40.5
Corporation tax at 19%	7.7
Less RDEC	(0.6)
Corporation tax liability	7.1

48.3 Calculation of the tax implications of the redundancy payments for Gig plc

IT employees

The 15 employees will receive a statutory redundancy of £12,000 and an ex gratia payment of £15,000. Therefore, the payments should be covered by the £30,000 exemption.

Frances

Frances' payments exceed £30,000 and therefore the excess would be taxable.

However, the exemption is reduced by her statutory redundancy pay as follows:

	£
Statutory pay	
Ex gratia payment	100,000
Less £30,000 – £12,000	(18,000)
Taxable payment	82,000

The taxable termination payment would form the top slice of Frances's income.

Tax relief for Gig plc

Tax relief for Gig plc for the payment of redundancy to the employees would be tax deductible provided the payments satisfied the general rule of a cost incurred wholly and exclusively for the benefit of the trade. If the employees were working wholly within the trade, then a tax deduction should be allowed.

48.4 Evaluation of the tax risks for Gig plc of the proposal to issue Frances and six of her team with contracts on a self-employed basis

The contractors may be deemed to be employees if they were recruited on a self-employed basis but failed to satisfy the employment status tests.

In determining the employment status, the employees' contracts should be considered by referring to eight tests of control. For example, whether the employees have financial risk, can send substitutes or have control over how they work are strong indicators of self-employment.

The implications of the self-employed status being questioned is that there could be additional tax liabilities under PAYE and NIC. These could ultimately be payable by Gig plc to the extent the tax is not recovered from the contractors.

Examiner's comments

48.1 The first issue on R&D did not cause any major problems. Some students treated Gig plc as a SME despite the question outlining that this was a large company. Many students correctly identified that the company would qualify for the above the line tax credit and made a good attempt at calculating the credit available; losing only minor marks by including 100% of the external worker spend rather than just 65%. These students discussed generally the operation of the R&D regime. Students demonstrated knowledge of the rules but a failure to apply them to the scenario.

The Ruritanian customer part of the question is changed due to a syllabus change.

The treatment of the IFA produced polarised answers with students either writing at length on how intangibles are treated for tax purposes without appreciating that rollover relief was available, to very detailed answers showing a detailed understanding of the intangibles regime and the resulting relief available and gain.

48.2 Follow through marks were awarded in this part but common mistakes noted were that the RDEC was deducted before corporation tax was applied and an add back of depreciation and capital being included even though students had started with the tax adjusted trading profit.

48.3 This part was very well answered with full marks often being awarded. Students demonstrated a good understanding of the treatment of termination payments.

48.4 Most of answers to this part focussed on the provisions of IR35 despite the question being silent on the presence of any intermediary companies. It merely referred to 'self-employed' so the IR35 approach conveyed confusion on the rules generally and a distinct lack of appreciation being self-employed as an unincorporated business and an incorporated entity.

Even though some students started off with the wrong approach, the position was recovered through a discussion of the employment indicator tests which resulted in the question being answered well (eventually).

The major observation from the approach to questions throughout the exam is that students do appear to have knowledge in the relevant areas but they fail to interpret the scenario presented and instead answer the question based on scenarios they have seen in past exams or the question banks they have practiced in preparation for the exam.

December 2017 exam answers

49 Philip and Estelle

Scenario

The candidate is in tax department of a firm of ICAEW Chartered Accountants acting for clients Phillip and Estelle Thompson who are directors and shareholders of a company.

This question considers ways in which Phillip and Estelle may effect their retirement from the company by disposing of shares to a current employee of the company and gifting the shares to their son and daughter. The question tested a range of taxes; Capital Gains, Inheritance Tax, and Income tax. These are mainstream topics and candidates should have been able to deal with the question very well.

Various elections and reliefs featured in the question. The question was purposely silent on a number of issues in an attempt to get candidates to think about the further information they would require to make a decision and recommendation to the clients.

Marking guide

	Technical	Skills	Marks
Pre-sale distribution			
All cash	2	3	
Reduced cash		2	
Sale to Francis			
Gains	2	3	
Impact of pre-sale distribution	1	2	
Entrepreneurs' relief impact		2	
Entrepreneurs' relief conditions	3	2	
Conclusion	1	3	
Gift to children – personal gift			
Gift relief	1	2	
Restriction of gift relief	1	2	
Other gains aspects	1	1	
IHT – PET	2	3	
BPR	2	2½	
Gift into trust			
Type of trust		2	
BPR		1	
Capital gains tax	1	1	
Income tax		1	
Exits/conclusion	½	1	
Recommendation		3	
Total marks	17½	36½	54
Maximum			40

Notes in preparation for a meeting with Philip and Estelle Thompson

Retirement planning

The plans set out in the client's email have a number of different tax consequences, I have considered the consequences under separate headings below and provided a summary of my final recommendation at the end of the notes.

Cash distribution before sale/transfer

The company has a cash balance of £300,000. Assuming that all of this cash could be distributed before the sale/transfer of the shares, this would give rise to a potential dividend of £150,000 each. If this were to be received before 5 April 2019, the dividend would form part of Philip and Estelle's taxable income for 2018/19.

The first £2,000 of dividend income each would be taxed at 0%. The remaining £148,000 of dividend income would be taxed on the clients, as higher rate taxpayers, at 32.5% and any dividend falling into the additional rate band would be taxed at 38.1%.

In addition, as adjusted net income would exceed £123,700 they would lose their entire personal allowance of £11,850, if they were to take the full dividend. This would increase the effective rate on the dividends.

The alternative would be to pay a dividend below the full £150,000 available, to take advantage of the 0% dividend nil rate band of £2,000, and also to preserve personal allowances.

We would need to know the exact level of the clients' income for 2018/19, before taking account of the dividend, to be able to calculate this amount.

Sale of shares to Francis

The sale of the shares to Francis would give rise to a substantial capital gain.

The gain would be split between Philip and Estelle. They would each have sale proceeds of £400,000, less a base cost of £20,000 (£50,000 × 20/50). Giving a gain of £380,000 each.

They would each be entitled to a capital gains tax annual exempt amount of £11,700 and to be able to deduct capital losses brought forward of £10,000. This would leave each of them with a gain of £358,300.

As higher rate or additional rate taxpayers, Philip and Estelle would be taxed at 20% on these gains, giving rise to a capital gains tax liability of £71,660.

If there was a distribution of the cash reserves before sale, this might reduce the amount that Francis was willing to pay for 40% of the business. If so, this would reduce the amount taxable at 20%. However, the tax on the cash distribution would be at 32.5% or 38.1% and effectively higher, due to the potential erosion of the personal allowance.

It would therefore be more tax efficient to keep the majority of the cash in the company and receive capital sale proceeds for the shares, rather than dividend income.

In addition, the disposal to Francis may qualify for entrepreneurs' relief, which would reduce the tax payable on the gain to 10%, for each of Philip and Estelle; Tax payable of £35,830 each.

However, the conditions that need to be satisfied for entrepreneurs' relief to be applicable are that:

- The shares must be in a trading company: we need to establish that the holding of a substantial cash balance and the residential investment properties does not render this company to be considered as an investment company by HMRC.

- Philip and Estelle must both be officers or employees of the company. We need to clarify the exact roles that Philip and Estelle hold.

- The shares are unquoted and have been held by Philip and Estelle for at least 12 months.

The sale of shares has stamp duty implications for Francis at ½% of the £800,000 purchase price – a cost to Francis of £4,000.

Philip and Estelle will both have cash in their estates rather than shares after the sale. The shares in Thompson Ltd may qualify for business property relief at the rate of 100% (assuming the company is a trading company and not an investment company). However, cash does not qualify. Therefore their estates will suffer a greater inheritance tax charge on death if cash is held.

The rate of IHT on death is 40%, but the amount chargeable is determined after considering the amount of nil rate band available and the value of the other assets in their death estates. The £325,000 nil rate band will have been used up against the value of the gift of the shares to their children, if the shares do not qualify for business property relief.

Gift of shares to children: personal gift or gift into trust?

In addition to selling 40% of the company to Francis, Philip and Estelle intend to give 60% of the company to Alan and Sandra (30% each).

Personal gift of the shares to the children

If they give the shares directly to their children, they will incur capital tax consequences, as follows:

A personal gift of the shares to the children gives rise to a capital gain for each of Philip and Estelle, of £570,000 (600,000 – 30,000).

This gain may be reduced by claiming gift relief, assuming that Thompson Ltd qualifies as an unquoted personal trading company for the purposes of gift relief.

However, the amount of gift relief available is restricted because of the cash and investments held by the company.

The gain eligible for gift relief would be calculated as:

Gain on gift of shares × MV CBA/MVCA
£570,000 × (250,000/ 1,000,000) = £142,500.

Therefore £427,500 of the gain would be taxable and £142,500 could be held over against the base cost of the shares for Alan and Sandra.

The tax on this gain (assuming the annual exempt amount and capital losses have already been used against the gain on the sale of shares to Francis) would be 20% × £427,500 = £85,500 each. This would reduce the amount of cash they have available for retirement.

Entrepreneurs' relief could be claimed on this gain, reducing the CGT due to £42,750 (10% × £427,500), assuming that the lifetime limit for entrepreneurs' relief has not been exceeded.

This gift would also be a potentially exempt transfer for inheritance tax purposes. The value of the PET, would be the diminution in value of Philip and Estelle's estates. The related property rules apply as the 60% of the shares are held by Philip and Estelle after the sale to Francis. The value of a 60% holding is £1.75 million, a value of £875,000 each to Philip and Estelle.

No tax would be payable in lifetime and tax might be payable, (after deduction of a maximum of £6,000 of annual IHT exemptions and a maximum of £325,000 of nil rate band) at 40% on death.

IHT payable would be £217,600, assuming the nil rate band and two annual exemptions were available against the transfer.

If business property relief is available at the rate of 100%, the value of the gift would be nil. We need to know more about the company and its activities to judge if BPR is available.

HMRC regard a company as trading in this context if it is wholly or mainly a trading company. This may look at the level of income generated, the assets of the business or the level of activity.

So the company may be regarded as trading and the value of the shares eligible for BPR, but there is no certainty.

Even if the shares qualify as business property, any assets not used for business purposes will not be eligible for BPR and will be treated as excepted assets, proportionately reducing the BPR available – in this case the residential properties are unlikely to count as business assets, as they are held as investment properties. The cash balance of £300,000, as it is not held for working capital needs, but, instead, held for the purpose of investment, would count as an excepted asset, if the cash were still held as part of the business at the date of the gift.

If BPR is available we need to ensure that the donees retain the shares, or replacement property for 7 years or at least until Philip and Estelle both die, in order to retain the eligibility to BPR eligibility should they die within 7 years of the gift.

Gift into trust

If they created a trust and transferred the shares to the trust, it could either be an interest in possession or a discretionary trust.

For IHT purposes the creation of a trust is a chargeable lifetime transfer, charged to IHT at the rate of 20% or 25% depending on whether the trust or the donor pays the IHT due in lifetime.

Assuming that both donors still have a nil rate band of £325,000 available and also have two annual exemptions available, the tax payable in lifetime would be £108,800 ((£875,000 – £6,000 – £325,000) × 20%) or £136,000 if Philip and Estelle pay the lifetime tax (25%).

Business property relief at the rate of 100% could reduce this tax to nil, if the company is regarded as a trading company with no excepted assets.

The creation of the trust would bring about the same CGT consequences as mentioned above, except that gift relief is available on the creation of the trust due to the immediate charge to IHT on the creation of the trust. In these circumstances the cash and investments would not restrict the amount of available gift relief and the full gain of £570,000 each is eligible for gift relief.

Once the shares are in the trust the trust will pay tax on any dividend income arising from the shares (at the rate of 38.1% for a discretionary trust and at 7.5% for interest in possession trusts). Payments to beneficiaries will be paid under deduction of a tax credit.

There will be capital gains tax consequences to remove the assets from the trust.

Inheritance tax will also be payable on every exit from the trust and every 10-year anniversary of the creation of the trust.

The advantage of creating a trust would be the ability to ensure that the assets remain within the family, however there could be a substantial tax cost involved in using a trust.

Recommendation

Although we would need to have additional information, where indicated, to give final advice about the tax consequences of the transactions stated, the current position would appear to be:

It would not appear to be beneficial to distribute the cash in the company as a pre-sale/transfer dividend due to the higher and additional rates of income tax chargeable on a dividend, compared to rates of CGT on the sale of shares.

The sale to Francis will give rise to CGT and entrepreneurs' relief may be available to reduce the CGT payable to the rate of 10%.

The transfer to Alan and Sandra will give rise to both CGT and IHT consequences. Although the CGT on transfer into the trust is lower than on transfer directly to Alan and Sandra, the additional tax costs of operating through a trust may outweigh this initial tax saving.

The IHT due on the transfer into trust could be substantial and the whether BPR is available or not would be a deciding factor in determining whether a transfer into trust was advisable or not. We could apply to HMRC for advance clearance that BPR is available.

Examiner's comments

49.1 Overall candidates approached this question very well by dealing with the three aspects of the plan in the order presented in the Exhibit. The sale and gift of shares were dealt with well, with the strongest candidates being able to correctly identify and apply the restrictions to gift relief for CGT, and BPR for IHT, in respect of the gifts. Many candidates identified the difference in how the gifts are valued for CGT and IHT purposes, but only the strongest candidates were able to correctly apply the diminution in value and related property principles to the scenario. This was surprising as this is a basic concept that candidates cover at Tax Compliance.

The distribution of surplus cash balances within Thompson Ltd was answered less well. Many candidates were confused by what such a payment was. The better answers correctly identified that there would be a dividend strip and went on to consider the income tax implications. Weaker candidates incorrectly believed that the payment would be a disposal by the company, or a potentially exempt transfer by the company. Another common problem, was candidates seeing this as a profit extraction question and producing detailed analysis of bonus v dividend. This was not the case and it was very explicit in the scenario that a dividend was going to be paid. This was a classic example of candidates answering the question they wanted as opposed to the question set.

49.2 Most candidates were able to make sensible suggestions based on their analysis of the tax implications. Those candidates concluded that a gift to the children was preferable to a gift into trust, and that a pre-sale dividend would likely result in higher tax than simply keeping the cash within the company. Stronger candidates identified that a pre-sale dividend would reduce the surplus cash balance within the company, which would increase the availability of BPR on a subsequent gift to the children.

49.3 Most candidates correctly identified the information required to conclude their recommendation, although answers were generally quite rushed due to mis-management of time. Weaker candidates also produced very general 'lists' which were not focussed to the information in the scenario.

50 TabletTech Ltd

Scenario

The candidate is an ICAEW Chartered Accountant employed by TabletTech Ltd (TT). TT have identified a potential business to purchase; PhoneCharger Ltd which was incorporated by Alice Crane. Alice still holds 100% of the share capital. The purchase of the company can be effected either by the purchase of shares or the purchase of trade and assets. The question covered CGT, IT, CT and also ethics focussing on enablers of offshore tax evasion; which was a new section in the learning materials this year.

ICAEW 2019   December 2017 exam answers 357

	Technical	Skills	Marks
50.1 Entrepreneurs' relief	2	2	
Calculation	2	3	
Liquidation	1	3	
Asset summary	2	2	
Consideration	1	2	
	8	12	
Max			16
50.2 Share purchase v asset purchase sale	1	3	
VAT – shares	1	1	
VAT – assets	1	2	
Stamp duty	-	2	
SDLT	-	1	
Conclusion	-	2	
	3	11	
Max			12
50.3 Ethical consideration	-	3	
Tax evasion	1	1	
Actions	1	3	
	2	7	
Max			7
Total marks	13	30	43
Maximum			35

50.1 Calculation of the consideration required so that Alice Crane can receive after tax consideration of £20 million

Share purchase

Alice would be liable to capital gains tax on the disposal of the shares. She is eligible for entrepreneurs' relief on the disposal of the shares, because:

* the shares are in her personal trading company; and
* she has held the shares and worked full time for the company for at least a year.

The gains on sale of the shares could be taxed at 10%, up to the lifetime limit of £10 million.

Gains over the £10 million would be taxed at 20%, because Alice is not a basic rate taxpayer.

Working back from the net proceeds required of £20 million, the gross consideration (G) required by Alice is calculated as follows:

After tax cash needs to be £20 million. The first £10 million of the gain is taxed at 10% with the remaining amount of the gain being taxed at 20%. Therefore:

G – (£10m × 10%) – 20% [(G – £2m) – £10m] = £20m
G – £1m – 0.2G + £400,000 + £2m = £20m
0.8G = £18.6m

Therefore G = gross consideration = £23.25 million

Asset purchase

Under this scenario, the total cash sale proceeds would be paid to the company and Alice would then have to extract the cash from the company. As PhoneCharger Ltd would cease to trade, the method of extracting cash would be through a liquidation of the company and a payment to Alice post liquidation. This payment will be taxed as a capital gain as the distribution of funds would be after trade has ceased. Again, as the gain is eligible for entrepreneurs' relief, the first £10 million of gain would be taxed at 10% and the remainder at 20%. The funds required to be distributed would be as follows.

The proceeds received by Alice, on liquidation would again be £23.25 million then she would be taxed on a gain of £21.25 million, as calculated above, giving after tax proceeds of £20 million as required.

The cash in the company from the assets purchased by TabletTech Ltd would be:

	£'000	
Net current assets	11,600	These assets do not give rise to any capital gain
Plant and equipment	1,000	There might be balancing charges or allowances, we would need more information to be able to calculate this.
Property	3,509	Gain £3.6 million – 3.12 million = £480,000. This will be taxed on the company at 19% (£91,200).
Total	16,109	

The balance of consideration paid would be for goodwill. The goodwill has no base cost, because it has been generated since incorporation. The goodwill would therefore be taxed in full as part of PhoneCharger Ltd's trading profit at 19%.

The cash available to Alice would therefore be 81% of the consideration paid for the goodwill plus £16.109 million, totalling £23.25 million. Goodwill would therefore have been sold for £8.82 million ((£23.25m – £16.109m)/0.81).

The total consideration payable by TabletTech Ltd would be:

	£'000	Tax@ 19% £'000	After tax £'000
Goodwill	8,820	1,676	7,144
Property	3,600	91	3,509
Plant	1,000	0	1,000
Net current assets	11,600	0	11,600
Total	25,020	1,767	23,253

Therefore, to purchase the assets, instead of the shares, would cost TabletTech Ltd an additional £1.767 million over and above the cost of purchasing the shares, if the net, after tax consideration payable to Alice is to remain at £20 million.

50.2 The purchase of TabletTech Ltd could take the form of either a share or an asset purchase. Given the need for net, after tax proceeds of £20 million, the respective cost of acquiring either shares or assets depends on the tax suffered by Alice.

In part 1 the calculation showed that purchasing the shares would cost £23.25 million whereas purchasing the assets would cost £25.02 million (£23.25m + £1.77m).

The property would be acquired at its current market value and any subsequent gain on sale would be calculated using a cost of £3.6 million. If TabletTech Ltd had purchased the shares, the property would have retained its indexed cost of £3.12 million to use in calculating any gain on sale. This will therefore save tax at 19% of the difference ie, £91,200.

There would be no amortisation allowable on the goodwill.

VAT

Share purchase

No VAT arises on the purchase of shares, because shares are exempt from VAT.

PhoneCharger Ltd could join a VAT group with TabletTech Ltd.

Sale of trade and assets

PhoneCharger Ltd is registered for VAT. A purchase of the trade and assets would however give rise to no VAT provided the purchase qualified as a transfer of a going concern (TOGC). To qualify as a TOGC PhoneCharger Ltd must be transferring the whole of its business, as a going concern and there must be no significant break in trade. The purchasing company must also be registered for VAT.

The property transferred is more than three years old and there is no VAT as part of the TOGC.

Stamp taxes

Sale of shares

TabletTech Ltd will pay stamp duty at 0.5% on the purchase price of the shares in PhoneCharger Ltd ie, £116,250 (£23.25m × 0.5%).

Sale of assets

Stamp duty land tax (SDLT) will be due on the transfer of the property giving an additional cost to the purchaser of £169,500 (((£250,000 – £150,000) × 2%) + ((£3.6m – £250,000) × 5%)).

Conclusion

At the point of purchase, the purchase of shares is cheaper than the purchase of assets.

However, the purchase of shares brings with it the history of the company, which might expose TabletTech Ltd to costs arising from past actions of PhoneCharger Ltd. It might, therefore be safer to purchase the trade and assets of PhoneCharger Ltd, even though the purchase of trade and assets might initially seem more expensive.

50.3 Ethical considerations of the payment of £5 million of purchase consideration to a nominated bank account in the Cayman Islands

The contract for the purchase of the shares or the assets will show the full purchase consideration. This contract will be available to HMRC and used to calculate taxes such as stamp duty. Therefore this payment will be visible to the UK tax authorities.

As an ICAEW Chartered Accountant I am bound by the ethical rules of my professional body.

My actions should not support a loss of revenue to HMRC.

The information given does not explain the reasoning behind the funds being sent to the Cayman Islands. We cannot simply assume that this request is to further some form of tax evasion and we should make enquiries of the vendor to determine the reason behind funds being sent to an offshore tax haven.

We should document our enquiries about this sum, with the client.

If we believe, upon enquiry, that the reason for sending these funds to the Cayman Islands is to evade tax, we should decline to make the payment to the Cayman Islands.

If the client goes ahead with arranging for funds to go to the Cayman Islands and we suspect that this is to evade tax, we should consider if this will constitute a money laundering offence and if we should report this to our MLRO.

Examiner's comments

50.1 Most candidates understood this requirement and approached calculating the gross proceeds in a sensible way, beginning with the net cash required and working backwards.

On the sale of shares, the standard of attempt was good. However only a small proportion of students correctly identified that the gain would be subject to 10% and 20% CGT due to exceeding the ER limit. A surprising number of candidates interpreted the sale of shares by Alice as a repurchase by the company, and therefore wasted time setting out the conditions for capital treatment of a company purchase of own shares.

The sale of trade and assets was dealt with well, with most candidates making a reasonable attempt to calculate the value of goodwill in the company. Weaker candidates considered the possibility of a pre-liquidation dividend, when this was clearly not relevant.

50.2 This section was generally answered less well. The general approach tended to be to discuss group aspects of corporate tax without focussing on the detail in the scenario. Stronger candidates produced a well-structured answer, comparing costs of the two possibilities, and correctly setting out the VAT and stamp tax issues. Weaker candidates produced a confusing answer, with little detail.

50.3 Ethics was answered very well. Candidates have improved in this area in recent years. Answers were very logical and structured. The higher scoring answers outlined the potential implications and the penalties/sanctions that would be applicable.

51 Elm plc

Scenario

The candidate is in practice in a firm of ICAEW Chartered Accountants acting for the Elm plc group of companies and has been asked to prepare notes for a meeting between their manager, Lewis Gordon and the Elm plc board. The candidate is required to deal with the features of group relationships and several issues in finalising the CT computation. These included; incorporation of a foreign PE and exit charges, share disposals and the SSE, including investment companies and gains groups.

	Technical	Skills	Marks
Issue 1			
Cessation of trade		1	
Capital allowances		1	
Gains conditions	2	2	
Calculations	2	2	
Deferral of gains	1	2	
Factory disposal – crystallisation	½	1	
Share disposal – crystallisation	1½	3	
Issue 2			
Degrouping – gains	1	2	
Degrouping – SDLT	½		
Issue 3	1½	2	
Issue 4	2½	1	
Issue 5	1	2	
Total marks	13½	19	32½
Maximum			25

Issue 1

On incorporation of Walker SARL, Elm plc's permanent establishment (PE) ceased to trade.

Incorporation results in balancing adjustments arising on branch plant and machinery transferred to the non UK company.

Incorporation results in chargeable gains/losses in the hands of Elm plc.

Relief exists for chargeable gains on incorporation to be postponed where:

- the trade of a foreign PE is transferred to a non-UK resident company with all the assets used for trade except cash

- the consideration for the transfer is wholly or partly securities

- the transferring company owns at least 25% of the ordinary share capital of the non-UK resident company

- a claim for relief is made

Therefore, the conditions appear to have been met and the gains on the factory, warehouse, the gain on the fixed plant and machinery and the accounting profit on the 'new' goodwill are eligible to be postponed.

Gains are as follows:

	£
Factory	
MV	700,000
Cost	(250,000)
Indexation (0.379 × £250,000)	(94,750)
Gain	355,250
Warehouse	
MV	500,000
Cost	(550,000)
Loss	(50,000)
Fixed P&M	
MV	250,000
Cost	(200,000)
Indexation (0.076 × £200,000)	(15,200)
Gain	34,800
Goodwill	
MV	1,250,000
Cost	(Nil)
Intangible profit	1,250,000

Net gains to be postponed = £340,050 plus the profit on the new goodwill of £1,250,000.

As the entire consideration was in the form of shares then the whole gain and the intangible profit can be postponed.

However, as Elm plc has now disposed of some of the shares in Walker SARL (on 1 January 2019) and in addition, Walker SARL has disposed of the factory (on 31 December 2018) within 6 years of the transfer, the gains will become chargeable on the UK company and will be calculated as follows:

$$\text{Remaining balance of net gain deferred} \times \frac{\text{Gain on asset at incorporation}}{\text{Gross gains at incorporation}}$$

On sale of the factory the following gain will become chargeable:

$$£340,050 \times \frac{£355,250}{£390,050} = £309,711$$

The balance of the postponed gain carried forward is therefore £30,339.

In terms of the disposal of securities, the gain previously deferred is chargeable in addition to any gain arising on the disposal of the securities themselves. The disposal of the shares will not meet the conditions for substantial shareholding exemption (SSE) because the securities have not been held for the required period. Therefore a chargeable gain will arise on Elm plc as follows:

Balance of gain × A/B where A = MV of securities disposed of and B is total MV of securities held immediately before disposal:

$$£30,339 \times \frac{£1,350,000}{£3,450,000} = £11,872$$

There will also be crystallisation of the intangible profit.

$$£1,250,000 \times \frac{£1,350,000}{£3,450,000} = £489,130$$

In addition, the disposal of the securities themselves will realise a chargeable gain and in this situation, the SSE does not apply. The gain will be £582,000 (£1,350,000 – £(£3,200,000 × 72,000/300,000)).

Total chargeable gains are therefore £903,583 (£309,711 + £11,872 + £582,000).

Issue 2

A degrouping charge arises on the office block because Labrador Ltd is no longer a 75% subsidiary of Elm plc.

The charge on the office block arises under the chargeable gains rules. Because it does not arise as a result of a share sale, it arises in Labrador Ltd at the beginning of the accounting period in which it leaves the group.

	£
Proceeds (MV at transfer)	2,400,000
Cost	(1,400,000)
Indexation 0.392 × £1,400,000	(548,800)
Chargeable gain	451,200

Because Labrador Ltd leaves the group more than three years after the transfer of the property, there is no stamp duty land tax degrouping charge.

Issue 3

This is a disposal to an unconnected third party and a loss therefore arises on the disposal of £12m – £14m = £2m. The loss is not disallowed by the substantial shareholding exemption because Parrot Ltd is not a trading company. It has substantial non-trading activities due to its investment property.

A chargeable gains group exists where a principal company owns at least 75% of its direct subsidiaries and has an effective interest of more than 50% in each sub-subsidiary. Therefore, Elm plc, Terrapin Ltd and Cat Ltd are all part of the same chargeable gains group.

An election can be made to reallocate the allowable loss to another group company.

Issue 4

The disposal of the shares should be exempt under the substantial shareholding exemption. Bassett Ltd is a trading company, and the shares have been held for more than 12 months.

Although neither of the companies which sold shares owned a 10% substantial shareholding, the holdings of all group members are aggregated in determining whether that test is satisfied.

Issue 5

The brought forward capital losses in Terrapin Ltd of £36,000 are available to offset against the gain of £140,000.

The capital losses brought forward in Cat Ltd of £550,000 are pre-entry losses and not available for use by the group.

Gains and losses can be 'transferred' to other group members by making an election under s.171A TCGA 1992.

All profits and gains in the FY 2018 are taxed at 19%.

Examiner's comments

Overall this question was answered well by most candidates. Good use of open book allowed many candidates to pick up marks on the incorporation of the overseas PE, with the standard of calculations being very good. The weaker candidates misinterpreted the question to be focussed on CFCs. This was not relevant as the scenario had been purposely created so that the new subsidiary was not subject to a CFC charge. Some candidates also discussed migration of a company which displayed a misunderstanding of the issues in the scenario. The group aspects were also answered well, with the degrouping charge calculated correctly by the majority of candidates. The point on SSE being applicable where companies in a group can aggregate their shareholdings was only picked up by a minority of candidates. This is in the learning materials and it was surprising that it did not feature in the majority of answers. Candidates were very comfortable with this question.

March 2018 exam answers

52 2B plc

Scenario

The candidate is in working on a short-term contract at 2B plc covering the temporary absence of the financial controller. 2B plc has four investments and the candidate is asked to explain the tax implications of 2B plc's shareholdings in two companies which are tax resident in a tax jurisdiction with a lower tax rate than the UK.

The candidate should identify that although both companies qualify as CFC, the profits of both companies are unlikely to pass through the CFC gateway for different reasons; CS Inc because of its commercial independence; and UB Inc because its shares were recently acquired and fall within the exempt period.

The candidate is also asked to explain the tax implications of an interest free loan, a leasing arrangement and adjustments to selling prices to secure a tax advantage.

The question also has an ethical issue concerning the transparency over the changes made to intra group selling prices – the changes impact on the awarding of bonuses to employees. The financial controller appears to be pressurising junior staff and demonstrates a lack of transparency.

Marking guide

		Technical	Skills
52.1(a)	Loss surrender		1
	CS Inc		
	CFC and exemptions	2	2
	Gateway		2
	UB Inc		
	CFC and exemptions	1	2
	Gateway	1	3
(b)	Note 1		
	Transfer pricing	1	3
	DPT conditions	1½	2
	Mismatch	1	3
	Relevant alternative provisions	2	2
	Note 2		
	Transfer pricing conditions	2	2
	Calculations	1	1
	Pricing structure and administration		3

		Technical	Skills	Marks
(c)	Adjustments	—	2	
		12½	28	
	Max			32
52.2	Issue		3	
	Threats and tax avoidance	2	2	
	Actions		3	
		2	8	
	Max			8
	Total marks	14 ½	36	50 ½
	Maximum			40

52.1 Draft report to 2B plc Board

(a) Evaluation of tax implications of shareholding in CS Inc and UB Inc

2B plc has a 100% shareholding in CS Inc and 60% shareholding in UB inc – however both are non-UK resident companies resident in Utopia and it is unlikely that losses can be surrendered to these companies.

CS Inc

CS Inc is a controlled foreign company (CFC) as it is a company resident outside the UK and controlled by 2B plc a UK resident company.

It does not appear to meet any of the exemptions at the entity level – its profits are over £500,000, there is insufficient information regarding its profit margins, the briefing says that the company is 'efficient and profitable'. We would need to confirm Utopia's status as an excluded territory.

The tax rate in Utopia is 9% which is less than 75% of the UK rate 19% (75% × 19% = 14.25%).

Assuming none of the exemptions apply, the next decision would be whether an amount of its chargeable profits should be apportioned to 2B plc.

CS Inc does not have non-trading financing profits and its business profits derived from operating the call centre are from many customers not just 2B plc. It would seem likely therefore that although CS Inc appears to be a CFC, its trading profits are not within the CFC gateway and no CFC charge would apply to 2B plc because of its investment in CS Inc.

UB Inc was acquired on 1 July 2018 and is a company resident outside of the UK and controlled by persons resident in the UK. It is therefore a CFC.

It does not satisfy the low profit test nor the tax exemption and as with CS Inc we would need to confirm whether Utopia is on the list of excluded territories.

However, as the shares were only acquired in July 2018, its accounting period may fall within the exempt period which is intended to allow groups time to restructure to ensure that they are not subject to the CFC charge. The exemption only applies if there would otherwise be a CFC charge this period. In a subsequent period UB Inc is still a CFC but there is no CFC charge then, either because there are no chargeable profits or another exemption applies.

Whether in the future profits will pass through the gateway and become subject to a CFC charge depends on certain entry conditions:

- There is evidence that a group company, H-Brew Ltd is party to an arrangement with UB Inc to reduce the charge to UK tax in the accounting period to 31 March 2020 by a transfer pricing structure which sells beer to UB Inc at a lower price than to UK customers.

- The information does not explain who controls the assets and risks of UB Inc – however Gerry Maya appears to be deciding the selling price of beer to UB Inc from H-Brew Ltd Ltd which is one of its core ingredients.

- As UB Inc's only customer is 2B plc there is a strong reliance on the UK and therefore its capability without the UK would seem to be in doubt.

The exempt period will only apply if there is at least one future accounting period with no CFC charge. If there is no such period (which may be the case given the facts above), 2B plc could be subject to a CFC charge on its share of UB Inc's profits at the UK rate of corporation tax from the period of acquisition.

The recommendation to the board would be to review the pricing arrangement with UB Inc to ensure appropriate pricing structures and commerciality of transactions between the group companies.

(b) **Tax implications of issues in the Exhibit**

Note 1: loan and lease arrangement

Because 2B plc is a large company and it controls CS Inc and Toll Ltd, the arrangement comes within the transfer pricing legislation. The interest free loan from 2B plc to CS Inc will be subject to the transfer pricing rules and will require an adjustment to 2B plc's tax computation to increase NTLR for the interest income on the loan calculated at an arm's length interest rate.

The adjustment required is:

£25 million × 2.5% = £625,000 × 6/12 = £312,500

Lease arrangement

The lease arrangement in respect of the land would seem to be without commercial substance. Toll Ltd will be deemed to have diverted profits because the lease transaction lacks 'economic substance':

- Toll Ltd is UK resident;
- It has entered into an arrangement with CS Inc:
- At the time both CS Inc and Toll Ltd are controlled by 2B plc; and
- The transaction causes an 'effective tax mismatch outcome' as:

  - the lease rental of £3.6 million (£7.2 million × 6/12) is deductible in calculating Toll Ltd's trading profits and results in a tax saving of £3.6 million × 19% = £684,000.

  - the resulting deduction in UK tax exceeds the resulting increase in Utopia tax of £3.6 million × 9% = £324,000.

  - the resulting increase of £324,000 is less than 80% of the £684,000 decrease in UK corporation tax. (£684,000 × 80% = £547,200).

There is no evidence that CS Inc's staff are involved in the arrangement beyond creating a monthly invoice and all the legal arrangements were undertaken in the UK by 2B plc.

The transaction has 'insufficient economic substance' as it is reasonable to assume that the operating lease and the involvement of CS Inc are designed to secure a tax reduction.

There is no tax relief for the acquisition cost to Toll Ltd if it had acquired the land and property itself.

The tax implication of this arrangement is that Toll Ltd will be deemed to have taxable diverted profits. Toll Ltd will be required to pay 25% of the taxable diverted profits.

To calculate this, Toll Ltd would need to consider the 'relevant alternative provisions' ie, what would the UK corporation tax position have been if Toll Ltd had purchased the land and buildings directly.

If on applying the 'relevant alternative provisions' expenses of the same type and for the same purpose arise and there would have been no resulting UK taxable income then the 'taxable diverted profits' are nil if either:

- the arrangements are at arm's length; or
- a transfer pricing adjustment is made before the end of the DPT review period.

It appears that the transaction is not at arm's length – we would need to determine whether the rental charge is a market rent.

DPT is not self-assessed and Toll Ltd will have to notify HMRC within three months of the end of the accounting period – by 30 June 2019 if it is potentially within the scope of the DPT.

Toll Ltd could ensure that the arrangement is at arm's length or make an appropriate transfer pricing adjustment for the lease.

Note 2: transfer pricing

The 2B plc group is large for transfer pricing purposes as its revenue clearly exceeds £40 million and the requirement is for the group to exceed this limit. Therefore, the transfer pricing rules will apply to H-Brew Ltd as it is controlled by 2B plc.

If the pricing strategy is implemented then 2B plc would be required to adjust for the tax advantage it will gain by selling beer to UB Inc at a lower profit margin than in an arm's length transaction.

The sales to UB Inc are understated by £8,960,000 (£29,120,000 × 85%)/0.65 – £29,120,000.

H-Brew Ltd's sales revenue and therefore its taxable profit next year should be increased by £8,960,000 and will result in additional tax being payable by H-Brew Ltd at 19% = £1,702,400.

Tutorial note

The arm's length sales to UB Inc are calculated by determining what the costs of sale must be ie, (£29,120,000 × 85%) if the profit margin is 15%. These costs must be grossed up by 65% to determine the sales which give a 35% gross profit margin. Alternative calculations were also accepted in marking.

This adjustment does not affect the year ending 31 March 2019. However, I would recommend the board reviews the pricing strategy since the acquisition of UB Inc's shares in July 2018 to ensure that no adjustment is required for the year ending 31 March 2019.

Transfer pricing is self-assessed and the penalties for not ensuring that the correct adjustments are made are very severe.

It is advisable to seek an Advanced Pricing Agreement in respect of the transfer prices.

(c) **Adjustments**

31 March 2019

	2Bplc £m	Toll Ltd £m
Tax adjusted trading profit/Loss	150.000	25.00
Note 1		
Interest – £25 million × 2.5% = £625,000 × 6/12	0.313	
Lease – diverted profits adjustment requires further information		
Note 2 – impact is on future periods		
	150.313	

H-Brew Ltd's £5 million loss could be group relieved to either 2B plc or Toll Ltd.

52.2 Ethical implications

As UB Inc will be buying the beer at a lower price, UB Inc will make a higher margin on its sales in Utopia which are taxed at a lower rate of 9%. 2B plc is UB Inc's main customer and owns 60% of the shares in UB Inc and appears to control the price it buys the bottled product to sell in the UK. The strategy could result in greater profits arising in UB Inc, a company in which Gerry's brother has a 40% shareholding.

The pricing strategy impacts on the sales staff as it may result in a lower bonus being due to them. However, it is not clear whether the strategy affects the gross profit overall or whether indeed there is an operational reason behind the pricing strategy.

There is a transparency issue because Gerry intends not to disclose the proposed pricing structure to the staff and it is unclear how much the H-Brew Ltd or 2B plc board knows about the pricing structure.

Gerry is pressurising both Denise and the candidate which represents an intimidation threat.

The candidate has a self-interest threat to implement the price changes to ensure that his/her job is secured.

There are clearly transactions that are purely motivated by tax avoidance which come within the revised PCRT – as financial controller of a large group, Gerry Maya may be a member of a professional body. The candidate would need to consider whether there is a breach of the ethical code which should be reported.

Gerry may have responsibilities as the senior accounting officer. Non-compliance with these requirements will impact on 2B plc.

H-Brew Ltd has a minority shareholder - if profits are being diverted the H-Brew Ltd board has a statutory duty with regards to the interests of the minority shareholder.

Actions

The candidate should take steps to eliminate the self-interest threat by discussing the potential intimidation threat with his/her manager.

Find out what the respective boards of H-Brew Ltd and 2 B plc already know – is there any board approval for the changes. The full facts behind the pricing strategy should be obtained and documented to determine whether there are any genuine reason for the proposed changes.

52.1 There were both excellent and very weak answers produced for this section. Candidates who noted that CFC was an issue tended to copy at great length from the learning materials with little application to the scenario. This resulted in incorrect conclusions that CS Inc profits passed through the gateway and were therefore taxable. The scenario specifically stated that the profits of the call centre were derived from many customers. Better answers applied the CFC exemptions to the scenario noting when these were not met and what additional information may be required or facts to be confirmed. Exceptional candidates were able to think beyond the current period and to consider what might happen in the future – and to advise that some planning is required if UB Inc's profits are not to pass through the gateway in the following period.

Some candidates also went down the DPT route in this section and discussed the possibility of avoided PE for both CS and UB which was irrelevant. There were also lots of 'prepared answers' which bore no resemblance to the question posed. Candidates approached the question by considering 75% loss groups, chargeable gains and VAT groups and discussed PE exemptions and DTR at great length. This displayed a lack of ability to deal with the facts in the question.

Likewise, the loan and lease arrangement generated a lot of discussion on non-trading loan relationships and thin capitalisation. Whilst these were both relevant to some extent, answers focussed on the rules with very little application of the rules to the scenario. This subsection of the question was in fact about DPT but several candidates failed to acknowledge this and therefore lost marks. Even though the question asked for calculations in relation to adjustments, weaker candidates did not attempt to produce any calculations. Better answers applied the DPT rules to the scenario and were able to score very well in this section.

The transfer pricing point on the adjustment to the selling prices was dealt with very well with the majority of candidates recognising that this was an issue and there needed to be an arm's length adjustment. Candidates have become comfortable with this topic area over recent sittings.

52.2 The approach adopted by weaker candidates in this section was to repeat the answers they had drafted to the transfer pricing point. They therefore focussed on whether transfer pricing was avoidance and discussed the possibility of getting agreement first with HMRC.

All too often, where ethics was spotted as the salient issue, candidates jumped straight into tax evasion, money laundering and resigning from the engagement. This has been a common approach over many sittings with the candidates failing to appreciate their role in the scenario. This leads to very 'rote' learned answers being produced.

The question required the candidates to think about their position and the fact that there was a self-interest and integrity threat and a lack of transparency. Better candidates considered their role and perspective in giving their answer to this section.

53 Recruit plc

Scenario

In this scenario, the candidate is providing tax advice to an employee of Recruit plc on the UK tax implications of a proposed secondment to Poland. The candidate must assimilate information regarding the taxpayer's proposed investment and property income and the employee's future plans to provide planning advice regarding the disposal of a rental property and/or shares.

To answer this question well the candidate must both demonstrate a technical understanding of the tax implications of residency and be able to recommend a course of action.

The candidate must also demonstrate an understanding of the VAT implications of an e-commerce service to advise Recruit plc.

	Technical	Skills	Marks
53.1 Domicile and residence issue	-	2	
Full time work overseas	1	3	
Impact in 2020/21	-	1	
Split year treatment	1	1	
Impact in 2019/20	1	3	
Impact in 2021/22	-	1	
UK tax liabilities	2	2	
Calculations	3	1	
	8	14	
Max			15
53.2 Share sale	1½	2	
Property sale	-	1½	
Temporary non-residence	1	2	
	2½	5½	
Max			5
53.3 E-commerce	-	1	
Place of supply	1	1	
Reverse charge	-	2	
Other VAT points	-	2	
	1	6	
Max			5
Total marks	11 ½	25 ½	37
Maximum			25

Email to: Peter

From: MN ICAEW Chartered Accountants

Subject: Tax implications of two year secondment to Faktur and the proposed sale of either UK rental property or EEW shares and VAT issue.

53.1 As you are leaving the UK to work in Poland, and you expect to be working full time in Poland in 2020/21, you will be treated as resident for only part of 2019/20. To be completely clear in our advice we would need to confirm whether you are UK domicile and your residency in 2018/19.

Because you are full-time working overseas you are automatically non-resident in 2020/21.

The conditions to be treated as 'working full-time overseas' for the purposes of the UK residence rules are as follows.

You work on average at least 35 hours a week overseas (excluding annual leave, sick leave and UK workdays); your email suggests an average of 40 hours a week.

There are no significant breaks of more than 30 days in the tax year (excluding annual leave) when you do not work at least three hours overseas; there appear to be no significant breaks planned.

You have no more than 30 UK work days in the tax year.

Your total work days will be $12 \times 1 = 12$, which is less than 30 days.

You spend fewer than 90 days in the UK in the tax year.

Your total days in the UK (based on days when you are in the UK at midnight) will be:

(12×4) for weekend visits and 10 in December, $= 58$ (which is less than 90).

The full-time work overseas test should therefore be met, and you should be non-UK resident for 2020/21. You will, however, need to ensure that you limit the number of weekend and holiday days when you work in the UK, as you could conceivably exceed 30 UK workdays (ie, days on which you do at least three hours' work in the UK).

Split year treatment should apply to 2019/20. You will be treated as non-UK resident from the day on which you first work in Poland.

The above tests will be applied to the period starting with your first day working in Poland. The 30 UK workday and 90 UK day limits will be reduced for the number of complete months before your first overseas workday.

The issue here is whether your period of full-time work overseas is treated as starting from the first day that you work in in Poland in August 2019, or whether it starts in October 2019 on the first working day of your actual secondment.

If the period from 6 August 2019 to 5 April 2020 is tested in the context of the full-time work overseas rules, the 30 and 90 day limits must be reduced by 4/12 to reflect the number of months before the period of overseas work starts. These therefore become 20 and 60.

You would work in the UK before returning to start your secondment. Therefore, the number of workdays in the UK would be more than 20 days. This period does not constitute a period of full-time work overseas as both the maximum number of UK workdays and the maximum break from overseas work would be exceeded.

You will be resident in the UK until the day before you start work in Poland on 6 October 2019 as the conditions are met for this period.

Split year treatment should also apply to 2021/22. You will be treated as UK resident from the day after your last day working in Poland.

For your UK tax liabilities, this means that you will be taxed in the UK on your worldwide income as it arises, and your worldwide capital gains as they are realised, up to the day you start work in Poland.

From the date you start work overseas, to the date you finish working overseas, your income and gains will be taxed as follows.

UK income will be taxable as it arises.

You will not be able to make contributions to any tax-free ISAs whilst you are non-resident but you can maintain any existing ISAs you have. Therefore, if you intend to invest in ISA – you are advised to do so before 6 October 2019.

If the only UK income that you will receive whilst you are abroad is interest, you will then have no further tax liability due on your investment income. This will not be taxable due to the existence of the savings income nil rate band.

However, you also have UK property income which will be taxable.

Assuming your income remains the same for 2019/20 onwards your tax liabilities will be:

	UK £	Non-resident £	Total £
Salary – UK	35,000	–	35,000
Rental property rental income	7,500	7,500	15,000
Rent from house 5 × £1,900		9,500	9,500
	42,500	17,000	59,500
Personal allowance	(11,850)		(11,850)
	30,650	17,000	47,650

34,500 × 20%	6,900
13,150 × 40%	5,260
	12,160

In 2019/20 and 2021/22 there is no restriction for the personal allowance in the split year. This assumes that when you return in 2021/22 your salary remains at £70,000.

2020/21 – The property income arising in the UK will be taxed. You will also be entitled to a personal allowance to set against your rental income.

53.2 ER relief may be available to you on the sale of the EEW plc shares. I need to know how long you have held the shares for and what percentage shareholding you own. However this will not be available unless you work for EEW plc, which does not seem to be the case.

Both the sale of the EEW plc shares and your rental property will give rise to capital gains tax. Clearly if you sell the rental property the rental income will no longer be received and this will reduce your income tax liability.

Chargeable assets sold before you leave are subject to capital gains tax. You will be able to reduce the disposal proceeds by the cost and the annual exempt amount of £11,700. Both assets will produce the same gain – however the rental property will be taxed at 28% whereas the shares will be taxed at 20%.

With respect to the rental property, the part of the gain which arises after April 2015 will be taxable in the year of sale regardless of your residency status. This is may not be significant but I will need more information, such as how long you have owned the property and the date of acquisition.

You would need to obtain independent financial advice on which investment should be sold.

Because you will be non-UK resident for less than five years, capital gains which arise while you are non-UK resident will be taxed on you in the year of your return to the UK (2021/22). This only applies to any chargeable gains arising on assets which you held at the time when you ceased to be UK resident.

Therefore, if you sell either your shares or your property the gain on the asset (or, in respect of the property, that part of the gain not already taxed) will be liable to UK taxation on your return as you owned the asset before you left the UK in October 2019. However, the holiday home in Poland if it is bought and sold during your absence will not be liable to UK capital gains tax.

53.3 The supply of the software is a service supplied by e-commerce – there are special VAT rules governing the supply of e-commerce services for VAT.

The place of supply of services would usually be in the UK where Recruit plc is established. However special rules apply where the services are used outside of the EU and the service is treated as supplied where it is 'enjoyed'.

So, the supply should be apportioned between Recruit plc and Faktur (which are both located in the EU so these are treated as supplied in the UK), and R-India Ltd which is outside the EU.

The VAT on the EU/UK supply is accounted for using the reverse charge procedure – ie, $2/3 \times (£900,000 \times 20\%) = £120,000$.

This should have been claimed as output tax on the VAT return to 31 December 2018 and reclaimed as input tax on the same return.

HMRC should be notified of this error on the December 2018 VAT return.

Examiner's comments

53.1 This was the weakest answered part of the exam. Many candidates either discussed domicile and remittance basis at great length, or failed to appreciate that the full time overseas work test was at issue and discussed sufficient ties and number of days spent in the UK as part of the statutory residence test. They completely ignored the requirement to include calculations altogether in a significant number of cases.

Some candidates did make a competent attempt at applying the working full time overseas test to the scenario and correctly identified that split year treatment may be relevant in the year of departure and arrival back in the UK.

(Some elements of this question have been removed from the syllabus and so the mark allocation has been reduced.)

53.2 A significant number of candidates concluded that if an individual is non-resident then CGT is not an issue. This displayed a lack of knowledge on the anti-avoidance provisions of non-residents.

53.3 This was generally answered very well. Candidates dealt with this competently and full marks were often awarded.

54 Frank and Hari

Scenario

In this scenario, the candidate provides advice to partners in the DroneTx business regarding the incorporation of their partnership. Two alternative methods are proposed: Method 1 – an incorporation by transfer to a newly incorporated company. Method 2 – incorporation by transfer to an unconnected company in exchange for shares.

The salient point in this question was that under Method 1, no ER was available on goodwill as the new company would be a close company, but it would be available under Method 2. The employment position of the partners was also an important factor.

The candidate is also required to explain the tax implications of a gift of a business asset to a connected party.

	Technical	Skills	Marks
54.1 Income tax			
Cessation of trade		1	
Capital allowances (succession)	1	3	
Adjusted loss	½	1	
Frank – losses	½	1	
Frank – calculations	1½	2	
Hari – losses	1	2	
Hari – calculations	-	2	
Gains	1½	3	
Incorporation relief	1½	3	
Frank – options	2	2	
Frank – recommendation	-	1	
Hari	-	2	
Rue House – ER	1	2½	
VAT	1	1	
	11½	26½	
Max			25
54.2 Capital gains tax	1	1	
Inheritance tax	2	2	
	3	3	
Max			5
Total marks	14 ½	28 ½	44
Maximum			30

54.1 Income tax implications

For both Methods 1 and 2, when the partnership is incorporated on 6 April 2019, the trade will cease for income tax purposes. The final period of trade is the 12 months to 5 April 2019.

An adjustment may be required to the trading loss for a balancing charge on the disposal of the equipment.

As the TWDV is £Nil, the balancing charge will equal the disposal proceeds of £50,000.

Under Method 1, as the computer equipment is sold to DX Ltd, which is a connected party, it may be possible to make a succession election to transfer the equipment at tax written down value.

Under Method 2, as MK Ltd is not a connected party a succession election is not possible and a balancing charge will decrease the trading loss in the final period as follows:

	Method 1 £	Method 2 £
Trading loss	(56,250)	(56,250)
Balancing charge	–	50,000
Trading loss	(56,250)	(6,250)

The trading loss will be split equally between the two partners ie, £28,125 and £3,125 for Method 1 and Method 2 respectively.

Frank

Frank has trading losses brought forward of £67,500 at 6 April 2018. As the partnership has not made a profit in the year ended 5 April 2019, the loss for this period will increase Frank's trading losses at 5 April 2019 to either £95,625 (Method 1) or £70,625 (Method 2).

As the trade has ceased, a carry forward against future profits of the same trade is not possible at 6 April 2019. However, Frank could carry the loss forward against income from the company under s.86 ITA 2007. This would apply to both Methods 1 and 2.

Under Method 1, Frank should not use s 64 loss relief in 2018/19 because this would involve wasting his personal allowance.

His income in future years is likely to be higher and therefore the loss relief would be more effectively used by carrying forward.

Under Method 2, his share of the partnership loss is £3,125 and therefore s.64 could be used without the loss of personal allowance.

	Method 1 £	Method 2 £
Gross income from discretionary trust	25,000	25,000
Less loss relief s.64	-	(3,125)
	25,000	21,875
Less personal allowance	(11,850)	(11,850)
	13,150	10,025
Tax at 20%	2,630	2,005
Tax suffered on income from discretionary trust at 45%	(11,250)	(11,250)
Tax repayment	8,620	9,245

Hari

Under Method 1, Hari would be advised to use his share of the partnership loss for the year ending 5 April 2019 under s.64 loss relief against his other income.

His share of the loss, assuming the election to transfer assets at TWDV is made would be £28,125. Given his employment income at £124,000 he would receive higher rate reduction and enable him to regain his personal allowance.

The same recommendation would apply under Method 2 as Hari does not propose to continue working in the business he would not be receiving employment income from the company, although he would be able to use the loss against dividends under s.86 ITA 2007.

If he sells his shares by 31 December 2019, this would not be possible as the relief requires the taxpayer to own the shares for the tax year in which the loss relief is applied.

In any case, a higher effective rate is achieved by using the loss against other income in the current tax year because of the ability to use his personal allowance, at least partially.

	Method 1	Method 2
	£	£
Employment income	124,000	124,000
Less loss relief s.64	(28,125)	(3,125)
	95,875	120,875
Less personal allowance	(11,850)	(1,413)
	84,025	119,462
34,500 @ 20%	6,900	6,900
49,525/84,962 @ 40%	19,810	33,985
Less PAYE	(42,100)	(42,100)
Tax repayment	15,390	1,215

Capital gains tax

The incorporation of the partnership will give rise to a capital gain for each partner.

The partnership's only chargeable asset is goodwill which has a £nil based cost.

	Frank	Hari
	£	£
Gain on goodwill	975,000	975,000
Gain on sale of Rue House	–	160,000
Less annual exempt amount	(11,700)	(11,700)
Taxable gains	963,300	1,123,300

Incorporation relief is automatic if certain conditions are met.

These conditions appear to apply here as the business is being transferred as a going concern and all the assets other than cash are being transferred for consideration consisting of shares.

Each partner can decide whether to disapply incorporation relief depending on their tax position and intentions.

As all the assets of the business are transferred under both Method 1 and 2 incorporation relief would be available to defer the gain which relates to share consideration. The gain is deducted from the cost of the shares received. Incorporation relief does not need to be claimed as it is automatic. However, consideration should be given to whether to disapply incorporation relief.

Frank

Frank intends to work in the business under both methods and under both methods he will own more than 5% of the company's shares. This means that if he sells his shares in the future, entrepreneurs' relief is likely to apply.

If he does not disapply incorporation relief, the advantage would be that no gain crystallises in 2018/19.

Method 1

Disapplying incorporation relief would result in the gain being taxed at 20% as the goodwill is being sold to a connected party. DX Ltd appears to be a close company and so ER cannot be claimed.

Method 2

Entrepreneurs' relief may be available on the internally generated goodwill as MK Ltd is not a close company (the other 25 shareholders each have small shareholdings) and the partners are shareholders in MK Ltd. As a result, the gain would be taxed at 10% instead of 20%.

Frank should consider whether to disapply incorporation relief as although entrepreneurs' relief is available on the future disposal of his shares, this is based on current tax legislation which could change in the future. Disapplying the relief now would secure a 10% tax rate on the gain.

Hari

Under Method 1 the implications are as above – disapplying incorporation relief would result in the gain being taxed at 20% as the goodwill is being sold to a connected party. DX Ltd appears to be a close company and so ER cannot be claimed.

If Method 2 is chosen, Hari should disapply incorporation relief and pay tax at 10% on the gain on the goodwill.

If he sells his MK Ltd shares in December 2019, he would not have owned the shares for 12 months after incorporation and so will not benefit from entrepreneurs' relief on the sale of the shares.

Rue House

The gain on disposal of the office building is not eligible for incorporation relief as it is not a partnership asset.

However, provided that the sale of the partnership share qualifies for entrepreneurs' relief (ER) then the gain on the building should also qualify for a 10% tax rate, as this is an associated disposal. Hari is disposing of the whole of his interest in the partnership and Rue House has been used for the purposes of the business for one year prior to the date of the material disposal. Rue House has always been let rent free and full ER should be available.

From Hari's perspective, he will pay less tax if Method 2 is chosen.

VAT implications

The partnership will be registered for VAT and on the incorporation under Method 1 and 2, the conditions for a TOGC appear to be satisfied – the whole of the business is transferred as a going concern – we would need to confirm particularly under Method 2 that the assets are to be used for the same kind of business. Under method 1 DX Ltd would need to be registered for VAT - it is likely that DX Ltd would assume the VAT registration of the partnership.

We need to confirm that under Method 2 MK Ltd is registered for VAT.

54.2 Capital gains tax

As Frank would not be buying the asset from Hari, market value is substituted for sales proceeds to calculate a gain of £160,000.

As the asset is used by Hari in a business, it will qualify for gift relief. No gain would arise on the disposal of the asset and therefore no capital gains tax arises.

Frank's deemed cost of acquisition which is the market value at the date of the gift is reduced by the amount of the gain which would have been chargeable had gift relief not applied. A joint election must be made by both the donee, Frank, and the donor, Hari, for gift relief to apply.

Inheritance tax

The gift of the building will be treated as a PET for IHT purposes. If Hari dies within 7 years of making the gift it will be treated as a chargeable lifetime transfer and taper relief may apply. However, it is likely to be treated as relevant property for Business Property Relief.

If the partnership is incorporated under Method 1, the building will continue to be used in the trade. It is relevant business property because it is has been used as a business asset for a partnership in which Hari was a partner. (I would need to confirm that Hari had owned the property for at least two years before the gift.)

The relief available would be a 50%.

BPR will no longer apply to the gift of the building if Frank disposes of the building before Hari dies. However, a replacement business property can be treated as the original property if the original property was sold before death and the whole of the consideration received was used to acquire replacement property within the three years from disposal.

Examiner's comments

54.1 Candidates sometimes ignored the income tax implications of the losses and dealt only with the CGT elements of incorporation which left them exposed to losing a substantial number of marks. Whilst most candidates were comfortable in discussing the conditions for incorporation relief and the fact that it could be disapplied in favour of ER; candidates mistakenly concluded that for Method 1 the goodwill was entitled to ER and if was very frequent to see candidates concluding that the computer equipment was also subject to capital gains tax.

For Method 2, a minority of candidates concluded incorrectly that incorporation relief was not relevant as an existing company was purchasing the business and that ER would not be in point, failing to pick up the point on the associated disposal of the building.

The salient point in this question was that under Method 1, no ER was available on goodwill as the new company would be a close company, but it would be available under Method 2. The employment position of Hari was also a deciding factor. This question showed that the weaker candidates can copy out rules from the learning materials but cannot then apply the rules to the facts of the question and recommend the most tax efficient course of action.

54.2 This was generally very well answered with a significant proportion of candidates achieving full marks. The weaker candidates either omitted this part altogether of only focussed on the CGT or IHT implications.

55 Swell Gallery

Scenario

This question tests the decisions to be made on incorporation of a sole trader business, including whether to include all of the assets in the incorporation or not.

The answer considers the income tax, VAT, SDLT, capital gains tax and corporation tax issues surrounding incorporation and, in particular considers the tax costs of transferring property on incorporation.

There were a number of paths through the question and it was not expected that candidates would explore every possible alternative. Therefore the marking scheme was set up in order to award sufficient credit to students, whichever route they chose.

Marking guide

	Technical	Skills
55.1 Alternative 1		
VAT and SDLT		
• TOGC	1	3
• VAT and SDLT on purchase	2	2
• CGS at purchase	1	1
• CGS sale adjustment	1	1
• SDLT	–	1
Income tax		
• P&M and overlap profits	–	2
• Amount to be taxed to cessation	1	3
CGT on incorporation		
• Gains	–	2
• Incorporation relief conditions	1	1
• Disclaiming incorporation relief	–	3
• Rollover relief	–	2
• Incorporation relief calcs and advice	1	3
Corporation tax	1	1
Alternative 2		
VAT and SDLT	1	2
Gain on incorporation	2	3
Gain on Tide House	–	2
	12	32
Max		25

55.2 Alternative 1 costs	1	2	
Alternative 2 costs	1	1	
Conclusion	–	1	
	2	4	
Max			4
55.3 VAT reclaimed on purchase	1	1	
CGS	1	2	
VAT on rent	1	3	
SDLT	–	1	
Property income	–	1	
	3	8	
Max			8
55.4 Dividends v salary	–	2	
Cash on incorporation	1	1	
Finance	–	1	
	1	4	
Max			3
Total marks	18	48	66
Maximum			40

55.1 Alternative 1: Transfer Tide House to S Ltd on 1 July 2019, along with all the other trade and assets of SG. The company then sells Tide House for its market value on 1 July 2019.

VAT and SDLT on incorporation

The incorporation of SG would be outside the scope of VAT, provided the conditions for a transfer of going concern (TOGC) were satisfied.

The conditions for a TOGC would be satisfied in this case because:

- the transfer is of a going concern;
- the business is continuing;
- we presume that S Ltd would be VAT registered; and
- there would be no break in trade.

Tide House is an 'old', commercial building and as no option to tax has been exercised, the TOGC would also apply to the transfer of Tide House to S Ltd.

On the purchase of Tide House in 2012, VAT was charged of £350,000 × 20% = £70,000. This was wholly recoverable as SG was a wholly taxable business.

SDLT was also charged, on the VAT inclusive purchase price of £420,000, even though the VAT was recoverable. The SDLT rate on non-residential property costing between £250,001 and £500,000 in June 2012 was 3% on the entire property value. SDLT of £12,600 was payable. This cost is deductible in calculating any gain on the sale of Tide House.

Because Tide House cost more than £250,000, the VAT initial recovery of £70,000 was subject to potential adjustment under the capital goods scheme in the adjustment period of 10 intervals. The first interval would run from purchase to 31 March 2013 and for 9 intervals thereafter up to 31 March 2022.

On the transfer of Tide House to S Ltd on 1 July 2019, the TOGC rules would ensure that no adjustment on sale was required on incorporation. However, S Ltd would take over responsibility for any future adjustments relating to the property.

On the immediate sale of Tide House to a third party, by S Ltd, on 1 July 2019, there would be an adjustment on sale, calculated as follows:

£70,000/10 × (100% - 0%) × 2 intervals = £14,000. This would be payable by S Ltd.

On incorporation, the transfer of Tide House to S Ltd would have incurred SDLT of £12,000 [(450,000 - 250,000) × 5% + (£250,000 - 150,000) × 2%] payable by the purchaser, S Ltd.

Income tax

The plant and machinery owned by SG would be transferred to S Ltd at tax written down value, if a succession election is made. Therefore no adjustment is required to the trading profits of the year ended 30 June 2019.

Hugh was loss-making in the first three years of trade and so there would be no overlap profits brought forward to set off on cessation of trade.

Hugh would be taxed on the profits of SG up to cessation. The final accounting period was the year ended 30 June 2019, so Hugh would be taxed on trading profits of £125,000 in the tax year 2019/20. In addition he would also be taxed on a receipts basis on any salary or dividends he received from S Ltd from incorporation on 1 July 2019 to the end of the 2019/20 tax year. He would be taxed on his salary of £10,000 per month. This would add an extra £90,000 to his taxable income for 2019/20, making a total of £215,000 in 2019/20. Hugh would not receive the personal allowance because his gross income exceeds £123,700 and the personal allowance of £11,850 would be abated by £1 for every £2 of income over and above the limit of £100,000.

Capital gains tax on incorporation

On incorporation capital gains will arise on any chargeable assets transferred to the company.

SG has two chargeable assets, which would give rise to a gain on incorporation as follows:

	Gain £
Tide House (MV - Cost - 12,600 SDLT)	87,400
Goodwill (no cost)	500,000

The gains will arise as shown above, however the conditions for incorporation relief will have been met.

The conditions are as follows:

- SG is a going concern.
- all assets of the business are transferred to the company.
- the consideration received is wholly in shares.

As the conditions have been satisfied, incorporation relief will apply automatically, unless it is disclaimed by Hugh.

Hugh would only seek to disclaim incorporation relief if he were likely to sell the shares in S Ltd within the 12 months following incorporation, given that entrepreneurs' relief would then not be available on any subsequent share sale, because the shares would not have been held for the minimum 12-month period. In this case, we would need to ask Hugh about his intentions regarding the shares in S Ltd, to determine if disclaiming incorporation relief would be beneficial to Hugh. If incorporation relief were to be disclaimed, the entrepreneurs' relief rate of 10% would only apply to the gain on Tide House, because the relief is not applicable to goodwill on incorporation of a close company where the claimant owns at least 5% of the company after incorporation.

As S Ltd is selling a qualifying asset (Tide House) and reinvesting in another qualifying asset (Beach House), if incorporation relief is disclaimed, then rollover relief would be available to defer the gain on Tide House against the cost of Beach House. This would be restricted, as the business use of Beach House is only two-thirds of the building.

The effect of incorporation relief will be to reduce the base cost of the shares in S Ltd, by the amount of the gain. Although this means that Hugh will not pay capital gains tax on the incorporation, he will pay a larger amount of capital gains tax on any subsequent sale of the shares, in the future, because of the reduction in their base cost.

The reduced base cost will be:

	£
Market value of SG at 1 July 2019	1,100,000
Less gains on incorporation	(587,400)
Reduced base cost of S Ltd shares	512,600

S Ltd will then sell Tide House, almost immediately, to a third party. On the sale of Tide House there will be no gain arising on S Ltd, as the deemed cost of the asset would be its market value on 1 July 2019, which would equal the sale proceeds for the asset on 1 July 2019, the SDLT paid by S Ltd on incorporation of £12,000 would be an additional capital cost which would give rise to a capital loss in S Ltd. This could be set off against any capital gains in the year or carried forward against future capital gains.

Corporation tax

On acquiring the goodwill of SG, S Ltd will not be able to claim the amortisation of goodwill as an allowable expense.

Plant and machinery will be taken over a tax written down value if there is a succession election.

Alternative 2: Hugh retains Tide House on incorporation and sells Tide House personally on 1 July 2019

VAT and SDLT

The transfer of the trade and assets to S Ltd would be a TOGC, as above. However, as Tide House was not transferred to S Ltd, there would be no VAT CGS adjustment for S Ltd and no SDLT to pay by S Ltd.

SDLT would be payable by the third party purchaser and the sale of an old commercial building on which there was no option to tax, would be exempt from VAT. Hugh would have an adjustment on sale of Tide House of £14,000, as calculated above.

Gain on incorporation

The gain on incorporation would just be the gain on the goodwill of £500,000.

Incorporation relief would not be available to defer this gain, because not all of the assets of SG were transferred to the company.

Entrepreneurs' relief on incorporation cannot be claimed in respect of goodwill, where the goodwill has been disposed of to a close company and immediately after the disposal, the claimant owns at least 5% of the ordinary share capital of the close company.

Therefore the gain on incorporation of £500,000 less the annual exempt amount of £11,700 and capital losses b/fwd of £50,000, would be taxable at the rate of 20% on Hugh (as his taxable trading profits from the sole trader business for the 2019/20 year alone, before any salary from S Ltd, would put him into higher/additional rate taxation). This would give rise to CGT payable by Hugh of £87,660.

Gain on the sale of Tide House

In addition, Hugh would also be taxable on the gain on the sale of Tide House of £87,400 at the rate of 10% as this disposal is likely to qualify for entrepreneurs' relief as it is disposed of at the same time as the other assets when the trade is ceasing.

55.2 **Comparing the tax costs of Alternative 1 and Alternative 2**

Cost	Alternative 1 £	Alternative 2 £
VAT CGS adjustment on sale of Tide House S Ltd/Hugh	14,000	14,000
SDLT on purchase of Tide House	12,000	0
Capital loss in S Ltd	(12,000)	0
Gains taxable on incorporation	Deferred till shares sold – 587,400	438,300
CGT on incorporation	0	87,660
Gain on Tide House		87,400
CGT on Tide House		8,740

If Hugh chose Alternative 1 he would defer paying tax on any of the gain on incorporation until such time as he sells his shares in S Ltd. If this is more than 12 months after incorporation and the entrepreneurs' relief rules still apply at that time, then he may only pay tax on that gain at 10%. Therefore, although he incurs £14,000 of SDLT on the transfer of Tide House in order to do this, he potentially halves the rate of CGT payable on the gain and, in cash flow terms defers the payment of this tax.

If Hugh chooses Alternative 2, he saves £14,000 of SDLT, but has to pay CGT immediately, on incorporation, and, at 20% on much of the gain, potentially twice the rate of CGT he would pay had the gains been deferred under incorporation relief and then taxed with entrepreneurs' relief, at 10%.

Although Hugh would have to be advised of the difference between these two options, in most cases Alternative 1 would be the most tax efficient option.

55.3 The new commercial premises at Beach Lane will cost £650,000 when purchased, new from the developer.

The VAT chargeable on the purchase of new commercial premises would be £130,000.

This would be 100% reclaimable if the company made wholly taxable supplies.

As the company intends to rent out two-thirds of the building, the VAT reclaimable would be 1/3 × £130,000 = £43,333 because rental of the building would constitute an exempt supply.

If the taxable use of the building were to change over the first 10 intervals of use of the building, the amount of input VAT recovery would be adjusted.

If an election were made to opt to tax the building, then all of the £130,000 VAT could be reclaimed.

The rental income from tenants would be an exempt supply, unless there were an election to opt to tax the building.

An election to opt to tax the building would mean that output VAT would be charged on the rent charged to tenants and on the final sale price of the property on sale.

For non-VAT registered traders or exempt traders, such as insurance companies, this would make the rent or purchase price more expensive. However, the advantage to S Ltd would be the ability to reclaim 100% of the input VAT of £130,000 on the purchase of the property and 100% of the input tax on any expenses, such as maintenance, associated with the building.

S Ltd should therefore consider the VAT status of any likely tenants or future purchasers of the building. If the company is comfortable that opting to tax the building would not damage the prospects for finding tenants or future purchasers for the building, then the company should opt to tax the building in order to reduce the VAT costs attached to the purchase and maintenance of the building.

S Ltd will incur SDLT on the VAT inclusive cost of £780,000 at the rates of 0%, 2% and 5% - amounting to £28,500 [(780,000 - 250,000) × 5% + (£250,000 - 150,000) × 2%] on the purchase.

The company would also receive taxable property income, which would be included in the company's corporation tax computation on the accruals basis, net of any allowable property expenses.

55.4 Pay dividends instead of salary as remuneration from the company to reduce income tax and national insurance contributions.

Pay a maximum taxable salary/dividends from S Ltd in 2019/20 of £25,000 (£150,000 - £125,000), to keep taxable income out of the additional rate band.

Take cash as a proportion of the proceeds on incorporation in order to realise a gain equal to the annual exempt amount of £11,700 and capital losses b/fwd of £50,000 - this would not affect the availability of incorporation relief, but would produce a tax free gain of this amount.

Consider the tax implications of any finance that might need to be raised to buy Beach Lane.

Examiner's comments

In part 1 weaker candidates produced rote learned lists of 'relevant' points, for example, discussing the availability of losses on cessation of trade, without realising there were no losses to use. As BP:T is a skills-based exam, candidates need to tailor their answers to the scenario set.

The scenario involved the two possible alternatives for the disposal of a building. This should have led to answers focussing on the breadth of VAT and SDLT issues, but only the stronger candidates adopted this approach.

Surprisingly, not many candidates considered the possibility of dis-applying incorporation relief and opting for ER instead. This should have then led to a discussion on the availability of ER on goodwill as the new company would have been a close company. Very few candidates picked up this point. This is a core syllabus area and candidates should be getting to grips with the scenario and considering the relevant issues.

Many of the weaker candidates were confused between the corporate and individual tax rules on goodwill. Many candidates treated the goodwill as an intangible and discussed the CT rules, without spotting that the goodwill was generated by an individual sole trader. Many also failed to spot the possibility of rollover relief on purchase of the new building or the restriction of the relief. A common mistake was to completely ignore stamp duty land tax as a cost in computing the gain on the building or indeed recognising it in the first place.

56 Albion Ltd

Scenario

Part 1 of this question considers the UK income tax and Capital Gains Tax liability of a UK-resident, but non-UK domiciled individual, who is entitled to claim the remittance basis of assessment. This individual has also made investments, which will qualify for seed enterprise investment scheme income tax and capital gains tax reinvestment relief.

Part 2 of this question considers how the hybrid mismatch rules affect such arrangements and how failure to comply with these arrangements, could compromise the position of an SAO.

		Technical	Skills	Marks
56.1 Remittance basis				
Impact of domicile		–	1	
Impact of remittance basis claim		2	2	
Overseas dividends v RBC		1	2	
Income tax calculation – no claim		2	4	
Note 1 – personal allowance		1	–	
Note 2 – SEIS				
• Conditions		4	–	
• Relief		2	2	
Note 2 – Remittance from Oceania		1	2	
CGT calculation – no claim		–	2	
Calculation – with claim		–	2	
Conclusion		–	2	
		13	19	
	Max			25
56.2 Ethics				
SAO		1	2	
Hybrid mismatch		1	3	
Discussions and possible resignation		–	3	
Ethical considerations for firm		–	3	
		2	11	
	Max			10
Total marks		15	30	45
Maximum				35

56.1

> **Tutorial note**
>
> Please note, it was not necessary to prepare calculations, as shown, of both the arising and remittance basis IT and CGT liabilities. Candidates who identified that the £60,000 RBC would outweigh the advantage of not taxing unremitted foreign income and gains, would have received equal credit, provided this was explained as part of their answer.

Jim can choose between being taxed on his income and capital gains as a non-UK domiciled individual on the arising or the remittance basis.

Making a remittance basis claim would have the following impacts on Jim's IT and CGT liabilities for 2018/19:

1   Jim would be liable to pay a remittance basis charge (RBC) of £60,000 - because he was UK resident for at least 12 out of the previous 14 years.

2   He would lose entitlement to a UK personal allowance for income tax purposes and a UK annual exempt amount for CGT purposes.

3   He would only be taxed on foreign income, to the extent that it were remitted to the UK

Jim has unremitted foreign dividend income of £45,000. This is the only income or gains that would be omitted from the income tax and capital gains tax computations, if the remittance basis were to be claimed.

As such, the RBC would be much larger than any tax saving made by claiming the remittance basis.

Therefore, it is clear that the cost of claiming the remittance basis would be so high, that it would outweigh the advantage of making any claim.

(a) **Income tax and capital gains tax – no remittance basis claim, arising basis**

Jim Bell
Income tax computation 2018/19

	Non-savings income £	Dividend income £
Salary – Albion Ltd	100,000	
UK dividend – Albion Ltd		10,000
Overseas dividend – Bloomswell GmbH		45,000
Less personal allowance (Note 1)	-	-
Taxable income	£100,000	£55,000
Income tax:		
Non-savings income		
34,500 × 20%	6,900	
65,500 × 40%	26,200	
£100,000		
Dividend income		
2,000 × 0%	0	
48,000 × 32.5%	15,600	
5,000 × 38.1%	1,905	
£55,000		
	50,605	
Less SEIS investment (£100,000 × 50%) (Note 2)	(50,000)	
Income tax liability	605	

Notes

1   As Jim's adjusted net income is more than £123,700, he is not entitled to a personal allowance.

2   **Seed enterprise investment scheme**

As Jim has invested £150,000 in new, unquoted trading company shares, and his interest in the company is 30% or less of the company's shares/votes and he is not an employee or non-qualifying director of the company he can claim SEIS income tax relief of 50% of his investment in a qualifying company of up to £100,000.

For the income tax relief to be given, we need a compliance certificate from the company stating that it has spent at least 70% of the funds being invested.

In addition, the investment could be carried back to the previous tax year and 50% of the amount carried back could be given as a tax reducer in 2017/18 (assuming the £100,000 maximum investment allowance for 2017/18 has not already been used).

In addition to the income tax relief Jim can claim SEIS reinvestment relief equal to a maximum of 50% of his qualifying SEIS expenditure. For 2018/19 this would remove £50,000 worth of capital gains from tax. In addition, if he were to carry back any of the qualifying expenditure to 2017/18, he would also have been able to reduce gains in that tax year.

Jim would claim SEIS relief in preference to EIS relief as it gives a greater income tax reduction (50% rather than 30%).

3 **Taxation of remittance of £150,000 out of untaxed funds from Oceania to the UK**

Normally, when a remittance basis user remits funds to the UK out of unremitted and therefore untaxed foreign income or gains, the funds are taxed when they come into the UK. However a remittance basis user can bring funds into the UK without triggering a tax charge, if the funds are used to make an investment in an unquoted trading company, provided the funds are invested within 45 days of entering the UK. As Jim brought £150,000 into the UK and more than 45 days later invested the funds in an unquoted trading company, the investment exemption cannot be claimed and the £150,000 remittance is taxed in the UK. As this is a remittance of proceeds for a capital disposal, the amount of £150,000 would not necessarily be the amount of the gain that should be taxed. We would need to ask for more information from the client to ascertain the amount of the gain to be taxed.

Capital gains tax liability 2018/19

	£
Gain on sale of painting in the UK	75,450
Gain from remittance of funds from abroad	?
Less SEIS CGT exemption	(50,000)
Less annual exempt amount	(11,700)
Taxable gain	13,750
CGT @ 20%	2,750
Total tax payable (£2,750 + £605)	3,355

Note: This figure will be increased by the amount of the gain from foreign remitted funds at 20%.

(b) **Income tax and capital gains tax liabilities – remittance basis claim**

Income tax liability 2018/19

	Non-savings income £	Dividend income £
Taxable income: Re-stated to exclude overseas dividends	100,000	10,000

	Non-savings income £	Dividend income £
No PA – RB User		
Tax liability		
34,500 × 20%	6,900	
65,500 × 40%	26,200	
2,000 × 0%	0	
8,000 × 32.5%	2,600	
	35,700	
Less SEIS Investment (£100,000 × 50%) – max	(35,700)	
Income tax liability	Nil	

Capital gains tax liability 2018/19

	£
Gain on sale of painting in the UK	75,450
Gain from remittance of funds from abroad	?
Less SEIS CGT exemption	(50,000)
No annual exempt amount – RB user	
Taxable gain	£25,450
CGT @ 20%	£5,090

Total tax payable (remittance basis)   £65,090 (£5,090 + £Nil + RBC of £60,000)

Note: The gain on the proceeds of £150,000 remitted to the UK at 20% would again be added into the UK CGT liability. The issue being that when remittance basis was claimed in a previous year, this gain was excluded form UK taxation until remitted to the UK.

Jim will be liable to pay a higher remittance basis charge, because he was UK resident for at least 12 out of the previous 14 years.

By claiming the remittance basis, Jim increases his tax liability by £61,735, mainly because of having to pay the higher level of remittance basis charge of £60,000. As a result for 2018/19, Jim should not make the remittance basis claim.

56.2 Jim is SAO of Albion Ltd and, as such is required to certify the adequacy of the accounting systems for the purposes of accurate tax reporting and specify the nature of any inadequacies.

Jim would be personally liable for a penalty of £5,000 should he either fail to establish and maintain appropriate tax accounting arrangements; or provide a certificate that contains careless or deliberate inaccuracy.

Given the interest expense deduction being claimed by Albion Ltd for the year ended 31 December 2018, Jim is concerned that these interest deductions do not comply with UK tax law.

Hybrid mismatch arrangements, such as this one (where a deduction for corporation tax is given in the UK, with no corresponding income being taxed in the BVI) are counteracted, by refusing a deduction for the interest in the UK, because it is not taxed as income in the BVI.

Therefore Jim is correct to be concerned that he would be liable for a penalty of £5,000 for failing to provide accurate returns if he did not amend the corporation tax computation and return of Albion Ltd to disallow the interest expense as a deduction in the computation.

Jim has already discussed this matter with his fellow directors and their response implies that they will not comply with UK tax law. Jim should discuss the matter with them again, pointing out the hybrid mismatch legislation. If they will not support completion of the corporation tax computations and returns in line with UK tax law, he may have to consider if he should resign as FD and SAO. He could consult the ICAEW confidential ethics helpline.

Now that we are aware of this issue, it is also an ethical issue for us. We will have to ensure that the corporation tax computations and returns are completed in line with UK tax law. If they are not, we will inform the client of our concerns and the consequences of their actions, in writing. If we do not receive a satisfactory response from the client we will have to consider resigning from the engagement.

Examiner's comments:

56.1 This was answered very well with candidates showing they are comfortable with computational elements of the exam. Some of the most common mistakes were a failure to recognise the remittance basis charge or to include the incorrect amount of £90,000 instead of £60,000, deduction of the personal allowance under both the RBU and non RBU computations and inclusion of unremitted income in the RBC calculation.

The stronger candidates produced some very good answers which considered the special rules on reinvesting remitted funds within 45 days. This showed higher skills in dealing with the scenario.

56.2 Answers to this part were extremely disappointing. Whilst candidates had no problems dealing with the responsibilities of the SAO, answers in relation to the overall transactions varied wildly in standard. Some candidates attempted to discuss the correct accounting treatment, others immediately assumed it was tax evasion and discussed the common penalty regime and some spoke at great length about general avoidance and the Ramsey doctrine. Many also discussed the diverted profits tax regime.

Very few picked up the specifics on hybrid mismatch.

57 Dolphin Ltd

Scenario

This corporation tax question looks at the impact of expanding a company's trade and the expansion of the trade overseas, to a low tax jurisdiction, for commercial reasons. The question requires a decision about whether to trade overseas as a permanent establishment or as a subsidiary company and also whether to make up a long set of accounts or not on the change of a company's accounting reference date. Advice concerning these two options will also need to be taken together to achieve the optimum tax position for the company.

	Technical	Skills	Marks
57.1 PE v subsidiary			
Taxation of profits	1	2	
Exempt PE	–	2	
Subsidiary	1	3	
Recommendation	–	1	
	2	8	
Max			8
57.2 CT with R&D and DTR			
Recommendation	–	2	
Two sets of accounts	1	4	
One long period	2	6	
	3	12	
Max			12
57.3 Tax avoidance scheme			
DOTAS	1	1	
PCRT – standards for tax planning	–	2	
Aggressive tax avoidance	–	2	
Recommendation	–	1	
	1	6	
Max			5
Total marks	6	26	32
Maximum			25

57.1 Trading in Atlantica through an Atlantican permanent establishment (PE) or through a separate subsidiary incorporated in Atlantica

The trade in Atlantica is going to be profitable from the outset. So, to decide whether the trade should be carried on through a PE or whether it should be through a separate 100% owned subsidiary in Atlantica, consider the impact of the UK corporation tax rate on the profits to which it applies.

If the trade is carried on through a permanent establishment the profits of the trade will normally be regarded as part of the UK company's taxable profits and the profits will be included within Dolphin Ltd's corporation tax computation, because Dolphin Ltd, as a UK resident company, will be taxed on its worldwide profits. The UK taxation on these profits will be reduced by unilateral double taxation relief, to give relief for the 5% tax withheld on these profits in Atlantica.

It is possible that Dolphin Ltd could elect for the Atlantican PE to be exempt from UK taxation, however, this election would apply to all PEs set up by Dolphin Ltd, not just the current PE. As Dolphin Ltd intends to set up more PEs in the future, Dolphin Ltd would need to evaluate whether to make the PE exemption election or not. If Dolphin Ltd makes the election, this would preclude Dolphin from claiming loss relief for any losses made by any PEs in the future.

If the trade is carried on through a separate 100% owned subsidiary, the taxation of the profits will depend on where that subsidiary is considered to be registered for tax purposes. Assuming that the company is registered in Atlantica, and that the trade is carried on in Atlantica, the company will be taxed in Atlantica and subject to a corporation tax rate of 25%. These profits would only be taxed in Dolphin Ltd's UK corporation tax computation, if they were remitted to the UK. If remitted in the form of dividends they are likely to be exempt from tax in the UK. The worldwide tax rate suffered on these profits would therefore be 25%.

If taxed as a PE, Dolphin would suffer tax of 19% in the UK, less 5% WHT already paid in Atlantica as DTR. The worldwide tax rate suffered would therefore be 19%, subject to any variation for different rules relating to adjusting profits. For the purposes of the calculations it is assumed that taxable profits in Atlantic are calculated in the same way as in the UK.

It will probably be preferable to set up the Atlantican trade as a PE and suffer a total tax liability on the Atlantican profits of 19%.

57.2 **Making up a 15-month set of accounts to 31 March 2020 or two sets of accounts (12 months to 31 December 2019 and 3 months to 31 March 2020)**

The length of a company's accounting period, for corporation tax purposes cannot exceed 12 months. If a company makes up a set of accounts for a period in excess of 12 months, the company is taxed on the profits of the first 12 months of that period and then separately on the profits of the remainder of that period.

The way that trading profits are apportioned between the two separate CT computations is on a time basis, with capital allowances being computed on an actual basis.

In the case of this company, the difference between the two possible allocations of profits between the two separate corporation tax accounting periods, depending on the length of the set of accounts prepared is considered in the appendix, by preparing CT computations under each of the scenarios given.

If the company were to prepare one set of accounts for the whole 15-month period, the total tax due would be £9,500 less than if two separate sets of accounts were prepared. However, £166,176 more tax would be due in relation to the first 12-month period of account than if two sets of accounts were prepared. As this would mean that this tax would be due three months earlier, the tax saving may be offset by the impact of tax being paid sooner. The decision between which period(s) of account to adopt may therefore marginal.

Appendix:

Separate accounts made up for the 12 months ending 31 December 2019 and the 3 months ending 31 March 2020

Corporation Tax Computations (with Atlantican PE)

	12 months ending 31 December 2019		3 months ending 31 March 2020	
	£	£	£	£
Trading profits UK trade	2,100,000		550,000	
Less 130% additional deduction for R&D revenue expenditure				
£459,000 × 130%	(596,700)			
£100,700 × 130%			(130,910)	
Less capital allowances – per question	(345,000)		(45,000)	
Less 100% capital allowances R&D computer hardware	(400,000)		(95,000)	
		758,300		279,090
Trading profits Atlantica	100,000		1,450,000	
Less capital allowances	–		(500,000)	

	12 months ending 31 December 2019	3 months ending 31 March 2020
	£	£
	100,000	950,000
Taxable total profits	858,300	1,229,090
Corporation tax liability		
TTP × 19%	163,077	233,527
Less DTR		
Lower of:		
UK CT (19%)		
Foreign Tax (5%)	(5,000)	(47,500)
UK CT due	158,077	186,027
Total CT due for both periods £344,104		
Due date	1 October 2020	1 January 2021

One set of accounts for the 15 months ending 31 March 2019

	12 months ending 31 December 2019		3 months ending 31 March 2020	
	£	£	£	£
Trading profits UK trade	2,650,000			
Less 130% additional deduction for R&D revenue expenditure £559,700 × 130%	(727,610)			
	1,922,390			
Split between 2 separate CT Computations				
12/15 × £1,922,390		1,537,912		
3/15 × £1,922,390				384,478
Less capital allowances		(345,000)		(45,000)
Less 100% capital allowances R&D computer hardware		(400,000)		(95,000)
		792,912		244,478
Trading profits Atlantica	1,550,000			
Split between 2 computations:				
12/15 × 1,550,000		1,240,000		
3/15 × 1,550,000			310,000	
Less capital allowances		–	(500,000)	
Loss on overseas trade set off against UK trade profits				(190,000)
Taxable total profits		2,032,912		54,478
Corporation tax liability				
TTP × 19%		386,253		10,351

	12 months ending 31 December 2019		3 months ending 31 March 2020	
	£	£	£	£
Less DTR				
Lower of:				
UK CT (19%)				
Foreign Tax (5%)		(62,000)		-
UK CT due		324,253		10,351
Total CT due for both periods £334,604				
Due date		1 October 2020		1 January 2021

57.3 The tax-saving scheme has a hallmark of avoidance, which render the scheme reportable to HMRC under the DOTAS regime.

Confidentiality – the promoter wishes to keep the scheme confidential from others.

Although the promoter would be liable to report the scheme to HMRC under the DOTAS regime, this would give the scheme a number (the SRN) and there would be penalties, starting at £5,000, if this SRN were not to be disclosed on any returns made by Dolphin Ltd, if participating in the scheme.

The advice we have been asked for about investment in this scheme requires us to consider the standards for tax planning in Professional Conduct in Relation to Taxation. Although I am not the tax adviser promoting this scheme, I have been asked for my professional advice.

I should consider the following:

- Is the scheme lawful?

- Is there full disclosure to HMRC of all facts?

- Are the tax planning arrangements highly artificial and exploiting loopholes in the legislation or, are they achieving results not intended by Parliament?

In addition HMRC's guidance on tax avoidance signposts warning signs to guide taxpayers away from abusive or aggressive tax avoidance schemes. These are as follows:

- If it sounds too good to be true, it probably is.
- Secrecy or confidentiality agreements exist.
- The arrangement has a scheme number under DOTAS.

In the light of all these warning signs, I would advise Dolphin Ltd, not to enter into the scheme.

Examiner's comments:

57.1 Candidates dealt competently with the major differences between a PE and subsidiary. However, there is still a lack of ability to apply knowledge to question scenarios. Whilst the majority of candidates picked up that the election was available to exempt profits of PE's from UK tax; they failed to consider the implications for loss relief in the future. They also did not always reach suitable conclusions.

57.2 This part was attempted very poorly. Whilst the calculation of corporation tax is seen as a Tax Compliance topic, at BP:T we expect candidates to have brought forward knowledge from TC. This scenario required candidates to compute the corporation tax payable under two different accounting periods, with timing of R&D expenditure and capital allowances being the relevant deciding factors. This question needed candidates to compare two alternative courses of action and come up with a recommendation on the optimum position for the company.

It was really disappointing that candidates did either not attempt any calculations or when they did, they failed to show reasonable knowledge of the R&D regime or the existence of DTR. Both of these topics are covered again in detail in the BP:T manual.

57.3 Again, answers to this were very general and discussed evasion v avoidance. The scenario presented a very specific tax scheme, with a confidentiality clause which should have led candidates to discuss and consider DOTAS. The better answers did this but the weaker candidates again just 'knowledge dumped' without displaying any application skills.

September 2018 exam answers

58 Joe Gregory

Scenario

The candidate is in the role of a tax specialist working in practice.

The question tests the ability of the candidate to identify in which circumstances the IR35 anti-avoidance legislation would be applicable, in a variety of scenarios. The question focussed on the new rules for public bodies in particular which were introduced from April 2017.

The candidate is then required to give advice to the client on the future operation of the business considering differing business structures (unincorporated and incorporated businesses) and the net after tax income as a result of each.

The question also considers the managed service company anti avoidance provisions and their applicability to the scenario and the income tax and capital gains tax reliefs available for investment in venture capital schemes.

Marking guide

			Technical	Skills	Marks
58.1	(a)	IR35	1	1	
		Employed v self-employed	1	3	
		AM Ltd	1	2	
		Pennington LA	1	2	
		Jupiter Ltd	–	2	
		Deemed employment income	1	3	
		Employers NIC	1	1	
	(b)	Computation – sole trader	1	2	
		Computation – employee	1	4	
		NIC	1	1	
	(c)	Managed service company criteria	4	–	
		Application to criteria	–	3	
		Treatment of earnings	–	3	
		Comparison to IR35	–	1	
			13	28	
		Max			32

		Technical	Skills	
58.2	SEIS income tax	1	2	
	SEIS reinvestment relief	1	2	
	EIS income tax	2	2	
	EIS reinvestment relief	-	2	
	Conclusion	-	1	
		4	9	
	Max			8
Total marks		17	37	54
Maximum				40

58.1(a) The personal service company (IR35) legislation applies where an individual provides services to a client through an intermediary, and would be treated as an employee of the client if not for the existence of the intermediary. Where an individual provides services to more than one client it is possible that some or all of the services will be treated as relevant engagements on a case by case basis.

Self-employed/employed case law is considered for each separate contract. HMRC would consider the following in determining if the IR35 legislation is to be applied:

- Personal service
- Mutuality of obligation
- Provision of equipment
- Right of substitution
- Financial risk
- Degree of control
- Client portfolio

In this case, the intermediary is a company and the rules will apply because Joe owns at least 5% of the ordinary share capital.

Considering each of the contracts in turn.

AM Ltd

The personal service company legislation is likely to apply as AM Ltd has control, provides equipment and Joe cannot send a substitute. The deemed employment payment will be subject to income tax and NIC. The income received will be reduced by a flat 5% and any expenses which would be deductible under employment income rules in calculating the deemed employment payment. The purchase of equipment will also be subject to capital allowances.

Pennington Local Authority

Where an individual works via an intermediary for a public authority, IR35 applies but the responsibility for operating IR35 lies with the public authority. They must provide information about whether the scope of the engagement is within the IR35 rules. Therefore the fact that PAYE and NIC have been deducted appears to be correct in the circumstances. The flat 5% deduction does not apply to contracts for services provided to a public authority.

Joe can however take dividends from the company and dividends which are taken from income which has already been taxed as a deemed employment payment will be reduced by the amount which has already been taxed to ensure income is not taxed twice.

Jupiter Ltd

Further information is needed but it does appear that this would not fall within the scope of the legislation as there is flexibility in working arrangements, right of substitution and provision of own equipment and materials by Joe. Therefore no deemed employment income calculation is necessary and Joe may withdraw this income as dividends from the company if this is more tax efficient.

Deemed employment income calculation

	£	£
Total earned		80,000
Less 5% allowable deduction (AM Ltd only)		(4,000)
		76,000
Less expenses		(125)
Less capital allowance (100% AIA assumed)		(1,250)
Less salary	46,350	
Employers NIC	5,234	
		(51,584)
		23,041
Deemed employment income		
£23,041 × 100/113.8		(20,247)
Employers NIC		2,794
Income tax		
£20,247 × 40%		8,099
Employee national insurance		
£20,247 × 2%		405

(b) **2020/21 IT computation**

		Sole trader £	Company £
Employment income			24,000
Trading profits		145,000	
Dividends (W1)			96,269
Total income			120,269
Less personal allowance (W2)		Nil	(1,715)
Taxable income		145,000	118,554
Income tax			
£34,500 × 20%		6,900	
£110,500 × 40%		44,200	
£145,000			
£22,285 × 20%	(£24,000 – £1,715)		4,457
Dividends:			
£2,000 × 0%			Nil
£10,215 × 7.5%	(£34,500 – £22,285 – £2,000)		766
£84,054 × 32.5%	(£96,269 – £12,216)		27,318
Income tax payable		51,100	32,541
Cash		145,000	120,269
Less income tax		(51,100)	(32,541)
NIC (W3)		(5,539)	(1,869)
Net cash		88,361	85,859

Joe would have higher net cash if he continued to operate as a sole trader.

WORKINGS

(1) Dividend

CT will be:

	£
Trading profits	145,000
Less employment costs	(24,000)
Employers NIC (£24,000 – £8,424) × 13.8%	(2,149)
Taxable profits	118,851
CT @ 19%	(22,582)
Distributable profit	96,269

(2) Personal allowance

Personal allowance is restricted by £1 for every £2 over £100,000.

	£
Personal allowance	11,850
Less restriction	(10,135)
(£20,269/2)	1,715

(3) NIC

Sole trader

	£
Class 2: 52 × £2.95	153
Class 4: (£46,350 – £8,424) × 9%	3,413
(£145,000 – £46,350) × 2%	1,973
	5,539

Tutorial note

The exam front cover states that students should assume 2018/19 rates and allowances are to apply.

Employee NIC

Class 1 primary (£24,000 – £8,424) × 12% = £1,869

(c) A company will be treated as a managed service company if:

- it supplies the services of individual workers to third party clients;

- the worker receives the majority of the payments received by the managed service company from the client in relation to the workers services;

- the worker receives payments which are more than they would have been if they had been treated as employment income after the deduction of IT and NIC; and

- a managed service company provider is involved with the company.

It appears that Joe's company will be supplying Joe to third party clients and would receive all the payments as he is the sole shareholder. Given that the salary paid to Joe will be minimal in relation to the income it appears that the first three criteria would be met.

If the management company becomes involved and sources work for Joe then this will be a managed service company.

The implications of this are that any non-employment income paid out to the workers is treated as earnings for both IT and NIC, and the payment is chargeable when the payments are made. This is unlike a personal service company when payments are made at year end and the only deduction from the deemed employment payment are expenses which would be allowed under normal employment income rules.

There is generally a higher charge if a company is treated as a managed service company than there would be under the IR35 legislation.

58.2 Belle Ltd appears to qualify under SEIS as:

- the companies trade is new (carried on for less than 2 years)
- the gross assets before share issue do not exceed £200,000
- it has fewer than 25 full-time employees

Joe would be entitled to a deduction from his income tax liability equal to the lower of:

- 50% of the amount invested under the SEIS scheme; or
- the amount which reduces his liability to nil.

Relief can be carried back to the previous year so we would need to use information on Joe's income from the previous year to assess if this is worthwhile.

Income tax relief will be withdrawn if the investor disposes of the shares within three years of issue or receives value from the company in certain forms. Income tax relief is withdrawn by adjusting the assessment for the year in which the relief was claimed.

Reinvestment relief can also be claimed where an individual makes a qualifying SEIS investment in the same year. As Joe has disposed of other shares then he can claim relief of the lower of the amount of the gain so £9,500 or the amount invested on which income tax relief is claimed.

If Joe makes an election to treat the investment as made in the previous year for income tax purposes the investment is also treated as being made in the previous year for reinvestment relief.

Like the income tax relief, the reinvestment relief is also withdrawn if the SEIS shares are sold within three years and the original CGT computation would be adjusted.

The investment in Boo Ltd appears to qualify under EIS as the company:

- is unquoted and does not appear to control another company
- has gross asset value before the share issue does not exceed £15 million
- has fewer than 250 full-time equivalent employees at the date of issue
- has raised no more than £5 million under EIS and VCT

The income tax relief is the lower of 30% of the amount invested or the amount which reduces the tax liability to nil. Relief is normally given in the tax year that the investment is made but a taxpayer can claim to carry back the relief to the previous year. Like SEIS, income tax relief will be withdrawn if the investor disposes of the shares within three years of issue. Income tax relief is withdrawn by bringing the relief given back into charge in the tax year in which the disposal was made.

Like SEIS, capital gains tax reinvestment relief is available where an investment is made under the EIS schemes in the 12 months before and the 36 months after the date of disposal. Again, Joe could claim reinvestment relief to the value of the gain he has made on the disposal of Weiner plc shares.

In terms of tax relief, investment under SEIS gives a higher tax relief. However, commercially this could be a risky investment as it has no operating history and is a brand new start-up company.

58.1(a) Most candidates were able to identify the correct treatment of the contracts with AM Ltd and Jupiter Ltd. However, many candidates failed to identify that Pennington Local Authority was a Governmental body and that new rules apply to the tax treatment of intermediaries trading with governmental bodies. These rules are clearly stated in the relevant section of the ICAEW study material, and, as this is an open book examination would have been available to students in the exam room. It was therefore very disappointing that a significant number of candidates failed to identify and apply the new rules. The calculations in respect of AM Ltd and Jupiter Ltd, in relation to the deemed employment payment, were generally of a good standard. Candidates showed a good understanding of the operation of the rules in general and the resulting income tax consequences.

(b) Most students were able to prepare calculations of the net disposable income for Joe, bearing in mind the different business forms available (company v sole trader). However, only the better candidates were able to identify the amounts of the dividends payable to Joe under the incorporation alternative. Whilst it was a complex calculation and required candidates to think logically about the deductions from trading income in terms of corporation tax and the salary already paid to Joe, the weaker candidates tended just to ignore the availability of the dividend altogether. Some failed to do any calculations and instead just copied points from the manual describing the different tax and NIC treatment of operating a sole trader business compared to a company. These answers did not score well.

(c) Although many students were able to explain the managed service company legislation, most were unable to adequately apply this to Joe's situation and determine how the legislation would affect Joe's business. Again, this was a section which was often copied straight from the manual with few application skills displayed.

58.2 Many candidates produced excellent answers to this part of the question, correctly identifying SEIS and EIS investments and stating the conditions for these investments and the tax relief available. Fewer candidates recognised the opportunities to claim reinvestment relief for the gain on the sale of the shares in Weiner plc.

59 Foodpack Ltd

Scenario

The candidate is an ICAEW Chartered Accountant and works in practice for a firm of ICAEW Chartered Accountants.

The scenario required the candidate to deal with the corporation tax liability of Foodpack Ltd dealing with adjustments for patents and a sale of a short lease.

The scenario then focussed on disposal of shares in Foodpack Ltd by an individual majority shareholder, considering the tax consequences of disposal for the shareholder, the purchaser and the company overall under three alternative scenarios. The disposal of shares required candidates to deal with a range of taxes including IT, CGT, IHT, the various reliefs available and also the consequences of a company purchase of own shares.

The ethics element of the question was built around the Paradise Papers exposure and as BP:T is a commercial, topical exam, it should have been relatively straightforward for candidates to deal with.

	Technical	Skills	Marks
59.1 Adjustments			
Assignment of short lease	2	–	
Calculation of gain	–	3	
Patent box	2	3	
Calculation of profits	–	2	
Calculation of tax	1	2	
Taxable total profits	1	1	
	6	11	
Max			10
59.2 Alternative 1			
Gain and gift/entrepreneurs' relief	1	2	
Calculation	–	2	
IHT	–	1	
Stamp duty/qualifying loan	–	1	
Alternative 2			
CPOS – capital conditions	1	3	
PCP	1	1	
Calculation	–	2	
Stamp duty	–	1	
Alternative 3			
CPOS – shareholding reduction	1	3	
Calculation	1	2	
Stamp duty	–	2	
	5	20	
Max			18
59.3 Ethics			
Establish facts	1	2	
Residence issues	1	1	
Tax evasion	–	2	
Disclosure and Ramsay	–	2	
	2	7	
Max			7
	13	38	51
Maximum			35

59.1 (1) The disposal of the lease is the assignment of a short lease and so the calculation of the gain takes into account the wastage from April 2013 to April 2018.

The original cost to Foodpack Ltd used in the gains calculation must be adjusted for the amount of the deductions of deemed rent that the company has claimed over the five years of ownership of the lease.

Foodpack Ltd pays corporation tax on the gain on disposal of the lease in year ended 31 March 2019.

	£	£
Proceeds		40,000
Less cost	31,000	
Allowable deduction for trading profits		
$5/25 \times £31,000 \times (50 - 24)/50$	(3,224)	
Subject to wastage	27,776	
Wasted cost $£27,776 \times \dfrac{72.770\,(20)}{81.100\,(25)}$		(24,923)

Less indexation allowance

$$\frac{278.1 - 249.5}{249.5} = 0.115 \times £24,923 \qquad (2,866)$$

Gain   12,211

The £12,211 increases the taxable total profits of the company.

Corporation tax is therefore payable on:

	£'000
Tax adjusted trading profit	8,070
Gain on lease	12
	8,082

(2) Companies which own or exploit patents can elect for the profits from patents to arise within a patent box which suffers a lower rate of taxation.

Any patents created on or after 1 July 2016 are subject to an approach which deals with assets on a patent by patent basis (sub-streams) where there is a link between the R&D and the patent developed as a result of the R&D expenditure. This requires a high level of record keeping. Given that Foodpack Ltd has acquired patents and uses them to develop and manufacture packaging, it can elect to use/apply the patent box.

The profit relating to patents needs to be deducted from the tax adjusted trading profit and a separate calculation for each patent needs to be done:

	Patent 1 £'000	Patent 2 £'000
Patent box streamed profits		
Income	5,000	6,000
Less expenditure	(2,000)	(2,000)
	3,000	4,000
Less 10% return on costs	(200)	(200)
Less marketing royalty		
3% × £5m/£6m	(150)	(180)
Patent box profit	2,650	3,620
Nexus fraction		
60% × £2,650/80% × £3,620	1,590	2,896
Total patent box profits		4,486
Corporation tax payable		
£4,486 × 10%		449
Remaining patent box profits		
(£7,000 – £4,486) × 19%		478
Other profits		
(£8,082 – £7,000) × 19%		206
Total		1,133

59.2 Alternative 1

This will be treated as a disposal at market value as Ella and Daniel are connected persons.

The market price for the shares is £240,000. We would need to check this as Daniel is buying a reduced shareholding and therefore the reduced price of £9 per share (£9 × £20,000 = £180,000) may be justified.

Ella and Daniel could make a joint claim for gift relief as this is a sale at undervalue by £60,000. This would then reduce Ella's gain but would crystallise on Daniel when the shares were eventually sold. However, in addition Ella would also be entitled to entrepreneurs' relief because this is the sale of shares in a personal trading company which Ella has held for at least 12 months and for which she is an employee. There would therefore be a gain on Ella as follows:

	£
Market value	240,000
Less cost (£2 × 20,000)	(40,000)
	200,000
Gift relief	(60,000)
Chargeable gain	140,000
Less AEA	(11,700)
	128,300
Tax at 10%	12,830

This would also be a PET for IHT if Ella was to die within 7 years. However, BPR is likely to apply as these are shares is an unquoted company which have been owned for at least two years. Daniel however, would still need to own the shares at the time of Ella's death for BPR to apply.

There would be stamp duty payable by Daniel of 0.5% × £180,000 so £900.

The loan which Daniel has to take out from the bank is likely to be a qualifying loan as it is to purchase shares in a close company. Therefore, Daniel will be able to claim a deduction for this against his income for the purposes of calculating his income tax.

Alternative 2

As this is a company purchase of own shares, the sale will automatically be treated as a capital transaction unless one of the conditions is breached. The conditions are as follows:

- Foodpack Ltd must be an unquoted trading company.

- The buyback must be for the benefit of the trade.

- The shares have been owned for at least five years.

- Ella needs to be UK resident. Further information would need to be obtained to ensure that this is the case.

If Foodpack Ltd purchased Ella's entire shareholding of 70,000 shares then this is likely to meet the conditions for the capital route. The cost of these shares would be £840,000 (70,000 × £12). However, currently the retained earnings of Foodpack Ltd are only £790,000. Therefore, a PCP of £50,000 would be required. Before the buyback goes ahead, we would need to confirm that Foodpack Ltd's reserves have increased (we only have the statement of financial position at 31 March 2019) between the year end and the buyback going ahead.

If this is the case then the capital gains tax payable by Ella would be:

	£
Proceeds	840,000
Less cost (70,000 × £2)	(140,000)
	700,000
Less AEA	(11,700)
Taxable gains	688,300
Tax at 10%	68,830

Stamp duty of 0.5% × £840,000 = £4,200 would be payable by Foodpack Ltd.

Alternative 3

This is also a company purchase of own shares.

However, there is a requirement that the shareholding must be substantially reduced and therefore selling only 20,000 shares would not pass the substantial reduction test.

	Ella shares	Daniel shares	Hitchens shares	Total
Before buy back	70,000	20,000	10,000	100,000
Buy back	(20,000)			(20,000)
	50,000			80,000
Percentage before	70.0%			
Percentage after	62.5%			

As the post-sale percentage is more than 75% of the pre sale holding then the test is not met and the income distribution route will apply.

Tutorial note

Alternatively students could have discussed the 30% holding having been breached and so capital treatment does not apply.

As Ella is not the original subscriber then the situation is:

$20,000 \times (£12 - 1) = £220,000$
Tax charge = $38.1\% \times £220,000 = £83,820$, assuming the dividend nil rate band is already fully used due to other investments.

As the shares were subscribed for above nominal value, there is also a capital loss under this route.

	£
Proceeds (20,000 × £12)	240,000
Less net distribution	(220,000)
	20,000
Less cost (20,000 × £2)	(40,000)
Allowable capital loss	(20,000)

In terms of Foodpack Ltd, a buyback of the shares would result in stamp duty becoming payable of $0.5\% \times £240,000 = £1,200$.

59.3 First of all we would need check the validity of the newspaper article. If it is true it appears that Ella has attempted to avoid tax in both Barbados and the UK by setting up a BVI company. We would need to establish the facts to distinguish between planning and avoidance ie, is there any commercial purposes to setting up an overseas company.

If Ella is UK resident and has been exercising management and control of the company from the UK then despite where the company is registered, it will be deemed to be UK resident and subject to UK CT.

The fact that Ella has not informed us of the existence of the company means that she is unlikely to have declared any income/dividends to HMRC. This amounts to tax evasion for which there are serious penalties.

We must discuss the situation with Ella and advise her to disclose. We must also consider if a disclosure is needed to NCA.

Also consider the application of the Ramsay principle to this scenario.

Examiner's comments

59.1 The new, post BEPs, patent box rules were well understood and well explained by a lot of candidates. In particular the patent box calculations were well handled. Surprisingly, only a small number of candidates were able to competently explain the link with R&D. Some of the weaker answers did not deal with the information presented and erroneously assumed that the small claims treatment was available. The sale of the short lease is different to the original question set due to a change in syllabus content.

59.2 This considered three different ways in which Ella could divest herself of her shareholding – all with differing tax consequences. Candidates analysed this part of the question well and many scored highly, identifying a range of relevant issues. Common errors made involved candidates thinking that SSE was relevant. We do often see some confusion between corporate and income tax topics. It is worth reminding candidates that SSE only applies when there is disposal of shares by a corporate shareholder and is not a concept which is relevant when there is a disposal by an individual.

Candidates had also been given the SOFP for Foodpack Ltd so that they could consider if Foodpack Ltd had the available reserves to purchase Ella's shares. Most candidates did discuss this and the need for a permissible capital payment. Some candidates calculated the amount of shares that Foodpack Ltd could afford to purchase from Ella based on the SOFP in the question. Candidates were still given full credit where they adopted this approach.

59.3 As always the answers to the ethical issues in questions are of mixed quality. There are still some candidates who state a number of ethical platitudes, without relating their statements to the facts of the question asked. Although students should have a number of key ethical issues they can discuss, they should always be discussed in relation to the scenario set. It was encouraging to note however that candidates are now questioning the information presented and often stated that the credibility of the newspaper article would first need to be investigated before jumping to conclusions.

60 Gold Ltd

Scenario

The question concerned a close company with one subsidiary and required candidates to revise the corporation tax computation for the parent company, for three outstanding issues (the disposal of an overseas property, the issue of trade-related loan stock, and the write off of a loan to a participator). The second requirement was to explain the implications for the shareholder of the loan write off.

The question also included a VAT scenario involving the transfer of an 'opted to tax', tenanted building between the two group members. This required candidates to discuss the implications of the transfer and to identify the further information required to provide accurate VAT advice.

	Technical	Skills	Marks
60.1 Revised computation			
Calculation of TTP	1	2	
Working 1	1	1	
Working 2	1	2	
Working 3 – close company charge and interest	–	3	
Working 3 – NIC	1	1	
60.2 Distribution	–	2	
NIC	1	2	
60.3 VAT			
OTT	–	1	
VAT group	1	1	
No VAT group	1	2	
Third party disposal	–	1	
Capital goods scheme	1	1	
Negotiations	–	2	
Total marks	8	21	29
Maximum			25

60.1 Revised computation of the taxable profits of Gold Ltd

Year ending 31 March 2019

	£
TTP	760,000
Interest on Estelle's loan	(400)
Less trading loan relationship debits (W1)	
Incidental costs of finance	(8,000)
Interest	(4,500)
Forex (W2)	
Gain on property	1,250
NTLR – loss on bank account	(10,556)
NTLR – interest on Estelle's loan (W3)	400
Loan to director (W3)	80,000
Class 1 secondary NIC (W3)	(11,040)
Taxable total profit	807,154

WORKINGS

(1) **Trading loan relationship debits – debentures**

Any costs of raising finance will be treated under the loan relationships rule. Therefore, the cost of issuing the loan stock and the resulting interest payable can be treated as a trading loan relationship debit.

The incidental costs of raising finance of £8,000 plus interest payable of £12,500 (9/12 × £100,000 × 6%).

(2) **Forex**

Gain on investment property	£
Proceeds ($380,000/4)	95,000
Less cost ($300,000/3.20)	(93,750)
Gain	1,250

The movement in the exchange rate forms part of the capital gain as the asset is non-monetary.

Bank account

As the proceeds were held on deposit overseas, a foreign monetary asset is created at the date of disposal and is assessed under the loan relationship rules. Once the money is remitted exchange movements are crystallised and the loss of £10,556 (£95,000 – £84,444 ($380,000/4.50)) will be treated as a non-trading loan relationship debit.

(3) **Close company loans**

Gold Ltd is a close company. As a result loans made to its directors are subject to anti-avoidance rules. When the loans were issued, a penalty tax would have been payable to HMRC by Gold Ltd.

The amount paid would have been 25% × £80,000 = £20,000 as this was a pre 1 April 2016 loan. This is repayable (assuming Gold Ltd does not pay its corporation tax by quarterly instalments) nine months and one day after the end of the accounting period in whichthe loan is written off ie, by 1 January 2020. Therefore Gold Ltd should reclaim this tax on the corporation tax return for the year ending 31 March 2019.

The company receives interest of 1% pa on the loan and therefore to 30 September 2018 this is £400 (£80,000 × 1% × 6/12).

The loan write off is not an allowable debit against non-trading loan relationships, so the £80,000 should be added back in calculating the company's taxable profits made. The client should be notified about this.

A corporation tax adjustment is required for the class 1 secondary NIC on the loan write off.

Secondary NIC due is £80,000 × 13.8% = £11,040

60.2 For income tax purposes the loan is treated as a distribution. This treatment takes priority over any employment income charge and therefore no income tax should have been collected via the payroll. Instead for income tax purposes the distribution should be taxed at Estelle's highest marginal rate for dividends.

£80,000 × 38.1% = £30,480

As Estelle is also an employee, for NIC purposes the write off is subject to NIC class 1 primary and secondary contributions. Gold Ltd should be able to recover the primary NIC due from Estelle. However, if that is not possible the total NIC due should be included as a deduction in the adjusted profits figure rather than just the secondary NIC.

Class 1 primary NIC payable £80,000 × 2% = £1,600

60.3 The original input VAT at the time of acquisition by Gold Ltd would have been reclaimed in full as the option to tax (OTT) converted the rental business from an exempt into a taxable supply.

The VAT treatment on the time of transfer to Silver Ltd depends on whether both companies are part of the same VAT group.

If they were part of the same group the transfer would be disregarded and the OTT would continue to apply.

If they were not part of the same VAT group then the transfer would be chargeable to VAT as a disposal of a taxable building. The OTT would not have been transferred.

However, it might be treated as the transfer of a business as a going concern given there were tenants in situ. If so, provided Silver Ltd also made an OTT there would have been no VAT – more information is required about this.

The disposal outside of the group then depends whether the OTT was in place or not. It would be a taxable supply if Gold Ltd and Silver Ltd were part of a VAT group at the date of transfer or if they were not part of a VAT group at the time but Silver Ltd opted to tax the building prior to the disposal.

Otherwise it would be an exempt supply as the building is more than three years old by the time of sale. This would then lead to a claw back of input VAT under the capital goods scheme, assuming the original cost was in excess of £250,000, which seems likely – more information is required.

This could be avoided if it qualified as a TOGC but more information is needed. If this is the case the purchaser would take over the remainder of the CGS input period and potentially repay some of the VAT. If the tenants were to terminate the lease it would no longer qualify as a TOGC.

If it is a taxable supply then the potential recovery of input VAT will affect the price negotiations, so this should be borne in mind.

Examiner's comments

60.1 Despite the fact that there were only three issues to consider, many students struggled to identify the correct tax treatment for the exchange movements. Although this is an area of the syllabus that is examined infrequently, the learning materials are available to candidates in the exam. This part of the question should have been better answered than it was. The inability of candidates to identify which exchange rate was relevant to each part of the transaction was very disappointing.

The expenses of the trade related loan finance was a very straightforward issue to deal with and caused no issues at all.

The write off a loan to a participator is a core area of the syllabus and an area which is frequently dealt with in practice in respect of OMB clients. Again, this was dealt with well.

60.2 Most candidates were able to identify that Gold was a close company and were also able to, correctly, identify the consequences of writing off a loan to a participator, although many students failed to identify the NIC consequences of the write off.

60.3 A lot of answers rolled out a number of stock phrases about VAT on the sale of assets and mentioned option to tax, the capital goods scheme and transfer of a going concern. However, most answers did not understand how these items would interact, in particular when a company is part of a VAT group. Too many answers wasted time considering the capital gains tax consequences of inter-group capital transfers, instead of considering the alternative treatments depending upon the relationship of the group companies for VAT purposes.

REVIEW FORM – BUSINESS PLANNING: TAXATION QUESTION BANK

Your ratings, comments and suggestions would be appreciated on the following areas of this Question Bank

	Very useful	Useful	Not useful
Number of questions in each section	☐	☐	☐
Standard of answers	☐	☐	☐
Amount of guidance on exam technique	☐	☐	☐
Quality of marking guides	☐	☐	☐

	Excellent	Good	Adequate	Poor
Overall opinion of this Question Bank	☐	☐	☐	☐

Please return completed form to:

The Learning Team
Learning and Professional Department
ICAEW
Metropolitan House
321 Avebury Boulevard
Milton Keynes
MK9 2FZ
E learning@icaew.com

For space to add further comments please see overleaf.

REVIEW FORM (continued)

TELL US WHAT YOU THINK

Please note any further comments and suggestions/errors below.